KING SOLOMON'S TEMPLE
IN THE MASONIC TRADITION

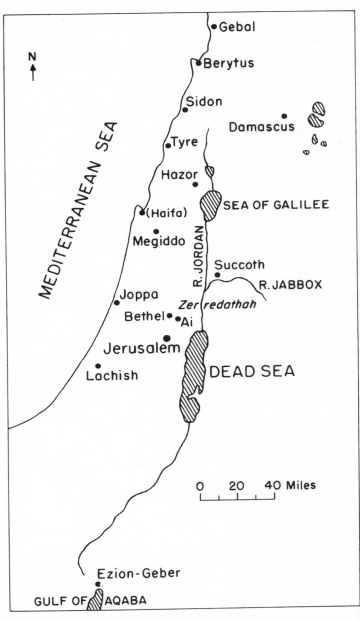

Frontispiece   Map of Palestine in Solomonic times

KING SOLOMON'S TEMPLE IN THE MASONIC TRADITION

By

ALEX HORNE

33°, Ancient & Accepted Scottish Rite, S.J., U.S.A.
Member, Quatuor Coronati Lodge No. 2076 (Research), London

Foreword by

HARRY CARR, P.J.G.D.

P.M. and Secretary, Quatuor Coronati Lodge No. 2076,
London

THE AQUARIAN PRESS
Wellingborough, Northamptonshire

First published 1972
Second Impression 1973
Third Impression 1975
Fourth Impression 1977

ISBN 0 85030 052 5

Printed in Great Britain by
Whitstable Litho Limited, Whitstable, Kent,
and bound by Leighton Straker Bookbinding Company Ltd.

DEDICATED

with affection and fond memories
to my MOTHER LODGE

Sinim Lodge, Massachussetts Jurisdiction
Tokyo, Japan
(formerly of Shanghai, China)

It is a privilege to have been invited to write the Foreword to a full-length book by a writer who has made his mark in more specialized works. The author, Alex Horne, has already received the accolade in Masonic studies as an elected member of the Quatuor Coronati Lodge, No. 2076, the Premier Lodge of Masonic Research, to whose Transactions he has contributed several important papers.

In the present work the author returns to a subject in which he has been closely interested for many years, King Solomon's Temple. It is a subject of the highest interest to Freemasons as well as to students of the Bible and of biblical archaeology. Indeed there has been such a spate of literature on almost every aspect of these themes that it might have been difficult to justify yet another work on the Temple were it not for the broad field of the present author's approach, via every possible aspect of his subject.

On the Temple itself and all the circumstances relating to its construction, the author presents his material based not only on biblical and extra-biblical sources, but supported by a most impressive range of authorities which represent the most up-to-date studies on each of his themes. All this is carefully related to the position which the Temple of Solomon occupies to this day as the allegorical, symbolical and spiritual background to the legends and practice of Freemasonry.

But Alex Horne has devised an additional and more unusual approach to his subject, based on extracts from the Masonic rituals and legends. Thus, starting from various passages in ancient and modern Craft ritual which make reference to the appurtenances, decorations and furnishings of the Temple, he traces their origins and evolution through to their counterparts in our present-day Lodge rooms, thereby solving many interesting problems en route and bringing all those complex details which surround the biblical

7

accounts of that revered building into a closer relationship with the ritual in which the Freemasons commemorate it.

If we visualize the Temple as the background to the Craft, it is as though the author, by this method, gives us a guided tour of each of its parts, in the course of which he provides answers to the innumerable questions that constantly arise among those who are interested in this field, and especially among the Lodge Officers who have the responsibility of mastering the ritual—presenting it in well-rehearsed and polished ceremonies, and teaching it eventually to their successors.

Every chapter of this deeply absorbing work is likely to find interested readers no matter what their approach may be. But it is for the Officers and Members of the Masonic Lodges especially that Alex Horne's work is likely to prove most immediately beneficial and most lastingly useful—and it is hoped that the book will have the success it deserves.

May 1970   Harry Carr

CONTENTS

PART IV

THE BUILDER OF THE TEMPLE

ILLUSTRATIONS

In offering the present work to the Masonic reading public, I find myself somewhat in the position of the sharp-quilled Laurence Dermott, the intransigeant originator and first Grand Secretary of 'The Grand Lodge of England according to the Old Institutions'— the so-called 'Antients'. This worthy wrote of himself, in his *Ahiman Rezon*—a variously-translated title for a work published in 1756— that, in order to be in the fashion and produce a work on Masonic History, he first 'purchased all or most of the histories, constitutions, pocket-companions, and other pieces (on that subject) now extant in the English tongue', and then, he went on to say, 'my next step was to furnish myself with a sufficient quantity of pens, ink, and paper: this being done, I immediately fancied myself an HISTORIAN. . . . '

However, an historian I am not—least of all, one who could merit being emblazoned in capitalized letters—but I do fancy that I have gathered together in these pages something that may be of interest to the Masonic reader, and may perhaps even furnish him with some food for thought, or at least stimulate some desire toward further exploration in this fascinating realm of masonic research.

The need for a serious and thorough discussion of this all-important matter of King Solomon's Temple comes quickly to the fore when we consider the largely uncritical view that the vast majority of Masons unfortunately take of the alleged 'history' and traditions of their institution. All this goes back through a long list of quasi-historical works beginning with the 'historical' portion of Dr. Anderson's first *Book of Constitutions* (1723) and which, Dr. Mackey tells us, was 'for a century and a half deemed an authentic history, and even at the present day is accepted by some over-credulous and not well-informed Masons as a real narrative of the rise and progress of Masonry'.[1] This was written perhaps a century

---

[1] A. G. Mackey, M.D., *The History of Freemasonry*, Its Legends and Traditions, Its chronological history. In seven volumes. New York and London. Vol. 1, p. 118.

ago or more, but is probably as true of the present generation of masonic readers as it was in Mackey's time.

But, in defence of these 'over-credulous' Masons, stigmatized by Mackey, it may be said that they can hardly be blamed for their excess of credulity, since the fault lies rather at the door of those who, knowing better, fail to correct that over-credulity with a modicum of true knowledge, and it is this correction—one of many such worth-while efforts—that the present work is aimed at effecting. On the other hand, the criticism as to the 'not well-informed Masons' is somewhat better-deserved, in these days of Research Lodges and their *Transactions*, of Study Clubs, of masonic books and periodicals, masonic Libraries and Speaker's Bureaux, in practically every Jurisdiction around the masonic world and in their principal masonic centres. With all this freely-proffered help toward a more correct and fuller understanding of masonic history and of its traditions, if any one still chooses to remain a 'not well-informed Mason', of his own free will and accord, he probably has no one to blame but his own lack of interest and industry.

As to the practical usefulness of such a study as I have here undertaken, a little thought will surely lead one to the conclusion that it is much more than of purely academic or antiquarian interest. There is no question but that a deeper understanding and appreciation of our traditions in the light of their biblical, historical, and even mythological background confers upon the various personalities and events involved therein an endowment of real flesh and blood and of historical validity that is far superior to the shadowy and purely nominal image we generally possess of them. Persons, events, and localities thus take on a four-dimensional depth that is far more satisfactory than the faint and uncertain picture generally held in our mind's eye—if we may add to our customary three-dimensional view the Einsteinian fourth-dimension of Time. And by this means our traditions themselves take on a dramatic reality that is highly satisfying. J. R. Rylands undoubtedly states a profound psychological truth when he says, in his comment on Gerard Brett's paper on 'King Solomon': 'That which is myth may be disproved; that which is legend may pass away, but that which is enshrined in ritual has exceeding permanence in the affairs of men.'[1] Thus both myth and legend—themselves unreal—establish a vicarious reality for them-

[1] *AQC* vol. lxvi. *Ars Quatuor Coronatorum*. Transactions of Quatuor Coronati Lodge No. 2076, London.

selves in Masonic ritual, and the study of myth and legend thereby begins to assume an ethical importance which overflows its own boundaries of imagination into the practical realities of everyday life.

As to the specific and delimited subject-matter of the present work, we can well insinuate ourselves into the sentiment expressed by Dr. Thomas Fuller, in a chapter on Solomon's Temple in his 1650 *Pisgah Sight of Palestine*:

'The subject whereon we enter is holy ground; may both writer and reader put off their shoes, and divesting themselves as much as may be of carnal corruption, come with simplicity and sincerity to the matter now undertaken.'

Some portions of the present work have appeared in the pages of *Ars Quatuor Coronatorum*, the Transactions of Quatuor Coronati Lodge of Research, London, and the author accordingly wishes to thank the Officers of the Lodge for permission to include them in this complete work. A summary of it was also presented before the American Lodge of Research, New York, at its meeting of May 28, 1959, under the title 'King Solomon and his Temple in Masonic and Popular Legend', and is to be found in vol. VII, Number 2 of their Transactions. (At that time, the present book-length work was referred to as still 'in process of completing'.) The 1659 work of Samuel Lee, *Orbis Miraculum*, briefly referred to in the present section on 'The Twin Pillars' and elsewhere, has similarly been more adequately treated in my paper on 'King Solomon's Temple, 1659 A.D.', in vol. VIII, Number 1 of their Transactions.

An extensive Index has been prepared, to provide, hopefully, a one-volume 'Encyclopedia' on the Temple of Solomon for easy reference.

San Francisco   A.H.

Dec. 1967

BIBLIOGRAPHICAL NOTES

Cyclopedia of Biblical, Theological, and Ecclesiastical Literature. M'Clintock and Strong. New York, 1894.

Encyclopedia Biblica. Cheyne and Black. New York, 1899.

Dictionary of the Bible. James Hastings. New York, 1905.

Dictionary of the Bible. Dr. Wm. Smith. London, 1893.

The Holy Bible . . . with a Commentary and Critical Notes. Adam Clarke, LL.D., F.A.S. London.

The Holy Bible . . . with Commentary. F. C. Cook. London, 1872.

The Interpreter's Bible, with Commentary. New York, 1954.

The Jewish Encyclopedia. Funk & Wagnalls. New York, 1901.

The Works of Flavius Josephus. Whiston's Translation (1737). Standard Edition, Philadelphia.

The History of Freemasonry, Its Legends and Traditions, Its Chronological History. In seven volumes. Albert G. Mackey, M.D. New York and London, 1898 edition.

The History of Freemasonry, Its Antiquities, Symbols, Constitutions, Customs, etc. In five volumes, Robert F. Gould. Yorston Pacific Coast Edition, 1905.

Encyclopedia of Freemasonry. Albert G. Mackey, M.D. Clegg Revised Edition, in two volumes. Chicago, 1946. With vol. III by H. L. Haywood.

Ars Quatuor Coronatorum, (AQC). Transactions of Quatuor Coronati Lodge No. 2076. London, 1886 to date.

The Early Masonic Catechisms, (EMC). Knoop, Jones, and Hamer. Manchester, 1943.

Quatuor Coronatorum Antigrapha, (QCA). Masonic Reprints of Quatuor Coronati Lodge No. 2076.

PART I

THE TEMPLE

' . . . The Temple of Solomon, so spacious and magnificent, and constructed by so many celebrated artists. . . . '

—Wm. Preston, *Illustrations of Masonry*, 1772.

I

THE TEMPLE OF SOLOMON IN MASONIC LEGEND

I T MAY perhaps be a pardonable exaggeration—but none the less an exaggeration—to say, as Robert W. Bowers does say, in an opening statement of his *Freemasonry and the Tabernacle and Temples of the Jews* (1899), that Freemasonry is blended 'indestructibly with the rites, ceremonies, and traditions of Hebrew worship'. This in fact is not entirely and literally true, in all respects, but, on the other hand, it is true that we do have, in our Craft Lectures, and in those of other associated Masonic Rites, as most of us know, numerous traditions respecting the building of King Solomon's Temple in which we find recited some of the architectural and ornamental details of 'that mighty edifice', and details of some of the personalities involved, from all of which we attempt to derive a suitable symbolism leading to an ethical and spiritual philosophy. The basis of all this is what Mackey and others have appropriately called the *Legend of the Craft*.

Some of the traditions associated with this Legend are factual in so far as they may be considered to be supported by scriptural or secular history, while others are purely legendary or even entirely mythical and imaginary, in so far as they, on the contrary, appear to have no scriptural or historical support. It is important that we attempt to separate, as much as we can, the one class from the other, thus extricating the historical from the purely legendary, while attempting to arrive at some answer to the oft-taunting question as to the primary origin of some of these Masonic traditions, and the manner of their transmission down to our own day.

The necessity to separate ascertainable history from mere legend and tradition is no doubt appreciated by all, though not always carried into practice, but a further necessity also exists to separate genuine tradition from mere fable. A genuine Masonic 'tradition', properly speaking, presupposes some measure of antiquity, whereas a mere 'legend' could be a recently-concocted one and still be a genuine legend of sorts. Or it could even be an ancient legend, and still have no appreciable significance for the Masonic ethic and philosophy.

'Traditional Masonic legends,' therefore, become the proper study of the Masonic mythologist, as opposed to those so-called 'legends' that have no satisfactory measure of Masonic antiquity behind them, or have no ascertainable association in Masonic ritual, symbolism, or philosophy. It is to the former class—in addition to the purely historical aspects of the question—that the present work will address itself.

These thoughts and conclusions are brought to mind by a consideration of such a work as Dudley Wright's *Masonic Legends and Traditions* (London, 1921), which inescapably centres itself around King Solomon and his Temple. Unfortunately, however, and despite the well-intended dichotomy in the title, the work itself is found to contain an uncritical and largely mixed-up jumble of both 'legends' and 'traditions', Masonic and otherwise, and without any serious attempt to distinguish editorially between them.

Our documentary heritage

The Masonic documents we have at our disposal for the purpose of our present study fall naturally into a definite chronological sequence:

First come the *Old Charges*, mostly of an Operative character, but with some undoubtedly 'Speculative' overtones, from the very earliest of them, and dominating in point of time the fourteenth to the seventeenth centuries. A large number of these *Old Charges* have now come to light, and many of them can be found reproduced in various works, easily accessible, and some of them in photographic facsimile, which gives them an added value and interest. They can thus be studied at first hand by those to whom the original manuscripts—in the British Museum, in Oxford's Bodleian Library, or in Masonic collections—are largely inaccessible. These *Old Charges*, H. L. Haywood reminds us, 'continue to be the key to the mysteries and symbolism of the Ritual of the Three Degrees, in which are enacted in a somewhat changed and elaborated form what was first written down in those documents'.[1]

---

[1] H. L. Haywood, *The Freemason*, Portland, Oregon, Jan. 1959. '*Somewhat* changed and elaborated' could perhaps be more realistically altered to '*vastly* changed and elaborated', but Haywood's estimate of the *Old Charges* otherwise is basically correct.

Secondly, we have the *Early Catechisms*, mostly of a non-operative and incipiently speculative character, and dominating the late seventeenth and first half of the eighteenth centuries, thus overlapping the closing period of the *Old Charges* and effectively forming a continuation thereto. Some dozen and a half of the most significant of these Catechisms have been collected and published under the title of *The Early Masonic Catechisms* (Manchester, 1943), edited by Knoop, Jones, and Hamer, and recently reprinted by Quatuor Coronati Lodge No. 2076, London, and are thus easily within the reach of all. This publication, in a sense, is even more significant for the elaboration of our ancient traditions than our *Old Charges*, and should be studied by every student interested in tracing the progressive evolution of our Ritual, and evaluating the bed-rock elements out of which this Ritual has emerged.

Straddling the era that closed the period of the *Old Charges* and opened that of the *Early Catechisms*, we have the first and second editions of the *Book of Constitutions*, edited by Dr. James Anderson in 1723 and 1738 respectively, with the approval of the Grand Lodge of England; this was the first work of its kind in the history of speculative Masonry, and the one which officially ushered in the speculative period of modern Freemasonry.[1]

Lastly, we have, in the United States, the *Monitors*, with their explanatory Lectures, and the several *Masonic Manuals* which serve the same purpose, in various Jurisdictions, and based on these *Monitors*. And, elsewhere, the three 'Explanations of the Tracing Board' which again serve the same purpose in the British Isles and in the 'Dominions beyond the Seas' wherever British work is practised. All of these are entirely speculative, but with operative undertones and recollections, and these carry us down to the present day.

With these various documents before us, and others of a cognate nature, both Masonic and non-Masonic, that will be identified as occasion arises, we can consider the details of King Solomon's

[1] *The Constitutions of the Free-Masons*. Containing the History, Charges, Regulations, &c. of that most Ancient and Right Worshipful Fraternity. For the Use of the Lodges, London, 1723. Reproduced in facsimile by Bernard Quaritch from the original edition, London, 1923, with an important Introduction by Lionel Vibert.

The second edition is titled *The New Book of Constitutions*, etc., and has been reproduced in facsimile as vol. vii of the Masonic Reprints of Quatuor Coronani Lodge No. 2076, London—*Quatuor Coronatorum Antigrapha (QCA)*—with an Introduction by W. J. Hughan.

Temple and its builders and their building activities, comparing the statements found in our Lectures with their scriptural parallels where such parallels do exist, as well as with the writings of 'the great Jewish historian Josephus', and the accumulated legendary lore that has grown up in the three thousand years behind us—in the writings of the Rabbis, the writings of the Christian commentators, and even in the myths of the *Arabian Nights*. The thread of narrative can thus be carried back, as far as possible, to the earliest times.

The Monitorial Lectures that will be cited, as a point of departure in our analysis, will be taken from various Monitors that are available, both official and unofficial, representing several Jurisdictions in the United States, as well as the efforts of several individual writers like Mackey, Cross, Simon, and others, who attempted to follow Webb in arranging a Lodge Manual more to their own liking, or that of the Jurisdiction they served. James Wright Anderson did the same for California work, and his *Masonic Manual*, 1893, will be largely used here for purposes of monitorial exposition, since his work, based on the official California Monitor, gives more details of King Solomon's Temple than perhaps some of the others.[1]

The fountain-head of all this monitorial work, in this country, is, of course, the famous *Freemason's Monitor, or Illustrations of Masonry*, by Thomas Smith Webb, a work that first appeared in 1797, and upon whose basis most if not all of the American Monitors and Manuals in use today have been evolved. Webb's work, in its first edition, was in turn based upon William Preston's still more famous *Illustrations of Masonry*, first published in London in 1772, the word 'illustration' being used, not in its pictographic sense, but in the sense of 'exposition' or 'elaboration'. This first edition of Webb's is in somewhat less elaborate form than his later ones, and in its first sixty-four pages of the 1797 edition is actually a reprint, almost verbatim, of a part of the work by Preston, probably of the 1792 edition. But subsequent editions of Webb were re-cast to some extent in Webb's own words, and, as in the case of Preston's later editions, were considerably amplified. Thus the second edition of Webb (1802) contains a good many items not found in the first, and the third edition (1805) contains still more. With the publication of this third edition, Webb had completed his monitorial arrangement,

---

[1] To distinguish the work of this American James Anderson from that of the British James Anderson of the English *Book of Constitutions*, the latter author will be designated when necessary by the commonly used prefix 'Dr.'

and later editions are found to contain nothing that had not gone before, except for the charts and illustrations. But despite these elaborations by Webb in his second and third editions, large portions of his work—even as reflected in the Monitors which are in use today—are almost verbatim reproductions of the corresponding passages in Preston, thus carrying our explanatory work to a period of approximately half-a-century from the official beginning of our speculative Masonry.

As to the historical portion of Preston's work—or what was intended to pass for historical—this was, in turn, based largely if not entirely upon the *Book of Constitutions* of Dr. Anderson. This latter work consists, first of all, of a seemingly 'historical' section, interspersed at convenient intervals with a number of legends and traditions. These are followed by a collection of 'Charges' and General Regulations for the government of the Craft, all of this having been re-cast, wherever possible, from a number of 'old records'—the *Old Charges*—amplified, in a few cases, as Anderson assures us, with some of 'the traditions of old Masons, who talk much of these things'.

To come down to specifics, Anderson's elaboration of the Solomonic and Temple legends—since this is what we are primarily concerned with in the present work—'has exerted a considerable influence upon other Legends subsequently framed', Dr. Mackey tells us, 'and especially upon all the rituals, and indeed upon all the modern ideas of speculative Masons'.[1] We might consequently be justified in saying that, during the speculative period of our development, everything goes back to Anderson.

Some of the specific copies of the *Old Charges* that Anderson must have had before him while he was preparing his work have actually been identified, from the verbal similarities that have been discovered. Lionel Vibert, who has made a very thorough study of Anderson's work and its operative background, cites particularly the *Cooke MS.*, one of our oldest of the *Old Charges*, and said to have been written down about 1410 A.D., but containing at least portions that appear to experts to be a copy of a still older work, from about the middle of the preceding century. The *Cooke* text is shown to have been exhibited in Grand Lodge in 1721, and thus must have been well known to Anderson at the time he was working on his own book.

[1] Mackey, *History of Freemasonry*, vol. I, p. 120.

The Masonic Legend of King Solomon's Temple can therefore be seen to go back to about 1410 A.D., as far as our own written records are concerned; and, inferentially, it may even go back, by way of 'from mouth to ear', to still earlier times, since these traditions may have been on the lips of men for an appreciable length of time before they came to be written down for posterity. Some of the details of this Legend of the Temple we can see for ourselves in a perusal of the *Cooke MS.*, reproductions of which, in modernized English, are today readily available (*Quatuor Coronati Pamphlet No. 2*, etc.); and when we say, as we so often do, 'Masonic tradition informs us . . . ' we are actually harking back to an immemorial past.[1]

This Masonic tradition of King Solomon and his Temple, as it finds itself reflected in the operative documents, beginning with the *Cooke MS.* and elaborating into the later versions, is conveniently summarized for us by George F. Fort in his reading of such of these *Old Charges* as he had examined:

> King David began the temple, called *Templum Domini*, now designated as the temple of Jerusalem. This monarch constituted himself a patron of the Masons, and by every means in his power endeavoured to show how highly he prized them. Although he adhered to the charges of Euclid, the Masons received from him enlarged powers for the internal government of the craft, and an increase of wages. Upon the accession of Solomon to the Israelitish throne, he pushed forward with vigor the projects of his father, and hastened the completion of the temple. This king collected from various countries of the world a larger class of skilled workmen, who numbered fourscore thousand hewers of stone. Among other changes made by Solomon, he selected three thousand of the most expert operatives, and placed them as governors or superintendents of the work. All these were classed

---

[1] Speaking of this manuscript, W. J. Crawley expresses the opinion that 'the assured tone with which the episode [of King Solomon's Temple] is introduced, backed up by specific references to the Bible in the vulgar tongue, gives us a clue to the date before which the Manuscript cannot have been compiled. . . . In short, the members of the Guild for whom this Manuscript was written were Lollards. . . .

'The reader, who sees in the . . . MS. the earliest authoritative identification of King Solomon with the Craft Legend, may recognize the long arm of coincidence in the fact that the first Book of the Lollards' Bible to see the light *in print* was the *Song of Solomon*. See Dr. Adam Clarke's *Commentary on the Holy Bible*; 1810'.—*AQC* xxvii, 163.

under the general term of Masons. At this time Solomon received many flattering indications of the friendly spirit of neighbouring rulers, and among others, Hiram, King of Tyre, who offered him the resources of the Tyrian kingdom. By this means the king of Israel was enabled to procure such timber as was essential in the construction of the temple. A son of Hiram, Aynon,[1] by name, was appointed master mason of this great work, and was especially distinguished for his geometric knowledge. He was chief master of all the masons engaged in the erection of the Jewish temple, and was a proficient master of engraving and carving, and all manner of masonry required for the sacred edifice. Solomon, according to old books of the craft, confirmed the ancient charges, and sanctioned the customs which had prevailed during his father's reign, which the chronicles affirm to be but little different from those then practised. In this manner the worthy science of masonry was introduced into the country of Jerusalem, and then propagated throughout many kingdoms.[2]

It is to be reiterated, however, that this long account is not to be found in any single one of the *Old Charges*, but is a compilation from a number of different versions. The way in which this apparently long Legend had become progressively elaborated from shorter and simpler beginnings will be demonstrated in one of the chapters that is to follow.

These *Old Charges* of the operative masons appear to have been available to others than the masons themselves, even in the very early days. Thus, Sir Walter Raleigh is said to have made reference in his *History of the World* to the building of King Solomon's Temple, wherein 'there were 80000 Masons and 30000 Carpenters and Joyners employed in that Work, and 35000 Master Masons or Directors to oversee and direct the Work.'[3] This citation, if it is

---

[1] Fort incorrectly thinks this to be a corruption of the name Hiram. The subject of these 'substitute names' found in the *Old Charges* will be fully discussed toward the end of this work.

[2] Geo. F. Fort, *The Early History and Antiquities of Freemasonry*. Philadelphia, 1877, pp. 162–163.

[3] Cited in 'The Perjur'd Free Mason Detected,' of 1730.—*EMC* 159. Sir Walter Raleigh's *History* is said to have been published between 1603 and 1616. —G. Ernest Wright, *Biblical Archaeology*. Philadelphia, 1957, p. 18.

The '35000' Overseers is no doubt a typographical error for '3500', which is nearer the 3600 number given in the *Book of Chronicles*.

accurately given, would appear to be a direct quote from one of the *Old Charges* that may have been current in Queen Elizabeth's time, since the wording obviously does not originate from the somewhat different account found in the Bible.

II

'WHENCE CAME YOU?'

THE theory of the origin of the Masonic institution from King Solomon's Temple is an old tradition indeed, and stems from the *Old Charges* of the operative Masons, a summary of which has been presented above. That the tradition was firmly believed in as historical fact by the old operative Masons who had these *Old Charges* before them is a natural assumption, and we are told in fact that it is quite probable, for example, 'that the hewers and setters who worked at Windsor Castle, or Westminster Abbey, or Eton College,' actually did think of themselves 'as practising a trade which had been carried on and regulated in the days of King Solomon.'[1]

The belief is expressed in the following words in the earliest of the *Old Charges* to carry the tradition—the *Cooke MS.* of *c.* 1410—where we read that

> at the making of Solomon's Temple that King David began . . . Solomon had four score thousand Masons at his work; and . . . Solomon confirmed the Charges that David his father had given to Masons. And Solomon himself taught them their manners [i.e., customs and practices], but little differing from the manners that now are used.

And all this, it is there also said, was on the authority of 'other chronicles, and in old books of Masonry', thus testifying, at least, to the prevalence—even at that early age—of an old tradition. 'And thus,' says the more elaborate tradition in the recently-discovered *Beswicke-Royds MS.* of the early sixteenth century, 'was the worthy craft of masons confirmed in the Cuntry of Jerusalem.'

That the tradition was firmly believed in by the practical operative Masons of old is perhaps indicated by the 'Apprentice Orders' of a purely operative body—Swalwell Lodge—wherein we read, in part, that

[1] Knoop, Jones, and Hamer, *The Two Earliest Masonic MSS.* Manchester, 1938, *Introduction.*

29

King David, and his son King Solomon at the building of the
Temple of Jerusalem . . . did not only promote the ffame of the
7 Liberal Sciences, but fformed Lodges, and gave and Granted
their Commissions and Charters to those of or belonging to the
science of Masonry, to keep & hold their Assembly's for . . .
making Masons within their Dominions, when and where they
pleased.

Wm. Waples, who furnishes a lengthy history of this old Lodge,
thinks that these Apprentice Orders probably date from the very
commencement of its existence.[1]

As to the dependence of the old operative Masons on their *Old
Charges* for the history of their origin, we find the *Edinburgh-
Kilwinning MS.* (*c.* 1670) very appropriately headed: 'Narration of
the Founding of the Craft of Masonry', and it was referred to, by
the Scotch Masons of that time, as 'the old buik'.

After the *Old Charges*, this tradition of Masonic origin came to
be taken up in the Early Masonic Catechisms, in the earliest of which
—the *Edinburgh Register House MS.* of 1696—we find the following
characteristic Question and Answer:

Q. Where was the first lodge?
A. In the porch of Solomon's Temple.

This formula we find repeated, without variation, in other
Catechisms of the period—in *A Mason's Examination* (1723), in
The Mystery of Free-Masonry (1730), and others; and with some
small elaboration in *The Grand Mystery of Free Masons Discover'd*
(1724), where we read:

Q. In what Part of the Temple was the Lodge kept?
A. In Solomon's Porch at the West-End of the Temple,
where the two Pillars were set up.

Some of the esoteric elements associated with the primitive
Lodge—in at least one Catechism, the *Dumfries No. 4 MS.* (*c.* 1710)

---

[1] Wm. Waples, 'The Swalwell Lodge,' *AQC* lxii. 'The history of the Lodge
begins with a tradition that the Lodge may have been formed in Sunderland in
1681. . . .' It was also previously known as the Lodge at the Two Fencers, and
the Lodge at the Rose and Crown, and took the name of the Lodge of Industry
in 1776. In 1845 it removed to Gateshead, in the North-east of England, and the
old Lodge is still known as the Lodge of Industry No. 48.

—are even found to have been ascribed to Solomon's predecessor, King David:

Q. which way came ye W[ord] first about
A. it was given to King david by report qn [when] he was hewing ye stones in ye mount [in order to be able] to know ye workmen from ye labourers

—that is, in order to be able to distinguish the true Masons 'who had the Word', (as in the Scottish tradition of the Mason Word), from the 'men of burden, or labourers' who had not.

That the tradition would similarly find expression in the later and more elaborate eighteenth-century Catechisms is perhaps to have been expected. Prichard's *Masonry Dissected* (1730) accordingly gives, at one point:

Q. Did you ever work?
A. Yes, in the Building of the Temple.

Q. Where did you receive your Wages?
A. In the middle Chamber . . .

Q. How came you to the middle Chamber?
A. By a winding Pair of Stairs, etc. etc.

Elements—or supposed elements—of King Solomon's Temple became in time the 'Master-Jewels' of the Lodge, and are thus explained:

Q. What are the Master-Jewels?
A. The Porch, Dormer and Square Pavement.

Q. Explain them.
A. The Porch [is] the Entring into the *Sanctum Sanctorum*, the Dormer the Windows or Lights within, the Square Pavement the Ground Flooring.

Similarly, *Jachin and Boaz* (London, 1762), as well as its companion-work *Hiram* (London, 1764; Belfast, 1765),[1] ask:

'Why do three make a lodge, brother?'
—to which the 'second reason' given is, because

[1] My own micro-film of *Hiram* is from the Belfast edition in the New York Public Library, a vast treasure-house of Masonic information.

'There were three grand masons at the building of Solomon's Temple.'

Jachin and Boaz then goes on to give, in the course of the Master's Lecture (with virtually identical wording in the case of the *Hiram Catechism*):

Q. What support our lodge?
A. Three pillars.
Q. Pray what are their names, brother?
A. Wisdom, strength, and beauty.
Q. What do they represent?
A. Three grand masters; *Solomon*, King of Israel; *Hiram*, King of *Tyre*; and *Hiram Abiff*, who was killed by the three fellow-crafts.

Q. Were these three grand masters concerned in the building of *Solomon's temple*?
A. They were.
Q. What was their business?
A. *Solomon* found provisions and money to pay the workmen; *Hiram* King of *Tyre* provided materials for the building, and *Hiram Abiff* performed or superintended the work.

The first official elaboration into a connected account of the Solomonic Temple Legend in our Masonic tradition—with names, places, and dates; numbers of workmen and conditions of work; and incidents of one kind or another associated with the erection of such an important edifice—can no doubt be credited to our redoubtable Dr. Anderson. In the first edition of his *Book of Constitutions* (1723), he devotes no less than five pages to these sundry details. In this work—sanctioned by the Grand Lodge of England, and screened by 'fourteen learned brethren'—Dr. Anderson speaks confidently of King Solomon as 'Grand Master of the Lodge at Jerusalem,' while in his second edition (1738), he develops his theme to an even greater extent. Now we hear of Adoniram as the 'Junior Grand-Warden,' as well as of 'Hiram Abbif, the most accomplishd' Designer and Operator upon Earth, who in Solomon's Absence fill'd the Chair as Deputy Grand Master, and in his Presence was the Senior Grand Warden, or principal Surveyor and Master of Work.

'Solomon partition'd the Fellow Crafts into certain Lodges, with a Master and Wardens in each,' etc. etc., and later, Dr. Anderson informs us, 'many particular Lodges were constituted under Grand Master Solomon, who annually assembled the Grand Lodge at Jerusalem for transmitting their Affairs to Posterity. . . .'

Thus was the belief in the origin of the Masonic institution from the building of King Solomon's Temple firmly established, 'according to the Traditions of old Masons, who talk much of these Things.'[1]

This theme then came to get further elaboration at the hands of Wellins Calcott, in his *Candid Disquisition of the Principles and Practices of the Most Antient and Honourable Society of Free and Accepted Masons*—generally referred to in our literature by its abbreviated title, *Candid Disquisitions*—first published in 1769.[2] Here, the imagined establishment of Masonic principles, customs and practices, at the time of the building of this edifice, is described with such an air of seriousness (following, no doubt, the example previously set by Dr. Anderson) that the unsuspecting reader falls under the spell of an imagined on-the-spot report of a representative from *Reuter's Agency*. But even Dr. Oliver, fully a century later, and with smaller excuse, fell into the same pit.

Dr. Oliver's predecessor, in this respect, was the Rev. Jonathan Ashe, who brought out, in 1814, his *Masonic Manual, or Lectures on Freemasonry*. Mackey says that at least two-thirds of it is taken from Hutchinson, but, in respect to this question of Masonic origin, at least, Dr. Ashe, too, follows the tradition as expressed by Anderson, wherein we find that Solomon is said to have 'partitioned the fellow-crafts into certain Lodges, appointing to each, one to preside as a master, assisted by two others as wardens, that they might receive commands in a regular manner, take care of the tools and jewels, and be duly paid, fed, clothed, etc.,' following in this, Anderson's (and Calcott's) wording, almost verbatim. But Ashe goes one better than Anderson, in that in addition he sees 'our wise Grand Master' instructing 'the craftsmen in principles of the most sublime speculative philosophy, tending . . . to unite the Speculative and Operative Masons. . . .' Thus, not only is the operative Craft here said to have been firmly established, but our speculative Science also, in the days of King Solomon.[3]

[1] Anderson, *The New Book of Constitutions*, 1738. *Quatuor Coronatorum Antigrapha (QCA)*, vol. vii, p. 13.
[2] Vol. vi of the Universal Masonic Library, New York, 1855, pp. 19–22.
[3] Jonathan Ashe, D. D., *The Masonic Manual; or, Lectures on Freemasonry*. New Edition (Oliver), New York, 1855. Universal Masonic Library, vol vi, pp. 15–20.

But the most prolific and exuberant advocate of the origin of modern Freemasonry from the construction of King Solomon's Temple is our Dr. Oliver. In his *Antiquities of Freemasonry*, he appropriately devotes his concluding chapter to a discussion of the Temple, in its supposed relation both to the origin of our institution as well as to its later development through the succeeding millennia, and in respect to its institutional arrangement, its moralism and philosophy, its symbolism and its legendary values. This he goes into, in still greater detail, in his *Historical Landmarks*, where five whole chapters are devoted to this subject in Volume I, and two additional chapters in Volume II. His writings are not without interest for the curious reader, both for his studious collection of historical and legendary narratives, and his religious and philosophical disquisitions thereon, as well as for his imaginative inventiveness in developing such 'legends' as might best illustrate the propositions he wishes to establish, wherever such 'legends' do not previously happen to find themselves in the Masonic repertory. On the one hand, his listing of the builders engaged in preparing and erecting that mighty edifice is largely in accordance with Dr. Anderson's enumeration, and almost a verbatim copy of Calcott's, and all of this more or less in accordance with biblical information. But on the other hand, his listing of such items as 'seven hundred and fifty lodges' in operation at the quarries, and the still more impossible 'four hundred and twenty lodges' in the forests of Lebanon—where the workers, as pointed out by Mackey, were necessarily wood-cutters rather than stone-masons—must be pure fiction, and probably his own invention. Similarly, his reference to an 'ancient masonic tradition' listing no less than nine Grand Masters, each in charge of a different 'Degree', from Entered Apprentice to 'Super-Excellent Mason', must also be somebody's dream, if not his very own.[1]

As to the vastly exaggerated accounts that are given in our eighteenth-century rituals relative to the ornaments of King Solomon's Temple, and their monetary value, Oliver goes to great lengths

---

[1] Rev. Geo. Oliver, D. D., *The Antiquities of Freemasonry*. New Edition, New York, 1899. See especially pp. 224-226.

Oliver, *The Historical Landmarks and other Evidences of Freemasonry*. Lodgeton, Kentucky, 1856. Vol. I: Lectures viii, xv-xvii, xxiv. Vol. II: Lectures xxxi and xxxii. (These are respectively volumes 11 and 12 of the Universal Masonic Library).

to show the relative wealth and splendour of other Oriental courts and temples, in an attempt to prove that 'the accounts contained in Freemasonry are not to be considered as an exaggeration of facts'. But even he gags at times at some of the more ebullient expressions found in our Lectures and Catechisms, of his own day.

These early eighteenth-century Catechisms had become quite elaborate with the advent of William Preston (1742-1818). In *Henderson's MS.*, which purports to be Prestonian, and which is actually an extensive discourse that answers for the most part to the questions raised and the Syllabus outlined in Preston's *Pocket Manual* (1790 and 1792), Preston describes King Solomon's Temple as 'that greatest of Masonic edifices', and proceeds in due course to describe how 'the fellow crafts in former days went to receive their wages in the middle chamber of the Temple, reaching it by way of a porch and a winding staircase . . .' etc. Later on, he explains that

Degrees were established or recognised in our Order at the time of the building of the Temple of Solomon, when all the persons employed in the Temple were divided into three classes, rulers, overseers and craftsmen. . . . Our system of government took its rise from the system as established during the building of the Temple of Solomon.

In 1787, Preston created a Chapter of the 'Ancient and Venerable Order of Harodim,' as a sort of Lodge of Instruction for the study and rehearsal of his system of Lectures. In the spirit of the tradition we are here recounting, he declared this order of Harodim to be 'coeval with the building of Solomon's Temple and that it was established by the 3,300 eminent Masons who collaborated in its erection', thus tying it in with the biblical account.[1]

Of all the prominent early writers on the organization and development of the Masonic institution, only one seems to have departed somewhat from the traditional view—a contemporary of Preston himself, William Hutchinson. Writing in his *Spirit of Masonry* (1775), he categorically denies the development of our speculative institution from out of an operative past, and specifically contests the then-current and traditional view that its organization stemmed from the time of the building of King Solomon's Temple. But this is only with respect to its primary *origin*, which he relegates to an

[1] Wm. Preston. *Pocket Manual*, Introduction.

indefinite past, buried among the primitive religions and mysteries of the ancients. But even Hutchinson accepts the tradition of an operative body of Masons in existence at the time of the building of King Solomon's Temple, though he assigns to this activity a purely secondary function. But, in the course of this operative function, Hutchinson admits that Solomon managed to give to the workers 'particular signs and secret tokens, by which each rank should be distinguished, in order that the whole might proceed with propriety, and without confusion; . . . [and] the whole was conducted with that degree of holy reverence, that even the noise of a tool or instrument was not permitted to disturb the sacred silence on Moriah. . . . From thence, the masons of Solomon would be dispersed into different states, to superintend the works of other princes; and they would in consequence, convert infidels, initiate brethren in their mysteries, and extend their order over the distant quarters of the known world.'[1]

After Hutchinson and Preston, the story of our origin from King Solomon's Temple came to be carried on in the somewhat later eighteenth century English Catechisms.

In an interesting Lancashire Catechism of this period,[2] we find the following excerpts, illustrative of this question of 'origin':

Q. What is an excellent Master M's name?
A. G. . . .

Q. Who conferred that name upon him?
A. K.S.

Q. For why?
A. For the excellency in all manner of workmanship[3]. . . .

Q. What do you dedicate your L. with?
A. Corn, wine & oil.

Q. Why so?
A. . . . Corn, wine & oil, were the merchandise which

---

[1] William Hutchinson, *The Spirit of Masonry* (1775). Oliver Edition, Lodgeton, Kentucky, 1856, pp. 97-99.
[2] This is sometimes referred to as the 'Lodge of Lights' working. See the bibliographical note on p. 304 below.
[3] Obviously, from the context, in connection with the building of K.S.T.

S.K.I. sent H.K.T. in return for the stone & timber he received from him to build the T.

After this, some seventy-seven Questions and some very elaborate and lengthy Answers are given respecting the construction, the furnishings, and the religious service in connection with the Temple, including the details of its Dedication, some of this showing direct reflection from the analogous 'Questions concerning the Temple' in the *Dumfries No. 4 MS.* of *c.* 1710.

Some details of King Solomon's Temple have also managed to over-flow the boundaries of the Craft Degrees and spill over into the so-called 'Higher Degrees' of the Scottish Rite and the Royal Arch. Not only the Craft material, but even that of the Ineffable Degrees, now in the Scottish Rite system, is sometimes said to have had its origin at the time of the Temple's beginning, as Dr. Oliver reminds us. 'But,' he admits, surprisingly for him, 'there are insuperable objections to such an opinion.'[1] This could be said, with equal force, of the Craft material as well.

Current belief as to the Temple origin

Yet, despite all indications to the contrary respecting Masonic origin from King Solomon's Temple, we find this tradition to be believed in at the present time as well. This appears to be as true of some of our more eminent Masons, as of those that are less informed. As recently as 1873 (and perhaps even more recent examples might be found), the Rev. A. N. Keigwin, in the course of an important sermon delivered at the dedication of the Masonic Temple in Philadelphia, soberly expressed himself as saying that 'historically, Masonry dates from the building of the Temple of Solomon. No one at the present day disputes this claim.'

'I cite this out of hundreds of similar passages in other writers,' says Mackey, in comment on this astounding statement, 'to show how universal among such educated Masons is the belief in the Temple theory.'[2]

More to the point, however, is Mackey's own statement—not unlike the Rev. Keigwin's—written apparently at a time when he was still under the influence of his erstwhile *alter ego*, Dr. George Oliver. 'Speculative Freemasonry,' he confidently said at the time, in his *Symbolism of Freemasonry*, 'dates its origin from the building

[1] Oliver, *Antiquities of Freemasonry*, p. 227.
[2] Mackey, *History of Freemasonry*, I, 151, 163.

of King Solomon's temple,' thereupon compounding the felony by adding a footnote: 'This proposition we ask to be conceded; the evidences of its truth are, however, abundant' [!][1]

Several years later, however, he was not so sure. Writing in his more sober and realistic *History of Freemasonry*, he says of the Temple-origin theory that 'it is, in fact, very true that only those scholars who have made the history of the Order an especial study'— and he now surely numbers himself in that category—'have any doubts upon the subject'. And, on the more positive side, he has categorically laid down the maxim that 'the claim that Freemasonry took its origin at the building of the Temple is without any historical authority.'[2] But in spite of this denial, he appears to have made this very same belief the explanatory basis of his own 'Twenty-fourth Landmark', which he calls 'The Foundation of a Speculative Science upon an Operative Art'. Here he says, in elaboration, that 'the Temple of Solomon was the cradle of the Institution, and, therefore, the reference to the operative Masonry, which constructed that magnificent edifice, to the materials and implements which were employed in its construction, and to the artists who were engaged in the building, are all component and essential parts of the body of Freemasonry, which could not be substracted from it without an entire destruction of the whole identity of the Order.'[3] This is confusing legend and history with a vengeance! And giving it the dignity of a serious discussion on the Ancient Landmarks would seem to be carrying the 'confusion in the temple' to the heights indeed.[4]

---

[1] Mackey, *Symbolism of Freemasonry*, Chicago, 1952, p. 86. This work is supposed to have been first published in 1869 (*s.v.* the article 'Mackey' in Mackey's *Encyclopedia of Freemasonry*), a quarter of a century after his first Masonic publication, but may have actually been written earlier. It bears all the marks of an immature knowledge, and an adherence to the Oliverian system of thought which he later seems to have repudiated.

[2] Mackey, *History*, 1, 151, 163.

[3] In this connection, Luke A. Lockwood's description of his own Third Landmark, though similar in intent to Mackey's 24th, is more sober and realistic in its declaration, when he describes it as 'the inculcation of the moral virtues . . . by means of symbols derived from the Temple of King Solomon. . . .'—Lockwood, *Masonic Law and Practice*. Cited in Silas H. Shepherd's *The Landmarks of Freemasonry*, Bk. II, p. 99. Little Masonic Library, Kingsport, Tenn.

This, in fact, relegates the symbols to their proper place, and gives them their proper value, without dogmatizing as to their historical basis.

[4] Cf. Mackey, *Jurisprudence of Freemasonry*. Chicago, 1953, pp. 18–19. 13th Edition, revised.

Despite some positive disclaimers from our recognized historians
—including Mackey, when he elects to write as an historian—we
find a recently published work—*Our Ancient Brethren, the Origina-
tors of Freemasonry*, by the Rev. F. de P. Castells, P.M., P.Z., etc.—
once again flogging the dead horse of our Temple origin. Castells
takes this alleged origin of Freemasonry quite seriously and literally—and even, be it conceded, reverently—and builds out of it a
whole *mishmash* of Kabbalistic allegory and symbolism—a theory
of origins so fantastic in his account that it can only be designated
by the three 'imps'—implausible, improbable, and impossible.

But such a denial is believed by some to be unnecessarily icono-
clastic and overly sceptical. Thus, in a *History of Freemasonry*
which aims at being a sober and realistic appraisal of Masonic
history, but turns out to be anything rather than that, in some
respects at least, the author (ostensibly Alexander Lawrie, but in
reality Sir David Brewster) expresses precisely such a view as
Mackey has criticized in his more mature moments. For, after
describing in some detail the Mysteries of Egypt and of Greece,
and the professional accomplishments of the Dionysian architects,
as a suggested prelude to a better understanding of the Masonic
institution, both in its speculative and in its operative aspects, the
author of the *History* comes to the conclusion that

> the opinion, therefore, of Freemasons, that their Order existed,
> and flourished at the building of Solomon's temple, is by no means
> so pregnant with absurdity, as some men would wish us to
> believe. . . .
>
> Nothing indeed can be more simple and consistent than the
> creed of the Fraternity, concerning the state of their order at this
> period. The vicinity of Jerusalem to Egypt; the connection of
> Solomon with the Royal Family of that kingdom; the progress of
> the Egyptians in architectural science; their attachment to
> mysteries, and hieroglyphic symbols; and the probability of their
> being employed by the King of Israel, are additional considerations,
> which corroborate the sentiments of Freemasons, and absolve
> them from those charges of credulity and pride, with which they
> have been loaded.[1]

The superficial plausibility of the argument is perhaps one of
the reasons the tradition has been accepted from the earliest times.

[1] Lawrie's *History of Freemasonry* (1804). Boston, 1829, pp. 68, 70.

Charles W. Moore, who provides some 'Notes, Critical and Historical' for the edition of Lawrie's work from which I am quoting, here adds in a footnote: 'That Freemasonry existed at the time of the building of the first Temple, the internal structure of the institution furnishes the most conclusive evidence. . . .' And Jeremy L. Cross, who produced a valuable *Masonic Chart* (first published in 1819) after the fashion of Webb's *Freemason's Monitor*, incorporates therein an uncritical 'History of Freemasonry' by 'A Brother' which cites verbatim the paragraph I have just quoted.

Thus also we find the irrepressible Dr. Oliver—who, as previously indicated, was Mackey's shining light in his earlier days—speaking soberly some one hundred years ago of King Solomon as organizing his workmen 'into orders, lodges, and messes'; adding that 'they were distinguished by signs, words, and tokens, and their work by marks; all of which was necessary to produce regularity and decorum, that alone could render effective the united services of such an immense body of men'—which again sounds plausible enough, on the surface, except for the discouraging fact that there is no shred of evidence, biblical or otherwise, in support of the tradition thus expressed, and which remains, at best, only a legend.[1]

This latter statement is by no means a recently arrived at conclusion, and goes even further back than the sometimes more sober statements of Dr. Mackey. The non-historical character of the tradition has in fact been occasionally recognized from the earliest 'speculative' times, and has led to criticism and even to ridicule of the pretensions of some Masonic writers. Such works as the *Briscoe* pamphlet of 1724, the *Free-Masons Accusation and Defence* of 1726, *An Ode to the Grand Khaibar* of 1726, and a letter of 'A.Z.' in *The Daily Journal* of Sept. 5, 1730, 'poked fun at contemporary versions of masonic history', Knoop, Jones, and Hamer tell us, 'and ridiculed the idea of any connection between modern freemasonry and King Solomon.'[2]

In more recent times, Geo. F. Fort, who has made a valorous but rather unsuccessful attempt to trace the origin of Masonic institutions to the Teutonic and Scandinavian countries, in opposition to their reputedly Solomonic origin, makes much of the fact that the

[1] Geo. Oliver, *Historical Landmarks*, II, 174.
[2] Knoop, Jones, and Hamer, *The Genesis of Freemasonry*, p. 3, Manchester 1949.
    All these documents referred to in the quotation above are reproduced in the collection of *Early Masonic Pamphlets* by the above-named editors.

building of the Temple is nowhere mentioned in the oldest of our *Old Charges*, the *Regius MS.* or Halliwell Poem, and is similarly not mentioned in any of the old documents of the Continental operative masons:

> It is a notable fact that the oldest and most authentic document, which is historical of the year 1254, as well as the most ancient records of German Masonry, about the middle of the fifteenth century, and confessedly drawn up from much older traditions, neither mention, nor in the remotest manner indicate, that the fraternity of Masons was put upon a substantial basis at the building of Solomon's Temple.[1]

In his own attempt to demonstrate, rather, that 'the junction of Byzantine corporations with Teutonic guilds afforded the substantial basis of subsequent lodge appointments and ritualism, such as have descended to modern Freemasonry,' and not the operations at the building of King Solomon's Temple, Fort builds up an elaborate but on the whole not very convincing picture of the absorption by the Byzantine architects of Jewish learning and traditions—with particular respect to the history of the Temple and the legend of Hiram the Builder, and the later transfusion of that lore to the Teutonic building guilds of Lombardy. But if all this is so, one would be tempted to ask, were the author available for questioning: How does it happen that, on his own showing, there is no Solomonic tradition or legend among the German Steinmetzen? But all this takes us somewhat far afield from our main line of thought.

Non-Masonic writers have been found to entertain the same opinion of the attempt made by some Masonic writers to trace their institution to the building of King Solomon's Temple as has been expressed in the *Briscoe* pamphlet and similar works. Thus, Agostino Sagredo, in his work on the building guilds of Venice, makes reference to the mediaeval Freemasons who, he says, 'to enoble themselves, ... dated their origin from Solomon's Temple.'[2] But he may have been only repeating the legend of the British Freemasons, or perhaps that of the French *Compagnonnage*, who have a similar tradition.

[1] Geo. F. Fort, *The Early History and Antiquities of Freemasonry*, As connected with Ancient Norse Guilds, and the Oriental and Mediaeval Building Fraternities. Philadelphia, 1877, pp. 180–181.

[2] Cited in Leader Scott's *The Cathedral Builders*, p. 387.

The tradition we have been recounting, however, such as it is, appears to be no mere Masonic conceit, entertained solely by a fraternity striving to derive some glory from a romantic and far-off past. The belief in fact has been expressed by those apparently not of the Craft as well, and even in these more scientific and sophisticated times; by those who delve into and write of the civilizations of antiquity, and theorize on the possible relation between the institutions of the present and their analogical forebears in the distant past. Thus Leonard Cottrell, writing on *The Anvil of Civilization* (New York, 1957), points to the rise, towards the very beginning of our Mediterranean civilization, of 'a new class of specialists, craftsmen ... bound together in "secret societies", sanctified and set apart by religious or pseudo-religious ritual, [who] jealously guard the mysteries of their craft and transmit them only to their chosen successors'—and adds, in a significant footnote, 'Cf. the modern Freemasons.' And not so very long ago, H. J. Da Costa strove to connect the builders of King Solomon's Temple with the Dionysian Artificers and with the Ancient Mysteries they are supposed to have practised as followers of the god Bacchus[1]— a theory that made much impress upon so learned a brother as the Rev. Joseph Fort Newton, prompting him to write that, if 'the laws of building were secrets known only to initiates, there must have been a secret order of architects who built the temple of Solomon,' namely 'the *Dionysian* Artificers. . . .'[2]

The connection between some architectural features of King Solomon's Temple and corresponding features in mediaeval European architecture is brought out in a Review of Leader Scott's work, *The Cathedral Builders* (London, Second Edition, 1899), by Hamon Le Strange, wherein the reviewer summarizes one portion of the Scott argument thus: 'The use of spiral columns, derived from the Byzantines, may, Leader Scott thinks, be a Masonic link with the ancient traditions of King Solomon's Temple. The Byzantines may have taken their symbolism from the Hebrews, so that, after all, there may be some grain of truth in the traditional connection of Freemasonry with King Solomon's Temple.'[3] The preliminary statement with respect to the spiral columns and similar

---

[1] H. J. Da Costa, *Sketch for the History of the Dionysian Artificers*. London, 1820 reprinted, New York, 1936.
[2] Joseph Fort Newton, *The Builders*, Cedar Rapids, Iowa, 1914, p. 76.
[3] *AQC* xii, 125.

architectural features may be very true, but—it must be pointed out—a history of architecture is not a *history of Freemasonry*. The latter is essentially the history of an organization rather than the history of an art, despite the many points of contact between the two. It is to be noted, finally, that the Freemasons are not the only ones to have claimed descent from the builders of King Solomon's Temple. In France, the previously-mentioned *Compagnonnage*— an association of journeymen, whose members are called *compagnons*, companions—does precisely the same. This Guild—which is still in existence, though not in a flourishing state, and is composed not only of stone-masons but of other building crafts as well—has a Legend very closely analogous to that of the Freemasons, but with some additional elaborations that have no bearing on the present discussion. They, too, look to King Solomon as their Founder, along with two others, and they have, as well, a Hiramic Tradition that is in some respects very similar to ours.[1] In fact, one branch of the *Compagnonnage* claims direct descent from the stone-masons of Tyre, but the question whether the French *Compagnons* borrowed some parts of their Legend from the British Freemasons, or the reverse, has never been determined. 'A legend of the craft being at King Solomon's Temple, where he gave them a Charge, was apparently the common property of the building trades' in France, as it was in England. So says Lionel Vibert, who has made an astute study of the organization and its legends. The question of its reciprocal relationship with Freemasonry will be more adequately treated in our final chapter.

It is curious to note, as we have done, that we find no such comparable Legend of Solomonic origin among the Steinmetzen—the operative stone-masons of Germany. But perhaps this is no more than a matter of geography. France and England are separated by only a narrow channel, and their kings sometimes straddled each other's thrones, and exchanged masons, working on each other's edifices. Germany is somewhat further inland, and, in the middle ages, had no such political connections.

The 'Tower of Babel' origin

But King Solomon's Temple did not always hold the pre-eminent position it enjoys today as the legendary base of reference to which practically all our institutions—including our very beginnings—are

[1] For details, see Chapter XIV, p. 324 *et seq.*, below.

traditionally assigned. That position, in fact, was once held by the Tower of Babel. Thus, in the very oldest of our *Old Charges*—the *Regius MS.* or Halliwell Poem, said to date about 1390 A.D.—our 'first most excellent Grand Master' is declared to have been King Nimrod himself, the builder of that famous Tower; and it was he, and not King Solomon, who is there said to have given the operative Masons of his day their first 'Charge'—the rule of conduct and the regulation of the mason craft by which they and their descendants were going to be governed.

This is even more pointedly brought out in some of the later versions of these *Old Charges*. Thus, the *Thistle MS.*—dated 1756, and therefore towards, if not beyond, the end of the 'operative' period—elaborates upon the simpler account given in the original *Regius MS.*, and tells us that Nimrod not only 'made Masons' but also 'taught them signs and tokens, so that they should Distinguish one another from all the Rest of mankind. . . . ' In fact, it goes on to say, 'this was the first time that Masons had care of their craft',[1] and it was therefore from this earlier day that our Masonic institution was for a long time believed traditionally to have originated, with only a subsidiary position, in point of origin, relegated to King Solomon's Temple.

This earlier form of the Legend, says Dr. Mackey, 'prevailed during perhaps the whole of the eighteenth century. . . . But about the end of the last [i.e., the eighteenth] century, or perhaps, still later, about the beginning of the present [the nineteenth], this legendary account of the origin of Freemasonry began to be repudiated, and another one, in contradiction of the old manuscripts, was substituted for it. Masonry was [now] no longer believed to have originated at the Tower of Babel; the Temple of Jerusalem was considered as the place of its birth; and Solomon and not Nimrod was called the "first Grand Master" '.[2]

Mackey makes no attempt to evaluate the reason for the switch from King Nimrod to King Solomon, and from the Tower of Babel to the Temple of Jerusalem. My own estimate of the situation would be that when the Legend of the Craft, as exemplified in the *Old Charges*, ceased to preoccupy itself primarily with the art of building and its history, and became, instead, a story with a moral and with a spiritual interpretation, as later exemplified in the *Early Catechisms*

[1] Herbert Poole, 'The Thistle MS.' *AQC* xxxv, 41, 43.
[2] Mackey, *History of Freemasonry*, I, 60.

(inspired perhaps by Samuel Lee's *Orbis Miraculum* and John Bunyan's *Solomon's Temple Spiritualiz'd*, which had just come out about the time the Craft was in process of transition from operative to speculative), it no longer suited our 'ancient brethren' to find the prototype of our Craft in an institution connected with the building of the Tower of Babel—a heathen structure erected in overt defiance of Heaven—but they, on the contrary, had no difficulty in seeing our origin in an institution connected with a Temple erected to the glory of the one true God. Now they could no longer look to the heathen and rebellious King Nimrod as our 'first most excellent Grand Master', but could easily feel justified in conferring this honour upon King Solomon—our 'wise King Solomon', as he is spoken of in *A Mason's Examination* (1723)—'in his Time Grand Master of Masonry and Architecture. . . . '

That this estimate of mine is not entirely a fanciful speculation appears to be indicated in such a Catechism as *The Whole Institutions of Free-Masons Opened* (1725), where certain 'words' are given and explained, and the question is then asked:

[Q.] What mean you by these Words—
[A.] We differ from the Babylonians who did presume to Build to Heaven, but we pray the blessed Trinity to let us build True, High, and Square, and they shall have the praise to whom it is due

—an answer we find repeated in almost identical terms in the *Graham MS.* (1726).

This original preference for the Tower of Babel seems rather strange to us now, especially in view of the popularity that King Solomon had always enjoyed in the public fancy, as well as in the Masonic mind, as we shall presently see in greater detail. During the twelfth to the fourteenth centuries, the fable-makers and song-writers of Europe had been composing stories and romances and sonnets surrounding the character, wisdom, and artistic prowess of the fabulous Solomon, who seemed to have caught the imagination of that romanticizing period, and it was precisely at that time that the framers of the Masonic Legend were at work in developing the various aspects of the traditional history of their Craft. Mackey thinks it is only natural that the hero of so many of the mediaeval romances should eventually have found his way into what has come to be known as the *Legend of the Craft*—a Legend we find to be in general conformity with the historical atmosphere of the period it refers to, though inaccurate in many respects as to detail. We find in this *Legend of the Craft* a prolific confusion of dates, and of names, and of historical events, all of which can easily be ascribed to the generally low level of knowledge enjoyed by the public at large at the time these legends were composed or elaborated upon. But they are not altogether idle fancies or imaginative inventions, and, as far as many of the details now recounted in our Lectures are concerned, are to be found largely if not universally supported by the biblical authority on which they claim to rest.[1]

Some hints from the Bible

To turn finally to one aspect of the problem of Masonic origins, there is a significant circumstance that tends to indicate, if faintly, that the operative Masons—and, after them, the Speculatives— may not have been altogether fanciful or inventive in ascribing the origin of their institution to a Craft organization formed at the time of the building of King Solomon's Temple.

Smith's *Dictionary of the Bible* (London, 1893), under the article 'Solomon', gives the biblical account which describes the King as having reduced to bondage the 'strangers' in the land, the remnant of the Cannanite races, one hundred and fifty-three thousand of these being sent off to work in the mountains and in the forests of Lebanon, to prepare the stone and lumber for the construction of the Temple. 'One trace of the special servitude of these "hewers of stone" ', says Dr. Smith, 'existed long afterward in the existence of a body of men attached to the Temple, and known as "children of Solomon's Servants", and they are so classified in the enumeration of the various bodies of men returning from the Babylonian Cap- tivity, to rebuild the Temple, some five hundred years after its destruction.[2] Alongside these 'Solomon's Servants', in King Solomon's time, there had been another class, the *Nethinim*. These were the simple hewers of *wood* and drawers of water, and they had originally constituted an adequate class for the service of the Tabernacle in the Desert, in its time. But 'for the construction and repairs of the Temple, another kind of labour was required, and the new bondmen were set to hewing and squaring *stones*. Their descendants', Dr. Smith goes on to speculate, 'appear to have

---

[1] Cf. Mackey, *History of Freemasonry*, I, ch. xix.
[2] *Ezra* ii, 55, 58; *Nehemiah* vii, 57, 60.

formed a distinct order, inheriting probably the same functions and the same skill'.[1]

All this is very curious. No Masonic writer, to my knowledge, has taken any notice of these 'Solomon's Servants' mentioned in the Bible, or of their descendants during the Captivity, and of the 'Order' they are supposed to have formed. Several other biblical commentators, however, do speak of these 'Servants of Solomon', in the same strain that Dr. Smith does, though not always with the implication of an hereditary 'Order', which is really the nub of the question. Cheyne and Black, for example (*Encyclopedia Biblica*, New York, 1899), speak of 'a guild of persons attached to the *second* temple', but think that 'the probability is, however, that the phrase ["Children of Solomon's Servants"] has nothing to do with Solomon, but is corrupt'. Corrupt or no, some *tradition* of these 'Solomon's Servants'—and perhaps even of an 'Order' connected with them—may have remained, perhaps in some mutilated and even exaggerated form, and without the disturbing implication of bondage so abhorrent to the mediaeval operative Mason; and this tradition may have helped build up in the minds of our operative brethren the mistaken memory of an Order of operative Masons from which they themselves were descended, through those 'travelling masons' whose journeys and exploits are given such detailed description in some of our *Old Charges*, down to Anderson's *Constitutions of the Freemasons*, 1723. This tradition of an Order of 'Solomon's Servants'—if it had indeed come to the notice of any of our 'ancient brethren' (and regardless of whether or not it had any basis in historical fact)—may be the source of our mediaeval and present-day belief as to the origin of our Masonic Craft in the correlative organization said to have been in existence during the building of King Solomon's Temple.

This strange account would bear further investigation among the maze of Rabbinic and Talmudic legends that have come down to us through the centuries.

Other allusions to King Solomon's Temple

From this specific question of 'origin' we may conveniently turn to the subsidiary question of 'dedication', which is, in a way, connected with it.

Here we have the tradition, as we find it stated in the California

[1] Smith, *Dictionary of the Bible*, s.v. 'Solomon's Servants, Children of.'

Masonic Manual, that 'Lodges were anciently dedicated to King Solomon, as it is said that he was our first Most Excellent Grand Master'.[1] The *Emulation* Lectures in England are even more specific in this respect, and they there say that Lodges are dedicated to King Solomon, 'he being the first Prince who excelled in Masonry, and under whose royal patronage many of our Masonic mysteries obtained their first sanction'.[2] This follows along the lines of an almost identical statement in Browne's *Masonic Master-Key* of 1802.

But there are many additional allusions in our Masonic system that similarly refer directly to King Solomon's Temple. There is, for example, the Mosaic Pavement with its Indented Tessel, this having formed, it is said, 'the ground floor of King Solomon's Temple'. And every Masonic Lodge is said, more specifically, to be a representation of that ancient edifice, its orientation due East and West being similarly in imitation of the orientation that is said to have prevailed in the case of that earlier Temple. The North side of a Mason's Lodge, again, is always 'dark', we say, because of the geographical position of the Temple in relation to the rays of the Sun and Moon at meridian height. The three Officer's stations represent the three gates of the Temple, and so forth. And in England and Scotland they furthermore say that the ground of a Mason's Lodge is considered to be 'holy ground', and they assign to this three specific reasons, all having to do with the spot upon which it is said King Solomon's Temple was reared, and the particular circumstances (all mentioned in the Bible) which made that spot 'holy'.

These various allusions, all having to do with the Lecture in the First Degree, are followed, in the Second, with a progress made by the Candidate through a specifically marked-out representation of King Solomon's Temple; and, in the Third, he is told of an occurrence 'which, Masonic tradition informs us, actually took place' at the building of King Solomon's Temple.

W. H. Rylands, in his paper on 'Some Notes on the Legends of Masonry',[3] here raises the pertinent question of 'why the Temple

---

[1] James Wright Anderson, *A Masonic Manual of the State of California*. San Francisco, 1893, p. 232.
[2] *The Lectures in Craft Masonry*. 'Emulation' Working. A. Lewis, London, 1919, p. 44.
[3] *AQC* xvi.

of Solomon and its builders have been selected to play an important part in one division of our legendary history'. He suggests that, if it could be shown 'with ordinary probability why the Temple and its builders, or even the building of the Temple alone could naturally be selected by the Freemasons' for that purpose, it might be possible to arrive at some solution of the problem in its various aspects.

This question of the importance of King Solomon's Temple to our Masonic traditions, and the reasons why it is so important, is basic to our present inquiry, and is of particular interest to us because of the place it now enjoys in our Lectures and in our literature.

III

KING SOLOMON IN POPULAR AND MASONIC LEGEND

IN SOME cases, our Masonic Legends respecting King Solomon can in fact be found to be a reflection of the Rabbinic and Kabbalistic lore that had been current among the Jews from very early times, and among the Arabs as well, to whom 'Suleimann' (considered by them to have been a Moslem) is almost as fabulous a figure as he is to his own kinsmen and to Masonry. Both to the Jews and the Arabs he is the Wise Man *par excellence* and Master-Magician, and many are the tales told of his prowess and his wisdom, his miraculous domination of the demons and the *jinns*, his occult and superhuman faculties and powers. Of especial interest to Royal Arch Masons, for example, is the Rabbinic legend to the effect that Solomon, in his capacity as prophet and seer, foresaw the destruction of his Temple by the Babylonians, and accordingly caused an underground receptacle to be built below the Temple in which the Ark was eventually hidden. This Rabbinic legend—which Dr. Oliver quotes verbatim from Rabbi Mannaseh ben Israel, 1604–1657[1]—has been preserved in Moore's *New Masonic Trestle Board* (Boston, 1868), in the Lecture on the Royal Arch Degree, and a somewhat different version of it is given in an 'old ritual' cited by Dr. W. W. Westcott, which will be referred to again, in another connection, somewhat later. The 'old ritual' is not otherwise specified, but is probably of Irish or Scottish origin, its critical reference to 'English masons' being an obvious indication.

But the public at large had not entirely lost its fascination for our ancient 'friend and brother', in both mediaeval and more modern times. In the mediaeval period, two factors had figured to sustain this interest: first, the force of oral tradition; and secondly, Art, and particularly the Art associated directly or indirectly with the religious impulse, in painting, sculpture, and architecture. As to oral tradition, Gerard Brett reminds us that, before the late fifteenth century, the number of those who had access to an actual Old

[1] Oliver, *Historical Landmarks*, II, 183. Cf. *Jewish Encyclopedia*, s.v. 'Solomon'.

Testament must have been very small. Consequently, up to about the year 1500, he thinks, we must regard the spoken word as the most important element in the transmission of the Solomonic tradition. But there was also the influence of Art, and Brett cites and illustrates numerous examples of European Art in which the personality of King Solomon is figured in conjunction with his Temple, in tapestry and stained-glass, in carvings of wood and stone.

But to those few who could read, there was always of course the additional influence of the written word, and we do find a rich though sparse European literature connected with Solomon and his Temple, beginning with the Church Fathers Clement and Eusebius (second and fourth centuries respectively). Both of these ecclesiastics tell us the now Masonically-forgotten story of the 80,000 workmen sent to King Solomon by the King of Egypt (whose daughter King Solomon had married), in addition to the 80,000 sent by the King of Tyre. Eusebius embellishes this story with a long description of the Temple, and with particular reference to the two brass pillars, which we here find to have been gilded with pure gold—perhaps in imitation of the two pillars Herodotus had reported seeing standing before the Temple of Hercules, in Tyre, one of which is said to have been 'of pure gold'. Eusebius wrote in the period of the *Testament of Solomon*, a work principally of Solomonic magic and folk-lore, the burden of which is to the effect that it was for the specific purpose of building the Temple that King Solomon had acquired his wondrous powers over the demons, with whose aid 'the mighty edifice' was erected. Gregory of Tours, in his *History* (sixth century) cites King Solomon's Temple as one of unequalled magnificence and splendour, and in another of his works describes it as one of the Seven Wonders of the World.

But it is in the lengthy *De Templo Salomonis* of Bede (672–735 A.D.) that we first meet with the allegorical approach to the Temple story to which more detailed reference will shortly be made. Comestor (twelfth century), like Gregory of Tours, gives a detailed story of the building and magnificence of the Temple, while Alcuin, in the same century, recites the whole history of Solomon, incorporating into it many of the legendary accretions of later times.[1]

[1] Gerard Brett, 'King Solomon'. *AQC* lxvi, 89. The author (Director of the Royal Ontario Museum of Archaeology, in Canada), thus partly refutes the statement of W. J. Chetwode Crawley to the effect that 'between the third and

Some two centuries later—that is, in the late fourteenth century—we find the vernacular translations of the Bible beginning to make their appearance, and these of course had the at least partial effect of making the tradition of King Solomon better known and more popular than ever. But even before that time—say, from the eighth to the thirteenth centuries—there had already been in existence 'a kind of background of literary speculation and artistic imagery which indicate that the Temple of Solomon may—even at that early period—have formed the basis upon which a body of Masonic legend and tradition was gradually evolved'.[1]

But even more recent times have shown an inordinate interest in the romantic King Solomon and his fabulous Temple. This is well indicated by the project said to have been instituted by the French writer Gerard de Nerval, in connection with his libretto for a Grand Opera on the subject of King Solomon's Temple, discussed in some detail in our concluding chapter.[2] The plot of his projected Opera is given, with its Hiramic and romantic details, in his *Voyage en Orient*, under the title, 'History of the Queen of the Morning, and Soliman, Prince of the Djinns', and is also found in an English translation in volume two of *The Women of Cairo*, by the same author (London, 1929).

While Nerval's original operatic venture, for which Meyerbeer was to have supplied the music, never materialized, two other French writers, Barbier and Carré, took up the scheme about 1862 and produced an opera, *The Queen of Sheba*, with music by Gounod, and on the basis of Nerval's libretto. In it, is the love-affair between the Queen of Sheba and Hiram, the craftsman (called, in the opera, by the name of Adonhiram—a customary French 'substitute' for the Master Hiram)—and it is Solomon's jealousy as a result of it that is the cause of the murder by three conspirators, of the King's master-workman.[3] Still another opera of the same name as Gounod's has appeared more recently, with music by Goldmark, but there is

the thirteenth century ... references to Solomon or to his Temple ... are neither complimentary to the wisdom of the King, nor laudatory of the splendour of the edifice'—*AQC* xxvii, 163.
[1] H. Carr, *AQC* lxvi, 99.
[2] See p. 312 *et seq.*, below. Cf. the commentary by W. H. Rylands, *AQC* xiv, 179.
[3] Cf. John T. Thorp, 'Freemasonry in Gounod's Opera: "Irene, the Queen of Sheba".' *AQC* xvi.

here no connection between the two plots, though still based on the Solomonic motif.

In the philosophical field, and in the Elizabethan era of William Shakespeare, the influence of the 'wise King Solomon' is indicated by the work of Francis Bacon that appeared under the title of *The New Atlantis*, which is said to have been one of Bacon's greatest achievements, and to have exerted a great impetus on the founding of the Royal Society. As to this *New Atlantis*, and as stated in his Introduction, Bacon endeavoured to 'exhibite therein, a Modell or Description of a College, instituted for the Interpreting of Nature, and the Producing of Great and Marvellous Works for the Benefit of Men'. And when Bacon cast about for a suitable name for this House of Wisdom, he significantly could find nothing more apt or descriptive than to call it 'Salomon's House'[1]—a circumstance that has brought some to the unwarrantable conclusion (as in the theory of Nicolai)[2] that Bacon, so near to the time of the 'Accepted Masons', must in fact have been the prime if not the sole originator of speculative Masonry.

Some further indication of the continuing interest in King Solomon in non-Masonic circles is furnished us in the current collection appearing under the title of *Tales of King Solomon*, by St. John D. Seymour, and published by the Oxford University Press (London, 1924). In the Introduction, Dr. Seymour tells us of the enormous spread of territory from which these tales have been gathered—countries as far apart, geographically and culturally, as Ireland and the Malay Peninsula—and taken down by living writers from oral narration. All this goes to show, he thinks, 'that after three thousand years Solomon is still so important a figure in tradition that stories are related of him'.

Edmond Fleg's *Life of Solomon* is similarly a collection of legends concerning King Solomon rather than a biography, but it suffers from the fact that the compiler has permitted his own poetic fancy to obtrude itself upon the traditional legends, as he himself tells us he has done. The result makes for a more enjoyably readable account, no doubt, but something less trustworthy from the standpoint of genuine folklore. More recently, *Solomon and Sheba*, by

[1] *Encyclopedia Britannica*, s.v. '*Bacon*'.
[2] Cf. Mackey, *History of Freemasonry*, II, 304. New York and London, 1898. See also the curious but completely uncritical work by Geo. V. Tudhope, *Bacon Masonry*.

Jay Williams (Random House, New York, 1959) has brought the romantic story of this couple to the novel-reading and movie-going public.

Masonic interest in King Solomon

As for our own Masonic interest in all this lore, the Legend of King Solomon's Temple has now become so inseparable a part of our system of symbolism and philosophical allegory that it will probably never be displaced, and at present its elimination is well-nigh unthinkable, and most certainly undesirable. It becomes doubly important, therefore, to be able to trace the origin and development of the various traditions that compose that Legend as they have manifested themselves in the thinking of operative and speculative Masons alike.

Attention has frequently been called to the great interest manifested by the general public in King Solomon's Temple, both in England and on the Continent in the early part of the eighteenth century, just about the time the institution of speculative Masonry was beginning to take definite shape. The appearance of so much detail respecting every phase of the Temple, and of the personalities involved in its erection is sometimes believed to be but a secondary manifestation of that great interest. The two famous models of King Solomon's Temple which were exhibited in London at about that time—Rabbi Leon's, first in 1675, and again about eighty years later; and Schott's, in 1725, said to have been 20 ft. × 20 ft. × 12 ft. in size (W. H. Rylands)—are also said to have contributed a good deal to that general interest. But it seems to me that this interest must be looked upon as an effect rather than as a cause. The enormous labour and expense that must have gone into these models could hardly have been felt justified unless there already was in evidence a tremendous amount of speculation and curiosity concerning King Solomon's Temple. That these models reciprocally stimulated a still greater interest in the Temple, of course, also goes without saying.[1]

Schott's model, as advertised in *The Daily Courant*, around 1729–1730, was described as follows:

[1] For details of these two early models, see the article 'Rabbi Jacob Jehudah Leon,' by W. J. Chetwode Crawley, and 'Schott's Model of Solomon's Temple', by W. H. Rylands, in *AQC* xii, 150, and xiii, 24, respectively.

To be seen at the Royal-Exchange *every* Day, The Model of the TEMPLE of SOLOMON, with all its Porches, Walls, Gates, Chambers and holy Vessels, the great Altar of the Burnt Offering, the Moulton Sea, the Lavers, the Sanctum Sanctorum; with the Ark of the Covenant, the Mercy Seat and Golden Cherubims, the Altar of Incense, the Candlestick, Tables of Shew-Bread, with the two famous Pillars, called Joachim and Boas. Within the model are 2000 Chambers and Windows, and Pillars 7000; the Model is 13 foot high and 80 foot round. . . .

The Publick is desired to take Notice, that the Sanctum Sanctorum, with all the holy Vessels is new gilt, and appears much finer and richer than before.[1]

A much earlier Model than the two just mentioned is also known to have been in existence in Ireland. R. E. Parkinson offers the following interesting quotation from the *Annals of the Four Masters* (1129 A.D.):

The Altar of the great church at Cluain-mic-Nois was robbed, and the jewels were carried off from thence, namely the *carracan* (model) of Solomon's Temple, which had been presented by Maelseachlainn, son of Domhnall

—who died in 1022. In fact, says Parkinson, in comment, 'there are many references to a Solomonic tradition in Irish literature'.[2]

Professor Stinespring gives a lengthy and expertly critical description of the various attempts at reconstruction of the Temple in model form, with illustrations of various recent examples.[3] Several models have been exhibited in our own era: one, at the 1939 New York World's Fair, and another at the 1964—65 World's Fair in the same city. Still another—Hudson's Model—is on permanent exhibit in the Museum of the Grand Lodge of California, at San Francisco, and a much larger one, measuring 20 ft. × 20 ft. is on exhibit in the Memorial Room of the Masonic Temple in Montreal, an illustrated account of which was given in *The New Age* Magazine for January 1967.

A more critical approach towards reconstruction is that represented by the Howland-Garber model, on exhibit at Agnes Scott

[1] Cited in Bernard E. Jones, *Freemasons' Guide and Compendium*, p. 404.
[2] *AQC* lvii, 65.
[3] *Interpreter's Dictionary of the Bible*, New York, 1962. Vol. R-Z, s.v. TEMPLE, JERUSALEM.

College, at Decatur, Georgia, and is based on the researches of Professor Paul Leslie Garber, who reputedly refused 'to put into the model any feature for which we were unable to secure authorization from the work of some recognized scholar'.[1] A similarly scholarly attempt is that represented by the Wright-Stevens model, based likewise on archaeological and literary research.[2]

Reverting to the models that were exhibited in Europe in the seventeenth and eighteenth centuries, and the literature respecting King Solomon and his Temple that was widely prevalent in that era, can we conclude that our legends may have been absorbed from that non-Masonic source? Professor Johnston does not think so. Although the description of the Temple, he admits, excited a very considerable amount of attention and interest throughout Europe generally in the seventeenth century, 'there was little if anything of special Masonic importance' in this. From this he concludes that the legends concerning the Temple 'were not taken wholesale into our system from an outside source' but were indigenous to the genius of the Masonic institution itself.[3]

Dr. Herbert Poole comes to a similar conclusion in his discussion of the genuine antiquity of the Craft—a subject of undying interest —as against the possibility that has been suggested in some quarters to the effect that some of our traditions may have been artificially injected into Freemasonry from non-Masonic sources by some of our seventeenth-century 'speculatives' as late as that 'Century of Transition' from operative to speculative Masonry. He thinks in fact that 'speculative' interest within the Craft is actually older than this Century of Transition. 'I find it extremely difficult to believe', says this important authority, 'as is so often maintained, that any large portion of the speculative material was imported into the Craft by the literary speculatives of the seventeenth century. . . . ' He admits, in line with Prof. Johnston's findings, that 'there was considerable interest in King Solomon's Temple displayed among the learned in the seventeenth and early eighteenth centuries, and a perfect flood of "Temple" literature, [yet] a study of this reveals

---

[1] P. L. Garber, 'Reconstructing Solomon's Temple'. *The Biblical Archaeologist*, Feb. 1951, p. 3. See also 'A Reconstruction of Solomon's Temple' by the same author, in *Archaeology*, vol. 5, No. 3, pp. 165–172.
[2] G. Ernest Wright, *Biblical Archaeology*. Philadelphia, 1957, pp. 136–145.
[3] Swift P. Johnston, 'Seventeenth Century Descriptions of Solomon's Temple'. *AQC* xii, 142.

nothing which could either have been borrowed from, or have given rise to, our principal Craft legend, nor our technical description of Temple detail. On these grounds,' he goes on to say, in conclusion, 'I am more and more inclined to believe that the speculative content of the Craft at the time when, for instance, Ashmole was admitted [1646], was substantially the same as, though very likely much less elaborate than, it is today; and that, if so, then it must have been there at least a hundred years earlier', that is, in the operative period.[1]

We have already seen how this interest in King Solomon's Temple had been manifesting itself among the operative Masons of the preceding centuries, leading back at least to the fourteenth, when the Legend had begun to make its appearance in the *Old Charges*, but the operatives could not have had an absolute monopoly of this interest, which must have been fairly universal among clergy and laity alike. The romanticizing of the personality of King Solomon, that Mackey calls attention to, must have aided and abetted this interest, and the rapid dissemination of the first printed text of the Bible which took place at about this time must have contributed its influence as well.

J. E. S. Tuckett here draws some interesting parallels between the essential difference that manifests itself in our two earliest *Old Charges* in this respect, and the change that was at that time coming about in the religious complexion of Europe as a whole. The evidence, he says, in his paper on 'The *Old Charges* and the Chief Master Mason', seems to present itself as follows:

The two earliest *Old Charges*—the *Regius MS.* (*c.* 1390) and the *Cooke MS.* (*c.* 1410)—reflect two opposing schools of thought, in the religious sense, and demonstrate two opposing attitudes towards this problem of King Solomon's Temple. The first of these *Old Charges*, representing the older school and the then established Roman Church (the manuscript itself is believed to have been written by a priest), 'betrays no tendency to side with the Reformation movement, and contains no reference to King Solomon, King Hiram, Hiram the Builder, or the Temple at Jerusalem. Between this and the appearance of the next *MS.*, the *Cooke* (early fifteenth century), times have changed [they, of course, had been changing for some time]; Reformation is on its way and interest in the Old Testament narrative has been awakened by the Wycliffe translations

[1] Dr. Herbert Poole, 'Antiquity of the Craft'. *AQC* li, 16–17.

of the Bible from the Latin of the Vulgate, which from about 1380
were widely circulated in manuscript amongst those favourable to
the coming revolution'. It is in this *Cooke MS.*, as we shall presently
see in detail—representing, for the first time, the 'Protestant' as
opposed to the 'Roman Catholic' element in the Masonic tradition—
that we are introduced for the first time to the Masonic Temple
Legend.[1]

By the end of the seventeenth century, this interest in King
Solomon's Temple must have been at very high pitch, comparatively, especially as far as the operative-speculative Masons are
concerned, if we are to judge from one of the Early Catechisms, the
Dumfries No. 4 MS. (dated by Knoop, Jones, and Hamer as of
about 1710 A.D.), and this one is of particular interest to us because
it demonstrates, clearly and unequivocally, in conjunction with
several other Catechisms of that period (the *Edinburgh Register
House MS.* is even dated some fourteen years earlier; i.e., 1696),
the existence of a speculative Masonic science as an already
well-established institution, and not as something created out of
nothing as an aftermath to the establishment of Grand Lodge in
1717.

Here, in this *Dumfries No. 4 MS.* of 1710, a whole section is
devoted to 'Questions concerning the Temple'; and, out of a total of
some seventy-two general 'Questions Propounded and Answered',
no less than twenty-seven of them are on the Temple itself. These
not only describe with a great profusion of detail its various ornaments and religious features and appurtenances, but make an
attempt also to moralize upon them and give them mystic and
symbolic significance, very much after the style of Samuel Lee's
Orbis Miraculum and John Bunyan's *Solomon's Temple Spiritualiz'd*
(both of the seventeenth century), which may thus have contributed
no little share of influence in the development of our speculative
science. The compilers of the collection, *The Early Masonic
Catechisms*, think that the treatment of this topic of King Solomon's
Temple 'is apparently to some extent connected with a traditional
interpretation existing in the early Middle Ages, as found, e.g.,

[1] *AQC* xxxvi, 187. The following is a somewhat complete list of the other
important papers and Notes published in *AQC* that have to do with some
element or other of King Solomon's Temple:

xii, 135, 150; xiii, 24; xiv, 172; xvi, 4; xxi, 6, 264; xxiv, 24; xxxiii, 114; xxxvi,
179; xliii, 158; lxvi, 189; lxviii, 85; lxxv, 221; vol. 78: 226, 229.

in a treatise entitled *De Templo Salamonis* . . . and attributed to Bede', as has already been mentioned, and which thus brings the general non-Masonic interest in King Solomon's Temple, in England, back to as far as the seventh century. Furthermore, the authenticity of this *Dumfries* manuscript, the authors think, can hardly be questioned in respect to its Masonic application; the document belonged to the Old Lodge of Dumfries and was discovered in 1891 among the Lodge muniments. It is now said to be in the possession of its successor, Lodge Dumfries Kilwinning No. 53—and hence is often referred to as the *Dumfries-Kilwinning MS. No. 4*—and was printed by John Lane in *AQC* vol. vi in 1893. But Lane himself thought that the peculiar explanations of theological symbolism relating to the Temple of Solomon were, in his opinion, 'too "mystical" to have been in general use in Masonic Lodges'. That may very well be. However, in regard to the Old Lodge of Dumfries in particular, Knoop and his collaborators call attention to the physical condition of this MS. and the signs of its having been much used; they feel, no doubt justifiably, that it was most certainly thus used for ritualistic purposes.[1]

The late R. J. Meekren, too, thought that this MS. represented in its time at least current Masonic thinking with respect to King Solomon and his Temple. Speaking of the period 'between 1530 when the Coverdale and Mathews Bibles appeared with the references to Hiram Abi, and (let us say) 1710, the approximate date of DK'—the *Dumfries-Kilwinning MS.*—he says that he finds at this period

> an apparent, even if not very definite, increase in emphasis in the references to Solomon and his building operations in the Old Charges. . . . But when we come to DK we find this interest fully developed in considerable detail. And while it may well be possible that this document contains only the record of some particular individual opinion [following John Lane's argument], and to have had no currency outside the old Lodge of Dumfries, yet considering the intense interest in religious matters in general and the Scriptures in particular all through the country, we can hardly doubt that such an effort would at least be in harmony with the prevailing ideas among Scottish masons of the time.[2]

[1] Knoop, Jones and Hamer, *Early Masonic Catechisms*, p. 45.
[2] R. J. Meekren, 'The Lodge', *AQC* lxi, 50.

An example of the type of moralizing practised in the *Dumfries MS.*, and its backward reflection into the seventh-century moralizing of the Venerable Bede, may here be given. It is in *De Templo Salamonis*, Gerard Brett tells us, that 'we first meet the allegorical interpretation of the Temple story which has been a feature of the Western approach to it ever since. Bede states the basis of the allegorical approach in his first chapter:

' "The House of God which King Solomon built in Jerusalem represents the Holy Universal Church, which, from the first of the Elect to the last man who shall be born at the end of the world, is built daily by the grace of her peaceful King, that is, her Redeemer." '[1]

In somewhat parallel terms, the *Dumfries No. 4* has the following in the course of its Catechism:

Q. what signifies the temple

A. ye son of god & partly of the church ye son soffered his body to be destroyed & rose again ye 3d day & raised up to us ye christian church w^c [which] is ye true spiritwal church.

Q. what meant ye golden dore of ye temple Qr [where] they went in to [the] sanctum sanctorum

A. it was another type of Christ who is ye door ye way and the truth & ye life by whome & in whom all ye elect entreth into heaven

Knoop and Jones bring out some further parallels between the *Dumfries No. 4* and *De Templo Salamonis*, attributed to Bede, and which, they think, 'prove that allegorical or symbolical study of King Solomon's Temple was not unknown in the Middle Ages'. Thus, they say, it is explained in *De Templo* that 'cedar wood was employed because *cedrus arbor est imputribilis omnino naturae. Dumfries No. 4 MS.*, approximately a thousand years later, has the same explanation: "the cader, cyprus and olive wood was not subject to putrifaction nor possible to be devoured by worms". Bede, if indeed he was the author of *De Templo*, takes the cherubim in the Temple to have been symbols of the Old and New Testaments; so does *Dumfries No. 4 MS.* Both authors regard the laver as a symbol of baptism and the twelve oxen as foreshadowing the

---

[1] *AQC* lxvi, 92.

While Bede's ecclesiastical history has been translated into English, it is unfortunate that this Masonically more interesting work still remains in its original Latin.

Apostles; and both explain the pillars, Jachin and Boaz, as representing the churches of the Jews and Gentiles. . . . '[1]

This *Dumfries No. 4 MS.* is of additional interest because it combines the elements of the *Old Charges* with those of the *Catechisms* and thus constitutes a living bridge, as it were, between both types of document, being unique in this respect. It thus also forms a bridge, as already indicated, between the operative and speculative period, and offers the first lengthy Masonic exposition of the current practice of moralizing upon architectural details, and of symbolical interpretation. We will have occasion, in the course of our investigation, to make frequent reference to this important document, and its pre-Grand Lodge dating must always be borne in mind.

Another *Catechism*, not much later in date, and perhaps even earlier—the *Graham MS.*, whose enigmatical dating has been interpreted as signifying either 1726 or 1672[2]—carries an indication that King Solomon's Temple may even have been used as a Masonic 'hieroglyph', much in the style of our present Lectures; a hieroglyph representing—in a slightly different variant of our 'three great pillars'—the pillars 'Strength, Beauty, and Love'; and for proof it refers us to I Kings 7:6, 'where you will finde the wonderfull works off hiram at the building off the house of the Lord. . . . '

It is interesting to observe how early in the history of our speculative institution the symbolism surrounding our legend of King Solomon's Temple begins to assert itself. This is brought out very significantly in a 'confession' made at one time by John Coustos to the Holy Office of the Inquisition. Coustos was a naturalized British subject of Swiss birth who had come to Lisbon in 1743, joining a local Lodge in that city and becoming its Master. He was denounced as a Freemason, in keeping with the practice at that time and place, seized and imprisoned by the Inquisition and put to the torture during a period of two months, in an endeavour to elicit from him the 'secrets' of Freemasonry. He was subsequently sentenced to serve as

---

[1] Knoop and Jones, 'Masonic History Old and New'. *AQC* lv, 286.

Of course, this biblical symbolism of Bede's is sometimes carried to excess, and we find it adequately excoriated by Thos. Fuller. Hiram, he says on one occasion, 'could not so soon fit a pillar with a fashion, as a friar can fit that fashion with a mystery.'—Thos. Fuller, *A Pisgah Sight of Palestine*. London, 1869 (originally published in 1650), p. 353.

[2] For discussion, see p. 186, below.

a galley slave for four years, but released after about a year, upon demand of the British Minister.[1]

While the 'confession' is of date 1743, it was elicited therein that the information upon which it was based originated from his Masonic activities while in London some fourteen or fifteen years earlier, which would bring this down to about 1728. Among the information so disclosed, Coustos tells his inquisitors that on the floor of his Lodge there were fashioned two Columns, with the letters 'J' and 'B', representing the two Columns of bronze built by King Solomon for his Temple, 'thus distinguishing between the Officers and Apprentices who took part in the work of building, and so able to distinguish one from the other for the payment of wages due', etc.

'He further said,' the "confession" continues, 'that the first Institution and Origin from which were derived the signification of the Apron, Gloves, and other ceremonies the Officers and Apprentices use, as also the signs of the Masters, come from the time when Solomon built his sumptuous Temple, whereby for the better administration of the work, and distinguishing between Officers and Apprentices labouring therein, he, Solomon, made the separation of Signs above described, and which were initiated by a Master named Hiram who was next in government to Solomon and to whom alone was revealed the Sign which pertained to him as Master in order thus to be differentiated from the other and inferior Officers who worked in the same undertaking'.

A few days later, Coustos amplified his 'confession' by adding 'that when the destruction took place of the famous Temple of Solomon there was found below the First Stone a tablet of bronze upon which was engraved the following word—JEHOVAH, which means "God", giving thereby to understand that that Fabric and Temple was instituted and erected in the name of the said God to whom it was dedicated. . . . ' a legend that now forms the basis of the Thirteenth Degree of the Scottish Rite—the Royal Arch of Solomon.

So much for Coustos, and for Masonry and the Temple of Solomon, *circa* 1728.

---

[1] The full story is given in his 1746 publication, *The Sufferings of John Coustos for Freemasonry*, etc., London. An excerpt is to be found in Mackey's *Encyclopedia*, I, 247, and a transcript of 'The Trial of John Coustos by the Inquisition' is given in *AQC* lxvi, 107–123. Additional and more recently discovered documentation is offered in the paper, 'John Coustos and the Portuguese Inquisition', by Dr. S. Vatcher, in the 1968 volume of *AQC*.

Mackey accuses Dr. Anderson of having invented many of the 'traditions' respecting King Solomon's Temple. But many aspects of this Legend of the Temple must already have been in full bloom when Anderson came upon the scene with his *Book of Constitutions*, designed to digest the old Gothic Constitutions 'in a new and better method'.

We are now ready, in fact, to offer some suggestion of an answer to the question one time posited by W. H. Rylands; the question, namely, why the Temple of Solomon, and the builders of the Temple, had been selected to play a prominent part in one particular section of our legendary history—by which he alluded, obviously, to the origin and background of our Hiramic Tradition. He suggested that if it could be shown, 'with ordinary probability why the Temple and its builders . . . could naturally be selected by the Freemasons' for this very purpose, it might be possible to arrive at some solution of the problem in its various aspects.[1]

But from all that has gone before, it would appear that the answer now stares us in the face, and in no uncertain manner. Is it not this very inordinate interest that had for so many centuries during the operative period centred itself on every phase of King Solomon's Temple, and the moralizing opportunities it has constantly offered the pious and inquiring mind (from Bede to Samuel Lee and John Bunyan) during the speculative period; is it not this very combination of circumstances that may have naturally and almost inescapably forced upon the Freemasons—essentially a body of 'builders', whether operative or speculative—the adoption and elaboration of the Hiramic Legend? Rylands himself has just some such theory in mind, and calls attention to the near-veneration that European builders and architects have always felt for King Solomon's Temple, which to them appeared to be the highest ideal of ecclesiastical art, always to be imitated, and, if possible, to be surpassed. Thus it is said of Justinian that, when he had completed his church of Santa Sophia in Constantinople, he cried out, in exultation: 'I have surpassed thee, O Solomon!'[2]

[1] W. H. Rylands, 'Some Notes on the Legends of Masonry'. *AQC* xvi, 4.

[2] So W. H. Rylands (*AQC* xvi, 5), on the authority of Codinus. Gibbon, however, ascribes the ejaculation to Diocletian (*Decline*, IV, 86).

Dr. F. W. Farrar, writing on *Solomon: His Life and Times*, p. 81, similarly refers to the Khalif Omar's boast, as he pointed to the Dome of the Rock, which had replaced the Temple of Jerusalem: 'Behold, a greater than Solomon is here.'

IV

DID THE TEMPLE EVER EXIST?

An archaeological survey

IN HIS *Archaeology of Palestine*, Professor W. F. Albright—who has been described by another worker in that field as 'one of the most competent and versatile archaeologists of the modern period' —tells us that 'the age of Solomon was certainly one of the most flourishing periods of material civilization in the history of Palestine',[1] and it is not surprising, therefore, that his English counterpart,. Dr. John Garstang, has found sufficient material at his command to devote an entire work to the subject.[2]

This appraisal of Professor Albright's, however, is mainly on the strength of the biblical record itself, since contemporaneous extra-biblical chronicles are strangely silent with respect to this period, as Professor Adams has shown. With respect to any extraneous references to David and Solomon in the annals of the neighbouring States—and despite the close ties that David, and especially Solomon, are said to have had with Phoenicia and with Egypt—it is as if these two Jewish kings had never lived.[3]

It is illustrative of this absence of extra-biblical confirmation for the particular period now under discussion that Dr. Samuel A. B. Mercer's *Extra-Biblical Sources for Hebrew and Jewish History* (New York, 1913) has nothing to offer in this regard, though scanning the entire gamut of Babylonian, Assyrian, Egyptian, Semitic, Greek, and Latin sources. One short reference to Sheshonk I., King of Egypt—the 'Shishak' of the Bible (*I Kings* 14:25-26)— does, however, have some, if limited significance in this respect. It is this Sheshonk, or Shishak, that gave his daughter to Solomon

---

[1] W. F. Albright, *The Archaeology of Palestine*. Penguin Books, 1949, pp. 123-124.
[2] John Garstang (Institute of Archaeology, University of Liverpool), *The Heritage of Solomon*. London, 1934.
[3] J. McKee Adams, *Ancient Records and the Bible*. Nashville, Tenn., 1946, p. 297.

in marriage,[1] making her at the same time a gift of the town of Gezer, which he had conquered and destroyed.[2] Sheshonk is said to have subsequently invaded Palestine after the death of Solomon and sacked the king's palace and the royal buildings, as well as the Temple. (Fathers-in-law and sons-in-law have often been at odds, and 'there is nothing new under the sun'.) At any rate, the Great Karnak Relief, on the walls of Luxor, lists the towns Sheshonk had conquered in this campaign, and it shows the pharaoh before his god Amon, smiting the Asiatics, but the inscription indicates nothing specifically of Solomonic identification, and we are confined entirely to the story in the Bible itself for the other details enumerated. Solomon himself is nowhere mentioned.[3]

As for the Temple of Solomon, it must be confessed that archaeological excavations have similarly not so far turned up any unquestionable evidence of its ever having existed. The same can be said with respect to his other building activities in Jerusalem, all of which are said to have occupied him for a period of twenty years. By comparison, Ahab, king of northern Israel (875–853 B.C.), and thus not far removed from the reign of Solomon (971–931 B.C.), appears to have had a palace whose foundations at least have been successfully excavated and well authenticated;[4] but not so with respect to the Palace of King Solomon.

One recent attempt at a reconstruction of the Temple—the Howland-Garber model, at Agnes Scott College, Decatur, Georgia —is said to be based on 'the latest findings of textual study and the relevant data from biblical archaeology', as Professor Paul Leslie Garber states, in his article 'Reconstructing Solomon's Temple', in *The Biblical Archaeologist* for February 1951. But in a private letter he admits that the evidence, such as it is, is of a literary character only, and based on no actual discoveries that may have been made in

[1] Cf. *I Kings* 3:1. Shishak, however, is here referred to only as 'Pharaoh, king of Egypt', and is not specified by name.
[2] Cf. *I Kings* 9:16. Though Shishak is here again not mentioned by name, the identification is made on the basis of the chronology of the Egyptian kings.
—'The Kingdom of David and Solomon', Abraham Malamat, in *The Biblical Archaeological Reader*, vol. II, New York, 1964, p. 93.
[3] Samuel A. B. Mercer, *Extra-Biblical Sources for Hebrew and Jewish History*. New York, 1913, p. 140.
[4] R. A. S. Macalister (formerly Director of Excavations, Palestine Exploration Fund). *A Century of Excavation in Palestine*. London, 1925. See the photograph opposite p. 222, *op. cit.*
5

connection with the physical excavations on the site, the 'relevant data' being from indirect sources. 'No certain traces of the Temple of Solomon,' Professor Albright states pointedly, ' . . . have so far been recovered by archaeologists'.[1] This is generally ascribed to the fact that the Temple had been completely destroyed, and its valuable materials and ornaments carried away, in the total destruction of Jerusalem by Nebuchadnezzar. But, as Professor Adams has pointed out, the conqueror, who carried its people away to captivity in Babylon, did not even deign to commemorate his triumph, as Titus did, some six hundred years later, with respect to a similar destruction of the Temple of Herod.

Yet similar records of temple spoliations are not without parallel, on Assyrian reliefs, even in Nebuchadnezzar's approximate time. There is, for example, the stone slab from Khorsabad, which records the sack of the temple of Musasir by the troops of Sargon II. But Nebuchadnezzar's own sack of the Temple of Jerusalem, which must have been immensely more extensive and valuable, is not so recorded, anywhere. Similarly, the later return of temple treasure to its original owners is also sometimes recorded—as in the cuneiform inscriptions telling of the restoration by Cyrus to several Mesopotamian shrines of the statues of the god which Nabonides, king of Babylon, had stolen and set up in his own capital, as shown in the Rassam Cylinder in the British Museum.[2] But the parallel story of the restoration by this same Cyrus, after his capture of Babylon in 539 B.C., of 'the vessels of the house of the Lord, which Nebuchadnezzar had brought forth out of Jerusalem, and had put them in the house of his gods' (*Ezra* 1:7) does not appear to be so recorded, elsewhere.

However, as to Nebuchadnezzar himself, there may be something in the suggestion put forward by Dr. G. Ernest Wright, to the effect that 'it was not Babylonian custom to brag about military exploits in the way the Assyrian emperors had done'. They were more inclined, instead, to record the good deeds they had done for the gods in the building and repairing of temples, and other works of a constructive nature. If this suggestion is accepted, it goes far towards minimizing the plaint that Professor Adams gives voice to, in remarking upon the silence of Nebuchadnezzar in respect to his

---

[1] W. F. Albright, *op. cit.*, p. 154.
[2] *Revue Biblique*, 1937, p. 31. Cited by André Parrot in *The Temple of Jerusalem*. New York, 1955, p. 69.

spoliation of the Temple. In addition, we have the indirect testimony of the 'Babylonian Chronicle', which is, in Dr. Wright's words, 'apart from the Bible, our main source of information about the Neo-Babylonian Empire'. In 1956 the discovery of some additional tablets of the Chronicle was announced, and 'for the first time outside the Bible, Nebuchadnezzar's capture of Jerusalem in 598–597 B.C. is described', to the extent that we now in fact 'can have no doubt but that the devastation was as complete as the Book of Lamentations suggests that it was'.[1] 'The fifth paragraph of this Babylonian chronicle of the sixth century B.C. tells of the capture of Jerusalem on March 16, 597 B.C. by Nebuchadnezzar, and of the appointment of Zedekiah as king and the removal of Israelite prisoners, among whom [is] Jehoiachin, to Babylonia.'[2]

Dr. Wright similarly finds that the excavations at Tell ed-Duweir (the 'Lachish' of the Bible)—a frontier fortress guarding the approaches to Jerusalem and Hebron—have produced evidence to the effect that the destruction of the city at one particular level 'must be attributed to Nebuchadnezzar's second invasion in 589–587 B.C. The evidence of the city's complete demolition is as vivid as that at Tell Beit Mirsim (Debir), eight miles away'.[3]

'In Lachish,' says J. A. Thompson, 'we have the best picture of the destruction . . . and so fierce was the fire which destroyed the city that the limestone of the buildings turned to lime. The most important item [found] in the town of Lachish was the collection of inscribed potsherds or ostraca'—generally referred to as the 'Lachish Letters'—discovered in 1935 in a layer of charcoal and ashes belonging to a level representing the final destruction of the city. 'These turned out to be military letters quickly written out in the days of feverish haste as the Babylonian armies were closing in. As we read these short notes, we gain the impression that southern Judah was in a state of stress. There were urgent orders passing to and fro, special arrangements being made for fire signals, the sending of a military mission to Egypt (*Jer.* 26:20–23), the inspection of guards, and general increase of military activity. The whole

[1] G. Ernest Wright, *Biblical Archaeology*. Philadelphia, 1957, pp. 176–177.

[2] J. A. Thompson, *The Bible and Archaeology*, Grand Rapids, Mich., 1962, p. 165. See the photograph of this 'Babylonian Chronicle' to be seen in the British Museum.

[3] G. Ernest Wright, 'Judean Lachish'. *The Biblical Archaeologist Reader*, II, p. 306.

correspondence suggests an atmosphere of nervous tension in the early stages of the war before Jerusalem fell.'[1]

We thus find that we do have, in effect, extra-biblical evidence —in the 'Babylonian Chronicle' and in the Lachish Letters—of the destruction of Jerusalem itself, by Nebuchadnezzar, at the time of his destruction of the Temple, precisely as described in the Bible, though not so recorded by Nebuchadnezzar himself. His similar failure to have recorded the destruction of the Temple may thus no longer be taken as an argument in favour of the belief that there may have been no Temple to destroy in the first place. One might, in fact, argue with equal cogency that Jerusalem had never suffered complete destruction, as the Bible says it did, simply because Nebuchadnezzar had failed to record it.

The extra-biblical record

But, bearing in mind, in all of our investigation, this continued non-existence of any direct archaeological evidence in favour of King Solomon's Temple, we can now continue to turn the coin over, to see what may perhaps be on the other side. We direct our attention, again, to the extra-biblical record, fragmentary as it may be.

One *quasi*-extra-biblical account—if it can be called even that, since it is second-hand at best, and is no longer extant and capable of verification—is the reference we find in Josephus—'the great Jewish historian Josephus', as we speak of him in our American Lectures—wherein he tells us of 'records among the Tyrians that take in the history of many years . . . public writings . . . kept with great exactness' concerning their transactions with other nations. 'There it is recorded,' says Josephus, specifically, 'that the temple was built by king Solomon at Jerusalem, one hundred forty-three years and eight months before the Tyrians built Carthage; and in their Annals, the building of our temple is related; for Hirom, the king of Tyre, was the friend of Solomon, our king, and had such friendship transmitted down to him from his forefathers.' But, unfortunately, Josephus gives us no definite references. However, sensing this difficulty, and in order that his statement 'may not depend on my bare word', Josephus does go on to quote Dius by

[1] J. A. Thompson, *The Bible and Archaeology*, pp. 150–151. See also Harry Torczyner's *Lachish I, The Lachish Letters*, 1938. Some of this correspondence, in translation, is given in Thompson's work.

name, who is 'believed to have written the Phoenician History after an accurate manner'; and, in another one of his works, Josephus quotes still further from Menander the Ephesian, who is said to have 'translated the Tyrian archives out of the dialect of the Phoenicians into the Greek language'. But even here, the specific quotations he offers disclose upon examination only a reference to the King of Tyre, and to Solomon, King of Jerusalem (as there stated), being completely silent on the subject of the Temple itself. The testimony, then, by any acceptable standards of historical criticism, is highly unsatisfactory.[1]

Another—and perhaps the only other—approach to so-called 'extra-biblical' testimony as to the one-time existence of King Solomon's Temple is in the 'rescript by Cyrus, which the Jews seem to have brought with them on their return from the Captivity', as the architectural writer, James Fergusson, tells us.[2] Even the measurements mentioned therein, he thinks, are reliable, and it would be most improbable 'that these should .be any other than those which the Assyrians had noted when they took Jerusalem, and which were found in the record chamber of Babylon or Ecbatana, under the circumstances detailed in the narrative'—as found in *Ezra* vi; *et seq.*, and *I Esdras* vi:22 *et seq.* The *Book of Esdras* is the non-canonical counterpart of the biblical *Book of Ezra*, and the account of the rebuilding of the Temple, under Zerubbabel, mentioned by Fergusson, is essentially the same in both.[3] As a result, Fergusson himself is convinced that 'everything tends to show that the edict of Cyrus was based on documents he found in the record office, and that these did describe the Temple which had existed in Jerusalem down to the Captivity'. But it is clear that the evidential value of this supposedly non-Jewish testimony is considerably minimized by the fact that it is now to be found only in the biblical narrative itself, and is thus not in reality 'extra-biblical' in the true sense, just as the allegedly extra-biblical references in Josephus are now only found in the works of Josephus himself. As to this 'rescript by Cyrus', Josephus also gives a similar (but not identical) 'epistle to the governors that were in Syria', which Whiston notes

---

[1] Josephus, *Against Apion*, Bk. I: 17, 18; *Antiquities of the Jews*, Bk. VIII, 5:3. Whiston Translation, Philadelphia.

[2] James Fergusson, F.R.S., *The Temples of the Jews*. London, 1878, p. 30.

[3] Cf. *The Apocrypha*. Oxford University Press, 1895. This account is of obvious interest, especially, to the Royal Arch and Scottish Rite Mason.

is 'omitted in our other copies.'[1] On the other hand, the notion that this extra-biblical and extra-Josephian evidence could have been fabricated merely to lend support to the traditional belief in a temple that never existed is hardly credible. If the story, in fact, had been fabricated, it would constitute one of the most stupendous hoaxes of history.

And if King Solomon's Temple never did really exist, this 'hoax' must have continued to be piously perpetrated through some six centuries or more of later biblical history, to a time even beyond the recorded period of its destruction. Thus we read of Joash, who 'stood by a pillar' of Solomon's Temple, at the former's coronation, 'as the manner was'[2]—a practice also mentioned in connection with Josiah (640–609 B.C.).[3] Josiah, we also find, had been involved in connection with the repair of the Temple and the restoration of the pure worship,[4] just as Hezekiah (712–687 B.C.) had previously embarked on a thorough-going clearance but was later forced to despoil the Temple to furnish tribute to Assyria.[5] Manasseh, on the

[1] Josephus, *Antiquities*, XI, 1:3.
[2] *II Kings* 11:14.
[3] Cf. *II Kings* 23:3.
[4] *II Kings* 23:4, 11, 12.
[5] *II Kings* 18:4.

The Hezekiah episode does receive dramatic extra-biblical confirmation in an inscription on an hexagonal clay prism, recording the annals of Sennacherib, dating from 686 B.C., found at Nineveh and now in the British Museum:

From II Kings 18: 13–16

'Now in the fourteenth year of king Hezekiah did Sennacherib king of Assyria come up against all the fenced cities of Judah, and took them.

' . . . And the king of Assyria appointed unto Hezekiah king of Judah three hundred talents of silver and thirty talents of gold.

'And Hezekiah gave him all the silver that was found in the house of the Lord, and in the treasures of the king's house.

'And at that time did Hezekiah cut off the gold from the doors of the temple of the Lord, and from the pillars which Hezekiah king of Judah had overlaid, and gave it to the king of Assyria.'

From the clay prism

'As to Hezekiah the Jew, he did not submit to my yoke. I laid siege to forty-six of his strong cities . . . and conquered them. . . . I reduced his country but I still increased the tribute . . . Hezekiah did send me later to Nineveh . . . thirty talents of gold, eight hundred talents of silver. . . .'

Cited by J. A. Thompson, *The Bible and Archaeology*, p. 144.

other hand, 'did that which was evil in the sight of the Lord, after the abominations of the heathen. . . . For he built . . . [heathen] altars in the house of the Lord, . . . of which the Lord said to David, and to Solomon his son . . .' etc.[1] *Ezra* and *Hagai* similarly tell the story of the restoration of the altar, immediately after the return from the Captivity; and eighteen years later, the Temple began to be rebuilt, under Zerubbabel, 'in the second year of Darius the king', when they began to 'build the house that was builded these many years ago, which a great king of Israel builded and set up'.[2] Obviously, you do not 'rebuild' a temple that never existed in the first place.

And, finally, there is the direct visual testimony of the prophet Jeremiah, who lived at the time of the Captivity, and personally witnessed the results of the destruction of the Temple (*Jer.* 52), though apparently out of the city at the time of the onslaught. Had the whole account of the destruction of the Temple, and the events surrounding it, been nothing but a blatant forgery, Jeremiah could hardly have escaped over-playing his hand, to the gleeful delight, no doubt, of our modern critics. If, in fact, such a 'hoax' was ever perpetrated, it was not only the most stupendous but also the most incredible hoax in history. No wonder Professor Albright is constrained to insist that 'conservative scholars are, we believe, entirely justified in their vigorous denunciation of all efforts to prove the existence of fraudulent invention and deliberate forgery in the Bible'.[3]

In addition to Jeremiah, J. A. Thompson thinks that there is archaeological reason to believe that Ezekiel, too, can be taken to have seen the Temple, and some archaeologists are of the opinion that the description of his ideal temple, though largely visionary, was not entirely so, because it incorporated many features and details that correspond with the Temple of Solomon, and so must have been a recollection of things that had actually been seen by him. At the very least, they point to some long-lost descriptions of Solomon's Temple which may have been available in Ezekiel's time.[4]

Ezekiel was a priest of Jerusalem (*Ezek.* 1:3), and, as such, must have been among the aristocracy whom Nebuchadnezzar carried

---

[1] *II Kings* 21:2–4, 7.
[2] *Ezra* 3:2; 5:11. *Haggai* 1:14, 15.
[3] W. F. Albright, *The Archaeology of Palestine and the Bible*. The Richards Lectures. New York, 1932, p. 176.
[4] G. Ernest Wright, *Biblical Archaeology*, pp. 136–137.

off to exile in Babylonia, after the first capture of Jerusalem (*II Kings* xxiv, 14). The most striking evidence of his personal knowledge of the Temple, in Thompson's opinion, comes from Ezekiel's description of the east gate of his ideal temple (*Ezek.* 40: 5–16). While this gate is of a size that may not have conformed to the proportions of Solomon's Temple, the pattern is the same; and archaeologists, says Thompson, 'point out that this type of gate . . . was quite common in the days of King Solomon . . . and is known in excavations at Megiddo, Ezion Geber, and Hazor, in the towns that go back to the days of Solomon.' But it also so happens that 'this type of gate disappeared in the ancient Near Eastern scene in the ninth century B.C. and was replaced by a new style of gate altogether, . . . so that by Ezekiel's day it would be almost impossible to find one. How then,' asks Thompson pertinently, 'would Ezekiel in a vision see a gate, the like of which was known in Solomon's day, but which had long since gone out of use in the East? The answer is that he must have seen the Solomonic gate in the Temple in Jerusalem prior to its destruction by Nebuchadnezzar in 587 B.C. The destruction of the Temple would have removed what was probably the last gate of this kind to be seen in the East.'[1]

The tradition of King Solomon's Temple appears to have persisted long after the destruction not only of the Temple of Solomon, as Fergusson tells us, but even the destruction of the Temple of Herod, rebuilt on the same site a thousand years later. This Temple of Herod (known generally as the Third Temple, the Second being Zerubbabel's) was not entirely demolished at the destruction of Jerusalem by Titus, in A.D. 70, and some of its features—and inferentially of King Solomon's Temple as well—continued to be pointed out and described by travellers for centuries afterwards. Thus, it is said that 'Antoninus Martyrus visited Jerusalem shortly after the buildings undertaken by Justinian in the Haram area had been completed, in or about the year 570 [A.D., and he wrote]: "Before the ruins of the Temple of Solomon, water runs down below the platform to the fountain of Siloam (by the Water Gate). Alongside of the portico of Solomon in the Basilica is the seat on which Pilate sat when he heard our Lord. . . ." The old judgment-seat of Solomon "alongside of his portico" was still known and correctly described in the sixth century.'[2]

[1] J. A. Thompson, *The Bible and Archaeology*, pp. 163–164.
[2] James Fergusson, *The Temples of the Jews*, p. 186.

Correctly or no, it must be re-emphasized that all this ascription to King Solomon's Temple is purely inferential, and traditional only—a 'backward glance', so to speak—and merely serving to point up the care that must continually be exercised in reading the written word, if one is to be realistic as to the knowledge to be obtained therefrom. The same comment can be made with regard to the 'Solomon's porch' in which Jesus is said to have walked (*John* 10:23); also, in our own time, with regard to the subterranean quarry in the Jerusalem area, popularly known as 'the Quarry of Solomon', and generally thought to be the source from which King Solomon obtained the stone for the building of his Temple. As a result, Masonic tourists visiting Israel are fond of bringing home with them souvenirs of this stone cut into various shapes—'ashlars' and 'gavels' and 'keystones'—thinking thereby that they are in possession of mementoes made from the same stone that built King Solomon's Temple three thousand years ago— while all we know about it, factually, is that 'from this quarry was obtained much of the stone of which Jerusalem was built',[1] nothing being said specifically, in this part of the account in the *Jewish Encyclopedia*, about the Temple itself. Charles A. Conover, writing on 'King Solomon's Temple', cites a description of these so-called 'Solomon's Quarries' as seen by a recent observer,[2] and 'the famous white limestone', says Professor Stinespring, 'is familiar to every visitor to Jerusalem, and is still quarried from the great cavern under the Old City now known, perhaps with some justification as Solomon's Quarries (called by Josephus the "Royal Caverns").'[3] But Selah Merrill, a long time resident of the city, and a student of its antiquities, thinks that this stone is not of a quality that would have been suitable for the walls of the Temple. 'There is a tradition, constantly repeated in Jerusalem,' he tells us, 'that the great stones in the Temple were taken from the so-called Solomon's Quarries near the Damascus Gate; but this is pure fiction.'[4]

The same comment, again, could be made with reference to the substructure of the Temple of Herod, called by the Arabs and others

[1] *Jewish Encyclopedia*, s.v. JERUSALEM. New York, 1916.
[2] *British Masonic Miscellany*, viii, pp. 106–107. Compiled by George M. Martin. Dundee.
[3] *Interpreter's Dictionary of the Bible*, vol. R–Z, p. 542.
[4] Selah Merrill, *Ancient Jerusalem*. New York, 1908, pp. 371–372.

'Solomon's Stables', and still known by that name,[1] but without any archaeological evidence that these 'stables' had actually been used by Solomon himself. J. A. Thompson, in fact, thinks that they were built by Herod,[2] and it is even thought that, in their present form, these so-called 'Stables of Solomon' were actually constructed at a later date than the Temple of Herod.[3]

But the most striking demonstration of false ascription, perhaps, is the famous 'Wailing Wall', immortalized in the painting by Bida, and so called because of the pious Jews who have been wont to stand and pray before it, for countless centuries, bewailing their lost glory.[4] 'The splendid masonry of the great retaining wall of the Temple esplanade,' writes Professor Albright (alluding to this "Wailing Wall"), 'was believed to be Solomonic when it was first partly cleared down to bed-rock by Sir Charles Warren.' Sir Charles, for example, speaks confidently in *The Recovery of Jerusalem*, of the 'wall of King Solomon', and of 'the marks of King Solomon', but does not state explicitly how this designation had been arrived at.[5] A discovery 'made at this place, which caused great excitement', says Professor Macalister, a later Director of Excavations of the Palestine Exploration Fund, 'was a group of marks painted on a foundation stone of the south-east corner of the great wall. These were supposed to be Phoenician characters, and to come from the hand of one of King Hiram's labourers. But although some of them—not all—superficially resemble Phoenician or Old Hebrew

---

[1] It is thought that they were so named because the Crusaders used to stable their horses in that area.—*Jew. Enc., s.v.* TEMPLE OF HEROD, and JERUSALEM. These 'stables' are not to be confused with Solomonic Stables at Megiddo, which have been archaeologically authenticated. See p. 76 below.

[2] J. A. Thompson, *The Bible and Archaeology*, p. 276.

[3] Jack Finegan, *Light from the Ancient Past*. Princeton University Press, 1949, p. 243.

[4] An excellent photograph of the Wailing Wall can be seen on p. 224 of G. Ernest Wright's *Biblical Archaeology*. The painting by Bida is reproduced in the *Jewish Encyclopedia*, VII, p. 143.

[5] *The Recovery of Jerusalem*. A Narrative of Exploration and Discovery in the City and the Holy Land. New York, 1871; a compilation of papers by Capt. Wilson, Capt. Warren, and others.

Sir Charles Warren was at one time head of the Palestine Exploration Fund, and in 1886 was the first Master of Quatuor Coronati Lodge No. 2076, London. Both the successes and the failures of Warren's Palestine Expedition are evaluated objectively in Professor R. A. S. Macalister's *A Century of Excavation in Palestine*. London, 1925, pp. 32–38.

characters, no one has ever succeeded in grouping them together, much less in making translatable words of them. Probably they were mere graffiti'—scribbling, doodling—'with no special significance.'[1] Yet even today, says Professor Albright, in commenting on this circumstance, there are 'a few specialists who believe that Warren did uncover fragments of the Solomonic structure. In the author's opinion, this is most improbable. . . .'[2] In an earlier work on the same subject, he speaks of 'the draughted blocks of the Herodian retaining wall'—this same "Wailing Wall" again—'actually dating from the last decade before the birth of Christ,' thus indicating its true 'Third Temple' origin.[3]

As for the 'Quarries of Solomon', it might be said to be, of course, a natural and perhaps forgivable inference that the quarries from which the stones were obtained for the building of Jerusalem (as stated in the *Jewish Encyclopedia*) could also have been used for the building of its Temple. The inference, in fact, is much less non-historical and improbable than the '1453 Columns of Parian Marble' —that is, from the Island of Paros, in the Aegean Sea—'that Dr. Anderson talks about in connection with the Temple',[4] and now a prominent feature of our American monitorial 'history'.

Books, on travel, of course, continue to show alleged sketches or even photographs of the so-called 'foundations' of King Solomon's Temple, but their validity, it is hardly necessary to say, is highly suspect. The same question can be raised with respect to the supposed 'corner-stone' and other so-called 'vestiges' of the Temple described with so much assurance by Robt. W. Bowers in his *Freemasonry and the Tabernacle of the Jews*.[5] It is true that he cites in support the excavations made by Sir Charles Warren in 1868, but some doubts have been raised in professional circles as to the accuracy of his findings in respect of their specific Solomonic ascription, as we have seen, although admittedly he has done some fine work in that connection. The whole subject is fraught with considerable uncertainty.

It is true, of course, that these false ascriptions that we have noted are by no means confined to features of King Solomon's

[1] R. A. S. Macalister, *op. cit.*, pp. 35–36.
[2] W. F. Albright, *The Archaeology of Palestine*, p. 155.
[3] W. F. Albright, *The Archaeology of Palestine and the Bible*, p. 23.
[4] *Book of Constitutions*, 1723. Facsimile Edition, p. 13.
[5] R. W. Bowers, *op. cit.*, 1899, pp. 37–39.

Temple, but are found equally prevalent in connection with other items of biblical interest, as Macalister has so well demonstrated.[1] But all this has had the effect, in some circles, of denying the very existence of King Solomon himself, let alone of his Temple, and has even led to the assertion that his name, Sol-Om-On—at a time when Sun Worship was a widely prevalent practice—is only the name of the Sun in three languages[2] (presumably Latin, Sanscrit, and Egyptian). But it would be difficult, if not impossible, to perpetrate such a linguistic pun in connection with the Arabic form of the name by which he is almost equally as well known to the Moslems—*Suleiman*. And what should we say with regard to the Hebrew original, *Sh'lomo*?

The Solomonic city of Megiddo

Despite these many questionable ascriptions that we have observed, there remain numerous archaeological pointers bearing evidence to the real existence and to the specific activities of King Solomon as a great builder. One of these pointers is the city of Megiddo, recently excavated, and which Professor Albright considers to be 'one of the most remarkable finds ever made in Palestine, which has illuminated a period regarding which archaeology has had very little to say, the age of Solomon'.[3] This excavation has been described in practically every recent archaeological work that has to do with the Bible. At one level, belonging to the early monarchy, P. L. O. Guy found in 1928-9 a remarkable complex, consisting of stables for horses, and space for chariots and grooms. The 'stables' were evidenced by dressed limestone pillars, which, however, when first discovered in 1903, were mistakenly taken to be cult-objects characteristic of Canaanite sanctuaries. But stratified excavation by Guy revealed a whole series of such pillars standing regularly in several blocks. 'Their true nature,' says Dr. John Gray, 'was indicated by the fact that each was perforated at its angle, and between each pair was a hewn limestone trough. It was obvious that these were not the standing-stones of a sanctuary but tying-posts of stables.'[4] We can

[1] R. A. S. Macalister, *op. cit.*, pp. 84-93.
[2] Cf. a letter received from one Charles Sotheran, in 1877, said to have been the 'Masonic editor of the New York Advocate', and cited in Mme. Blavatsky's *Isis Unveiled*, vol. II, p. 389.
[3] W. F. Albright, *The Archaeology of Palestine and the Bible*, pp. 46-47.
[4] John Gray (Lecturer in Hebrew and Biblical Criticism, Aberdeen University), *Archaeology and the Old Testament*. London, 1962, p. 133.

even visualize, with Dr. Wright, how these horses stood in a double row with heads inward, tied to their hitching posts, which also served as roof supports, with the stone mangers between them.[1] 'Adjacent to these stalls, the foundations and lower courses of the walls of other buildings were found which were obviously sheds for chariots, and barracks for grooms, with an open parade-ground. There was, in all, accommodation for 450 horses.'

Subsequent exploration by Professor Yadin has disclosed the fact that only the southern part of the stables were of Solomonic origin, the northern part being of somewhat later date. But even if not all of these stables is of Solomonic construction, comments Dr. Gray,' the stable accommodation at Megiddo . . . indicates that the statement that Solomon had 1400 chariots (I Kg. 10:26) is no exaggeration but an accurate report.'[2] 'In addition,' says Dr. G. Ernest Wright, 'the ruins of stables from the same period have been discovered at Taanach, near Megiddo, [and] at Eglon on the Judean border.'[3] Solomon, we are told, 'built chariot cities in which to keep his twelve thousand chariot horses. . . . Megiddo is one of the places mentioned in this connection. The splendour of the great king's reign, and the care with which he provided for the horses which he imported into Israel for the first time are both vividly illustrated by the discoveries at Megiddo.'[4]

But this does not by any means exhaust all the wonders found at this site, and Dr. Wright gives us some fascinating and colourful details of other Solomonic construction at Megiddo, so important for an indirect confirmation of the comparable building activity in Jerusalem itself—of which, unfortunately, in the latter case, we have so little direct evidence. 'The great city of Megiddo in the northern plain of Esdraelon,' Dr. Wright tells us, 'furnishes the best pictures of Solomonic building thus far excavated. . . . The whole town was apparently converted to governmental purposes,' and he illustrates this with numerous photographs, diagrams, and reconstructions, including that of an elaborate palace. 'Various

[1] G. Ernest Wright, *Biblical Archaeology*, pp. 130–132.
[2] John Gray, *op. cit.*, p. 134.
[3] G. Ernest Wright, *Biblical Archaeology*, p. 132.
[4] W. F. Albright, *The Archaeology of Palestine and the Bible*, p. 47. See the photograph of these stables in his smaller work, *The Archaeology of Palestine*. Plate 20. Larger and more impressive photographs are found on p. 104 of Thompson's *The Bible and Archaeology*; on p. 133 of Dr. Wright's work (above); and opposite p. 148 of Dr. Gray's. See Plates 1 and 2.

features of the construction bear witness to the help of the Phoenician architects whom Solomon engaged from Hiram of Tyre. . . . Megiddo is thus a remarkable illustration of the energy of the illustrious king.'[1]

Stone-masonry in the Solomonic era

Some evidence of the type of stone-masonry in use at the time is also available, from actual examples that have been recovered, ascribable to that general period of history. Thus we find the noted English archaeologist, Dr. John Garstang—one time Director of the Palestine Exploration Fund, and appointed, in 1920, Director of the Department of Antiquities in British-mandated Palestine—remarking soberly, in his *Heritage of Solomon*, that, though 'we may hesitate to accept in detail the account of Solomon's building activities as the contemporary record of eye witnesses', yet, he is forced to point out, 'the revival of civil and military architecture seems to date from the reign and activities of Solomon. It was accompanied by a better building technique, particularly evident in the improved dressing of the stone, ashlar replacing the old hammer-dressed blocks, with a correspondingly true alignment of the courses. Where the face of the stone was left rough or bossed, the margin was carefully squared.'

At Gezer, he goes on to say—its site was not re-discovered until 1873—'rare examples of ornamental stone dressing were observed in the Solomonic tower of the outer wall.' At Megiddo, where the true 'Stables of Solomon' have been unearthed (unlike the previously-mentioned and wrongly-ascribed 'Stables of Solomon' in the substructure of Herod's Temple), 'the coursing was actually indicated by red lines, painted doubtless along a stretched string[2] with the end stones *in situ* [that is, in place], and in the construction, two headers in one course alternated with one stretcher in the next.'[3]

The stables at Megiddo, Professor Albright similarly tells us, 'were constructed of hewn stones, with the long rectangular shape which we have learned to associate with the tenth and ninth cen-

---

[1] G. Ernest Wright, *op. cit.*, pp. 130–132.

[2] Analogous to, or perhaps identical with, the 'skirret' referred to in British Freemasonry. This 'Working Tool' has, unfortunately, been ignored in American work.

[3] John Garstang, *The Heritage of Solomon*, pp. 379, 384.

turies B.C. in Israel. This type of masonry was undoubtedly introduced into Palestine from outside, probably from Phoenicia, in the reign of Solomon, whose relations with Hiram of Tyre were so intimate.'[1]

'The masonry of these structures in [the Solomonic level of] Stratum IV,' says Dr. Wright, 'is entirely different from anything found in the preceding strata. . . . Characteristic of it is the use of well-cut stones laid in the header-stretcher method: that is, two, or three stones were laid across the thickness of the wall (headers), whereas above, below, and beside them, stones were laid lengthwise (stretchers). Such an alternation of stones laid made for great strength; it was a building device probably borrowed from the Phoenicians.' 'In the reign of Solomon, Megiddo was made the capital of his fifth administrative district. . . . An elaborate plan for the rebuilding of the city was evolved and carried out by extremely able architects.' A gate with four doorways has been found in which 'the masonry was massive and the workmanship excellent. The stones were cut and fitted together in a regular bonding pattern on the wall faces, while the interiors were filled with mud and rubble. The masonry was laid dry without mortar, but the joint between any two stones is said to have been so perfect that not even a thin knife blade could be inserted between them.'[2]

Professor Yigael Yadin, writing on 'New Light on Solomon's Megiddo', tells us that 'a similar gate was found during our excavations at Hazor in a level attributable to Solomon on the ground of stratigraphy as well as pottery, . . .' and still another gate, found by Macalister in Gezer, has also been ascribed to King Solomon. In this paper, Professor Yadin describes the results of some excavations as recent as those of 1960, uncovering the existence in fact of a big city—Hazor—'well defended by casemate walls, the formidable six-chambered city gate and the newly discovered Northern Fort which dominated from above the approaches to the city gate'— the Solomonic city, in fact, that is referred to in *I Kings* 9:15.[3] In a further paper, describing specifically his excavations at Hazor, Professor Yadin tells us that 'the outstanding find . . . in the whole

---

[1] W. F. Albright, *The Archaeology of Palestine and the Bible*, p. 46.
[2] G. Ernest Wright, 'The Discoveries at Megiddo, 1935–39'. *The Biblical Archaeologist Reader*, II, pp. 235, 237–239.
[3] Yigael Yadin, 'New Light on Solomon's Megiddo'. *The Biblical Archaeologist Reader*, vol. II, pp. 240–241, 246–247.

Israelite city, was the gate of Stratum X, belonging to the Solomonic casemate city wall. . . . Its plans and measurements (some twenty meters long) are identical with those of the Solomonic gate found at Megiddo, Stratum IV B,'—indicating 'that both gates were built by the same royal architect'.[1]

As to the type of masonry previously described by Dr. Wright, Professor Albright takes cognizance not only of this improved type found at Megiddo, but also of the Solomonic masonry found at Gezer mentioned by Dr. Garstang—in both cases an archaeological reference to the age of Solomon all the more significant because it comes from one who is so generally sceptical of facile Solomonic ascriptions when they are not fully warranted by accepted scientific standards.

Solomon's Copper Smelter-Refinery at Ezion-geber

Like the 'Stables of Solomon', now found at Megiddo and satisfactorily authenticated, another indirect archaeological corroboration for Solomonic activity is provided us in the recent discovery by Dr. Nelson Glueck of the smelting and working of metals in the Solomonic era, as evidenced by the finding of deposits of copper ore in the areas south of the Dead Sea, which appear to have been worked with particular intensity in the days of King Solomon.[2] This discovery is of even greater importance for the Masonic reader than that of the stables, because of its direct connection, this time, with Solomon's Temple activity. Here, in fact, we find the source of the raw material for Solomon's two brass pillars, his enormous Brazen Sea that stood before the Temple, the brass Altar, the elaborate 'ten bases of brass' and the 'ten lavers of brass'—'and the pots, and the shovels, and basons: and all these vessels, which Hiram made to King Solomon for the house of the Lord, [which] were of bright brass' (*I Kings* ch. 7).[3]

[1] Yigael Yadin, 'Excavations at Hazor'. *Op. cit.*, p. 199.
[2] Cf. Nelson Glueck (Professor of Bible and Biblical Archaeology, Hebrew Union College, Cincinnati, Ohio; sometime Director, American School of Oriental Research, Jerusalem), 'Explorations in Eastern Palestine', *Annual* of the American School of Oriental Research, vol. XV, pp. 42–45.
[3] Dr. Glueck thinks that the 'brass' and 'bronze' in our English Bibles is a mistranslation of the original, which, in his opinion, should be rendered 'copper' instead, since brass and bronze were not known in ancient times. (*National Geographic Magazine*, 1944, p. 233). This controversial and purely technical question need not detain us here.

1 Ruins of one section of the Solomonic Stables at Megiddo. *See pages 76, 77.*
From G. Ernest Wright, *Biblical Archaeology.*

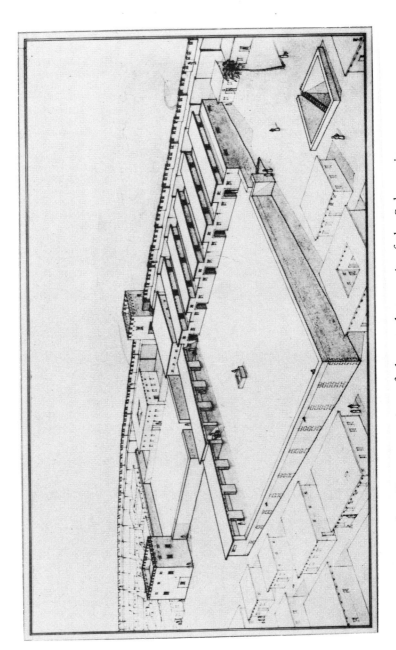

2   Reconstruction of the southern unit of the Solomonic
    Stables at Megiddo. *See page 77.*

Dr. Glueck describes his discovery at the present Tell el-Kheleifeh, at the tip of the Gulf of Aqabah, the north-eastern arm of the Red Sea, and which he thinks is in all likelihood the Ezion-geber of *I Kings* 9:26. The site itself is in a curious location, open to the full fury of the winds and sandstorms blowing in from the north as if forced through a wind tunnel, at the cost of much inconvenience and discomfort for its inhabitants, but an ideal site, for that very reason, for a natural smelter-refinery—a nature-and-man-made Bessemer furnace, in fact, with the fierce natural winds taking the place of artificially compressed air in the man-made structure excavated on this site.

The construction, too, was found to be as curious as its location, the walls being found pierced with two rows of flues, and inter-connected by a system of air channels, to take advantage of the prevailing wind-storms. 'It became evident,' says Dr. Glueck, 'that the building was an elaborate smelter or refinery, where previously "roasted" ores were worked into ingots of pure metal . . . devoted mainly to copper and in a lesser degree to iron . . . for home consumption and for export. Ezion-geber was the Pittsburgh of Palestine.'[1] The pottery, whereby the stratum of the site was dated, he thinks, belongs to the time of King Solomon.

It must have taken a great deal of business ability, as well as architectural, engineering, and metallurgical skill on the part of the developers of this Solomonic venture, says Dr. Glueck, 'to construct the factory town and seaport of Ezion-geber, and to keep the production line going. . . . Bricks had to be made by the thousands, and laid by expert bricklayers. (Some of the walls of the smelter have stood almost to their original height for nearly thirty centuries). . . . Thousands of laborers had to be assembled, housed, fed, and protected at the chosen building site. . . . Skilled technicians of all kinds had to be recruited. Great caravans had to be collected to transport materials and food. An effective business organization had to be called into existence to regulate the profitable flow of raw materials and finished or semi-finished products. There was, so far as we know, only one man who possessed the strength,

---

[1] Nelson Glueck, 'The Excavations of Solomon's Seaport: Ezion-geber' (1938–1940). *Annual Report*, Smithsonian Institution, 1941. A more easily accessible reference, to most readers, is perhaps the previously mentioned *National Geographic Magazine* (Washington, D.C.), vol. 85 (1944), pp. 233–256. It is beautifully illustrated.

wealth and wisdom capable of initiating and carrying out such a highly complex and specialized undertaking. He was King Solomon. . . . Ezion-geber represents one of his greatest, if indeed up to the present time his least known accomplishments.'[1]

As to the sea-port at Ezion-geber, the search for which initially led Dr. Glueck to the discovery of the smelter-refinery, 'it is interesting to learn from the Bible,' says J. A. Thompson, 'that Solomon had a port on the Red Sea at precisely this point. That a port existed here is borne out by the excavations at Ezion Geber,' disclosing such objects as copper and iron nails, pieces of rope and pieces of tar.[2]

The Temple of Solomon

So far, of course, we have not yet found any direct archaeological confirmation of the building of King Solomon's Temple itself—comparable, for example, to the excavation of the palace of Sargon II, King of Assyria, at Khorsabad, 'where 31 courts, 209 rooms, a ziggurat, and a temple have been uncovered'[3]—but we *have* found archaeological evidence of immense Solomonic activity in other directions—the Stables of Megiddo; several cities that exhibit the typical Solomonic style of stone-masonry; and, most important of all, the copper smelter-refinery at Ezion-geber that furnished him with the raw material for his brass ornaments and utensils for his Temple.

But there are still other avenues wherein we can explore the question of King Solomon's Temple itself, although, again, in an entirely indirect manner. This exploration takes the form of comparison with other temples in the Near East, where we successfully find some features associated with the Temple of Solomon reproduced in one way or another elsewhere. The two pillars which Herodotus says he saw at Tyre, standing before the Temple of Hercules—'one of pure gold, the other of emerald'[4]—has often

[1] *Loc. cit.*
[2] J. A. Thompson, *The Bible and Archaeology*, p. 106, citing Nelson Glueck, *The other side of Jordan*, pp. 50–113.
[3] James B. Pritchard, *Archaeology and the Old Testament*. Princeton, 1958, p. 134. Reconstruction.
[4] *History of Herodotus*. Tr. by George Rawlinson. New York, 1928, p. 96. Josephus, on the authority of Menander the Ephesian, says that Hiram, King of Tyre, erected a temple to Hercules (*Against Apion*, Bk. I, 18). This may have been the one that Herodotus (484–425 B.C.) says he saw. But current writers

been compared by writers with the Two Pillars in the Porch of King Solomon's Temple. A perhaps more significant parallelism between Solomon's Temple and others in the Near East, of approximately the same period in history, is the eighth century B.C. temple recently unearthed at Tainat in Syria—'the only temple contemporary with the kings of Israel ever found in Syria or Palestine,' says Dr. G. Ernest Wright, in describing it, 'and it is most important to note that its plan is very similar to that of the Temple of Solomon',[1] as can easily be seen from the accompanying reconstruction.[2] While this eighth-century temple, being later than Solomon's, may be considered to have been in imitation of Solomon's, rather than the reverse, the same is not true of a fourteenth-century B.C. temple that Professor Yadin has found in the ruins of the Canaanite city of Hazor. It is similar in plan, again, to King Solomon's, with its characteristic three chambers consisting of porch, main hall, and holy of holies. Significantly, 'in the porch, on either side of the opening leading to the main hall, we found two round pillar bases made of basalt. ... We have here,' comments Professor Yadin, 'a prototype of Solomon's temple, with the two pillars on the porch emphasizing the resemblance.'[3]

Additional resemblances between Solomon's Temple and others of the adjacent area show up in individual items of ornament or construction. 'The bronze altar was a Phenician innovation,' says Dr. G. A. Barton, in the *Jewish Encyclopedia*, while 'the Orthodox Israelitish altar was of earth or unhewn stone. ... Several temples in Babylonia, many in Egypt, and some of the Phenicians are now known. ... Solomon's Temple was not a copy of any of these, but embodies features derived from all of them.'[4] Thus, we read of the 'ten lavers of bronze and ten wheel-stands to hold them' that were cast by the brass-worker, Hiram. But 'such lavers have been found in the excavations' elsewhere, as Dr. Wright assures us, 'both with and without wheels. One unearthed at Ras Shamra in northern Syria has metal pomegranates hanging from the bowl,' not unlike

on archaeology and on the history of architecture, so far as I have been able to determine, appear to know nothing of such a temple, every vestige of it having apparently disappeared. In this other sense, it is in a class with the Temple of Solomon, which suffered a similar fate.

[1] G. Ernest Wright, *Biblical Archaeology*, p. 138.
[2] See: Oriental Institute Bulletin No. 1 (1937), p. 13.
[3] Yigael Yadin, *The Biblical Archaeologist Reader*, II, pp. 215, 218.
[4] *Jew. Enc.*, XII, *s.v.* TEMPLE OF SOLOMON.

those decorating the capitals of Jachin and Boaz. Other utensils mentioned in the Bible in connection with Solomon's Temple—shovels, flesh-hooks, and censers, for example—have also been found.

The method of building the wall of the Temple courtyard—'with three courses of hewn stone and a course of cedar beams' (*I Kings* 6:36)—'seems to be exactly paralleled at Ras Shamra in Syria, and several other sites have a comparable technique in using wood with brick or stone.

'Most Phoenician of all is the carved decoration: palm-trees and open flowers (also chains as in *II Chron.* 3:5) used for borders and panels with cherubim for filling. . . .

'The Temple of Solomon, therefore,' concludes Dr. Wright, 'was a typical Phoenician temple. Solomon, engaged as he was in the attempt to place Israel on the cultural map of the world, borrowed the whole religious equipment and paraphernalia of his culturally superior neighbours. Archaeology thus furnishes independent testimony to the fact which has previously been suspected from the Old Testament record that the reign of Solomon marked the greatest period of Israelite religious syncretism. . . . Solomon was a great cosmopolitan. . . .'[1]

We get the same story from the side of the history of architecture. 'Solomon's temple, however planned,' says Hugh Plommer, in his history of *Ancient and Classical Architecture*, 'was at any rate decorated like a north Syrian building. The brazen sea and bases recall the column bases of Senjirli; the decoration of the panelling with golden palms, several of the ivories from Nimrud.'[2]

Thus the problem of attempting to reconstruct in our mind's eye some realistic conception of what the Temple of Solomon may have looked like does not labour under some of the disadvantages of former times, when, as Dr. Wright tells us, many biblical students had to allow their architectural and artistic imaginations full play, because they had nothing more solid to go on.[3] 'Today,' he assures us, 'the situation is changed, for there are many new discoveries

[1] G. Ernest Wright, *Biblical Archaeology*, pp. 136–137, 140–141.

[2] Simpson's *History of Architectural Development*, vol. I. New York, 1955, p. 100.

[3] Cf. the paper by Rodk. H. Baxter, 'The Architectural Style of King Solomon's Temple', in *AQC* xxxiii, pp. 114–120. Cf. also, 'Some Notes on the Building of King Solomon's Temple', by Frank Trumper. *AQC* lxxviii, pp. 226–230.

which bear directly upon our problem.' And he illustrates this by devoting a number of pages, with photographs and diagrams, to an exposition of the problem, leading in the end to the Stevens reconstruction of the Temple of Solomon, as drawn from specifications prepared by Professor Albright and himself. All of this furnishes a most readable, and, what is more important, a most convincing account of the step-by-step process by which one can achieve a clear visualization of the Temple in all of its known aspects, architectural, archaeological, and religious.[1]

All this, of course, is without any direct benefit that might have been derived from any archaeological discoveries made on the site itself. While excavations have been made in the Jerusalem area, generally—as in the rest of Israel—comparatively little work has been done on the site of the Temple. The famous Rock 'where Abraham was about to offer up his son Isaac, and where David met and appeased the destroying angel', as we say in our American Lectures,[2] and which is traditionally, as well as in the acceptation of biblical scholars, taken to be the actual site where Solomon's Temple once stood, is now the site of the Mosque of Omar, as it is called, or Dome of the Rock.[3] It is from this very Rock, Moslems say, according to one of their traditions, that Mohammed ascended into heaven, and their reluctance to have this holy place excavated and disturbed is perhaps understandable. In his paper on 'Excavations of Jerusalem', Sir Charles Warren in fact describes the difficulties put in his way by native officialdom and superstition (Palestine was at that time under Turkish rule). 'This rock is very holy,' Sir Charles says at one point, 'and the dust gathered from it once a year is swept off by the pacha, and given or sold for the cure of ophthalmia.'[4]

Yet, in spite of the general dearth of direct archaeological and extra-biblical confirmation of the Solomonic era itself (of which the Megiddo and Ezion-geber and associated discoveries are dramatic exceptions), the archaeological discoveries of the *pre*-Solomonic and *post*-Solomonic days bear eloquent testimony, generally, to the

[1] G. Ernest Wright, *Biblical Archaeology*, pp. 136–145.
[2] Anderson, *Masonic Manual* (for the Grand Lodge of California), 1893, p. 248.
[3] See the photograph of the interior of the Mosque, showing the Rock, in the *Jewish Encyclopedia*, XII, p. 100. The outcropping of rock is some 58 ft. long, 51 ft. broad, and 4 to 6½ ft. high (Jack Finegan, *Light from the Ancient Past*. p. 151).
[4] *The Recovery of Jerusalem*, pp. 172–173.

historical accuracy of the biblical record in numerous instances. This is the basic import of such works as *Extra-Biblical Sources for Hebrew and Jewish History*, by Samuel A. B. Mercer; *The Bible as History*, by Werner Keller; and works of a cognate nature, some of which have already been drawn upon. The profusely-illustrated 450-page work of J. A. Thompson—one time Director of the Australian Institute of Archaeology at Melbourne, and associated with the American School of Oriental Research at Jerusalem—serves further to demonstrate the confirmation from extra-biblical sources originating in the surrounding lands, and touching on biblical events at innumerable points. This is found in inscriptions on slabs, cylinders, clay tablets, bas-reliefs, etc., many of which can conveniently be seen in the British Museum and elsewhere, and all of which enhance our comprehension and visualization of biblical history as a living record. One of these—the clay prism containing the annals of Sennacherib—has already been mentioned. The famous Moabite Stone—recording the revolt of the Moabites, and citing the specific instance of 'Omri, king of Israel, [who] humbled Moab many years';[1] it is now in the Louvre—is another case in point,[2] and Macalister has shown how important this Moabite inscription is for pointing up a period in Jewish history that is only barely alluded to in the biblical record.[3]

As to the demonstration of Solomon's copper and iron smelting activities, as disclosed by the discoveries at Ezion-geber: it was in the person of Solomon, more than that of anyone else before or after him, Dr. Glueck reminds us, that the promise to Israel contained in Deuteronomy was fulfilled, according to which, Israel was to inherit a land 'whose stones are iron, and out of whose hills you can dig copper'.[4] But, 'copper and iron in Palestine'? asks Werner Keller, in feigned amazement. 'Scientists themselves seriously doubted until quite recently that there was or had ever been such a thing in Palestine. Even some of the latest biblical commentaries gloss over this passage (*Deut.* 8:7–9), since they can make nothing of it. The work of the archaeologists has now produced evidence showing how true is this description that the Bible gives. . . .

[1] Cf. *I Kings* 16:16–28 and *II Kings* 3:5.
[2] J. A. Thompson, *The Bible and Archaeology*, pp. 122–123.
[3] R. A. S. Macalister, *A Century of Excavation in Palestine*, pp. 180–181.
[4] Nelson Glueck, *Bulletin* of the American School of Oriental Research, Oct. 1938, p. 12.

'King Solomon, whom Glueck describes as the "great copper king", must probably be reckoned among the greatest exporters of copper in the ancient world. Research on other sites completes the picture of Palestine's economy under King Solomon.'[1]

But, aside from such positive archaeological and extra-biblical confirmation as the above, which seems to be increasing with ever greater intensity with the passage of time, we may perhaps also do well to bear in mind the remarks of Professor A. H. Sayce, in his appraisal of the 'Higher Criticism', and his discussion of the archaeological evidence that has so far been turned up (or not turned up) in connection with the biblical record. In his work, *Monument Facts and Higher Critical Fancies*, he expresses his own estimate of the relative value of mere 'traditions' when they are not supported by either biblical or archaeological evidence, and he reminds us that ' "critical" difficulties and objections commonly turn out to be the result of the imperfection of our own knowledge. Archaeological research is constantly demonstrating how dangerous it is to question or deny the veracity of tradition or of an ancient record until we know all the facts.'[2]

Thus we can perhaps view with some patience and equanimity the present dearth of extraneous contemporary evidence with respect to the existence of David and Solomon and of the First Temple of Jerusalem, and we may have reason to hope that, with the passage of time, and the continued efforts of the archaeologists and historians, unequivocal corroboration of their existence as well will eventually come to light.

Towards the end of Professor Albright's significant work, *The Archaeology of Palestine and the Bible*, some of it based on his own discoveries, the author shows that recent archaeological finds have increased, rather than otherwise, our respect for the Bible as history. 'The excessive skepticism shown toward the Bible by important historical schools of the eighteenth and nineteenth centuries, certain phases of which still appear periodically, has been progressively discredited. Discovery after discovery has established the accuracy of innumerable details, and has brought increased recognition of the value of the Bible as a source of history.'

And he concludes his book with the significant and hopeful

[1] Werner Keller, *The Bible as History*. Translated by Wm. Neil. New York, 1956, p. 197.
[2] A. H. Sayce, *op. cit.*, London, 1910, p. 60.

prophecy: 'The progress of archaeological investigation will make the Bible stand out more and more brightly against the background of the ancient Orient,'[1] to which we might piously add,

So mote it be!

---

[1] W. F. Albright, *op. cit.*, pp. 47, 127–128, 177.

V

MASONIC TRADITION OF KING SOLOMON'S TEMPLE

as developed in the 'Old Charges' and the 'Early Masonic Catechisms'[1]

AS HAS been indicated in a previous chapter, the Masonic legend of King Solomon's Temple finds its origin among the earliest of our operative documents—the well-known and often alluded to *Old Charges* of the British Freemasons.

These *Old Charges* are a distinctive type of document, peculiar to the operative Masons, of which something must be said at the outset, for the benefit of those who may not have had previous opportunity to familiarize themselves with their principal features.

The documents generally comprise two essential elements. The first is a more or less legendary account of the origin and development of the art of building, and of the institution of Masonry as an organized Craft, with its established customs and practices, and rules and regulations—an account no doubt firmly believed in as genuinely 'historical' by those who made use of these documents, and who at the time had no better criterion than their own tradition.

The second essential element of these *Old Charges* consists of one or more sets of 'Charges' 'Articles' or 'Points', enunciated for the benefit either of Freemasons in general or Apprentices in particular, or both, and which consisted very generally of rules and regulations for the Mason's trade as well as an exposition of the reciprocal relationship between Master and Apprentice, and a few rules of good behaviour and moral conduct.

These *Old Charges* are said to have been used for two specific purposes in the old operative days, and for some time during the 'era of Transition' to the speculative.

Firstly, they were used to regularize the proceedings of any group

[1] The present chapter has appeared in *AQC*, vol. 80, and was presented in Quatuor Coronati Lodge No. 2076, London, at its meeting of January 1967.

of Masons acting as a 'Lodge', much as we nowadays establish our regularity by a similar possession and display of a Charter or Warrant. Thus, W. J. Hughan relates of the *Stirling MS.*, a seventeenth-century document belonging to the Lodge of Stirling, that a belief existed in that Lodge that a meeting would not be legal unless the MS. was exhibited in the Lodge Room;[1] and, at the Lodge of Hope, their own *Hope MS.*, also of the seventeenth century, was even 'for many years considered as an authority for conferring the Mark degree'[2]—a not unusual circumstance for the Craft Lodges of those early days, as far as these 'extra' degrees were concerned. D. Murray Lyon similarly tells us that 'in the early part of the last century [the eighteenth] it was a custom of the Lodge of Kilwinning to sell to Lodges receiving its charters, written copies of this document . . . the "Narration of the Founding of the Craft of Masonry" . . . which was termed "the old buik" '[3]—now known as the *Edinburgh-Kilwinning MS., c.* 1670—and which thus confirmed the regularity of these 'Daughter Lodges' of 'Mother Kilwinning'. There is also a MS. of the same version, only slightly altered, in the old minute-book of Atcheson's Haven Lodge, and carrying the endorsement, 'the 29th May 1666, by Jo. Auchinleck,' clerk of that Lodge.[4] Similarly, we find the *Alnwick MS.*, 1701, entered under the title of 'The Masons' Constitutions', and written in 'on the first twelve pages preceding the records of the "Company and Fellowship of Freemasons of a Lodge held at Alnwicke" '.[5]

Secondly, these *Old Charges* were used as reading material at the induction of an Apprentice into a 'Lodge', whereby he might come to know the history of the art he was embarking upon, and the association he was entering into, and would become acquainted with its rules and regulations, and the moral duties and rules of good conduct that were to become incumbent upon him. Perhaps these *Old Charges* were used again, in some cases, and perhaps in most, at the 'passing' of an Apprentice into full Fellowship at the end of

---

[1] Hughan, *Old Charges of the British Freemasons*, 1895; as told by Dr. Herbert Poole, *The Old Charges*; London, 1924, p. 26.

[2] H. Poole, *The Old Charges*, p. 26.

[3] D. Murray Lyon, *History of the Lodge of Edinburgh (Mary's Chapel) No. 1.* London, 1900, p. 115. (Since the first edition of this work came out in 1873, 'the early part of the last century' must refer to the eighteenth century, and not the nineteenth.)

[4] D. Murray Lyon, *loc. cit.*

[5] R. F. Gould, *History*, I, 69.

his period of indenture, at which time the reading would serve as a sort of 'refresher course', both to the newly-made Fellow and the older members. It is, in fact, difficult to see how this elaborate material could be completely intelligible to a young boy of thirteen or fourteen, entering upon his Apprenticeship, and hearing all this for the first time. Be that as it may, D. Murray Lyon, in presenting his readers with a print of the *Edinburgh-Kilwinning MS.* offers what he believes to be 'a transcript of the Masonic Legend and Charges which, with certain modifications, would in all probability be used by the Lodge of Edinburgh in the initiation of its intrants in the middle of the seventeenth century.'[1]

Most of the *Old Charges*, in fact, contain a built-in statement of the purpose to which they were dedicated. Thus, in the *Buchanan MS.*, in the course of telling the story of the Athelstan Constitutions of 926 A.D., it is said that Edwin, the king's 'son', who had obtained the Masons' Charter from the king, and had brought about an Assembly in the city of York, had 'caused a crie to be made after this manner that all old Masons and younge that had any writeings or understandings of the charges and manners that were made before in this Land or in any other that they should show them forth. ... And hee caused a booke to be made thereof: And how the Craft was found and hee commanded that it should be read or told when any free mason should bee made. ...'[2] Accordingly, the *Hope MS.* (*c.* 1680) presents an 'Apprentice Charge', the MS. as a whole being found to bear the significant title, 'The Constitutions, articles which are to be observed and fulfilled by all those who are made free by the R^t. Wor^l. Mrs Fellowes and Brethren of Free Masons at any Lodge or assemblie.'[3]

There is thus widespread evidence, from a number of independent and reliable sources, as to the double usage to which these *Old Charges* were put in operative times, and even well into the latter part of the 'Century of Transition' from operative to speculative Masonry—the seventeenth—and even into the early part of the eighteenth century.

The significance that all this has for our tradition of King Solomon's Temple as brought out in present-day Lodge practice is an obvious one, for it bears direct testimony to a similar tradition

[1] D. Murray Lyon, *op. cit.*, p. 116.
[2] The Buchanan MS. R. F. Gould, *History*, I, 100.
[3] Gould, *History*, I, 67.

having been continually recounted at meetings of our operative brethren as far back at least as the middle of the fourteenth century, when the original versions of the *Old Charges* began to form the basis from which the *Cooke MS*. had taken its rise.

The numerous versions of the *Old Charges* that we have in our possession today are a fairly recent acquisition in our investigation of the Masonic antiquities. When R. F. Gould wrote the first half of the first volume of his monumental *History of Freemasonry* in 1882— the best of its kind by all counts—he was able to say only that 'within living memory barely ten copies were known to be in existence',[1] but by the time of the publication of the Rev. Herbert Poole's *The Old Charges* in 1924—less than a half-century later— the latter was able to list as many as 101 separate versions, the newly-resurrected copies having been rescued in the interim from old chests stored away in attics, or otherwise brought to light.

We now have in our possession today, in the keeping of Lodges and other Masonic bodies, in some public libraries and museums and owned by private individuals in America as well as in the British Isles, perhaps a hundred and twenty-five versions of these *Old Charges*. They are all more or less of one basic pattern, having been mostly copied from one to the other, as additional copies came to be needed. And yet they are mostly all different, in some details, some more extensively so than others, the hand of the copyist showing itself in almost every case, either through inadvertence or by design; through misreading, or by the inclusion of some material picked up perhaps from some local tradition or out of his own learning or imagination. Thus the comparison of these different versions with one another has become an extremely fascinating study, and many diligent scholars have spent the better part of a lifetime in its pursuit, classifying and dividing these different versions into 'Families' and 'Branches', according to their similarities and peculiarities—much as a biologist divides our fauna and flora into Families and Genera and Species—and showing the indicated lines of descent of these different versions as copies are found to have been made from one probable source or another. In this lifetime endeavour, the names of Dr. W. Begemann, of Germany, and of R. F. Gould, W. J. Hughan, and, more recently, the Rev. Dr. Herbert Poole, of England, stand out as shining lights. To acquaint oneself with this question of the *Old Charges* in capsule form, there is

[1] R. F. Gould, *History*, I, 58.

probably no better work than the small book by the one last-named.[1]

Dr. Poole lists among the one hundred-and-one separate versions in his extremely readable little work, ten versions once known to exist but now missing. Two of these, originally listed among the missing, have since been found again, fortunately, but two others have now taken their place among the missing. These *Old Charges*, he tells us, carry us back to a period represented by the early part of the fourteenth century. They are in various forms. 'Some are on parchment and some on paper. Some are in book form and some in the form of rolls. A few have survived only by being printed, and the originals are now lost. But they are all substantially the same,' though there have been several revisions. And in some instances a particular version would be found to be, not a complete and more or less accurate copy from a single preceding version, but a compilation from two or more. Thus the study and comparison of these various versions, and the attempt at the detection of the intrusion of fresh elements, and the tracking of them down to their probable source, becomes an extremely fascinating game.

The peculiar interest all this has for the Masonic student stems from the fact, already indicated, that these *Old Charges* of the operative Masons were used in their day for ritualistic purposes, if we may so designate the very simple but no doubt impressive ceremony of admission practised by them in the operative days. But in addition they contain numerous germs of ideas which we now find full-blown in our own more elaborate rituals of today.[2]

This ritualistic use of the *Old Charges* among the operative Masons is very clearly indicated by a rubric found in practically all of them, generally in Latin—perhaps to give it added dignity —but sometimes in English, as in the following instance, from the *Alnwick MS.*, 1701:

[1] See also his 1933 Prestonian Lecture, 'The Old Charges in Eighteenth Century Masonry'. Quatuor Coronati Pamphlet No. 3.

[2] See, for example, the paper by E. L. Hawkins on 'The Evolution of Masonic Ritual', and by Rodk. H. Baxter, 'The Old Charges and the Ritual', in *AQC* xxvi and xxxi. This last-mentioned paper lists a large number of these *Old Charges* and where they can be found in print or facsimile. A similar list is to be found in Mackey's *Encyclopedia of Freemasonry*, s.v. 'Manuscripts'. R. F. Gould, in discussing all the versions of the *Old Charges* that were known in his day, also states 'where published', in each case. (*History*, I, ch. ii).

A 'Partial Bibliography' of the more easily accessible of these *Old Charges* is given at the end of the present chapter.

> Then shall one of the most ancient of them
> all hold a Book thatt he or they may Lay his or
> their hand or hands upon the said Book, and these
> p^rcepts followeing ought then to be Read.

The 'Book' in some versions is actually indicated as being the Holy
Bible, as in the following exhortation, from the *Lechmere MS.*
(seventeenth century):

> theise Charge[s] wch I haue rehearsed & all
> other yt belongs to masons you shall keepe, soe helpe
> you god & by this Booke to youre power

—while at least three versions specifically mention 'the Bible' or
'Holy Scripture', in so many words. But whether or not clearly
indicated in this manner, students are generally of the opinion that
the Holy Bible is intended to be referred to in each case.

The presence of the *Chetwode Crawley MS.* ritual (early eighteenth century), 'at the end of a copy of the Old Charges', Dr.
Poole thinks, 'goes far to support the view that these documents
supplied a part, at any rate, of the ritual of admission', in pre-
Grand Lodge days. In actual fact, it is thought that the *Sloane
No. 3848 MS.*, which is inscribed as having been completed on
Oct. 16, 1646—the very date recorded in Elias Ashmole's Diary as
the day of his own initiation—may have been prepared for that very
occasion, because of the coincidence of dates, and the further fact
that the scribe, whose name is appended to the document, is
believed to have been the son of one of those present in the Lodge
at the initiation, as listed in the Diary.[1] And the *Scarborough MS.*
bears witness to the fact that it was actually used at a meeting of
Freemasons for the purpose of initiation, for it bears the following
endorsement at the end of the Roll:

' . . . att A private Lodge held att Scarbrough in the County of
York the tenth day of July 1705 . . . severall p[er]sons whose names
are herevunto subscribed were then admitted into the said
ffraternity.'

Accordingly, we find Anderson's 1723 *Book of Constitutions*
opening with the heading:

[1] R. F. Gould, *History*, II, 266. See my short article, 'Elias Ashmole', in *AQC*
vol. 78, pp. 83–86.

The CONSTITUTION, History, Laws, Charges,
Orders, Regulations, and Usages . . .
to be read
At the Admission of a NEW BROTHER . . .

—to which Dr. Poole makes the comment that only a strong tradition on the practice of reading these long *Constitutions* or *Old Charges* at Admissions 'could have prompted Anderson to insert such a ridiculous direction' in his own day and age.[1]

But, it might be countered, with some degree of reason, that this direction could not have been so ridiculous in 1723 if it was in actual practice as recently as 1705.

The Masonic Tradition

We are now ready to examine a few of these *Old Charges* for evidence of the origin and development of the Masonic tradition respecting King Solomon's Temple. This tradition, it is true, is not to be found in the very oldest of our *Old Charges*—the *Regius MS.*, or Halliwell Poem, as it has been alternatively known. In this version, ascribed to a date of about 1390 A.D., there is no mention whatever of the Temple, nor of King Solomon, nor of any of the other personages connected with that edifice with which we are familiar from the biblical account. But in the very next version of the *Old Charges*—the *Cooke MS.*, of about 1410–20 A.D.—the tradition begins.

To be more accurate as to this matter of dating, the original text from which the *Cooke MS.* is thought to have been copied is believed by the experts to be actually older than that of the *Regius*, though written down in this particular MS. somewhat later than the *Regius* writing. The *Cooke MS.* is in fact a copy of an older version, now no longer in existence, as Dr. Begemann pointed out in calling attention to the repeated mistakes made by the transcriber of the *Cooke MS.* This investigator thought it could even be only a transcript of a still older transcript, because some of these mistakes were of such a character that they could not have occurred in a single copying only once removed.[2] The *tradition* represented by this *Cooke MS.*—regardless of the actual date at which the tradition may have come to be written down—would therefore extend backwards for some indeterminate but perhaps considerable length

[1] H. Poole, *The Old Charges*, p. 24.
[2] Dr. W. Begemann, *AQC* iv, 109–110.

of time. Both these two versions of the *Old Charges*, we are told by the joint authors of *The Two Earliest Masonic MSS*. must have been in fact 'composed, in large part, of materials current among masons, of customs, and perhaps traditions, which had been orally transmitted from generation to generation, much as manorial customs were commonly transmitted before it became convenient or necessary to set them down in writing'. And while 'examination of the handwriting suggests to the paleographical experts of the British Museum that the *Regius MS*. was written about 1390 and the *Cooke MS*. about 1400 or 1410 ... the comparatively brief common core, no longer surviving in manuscript, which was the foundation of all the MS. *Constitutions of Masonry* [an alternative and perhaps more accurate designation for the *Old Charges*], was probably first set down in writing in the third quarter of the fourteenth century, though the traditions and customs on which it was based may well have been considerably older'.[1] Lionel Vibert, in fact, is said to have expressed the opinion that this oral tradition may go as far back as the tenth century, having perhaps in mind the Athelstan Constitution of 926 A.D., and the tradition on which it is based.

The *Cooke MS*. is thus of considerable interest to us in our present study, being the first of the *Old Charges* to give us the story of King Solomon's Temple. The MS. itself lies in the British Museum, and is a book $4\frac{3}{8}$ in. $\times$ $3\frac{3}{8}$ in. in size, still bound in its original bare oak covers, but now with its clasp broken. Nothing seems to be known of its history prior to 1721, but on June 24th of that year, the Grand Master produced it at a Masonic dinner, and the antiquary, Rev. William Stukeley, recorded the event in his diary.[2]

The MS. has two direct descendants in the form of transcripts: The *Woodford MS*., 1728, and the *Supreme Council MS*., *c*. 1728, the latter being a very accurate copy.[3] In addition, it has given rise to a number of revised MSS. directly patterned after it, in whole or in part: the *Heade MS*., 1675; the *Plot* Abstract, 1686; the *Wm. Watson MS*., 1687; and the *Crane No. 2 MS*., *c*. 1781.[4]

The account of King Solomon's Temple in the *Cooke MS*. is part of the historical section originally written some time after 1350, and before 1390, but, as stated above, the MS. itself came to be

[1] Knoop, Jones and Hamer, *op. cit.*, p. 3.
[2] *Op. cit.*, p. 55.
[3] *Op. cit.*, p. 57.
[4] *Op. cit.*, p. 59.

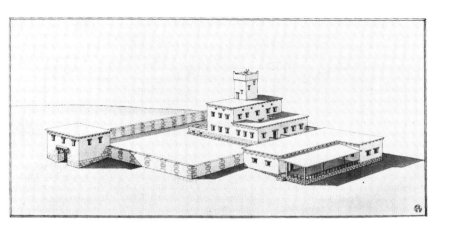

3a   Reconstruction of a Solomonic palace at Megiddo. First
half of the tenth century B.C. (Wright). *See page 77.*
Courtesy of the Oriental Institute, University of
Chicago.

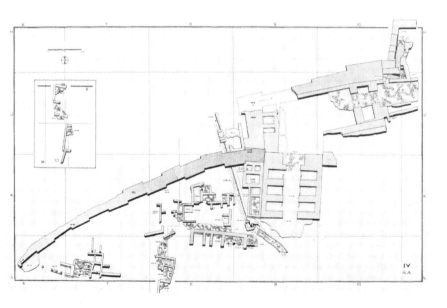

3b   Plan of the Solomonic city gate at Megiddo. It is exactly
like the east gate of Solomon's Temple enclosure in
Jerusalem as described in Ezekiel (Yigael Yadin). *See
pages 79, 80.*
Courtesy of the Oriental Institute, University of
Chicago.

4   From Prof. Paul Leslie Garber's pamphlet: *The Howland-Garber Model Reconstruction of Solomon's Temple*. Front view, with 'Molten Sea' at left, Altar of Burnt Offering at right. *See pages 55, 56*.

written about 1400–1420. In modernized English—the MS. is originally written in the 'Middle English' of Chaucer's time—it reads as follows:

> When the Children of Israel dwelt in Egypt, they learned the Craft of Masonry. And afterwards they were driven out of Egypt, [and] they came into the Land of Behest, which now is called Jerusalem. And there it was employed and the Charges held and kept. And at the making of Solomon's Temple that King David began—King David loved well Masons, and he gave them Charges right nigh as they are now. And at the making of the Temple in Solomon's time, as it is said in the Bible, in the III Book of Kings—*in tertio Regum, capitulo quinto*—(that) Solomon had four score thousand Masons at his work; and the King's son of Tyre was his Master Mason.

> And in other chronicles it is said, and in old books of Masonry, that Solomon confirmed the Charges that David his father had given to Masons. And Solomon himself taught them their manners, but little differing from the manners that now are used.

> And from thence this worthy Science was brought into France and into many other regions.[1]

So far we have a fairly straightforward, though simple, account. But several important points are worth noticing.

First and foremost is the insistence on the existence of traditional Masonic 'Charges'—that is, some sort of operative rule or custom, predicating some form of organized institution—in the time of King David and Solomon, 'but little differing from the manners [that is, the customs and practices] that now are used'. This, perhaps, is only a forgivable conceit, on a par with the practice of many of the guilds of that era, who similarly attempted to trace their origin to some ancient past; the French *Compagnonnage*, in fact— an institution comprising a number of building crafts, mainly operative in character, and still in existence in a somewhat modified form—similarly traces its origin to the building of King Solomon's Temple, as we shall have occasion to see in detail in our concluding chapter. And this tradition, preserved in the *Cooke MS.*, is in fact the source of our own present-day tradition that the origin of our

[1] Q.C. Pamphlet No. 5, *The Cooke MS. of c.* 1420. London, 1949. Rendered into modern English by Dr. Herbert Poole.

7

modern Freemasonry stems from the time of the building of King Solomon's Temple, and that some of our present-day practices similarly stem from corresponding practices in the 'Masonic Lodges' said to have been held in the Temple during that early time—a tradition firmly but uncritically still believed in by many today, even among those who should know better.

The second point to be observed is the attempt to bolster up the Temple account by reference to a specific passage in the Old Testament. Obviously, this 'Masonic' period was considered of some importance.

The third point to be noted is the reference to the 'Master Mason' in charge of the building of the Temple—so far unnamed—as the 'son' of the King of Tyre. This point is at first somewhat confusing, but is fairly easily disposed of. The reference in the Bible to our Hiram Abif, in the exchange of letters that took place between King Solomon and the King of Tyre, is, in the original Hebrew, in the form of *l'Huram abi*, and has been mistakenly rendered, in the literal English translation, as 'Huram my father's' —the word *abi* meaning 'father'. Thus the mistaken notion (though the reasoning is not very clear) that this Huram Abi—or, as we now say, Hiram Abif—was somehow the son of the King of Tyre—a notion that we find in all the subsequent versions of the *Old Charges* until we come to some of those of the eighteenth century.[1]

The fourth point to be noticed is the confident reference to 'other chronicles' and 'old books of Masonry'—an assertion of the belief that even in that early age the Masonic tradition recounted at that time was already of long standing.

Finally, it is curious to note one discrepancy between the Masonic tradition as herein recounted and the scriptural reference on which it claims to be based. ' . . . At the making of Solomon's Temple that King David began . . . ', the *Cooke MS.* says. But the Bible, in fact, makes no such reference to King David as having begun the construction of the Temple, but says instead:

> And it came to pass in the four hundred and eightieth year after the children of Israel were come out of the land of Egypt, in the fourth year of Solomon's reign over Israel . . . that he began to build the house of the Lord. . . .[2]

[1] This question of the name of Hiram Abif will be dealt with more fully towards the end of the work.
[2] *I Kings* 6:1. Cf. *II Chron.* 3:2.

Yet in most of the *Old Charges* that I have been able to see, following upon the *Cooke*, we have this Masonic tradition of the Temple having been begun by King David himself.[1]

This erroneous tradition is not rectified, in fact, till we come to the fairly late *Probity MS.* (of about 1736, or earlier, according to Hughan), and which may have taken its cue from Anderson's first *Book of Constitutions*, of 1723, both of which follow the biblical narrative correctly. The *Graham MS.*, of 1726, also does so, but this is not a true version of the *Old Charges* proper.[2]

This *Probity MS.*, which is supposed to belong to the Landsdowne Branch of the Grand Lodge Family of *Old Charges*, according to Dr. Begemann's classification,[3] comprises as well the *Landsdowne*, *Antiquity*, and *Foxcroft MSS.* (and, according to the later classification of Dr. Poole, the *Fortitude* as well), and should presumably be similar in context to the other members of the same Branch. The *Probity*, however, is the only one that makes the clearcut and biblically-correct statement: '. . . King Solomon began the temple . . .', while the other members of the same Branch hew to the same line as the preceding versions: '. . . King David began. . . .'

Another curious circumstance, in this same connection, is in the Spencer Family of *Old Charges*, which introduces a new element into the Masonic tradition, in the form of an actual citing of the 'reciprocations', or the exchange of letters that took place between King Solomon and the King of Tyre, preparatory to the building of the Temple, as we shall soon see in detail. In this exchange, King Solomon tells his brother-monarch of his 'Father having a will to build a Temple to God [but] hath been withdrawn from the performance thereof by the continual wars and troubles he hath had'—which is biblically correct. But this follows almost immediately after the customary statement, in accordance with the older versions: 'King David began', and is in turn followed, at the conclusion of the 'reciprocations', with a return to the traditional statement, wherein Solomon is said to have merely finished the Temple that his father had begun. The transcriber of the 'Spencer Family' version had, in fact, merely cut off the traditional version at one point, then had abruptly inserted the 'reciprocations', and finally

[1] I am indebted to my son Anthony for calling my attention to this discrepancy.
[2] Cf. p. 116, below.
[3] H. Poole, *The Old Charges*, p. 16. Cf. also Q.C. Pamphlet No. 3, 'The Old Charges in Eighteenth Century Masonry'.

picked up the original narrative in the traditional manner, without noting for one moment the very evident contradiction between these two sets of statements as regards the commencement of the building.

The apocryphal *Krause's MS.* attempts to correct the traditional 'King David began' by only speaking of the Temple of Solomon 'which his father had projected', and it is possible, of course, that this in fact was the thought in the mind of the first writer of the tradition we find in the Cooke and subsequent manuscripts of the *Old Charges*. But this is only a surmise. It may be supported, however, by the 'pattern' that David is said in the Bible to have left to his son Solomon for the various details of the Temple, and the fortune he had laid aside for its construction.[1] He had in fact 'begun' the Temple in that limited sense. Thomas S. Webb's *Freemason's Monitor*, however—the source of our American monitorial working—wisely follows the course of events more literally described in the scriptural narrative.[2]

Later versions of the 'Old Charges'

The reference to the building of the Temple, in the *Cooke MS.*, as we have noticed, is itself quite short. But when we reach the end of the fifteenth century, or the beginning of the sixteenth, and come to *Dowland's MS.*, of about 1500 (we do not now have in our possession any version of the intervening period), the tradition has become somewhat more elaborate.

The *Dowland's MS.* is here referred to as a manuscript of about 1500 A.D., but this dating requires explanation. The only text we have at present of this version is in the form of a print which appeared in the *Gentleman's Magazine* in the year 1815, set up in type from a manuscript prepared for the printer by James Dowland (hence 'Dowland's' MS.), and which he claimed to have copied from an earlier original. But neither Dowland's actual manuscript which he had prepared for the printer, nor the original from which he says he had copied it, are at present in existence. From internal evidence, however, Hughan and other experts were able to date this probable original as about 1550, while Woodford thought that it 'represents a MS. *circa* 1500'.[3] Despite this slight difference as to

---

[1] *I Chron.* 28:11–18.
[2] Webb, *op. cit.*, Providence, 1805, p. 163.
[3] Wm. J. Hughan, *The Old Charges of British Freemasons*. London, 1872. Preface by A. F. A. Woodford, xiii.

the probable dating, Gould does not hesitate to describe *Dowland*'s *MS.* as 'a transcript of probably the oldest original of any MS.', except of course the *Regius* and the *Cooke*.[1]

Woodford says of this version as a whole that it is the one from which 'almost all the remaining Constitutions derive their phraseology and arrangement . . . and [it] is probably the original of all the later forms modernized by the later transcribers'.[2] More specifically, the account of King Solomon's Temple in the *Dowland* version forms a pattern for many similar versions of a later date, and is therefore here given in full, in spite of the unavoidable repetitions, and in a version whose language I have taken the liberty to modernize:

Long after the Children of Israel had come into the Land of Promise, that is now called amongst us the country of Jerusalem, King David began the Temple that they called *Templum Domini*, and which is named with us the Temple of Jerusalem. And the same King David loved Masons well and cherished them much and gave them good pay. And he gave them the Charges and the manners as he had learned them in Egypt, as given by Euclid, and still other Charges that you shall hear of afterwards. And after the decease of King David, Solomon, that was David's son, completed the Temple that his father had begun, and sent after Masons into divers countries and of divers lands and gathered them together, so that he had fourscore thousand workers of stone, who were all named Masons. And he chose out of them three thousand who were appointed to be Masters and Governors of his work. Furthermore, there was a King of another region whom men called Hiram, and he loved well King Solomon, and gave him timber to his work. And he had a son who was called Aynon, who was a Master of Geometry, and Chief Master of all his Masons, and Master of all his engravings and carving, and of all kinds of Masonry that belonged to the Temple. And this is witnessed by the Bible, *in libro Regum*, the third chapter. And Solomon confirmed both the Charges and the manners that his father had given the Masons. And thus was that worthy Science of Masonry confirmed in the country of Jerusalem, and in many other kingdoms.

Curious craftsmen walked about full wide into divers countries

[1] Gould, *History*, I, 75.
[2] Wm. J. Hughan, *The Old Charges of Britith Freemasons*. London, 1872. Preface by A. F. A. Woodford, xiii.

. . . and so it befell that there was one curious Mason who was called Maymus Grecus who had been at the making of Solomon's Temple, and he came into France, and there he taught the science of Masonry to the men of France [etc. etc.].

We now see how the tradition has become somewhat elaborated. A characteristically Masonic tradition is here introduced—repeated in most if not all of the subsequent versions—to the effect that Solomon had 'sent after Masons into divers countries and of divers lands and gathered them together'. This is not entirely borne out by scriptural evidence (and fortunately now forgotten or ignored), since the Bible itself speaks only of indigenous workers, together with those of the Kingdom of Tyre. Furthermore, a group of Masons, to the number of three thousand, are now said to have been chosen out of the original eighty thousand, to be Masters and Governors (or Overseers) of the work. Hiram, King of Tyre, is now also mentioned by name, and his contribution of timber towards the work of building the Temple is added. His so-called 'son', who was the 'Chief Master of all his Masons', is also mentioned by name, but by a 'substitute name' only—Aynon, in this particular version, and by mostly similar but sometimes quite dissimilar 'substitute names' in other versions, until we come to the early eighteenth century, when the name of Hiram or Hiram Abif makes its appearance for the first time.[1] The reference to the Bible, in alleged support of the statement concerning this 'Chief Master of all his Masons . . . and of all kinds of Masonry that belonged to the Temple' is also scripturally inexact, if it has reference to our Hiram Abif, which it obviously does have. In the Bible, this craftsman is quite otherwise described, as only a brass-founder, and a master of other crafts, but not that of Masonry. That he was also the principal 'architect of the work' is mostly a Masonic tradition, carried out in all the *Old Charges* following upon *Dowland's MS.*, and is one, of course, that has come down to our own time.

[1] As to this name Aymon, and its variants, 'there are no indications', thinks Dr· Poole, 'that it was, as has sometimes been supposed, a corruption of an original Hiram, Hyram, or Huram; and a full investigation of the meaning and significance of the name seems likely to yield results of great value and interest'. (*The Old Charges*, p. 30.) This is precisely what J. E. S. Tuckett has done, in his paper, 'The Old Charges and the Chief Master Mason' (*AQC* xxxvi), and his demonstration has indeed yielded 'results of great value and interest', as we shall see towards the end of this work.

To return to this *Dowland's MS*. We now meet, for the first time, with a 'curious Mason' called 'Maymus Grecus' in this version, and by a similar but sometimes distorted form of the same name in the succeeding versions. ('Curious', indeed, since he is not only said to have been 'at the making of Solomon's Temple', but later also in contact with Charles Martel, of France, grandfather of Charlemagne—seventeen hundred years later! But historical anachronisms of this sort are no strangers to the *Old Charges*, in other respects as well. This story of 'Maymus Grecus' has fortunately not descended into our present-day 'speculative' account of the 'traditional history' and so may be dropped from further consideration at this time.)

Some anomalies

As has been stated, this *Dowland's MS*. (originally of *circa* 1500), in respect to the tradition of King Solomon's Temple, becomes the pattern for a great many other versions of a later date, so that it can virtually be called the 'standard version' of the *Old Charges* until we come to a comparatively late period.

There are, however, many curious anomalies. Some of these, as previously suggested, are obviously due to the failure of the transcriber to decipher the handwriting in the manuscript being copied, especially when he would come to some unfamiliar word—the word being, in some cases, in Latin. Thus, 'Templum Domini' becomes 'Templum Dei', in some versions, and 'Dom', 'Domi', 'Domin', 'Domino', 'Dominum', in some others; and is rendered, curiously, as the 'Temple of Diana', in at least four versions, and 'Temple Dianum', in one other. It is similarly Latinized into 'devinum templum', in one version, and 'Templum Deum' in another; and in some others, simply anglicized into the 'Temple of our Lord'. In one place, however, it has the completely incomprehensible name of 'Voo'. The transcriber of the *Carson MS*. throws up his hands, so to speak, over all these confusing variations, and prefers to give the Temple no name at all.

Another anomaly is in connection with the name of the so-called 'son' of HKT, as has already been mentioned; here given as 'Aynon', although it obviously refers to Hiram Abif. This 'substitute name' is repeated in a number of versions, and in some others it shows spellings somewhat comparable to it—such as 'Aymon', 'Annon', 'Annas', 'Amon' or 'a man', 'Hynon' and

'Ajuon'. 'Dynon' appears in one version, and 'Hyman' in at least two; also 'Ham' and 'Benaim'.[1] This last strikes one as at least having a Hebraic flavour, and as having some suggestive connection with the building craft. Perhaps it was even chosen by the transcriber for that reason—since *Bonai* (from which *Bonaim* can be developed, though not quite correctly) is the term used in *I Kings* 5:18 for the builders of the Temple.[2] But another 'substitute name'—Apleo—is quite incomprehensible, on the surface, and, curiously enough, is found not only in the *Carson MS.*, but also in the same *Stanley MS.* that gives the name of the Temple as 'Voo'. Two versions[3] call HAB 'Hiram of Tickus a masons sonne'—a variant that even W. J. Hughan said he was unable to explain—but perhaps I can offer a suggestion. For in the *Huddlestone MS.*, of 1730, we find HKT referred to as 'Hiram King of Tyrus', and the similarity in sound—Tyrus, Tickus—becomes at once apparent, if we give the 'i' the long sound.[4] The *Rawlinson MS.* (eighteenth century) tells us that 'this Hyram [HKT] had a Son called Amnon', while the *Antiquity MS.*, 1686, merely says that the King of Tyre 'had a son called . . . ', leaving the name entirely blank. The *Melrose No. 2 MS.*, 1674, similarly refers only to a 'son' of King Hiram, also leaving him unnamed. At least two others (the *Langdale* and *Foxcroft MSS*) also leave the 'Chief Master' unnamed, and this fact, combined with the numerous 'substitute names' in other versions, is what has suggested to J. E. S. Tuckett and others that the true name of the Master Builder may have had some esoteric significance to the operative Masons, and was left blank, or in a mutilated and outwardly unrecognizable form, for that reason.

It is only comparatively late in the operative period, and towards the beginning of the transition to the speculative, that we begin to

[1] This 'Benaim' is in a version known as *Papworth's MS.*, *c.* 1714. The Rev. Woodford, writing in the Preface to Hughan's *Old Charges* (1872, p. 11), thought that 'Mr. Wyatt Papworth's MS. is a copy of Dowland's modernized', but this is clearly impossible, in view of this change from 'Aynon' (in *Dowland's*) to 'Benaim'. Furthermore, 'Maymus Grecus' in *Dowland's* becomes 'Nimus Graneus' in *Papworth's*, and this, too, is palpably not a simple case of 'modernization'.

[2] Mackey's *Encyclopedia*, I, 144.

[3] *Clapham MS.*, *c.* 1700 and *Colne No. 1 MS.*, seventeenth century. The *Colne No. 2 MS.* (eighteenth century) merely calls him 'Hiram Ticku'.

[4] I subsequently found that Dr. Poole had had a similar idea. This 'HIRAM of TICKUS', found in a version of the *Old Charges*, he says, 'is clearly a corruption of HIRAM OF TYRUS. . . . ' (*AQC* xxxvi, p. 283).

meet with the true name of HAB; first, in the *Colne No. 1 MS.* (seventeenth century) and *Clapham MS.* (of about 1700), in both of which he is given this queer name of 'Hiram of Tickus'; then, in the *Dumfries No. 4 MS.* of about 1710, and the *Cama MS.*, of the first half of the eighteenth century, where the name is cleaned up to a plain 'Hiram', and finally in the Spencer Family of MSS. and prints (consisting of the *Spencer, Inigo Jones, Songhurst, Cole, Fisher-Rosedale,* and *Dodd* versions), where he is at last given the full name of Hiram Abif.

This previously-noted habit, found in the earlier versions, of referring to the Master Builder as the 'son' of the King of Tyre, has led to one still more curious anomaly—though logical enough in itself—in that this 'son' is referred to as being a 'Prince'. Being the so-called 'son' of a king, he naturally would be. This occurs in the *Harris No. 2 MS.* (late eighteenth century), where we find, after the more or less usual story of the Temple, a sectional heading, no doubt intended as a question, in this form:

Who was the first Prince that was a Mason [?]

with the answer following immediately thereafter:

Hyram the Son of Ahibbal King of Tyrus who sent to Solomon and gave him Cedar Trees and Timber wood to work, was a Master Mason

—and so forth. Here a second confusion is perpetrated. Hiram, King of Tyre was the son of Ahibbal, the *previous* King of Tyre, but in this version the two Hirams are obviously confused one with the other. This confusion is further suggested by the earlier *Thos. Carmick MS.*, 1727, which also speaks of 'the first Prince that was a Meason', but thereafter follows the customary version in naming him 'annas Son of hiram King of tyre. . . . He was master Meason and Master of Geomatry by Reason of his Great Skill and Cunning in Measondry.'

In connection with the name 'Hiram', one very curious anomaly occurs in the *Melrose MS. No. 2.* In all these *Old Charges*, as we have seen exemplified in the *Cooke* and *Dowland's MSS.*, the story of the Temple is almost invariably concluded with the statement: 'And thus was that worthy Science of Masonry confirmed in the country of Jerusalem,' or words to that effect. But there is this one very curious exception. In this *Melrose MS. No. 2*, of 1674 (but stated therein to have been copied from an original of 1581), the country is not 'Jerusalem', but 'the country of Hiram'. Now, *which* Hiram is meant? Hiram Abif is nowhere specifically mentioned by name, as we have seen, and in this MS. the 'son' of HKT remains anonymous. And the name, obviously, could not refer to the King of Tyre himself, since *his* was not the country in which the Temple was built and where the Charges had been laid down. One can perhaps conclude that this entry of the name of Hiram was by inadvertence—a slip on the part of the copyist. Unless, indeed, one prefers to develop still further the suggestion of J. E. S. Tuckett, already mentioned, in which the so-called 'son' is generally given a 'substitute name', through some belief in the esoteric character of the true name. In the *Melrose MS.*, it might appear as if an attempt was nevertheless made to bring in the true name through another and less obvious connection. Having kept it out at the front door, it is now, so to speak, brought in surreptitiously through the back door. And that is perhaps the correct interpretation of this otherwise anomalous 'country of Hiram'.

One very curious error in copying (or so it seems) occurs in a comparatively late version—the *Dumfries No. 3 MS.* (second half of the seventeenth century)—which is apt to cause some confusion. Here, a customary statement is first made:

> After ye Death of King David, Solomon Reigned, who finished ye Temple, and sent for masons into severall countrys. Thousands of Workers in Stone, wood, &c., and Chose out of them three hundred Whom he ordained masters over them and governers of the Work.

A few words are obviously left out between 'countrys' and 'Thousands', but this is relatively unimportant, since they can be easily supplied, and the 'three hundred' Overseers should as obviously have been referred to as 'three thousand three hundred', to conform to *I Kings* 5:16. However, the story then goes on to make the following very confusing statement, spaced exactly as given below:

> King Solomon's Charge Confirmed the Charge given by King David, Eucladus and King Nimrod.

> son to ye King of tyre, who sent to Solomon Cedar trees & other timber for the work, was a master mason, or master in

geometry, by reason of his great skill In yt syence, so yt King Solomon made him master over his masons.[1]

Here the 'son to ye King of Tyre' is somehow confused, on a quick reading, with King Nimrod; but of course the confusion is inadvertent. There is obviously something missing, again, between the words 'Nimrod' and 'son', perhaps because illegible in the original MS. from which the passage was copied. Or perhaps there was only one word preceding the word 'son'—the very name of that 'son'—purposely suppressed in this version, as in some others, for reasons that have already been suggested.

The Workmen

Still other anomalies crop up in the designation of the number of workmen employed in the building of the Temple, although here, too, as in the case of the name of HAB, the correct information could have been easily obtained from the Bible, according to the version given in the *First Book of Kings*, or the *Second Book of Chronicles*. Only a comparatively few of the MSS. cite the approximately correct number, given in *Dowland's MS.* as 80,000 workers of stone, out of which number 3000 'were ordayned to be maisters and governors of his worke'. One MS. even gives the number of stoneworkers as 80, obviously overlooking the word 'thousand', while several mention only 24,000—a somewhat understandable error if we were to assume that the 'four score thousand' given in some of the *Old Charges* had come to be misunderstood as 'four and twenty thousand'. An alternative explanation might also be suggested by the *Grand Lodge No. 1 MS.*, of 1583, which cites the number of workmen as 'iiij^{xx} Thousand', and which W. J. Hughan renders correctly in his printed version as 'four score thousand'. It is conceivable, however, that some ignorant copyist could make instead 'four and twenty' out of these same Roman numerals. We can also understand the possible frustration of the transcriber of the *Levander-York MS.* (*c.* 1740, from an original of 1560), who gave up the job entirely, merely referring to the workmen as the 'cunning men', without specifying the number. The *Thos. Carmick MS.* similarly refers to the 'artists and workers in stone', without saying how many there were; and the *Dumfries No. 3 MS.* merely says 'thousands of workers'.

[1] I have been unable myself to see this particular version, and the excerpt has been kindly supplied me by Mr. Harry Carr.

The number of those who were 'ordayned to be maisters and governors' of the work is given in some MSS. as 3000, as in the *Dowland*, but is corrected to 3300 in some MSS. (perhaps to make it conform to the *Book of Kings*), and to 3600, in other MSS. (as given in the *Book of Chronicles*). But in some other versions, the number has no rhyme or reason. It is given as 500, 1000, 3700, or 4000, according to the whim, apparently, of the copyist, while in at least seven versions it is found to be only 300, perhaps through the inadvertent dropping of a 3 in front, or a cypher, at the end.

The *Rawlinson MS.* (eighteenth century) perpetrates another curious error when it speaks of the 'twenty four thousand Elect and Nominated Master and Governour of the work', but there is an obvious omission of a few words between the 'twenty four thousand' and the 'Elect and Nominated', which destroys the sense. Thus the relevant passage, corrected from such a version as the *Thomas W. Tew MS.* (*c.* 1680), would read as follows:

> [And he sent after Masons of Diver's Lands and Countries and Gathered them togeather so that he had] twenty four Thousand [Masons and four Thous^d of them were] ordained to be Masters and Governo^rs of the Work.

These 'Masters and Governors', or Supervisors, Overseers, are generally taken to be chosen out of, and included in the 80,000 (or whatever the number was given to be) who were named Masons, but in the *Stanley MS.*, 1677, the *Clapham MS.* (*c.* 1700), and the *Huddlestone MS.*, 1730, they are said to have been in addition to them, so that the total number of Masons is there considered to have been greater.

Another unusual departure from the norm we find in the *Wood MS.*, 1610, where the 'fourscore thousand workers of stone' are entirely disregarded, and in their place the '70,000 who bore burdens' are mentioned. Now, both sets of figures follow the scriptural narrative accurately, and both sets of figures are given in our modern working, but the *Wood MS.* is the only one among the *Old Charges* that I have found to refer to thesê 70,000. In the others, it is only the 'workers of stone' who 'were all named Masons', together with the 'Maisters and governors' of the work, who are generally immortalized, but the 70,000 'bearers of burdens' were apparently unskilled labourers only, and, as Dr. Mackey explains, were thus not entitled (in the opinion of our operative brethren) to be similarly dignified by the title of 'Mason'.

But enough of anomalies, contradictions, and misreadings. There are numerous others, in this simple story of the Temple, as in other parts of the *Old Charges*, but it would be too tedious to go through all their multiform variations.

Hiram Abiff

We now turn our attention to a fairly late version of the *Old Charges* —the *Fortitude MS.*, ascribed to about 1750, and which is stated by Dr. Poole to have first attracted attention only as recently as 1934. It is of special interest because of an important accretion to our Solomonic tradition that occurs therein. This 1750 version repeats the story that we have so far been following, up to the time of the building of the Temple itself, including one of the very common anomalies we have also noted—'24,000 workers of stone' in place of the biblical four-score thousand—but at this point it takes a 'flash-back' (to use a movie expression) to speak of the prior 'reciprocations' that had taken place: the exchange of letters between King Solomon and Hiram King of Tyre which led to the building of the Temple, and wherein Hiram of Tyre had

> sent to Congratulate him [King Solomon] after his Accession to the Throne of his ffather, being right glad of his great wisdom and Zeal for the Lord, and verry willing to assist him with necessaries in his proceedings according to his ffathers directions and his own great Wisdom [and] prompted him on in the Speedy performance thereof; and the same Huram gave him timber to his work; and he had a Son called Huram that was master of Geometry and was chief Master of all his Masons (and was of one of the women of the Daughters of Dan) that belonged to the Temple

—and so forth.[1] Here we notice that, while the 'chief Master of all his Masons' is still mistakenly referred to as the 'son' of the King of Tyre, he is here given his proper name, Huram, instead of a 'substitute name', as in most of the previous versions we have so far considered. Moreover, his maternal lineage also is correctly given here—'one of the women of the Daughters of Dan', as stated in the *Book of Chronicles*.

[1] Q.C. Pamphlet No. 3, p. 25.

As already indicated, this is not our first meeting, chronologically speaking, with the true name Huram, as regards our *Old Charges*, as it had previously appeared in the *Cama MS.*, written about a quarter of a century earlier, where it is found in the more familiar alternative form 'Hiram', but still without the 'Abif' or 'Abiff'. In the still earlier *Clapham MS.*, of about 1700, and the *Colne No. 1 MS.*, of the seventeenth century, we found it to take the curious form of 'Hiram of Tickus'.

The *Inigo Jones MS.*, along with the rest of the 'Spencer Family' of *Old Charges* to which it belongs, is believed to have been based on a MS. similar to the *Cama*, above mentioned, according to the experts, and is of interest because it gives in full the actual 'reciprocations' which are found to be only alluded to indirectly in the *Fortitude MS.* This exchange of correspondence, however, is taken, not from the biblical account, but from the account left us by Josephus, basing his own account, perhaps, on some traditional version retained by the rabbis. The actual letters, themselves, are not likely to have been still in existence, a thousand years after they had been written.

These Josephian 'reciprocations', as taken from the *Inigo Jones MS.*, read in part as follows:

> Solomon to Hiram the King.
> . . . I Pray you, send me some one of yor Skilfullest men with my Servants to the wood Libanus, to Hew down Trees in that place; for the Macedonians [?] are more Skilfull in Hewing and preparing Timber, than our People are, And I will pay the Cleavers of wood according to your Direction. . . .

Immediately preceding these 'reciprocations', of which only a very short excerpt has been given above, the *Inigo Jones* gives the following introductory paragraph:

> After the decease of King David Solomon sent to Hiram King of Tyre for one who was a Cunning Workman (called Hiram Abif) the Son of a woma[n] of the Line of Naphtali and of Urias the Israelite. &c.

And towards the end of the story, it concludes with the statement:

> And Hiram King of Tyre . . . sent one that was named Hiram Abif a widows Son of the Line of Nephtali; He was a Master of

Geometry, and was [Master] of all his Masons, Carvers, Ingravers and workmen, and Casters of Brass and all other Metalls that were used about the Temple.

Our 'Cunning Workman' is now given his full name and title, as we have previously noted, and is no longer said to be the 'son' of HKT, but is given his true parentage, the latter according to the tradition also preserved by Josephus.[1] The '&c' in the citation given above, it should be noted parenthetically, may be only a decoration in the manuscript, and without significance. But in view of the remarks that will hereafter be made in connection with a similar 'etc.' in the *Thistle MS.*, it should be kept in mind.[2]

This *Inigo Jones MS.* produced a considerable amount of excitement at one time, not only because it was the first of the standard versions of the *Old Charges* found to carry the full double-name of Hiram Abif, but because of its being inscribed with the date 1607—thus indicating that the true name of the Master Builder was known to and openly used by the operative Masons in that early period, as against the many 'substitute names' otherwise found in the *Old Charges*. But more careful analysis has proven this early dating to be false. G. W. Speth even thought 'that the date on the title was done with a brush, although the rest was written with a very finely pointed pen', and may have been painted in quite a bit later. Dr. Begemann satisfactorily demonstrated that the 'reciprocations' in this document must have been taken from Thos. Lodge's translation of the works of Josephus, and probably from the edition of 1655 or 1670, because of a significant tell-tale error that appears in both the *Inigo Jones MS.* and in these two editions of Josephus. In the earlier editions, Josephus speaks of the 'Sidonians' who were 'more Skilfull in Hewing and preparing Timber', but in these two editions of 1655 and 1670, the word 'Sidonians' is mistakenly replaced by the word 'Macedonians', and the *Inigo Jones MS.*, as we have seen above, perpetrates the same error. Consequently, Dr. Begemann argued, the *Inigo Jones* could not possibly be earlier than 1655. On the basis of still other considerations, moreover, he thought the date of the *Inigo Jones* was more nearly 1725, and that the compiler of the MS.

[1] Jos., *Antiquities*, p. 244.
[2] It should be added, however, that there are numerous such 'decorations' in the MS., at the end of some lines, used to produce a uniform margin, but none of these other decorations give any such semblance of an '&c' as this one clearly does.

gratuitously inserted the name Hiram Abif, in place of the Huram in Josephus, as a result of his desire to 'introduce this Hiram Abif into the old history of the Craft, because of the newly invented legend of the Third Degree'.[1] Other experts are not quite so sure, however, that this legend of the Third Degree was only 'invented' about that time, but that is another story.

For the present, one further elaboration of the Masonic legend of the Temple is to be noticed at this time, as preserved in the *Inigo Jones MS.*, and taken obviously again from the Josephus 'reciprocations'. Solomon tells the King of Tyre, who had been a friend of his father David, that his father had been prevented from building a Temple to his God, because of the continual wars and troubles he had had, but that God had, on the other hand, foretold that the Temple would indeed be built, but not till Solomon's reign had come about. To which Hiram replies that he will indeed furnish the help that has been requested of him, and will send quantities of timber down by sea, to a port on the coast of Israel, from which place Solomon's subjects would be able to transport them inland to Jerusalem. It is worthy of note that these are precisely among the details that have been preserved in the American Monitorial Lectures.

We now turn to the previously-promised mention of the *Thistle MS.*, of about 1756, to discuss a curious omission, and the probable reason for it. This MS., which incidentally calls Solomon's Temple the 'temple of Diana' (perhaps through a misreading of 'Domini'), says little else in this connection beyond the statement that 'Solomon his son performed the temple that his father had begun', the rest of the story being covered by an enigmatic '&c'. Dr. Poole thinks it significant that the *Thistle MS.* omits all details of Solomon's gathering of workmen, as well as all reference to Hiram King of Tyre, and he is of the opinion that this omission may have some connection, perhaps, with the ritual of the period. This appears to be borne out, he further thinks, by a similar reticence indicated by 'the omission of the description of the two pillars in the *Thistle MS.*' The copying throughout is accurate, Dr. Poole assures us, 'but in two other places, words have been left with initials or a few letters and a dash. The words so treated are "T—", the brother of Naamah, who "found out the smith work", and the words "a

[1] *AQC* i, 202.

ORBIS MIRACULUM,

OR THE

TEMPLE

OF

SOLOMON,

POURTRAYED BY

Scripture-Light:

WHEREIN

All its famous Buildings, the pompous Worſhip of the *Jewes,* with its attending Rites and Ceremonies; the ſeveral Officers employed in that Work, with their ample Revenues : and the Spiritual Myſteries of the Goſpel vailed under all ; are treated of at large.

Pſal. 27. 4.
One thing have I deſired of the Lord, that will I ſeek after, that I may dwell in the Houſe of the Lord all the dayes of my life, To behold the beauty of the Lord, and to enquire in his Temple.

Pſal. 43. 3.
O ſend out thy Light and thy Truth, Let them lead me, let them bring me to thy Holy Hill, and to thy Tabernacles.

Pſal. 84. 1.2.
How amiable are thy Tabernacles O Lord of Hoſts : my Soul longeth, yea, even fainteth for the Courts of the Lord : My heart and my fleſh cryeth out for the Living-God.

LONDON,
Printed by *John Streater,* for *Luke Fawn,* at the Signe of the Parrot in Paul's-Church-yard,
MDCLIX.

5   Title page of Samuel Lee's *Orbis Miraculum*, 1659. *See pages 45, 115, 141, 222.*

6   Residence and Royal Chapel of the Princes of Hattina,
Syria, eighth century B.C.
See page 83.
Courtesy of the Oriental Institute, University of
Chicago.

Mental R— or Equi—" at the commencement of the Charge. Now,' says Dr. Poole, 'these are the *only* words in the whole of the MS. which are used with any special significance in our modern ritual; and it is more than probable that they were so used in 1756, and they were "heled" accordingly by the *Thistle* copyist'.[1]

We can now take a backward glance towards the *Inigo Jones MS.*, recently studied, where we found a similar '&c' after the first mention of Hiram Abif. Could this '&c' similarly indicate some element of the Hiramic Legend 'not proper to be written'? One wonders.

The Early Masonic Catechisms

This brings us by natural progression to a consideration of the *Dumfries No. 4 MS.*, a document of considerable interest and importance, and especially so because of its very elaborate development of the Temple theme. The MS. was discovered by James Smith in 1891 among the muniments of Lodge Dumfries Kilwinning No. 53, in Scotland, from which it takes its name, and 'at one time', the compilers of *The Early Masonic Catechisms* tell us, 'it was almost certainly employed for ritual purposes, as it shows considerable signs of use'.[2] It has been assigned a date of *circa* 1710, some half-dozen years before the formation of our first Grand Lodge, and is therefore of special interest because of this early dating, as well as because of its unusual contents. It has been listed among the 'sundry' versions of the *Old Charges*, since it does not fit into any of the usual patterns, and is not a true representative of the type of document we have so far been considering, but combines some of the features both of the *Old Charges* and the *Early Catechisms* that began to come into use about the time the Lodge reading of the *Old Charges* had begun to taper off, thus forming a bridge between these two types. This *Dumfries No. 4*, together with the *Thistle* and the *Thos. Carmick MSS.*, Dr. Poole tells us, all appear to have been compiled from materials taken from a number of previous versions of the *Old Charges*, and for this reason are not found to be copies from a single original.[3]

The *Dumfries No. 4 MS.* has been reproduced in full in vol. vi of *AQC*, as well as in the *Early Masonic Catechisms* collection, but a brief reference to some of its Solomonic features will here be made.

[1] *AQC* xxxv, 56.
[2] Knoop, Jones and Hamer, *The Early Masonic Catechisms*, p. 45.
[3] Dr. H. Poole, *The Old Charges*, p. 13.

8

The story of the Temple itself, in the *Dumfries*, adds little to what we have already observed in the *Old Charges* proper, but it does give the Master Builder his correct name Hiram, and his parentage, and does this some years earlier than the *Cama* or the Spencer Family of *Old Charges* or the 1723 *Book of Constitutions*.

> There was a king in Tyre called Hiram who loved Solomon well, and he gave to Solomon timber for his work, and likewise sent him an artist in whom was the spirit of wisdom. His mother was of the tribe of Naphtali and his father a man of Tyre. His name was Hiram. The world has not produced his equal to this day. He was a Master Mason of exquisite knowledge and generosity, and was Master Mason of all the buildings and builders of the temple, and Master of all graven and carved work in and about the Temple.[1]

The almost reverent tone accorded to the description of the Master Builder is particularly to be noted, something that has not been found in connection with any of the other builders mentioned in the *Old Charges*.

Subsequently, in the catechismal portion of the MS., we meet with a series of questions and answers, some of which have considerable interest for us today. They indicate an extensive expansion of the Masonic symbolism of the Temple, but this expansion could not have come about overnight; it must necessarily have been in process of elaboration for some time at least, though not evidenced by any of the standard versions of the *Old Charges*. In this Catechism we find questions and answers as to who laid the cornerstone of the Temple of Solomon (our own HAB, of course), and where it was laid; followed by some questions and answers relative to the Brazen Sea, and the golden door of the Temple, with their corresponding symbolisms. One of the significant questions and answers is here given:

> Q. Which way stands your Lodge?
> A. East and West; because all holy churches and temples stand that way, and particularly the temple of Jerusalem[2]

—followed by an explanation of the reasons for this orientation.

Another section is headed specifically, 'Questions concerning

[1] I have again modernized the original.
[2] The English has been modernized.

the Temple', and these are found to concern such items as the symbolic significance of the Temple itself, the white marble of which it was constructed, the 'cader' [cedar?], cyprus, and olive wood used in its construction, the gold and precious stones, and of course the cherubims, the veil, the ark of the covenant, the altar, the golden candlestick, the table of shewbread, etc.—all this being generally explained in the fashion developed earlier by Samuel Lee in his *Orbis Miraculum* (1659) and by John Bunyan in his *Solomon's Temple Spiritualiz'd* (1688).[1] Some fantastic dimensions for the temple building are then given—suggesting, perhaps, the inspiration for some equally fantastic figures found in Dr. Anderson's *Book of Constitutions* and carried down to our day in our *Monitors*—and the Catechism closes with the following reference to the Two Pillars in the Porch of King Solomon's Temple:

> Solomon set up two notable names. That on the right hand, called Jachin; that is, in it there is strength . . . for the time to come, God will establish . . . as . . . God would at length establish in His time, though as yet it had not attained to this stability. . . . This of the Gentiles, by Boaz, on the left hand . . .

—and so forth.[2] Not making too much sense, especially in this fragmented rendering, but at least the general drift is indicated.

A further interesting elaboration of the Solomonic Legend is that provided by the *Graham MS.*, a document brought to light as recently as 1936. As Dr. Poole points out, this one also is not a true version of the *Old Charges* proper, but does contain material found in some of them. It has a date inscribed thereon, but this is given in a somewhat enigmatic manner, which has led to some speculation, but is generally accepted as indicating the year 1726.[3] The MS. has proved to be of great interest to Masonic students because of its introduction of a Noachic Legend having many of the precise features of the Hiramic Legend with which we are familiar. The Solomonic story, however, is all that we are concerned

---

[1] For a fuller discussion of this question of Solomonic symbolism, see my paper, 'King Solomon's Temple, 1659 A.D.' in the *Transactions*, American Lodge of Research, viii, No. 1.

[2] The English has been modernized.

[3] See the important discussion of 'The Graham Manuscript' by Dr. Poole in *AQC* vol. 50, with facsimile. A transcript also is to be found in *The Early Masonic Catechisms* of Knoop, Jones and Hamer. See also p. 340 *et seq*, below.

with at present, and it is as follows (in modernized English, as before, but with some insignificant omissions, for the sake of brevity):

[It was] four hundred and four score years after the children of Israel had come out of the land of Egypt, in the fourth year of Solomon's reign over Israel, that Solomon began to build the House of the Lord which his father David should have built, but was not permitted to perform it because his hands were guilty of blood, wars being on every side—

... Now we read, at the 13th verse of the 7th chapter of the First Book of Kings, that Solomon sent and fetched Hiram out of Tyre, he being a widow's son of the tribe of Naphtali and his father a man of Tyre, a worker in brass, filled with wisdom and cunning to work all works in brass. And he came to King Solomon and wrought all his work for him. . . . So by this present scripture, it must be allowed that the widow's son whose name was Hiram had a holy inspiration, as well as the wise King Solomon or yet the holy Bezalleel. . . .

Then it goes on to describe an event that is said to have transpired at the building of the Temple, and which has managed to work its way into the basic legend of the present Mark Master Degree:

Now it is holden forth by tradition that there was a tumult at this erection which should [not have] happened between the laborers and the Masons about wages; and to calm all, and to make all things easy, the wise king should have said: Be all of you content, for you shall be paid all alike; yet give a sign to the Masons not known to the Laborers [who were not Masons] and whoever could make that sign at the paying-place was to be paid as Masons. The Laborers, not knowing thereof, were paid as aforesaid. This might have been: yet if it was so, we are to judge very mercifully on the words of the wise King Solomon, for it is to be understood and also believed that the wise king meant 'according to every man's deserving'. Yet the 7th verse of the 6th chapter of the First Book of Kings reads still better to me; where it is said: the House when it was in building was built of stone made ready before it was brought thither, so that there was neither hammer nor axe nor any tool of iron heard in the house when it was in building. . . . So the work went on and prospered, which it could not well go amiss, being they wrought for so good a master, and had the wisest man on earth to be their overseer. . .

This citation practically brings the MS. to an end, with a reference to the 'five points off free Masons fellowshipe' (which might well indicate a Scottish origin for this document, as these 'Five Points of Fellowship' are known to have been an early and peculiarly Scottish element of ritual, connected with the giving of the 'Mason Word'),[1] and which it is there stated take their strength from five primitive points, the fifth being 'hiram who was ffilled with wisdom and understanding'.

We can now turn our attention exclusively to the series of about a dozen-and-a-half mostly short Catechisms of the period beginning with the earliest of these, 1696 (many—perhaps most—of them being of Scottish origin), to discern the further direction which the legend of King Solomon's Temple now takes. For this purpose, a composite collection from these various Catechisms will here be presented, omitting some needless repetitions.[2]

Q. 10 Where wes the first lodge
An: in the porch of Solomons Temple
—*Edinburgh Register House MS.*, 1696

(This refers to the tradition, preserved in all the *Old Charges* since the *Cooke MS.*, and treated more fully in Ch. II, to the effect that the Masonic Craft had its principal origin at the time of the building of King Solomon's Temple.)

Q. 9th How stands your Lodge?
Ans.r.   East & West, as the Temple of Jerusalem.

Q. 20th Where are the words to be found?
Ans.r.   in I King. Chap. 7th verse 21. And 2 Chron: 3 Chapter Last verse.
—*The Chetwode Crawley MS.*, *c.* 1700.

Q. Where was the first Lodge kept?
A. In *Solomon's* Porch; the two Pillars were called *Jachin* and *Boaz*.
—*A Mason's Examination*, 1723.

[1] Douglas Knoop and G. P. Jones, *The Scottish Mason and the Mason Word*. Manchester, 1939, pp. 81–84.
[2] All of this is excerpted from *The Early Masonic Catechisms*, passim.

Q. What do they represent?
A. A Strength and Stability of the Church in all Ages.

Q. How many particular Points pertain to a Free-Mason?
A. Three; ... for which all Masons were ordain'd at the Building of the Tower of *Babel*, and at the Temple of *Jerusalem*.
—*The Grand Mystery of Free-Masons Discover'd*, 1724.

Jachin and *Boaz*, two Pillars made by *Heirom*. *Jachin*, signifies Strength and *Boaz* [signifies] Beautiful, ...

For proof of our two Pillars you may read the *7th* Chapter of the *1st* of *Kings* from the *13th* Verse to the *22d*, where you will find the wonderful Works of *Heirome* at the building the House of the Lord.

The reason why Masonary receiv'd a secret, was, because the building the House of the Lord pleas'd his Divine Majesty. ...
—*The Whole Institutions of Free-Masons Opened*, 1725.

None of these short Catechisms can be other than mere scraps of remembered information. The *Dumfries No. 4 MS.* and the *Graham MS.* are much more extensive, but have already been considered. The most complete of the Catechisms is Samuel Prichard's *Masonry Dissected*, 1730, but this only makes Solomonic reference, in the 'Fellow-Craft Part', to the Two Pillars, in the manner already seen in connection with the Catechisms given above. There is also a reference, in the form of a doggerel, to the Letter G, and which, like the Pillars, is given an origin connected with King Solomon's Temple. But the 'Master's Part' gives the story of the Master Builder Hiram, in connection with an occurrence that is supposed to have taken place at the building of the Temple, which will shortly be cited, and this is its only significant contribution.

Dr. James Anderson also makes reference to this occurrence in his 1738 edition of the *Book of Constitutions*, together with some other references concerning the Temple, and which he had commenced to discuss in his first edition of 1723. All of this, he assures us, was but a summation, so to speak, of what he had gleaned from the *Old Charges* of the operative Masons, together with what he had 'collected from their old Records and faithful Traditions', but some of which, as regards the story of the Temple itself, he could easily have extracted from the biblical account, aided and abetted, no doubt, by his own prolific imagination. Thus, when he tells us that, at the building of the Temple, 'Solomon partition'd the Fellow Crafts into certain Lodges, with a Master and Wardens in each', and furthermore adds, in a marginal note, that this was but 'according to the Traditions of old Masons, who talk much of these things',[1] we may reasonably question the reference, since there is no corroboration from independent sources, but perhaps there *may* have been some speculation along these lines on the part of those who were fond of speculating, in those early times, as there is in the present.

But Anderson also tells us—to confine ourselves this time to the more sober aspect of his discourse—of the '80,000 Hewers of Stone in the Mountain, or Fellow Craftsmen, and 70,000 Labourers' or bearers of burden, all working under the '3,600 Princes, or Master-Masons, to conduct the work according to Solomon's Directions'. And he goes on to speak of the levy of 30,000 working under Adoniram in the mountains of Lebanon, making 183,000 in all. 'For which great Number of ingenious Masons,' Anderson reminds us, 'Solomon was much oblig'd to HIRAM, or Huram, King of Tyre, who sent his Masons and Carpenters to Jerusalem, and the Firs and Cedars of Lebanon to Joppa, the next Sea-port.

'But above all,' he concludes, in the account given in his first edition, 'he sent his Namesake HIRAM, or Huram, the most accomplish'd Mason upon Earth'[2]—later elaborating the designation, in his second edition, to that of 'HIRAM ABBIF, the most accomplish'd Designer and Operator upon Earth'. And of the Temple itself, he tells us that

> It was finish'd in the short Space of 7 Years and 6 Months, to the Amazement of all the World; when the Cape-Stone was celebrated by the Fraternity with great Joy. But their Joy was soon interrupted by the sudden Death of their dear Master HIRAM ABBIF, whom they decently interr'd in the Lodge near the Temple according to antient Usage.[3]

This comparatively short account we find elaborated upon in Samuel Prichard's *Masonry Dissected*, 1730, which has been previously alluded to. It is given in the collection of *The Early Masonic Catechisms*, first published in a limited edition, and now fortunately

[1] 1738 *Constitutions*, Quatuor Coronatorum Antigrapha, London, vol. vii, p. 13.
[2] 1723 *Constitutions*, pp. 10, 11. Facsimile Edition, London, 1923.
[3] 1738 *Constitutions*. *QCA* vii, p. 14.

made more accessible through the reprint by Quatuor Coronati Lodge No. 2076 of London. It purports to represent the tradition as of 1730, but whether it does so or not, there is no way of knowing for certain, for lack of independent corroboration. It is here given for what it may be worth.

Speaking of 'the Death of our Master Hiram', the Catechism continues in the following terms:

Ex. [Examiner?] How came he by his Death?

R. [Response?] In the building of Solomon's Temple he was Master-Mason, and at high 12 at Noon, when the Men was gone to refresh themselves, as was his usual Custom, he came to survey the Works, and when he was enter'd into the Temple, there were Three Ruffians, suppos'd to be Three Fellow-Crafts, planted themselves at the Three Entrances of the Temple, and when he came out, one demanded the Master's Word of him, and he reply'd he did not receive it in such a manner, but Time and a little Patience would bring him to it: He, not satisfied with that Answer, gave him a Blow, which made him reel; he went to the ɔther Gate, where being accosted in the same manner and making the same Reply, he received a great Blow, and at the third his *Quietus*.

Ex. What did the Ruffians kill him with?

R. A Setting Maul, Setting Tool and Setting Beadle.

Ex. How did they dispose of him?

R. Carried him out at the West Door of the Temple, and hid him under some Rubbish till High 12 again.

Ex. What Time was that?

R. High 12 at Night, whilst the Men were at Rest.

Ex. How did they dispose of him afterwards?

R. They carried him up to the Brow of the Hill, where they made a decent Grave and buried him.

Ex. When was he miss'd?

R. The same Day.

Ex. When was he found?

R. Fifteen Days afterwards.

Ex. Who found him?

R. Fifteen Loving Brothers, by Order of King Solomon, went out of the West Door of the Temple, and divided themselves from Right to Left within Call of each other; and they agreed that if they did not find the Word in him or about him, the first Word should be the Master's Word; one of the Brothers being more weary than the rest, sat down to rest himself, and taking hold of a Shrub, which came easily up, and perceiving the Ground to have been broken, he Hail'd his Brethren, and pursuing their Search found him decently buried in a handsome Grave 6 Foot East, 6 West, and 6 Foot perpendicular, and his Covering was green Moss and Turf, which surprized them; whereupon they replied [*in Latin?* A.H.] *Muscus Domus Dei Gratia*, which, according to Masonry, is, *Thanks be to God, our Master has got a Mossy House*: So they cover'd him closely, and as a farther Ornament placed a Sprig of Cassia at the Head of his Grave, and went and acquainted King Solomon.

Ex.   What did King Solomon say to all this?

R.   He order'd him to be taken up and decently buried, and that 15 Fellow-Crafts with white Gloves and Aprons should attend his Funeral.

Ex.   How was Hiram rais'd?

R.   As all other Masons are, when they receive the Master's Word.

Ex.   How is that?

R.   By the Five Points of Fellowship.

Ex.   What are they?

[R].   Hand to Hand, Foot to Foot, Cheek to Cheek, Knee to Knee, and Hand in Back. Etc.

PARTIAL BIBLIOGRAPHY

of the 'Old Charges'
in readily accessible Masonic Libraries

Abbreviations

QC: Quatuor Coronati
AQC: Ars Quatuor Coronatorum
QCA: Quatuor Coronatorum Antigrapha

The Songhurst MS.	Q.C. Pamphlet No. 2	
The Talents MS.	„ „	
The Fortitude MS.	„ „	3
The Cooke MS.	„ „	5
The Dumfries No. 4 MS.	AQC vol. vi, p. 36	
The Thorp MS.	„ „ xi, p. 205	
The Rawlinson MS.	„ „ xi, p. 17	
The Levander-York MS.	„ „ xviii, p. 162	
The Bain MS.	„ „ xx, p. 249	
The Taylor MS.	„ „ xxi, p. 211	
The Henery Heade MS.	„ „ xxi, p. 161	
The Thos. Carmick MS.	„ „ xxii, p. 95	
The Beswick-Royds MS.	„ „ xxviii, p. 189	
The Colne No. 1 & No. 2		
MSS.	„ „ xxxiv, pp. 60, 66	
The Thistle MS.	„ „ xxxv, p. 41	
The Huddlestone MS.	„ „ lii, p. 160	
The Regius MS. (Halliwell)	QCA „ i Facsimile & Transcript	
The Cooke MS.	„ „ ii „	
The Landsdowne MS.	„ „ ii „	
The Harleian No. 1942 MS.	„ „ ii „	
The Wm Watson MS.	„ „ iii „	
The Cama MS.	„ „ iii „	
The Sloane No. 3848 MS.	„ „ iii „	
The Sloane No. 3323 MS.	„ „ iii „	
The Harleian No. 2054 MS.	„ „ iii „	
The Buchanan MS.	„ „ iv „	

The Harris No. 2 MS.	,, ,, iv Facsimile & Transcript
The Grand Lodge No. 1 & No. 2 MSS.	,, ,, iv ,,
The Dodd Print	,, ,, iv Facsimile Print
The Phillips No. 1, No. 2 & 3 MSS.	,, ,, v Facsimile & Transcript
The Scarborough MS.	,, ,, v ,,
The Wood MS.	,, ,, vi Facsimile
The Lechmere MS.	,, ,, vi Facsimile & Transcript
The Inigo Jones MS.	,, ,, vi Facsimile
The Buchanan MS.	R. F. Gould, *History*, i, p. 96
The Grand Lodge No. 1 MS.	H. L. Stillson, Editor, *History of the Ancient and Honorable Fraternity of Free and Accepted Masons*, p. 187
,,	Henry Sadler, *Masonic Facts and Fictions*, 1887, p. 199.
The Edinburgh-Kilwinning MS.	D. Murray Lyon, *History of the Lodge of Edinburgh (Mary's Chapel)* No. 1. 1900, p. 116.
The Atcheson's Haven MS.	,, p. 123
The Melrose MS. No. 2	W. Fred. Vernon, *History of Freemasonry in Roxburgh*, etc. 1893, p. 58.
The Col. Clerke MS.	Edward Conder, Jr., *The Hole Crafte and Fellowship of Masons*, 1894, p. 210.
The Holywell MS.	Rev. Herbert Poole, *The Old Charges*, 1924.
The Regius MS.	Knoop, Jones & Hamer, *The Two Earliest Masonic MSS.*, 1938.
The Cooke MS.	,,
The Wm. Watson MS.	*Masonic Old Charges* (compilation) Wm. J. Hughan
The Thos. W. Tew MS.	,,
The Clapham MS.	Wm. Watson
The Hope MS.	Wm. J. Hughan
The Waitsell MS.	,,
The Probity MS.	,,
The Hughan MS.	Wm. Watson
The Stanley MS.	,,

The Thos. W. Embleton MS.	Wm. J. Hughan
The Macnab MS.	Wm. Watson
The Jas. S. Haddon MS.	Wm. J. Hughan
The Drinkwater MSS. (No. 1 & No. 2)	Rev. Herbert Poole
The Levander-York MS.	„
York Rolls No. 1, 2, 4, 5 & 6	*Ancient Masonic Rolls*, York Lodge No. 236.
The Scarborough Roll	„
Dowland's MS.	Wm. J. Hughan, *The Old Charges of British Freemasons*, 1872.
The Lansdowne MS.	„
The York MS. No. 1.	„
The Grand Lodge MS.	„
The Sloane No. 3848 MS.	„
The Harleian No. 1942 MS.	„
.The Hope MS.	„
The Antiquity MS.	„
The Alnwick MS.	„
Papworth's MS.	„
Krause's MS.	„

PART II

THE BUILDING OF THE TEMPLE

VI

PREPARATIONS FOR THE BUILDING

THE MONITORIAL account of the preparations made for the building of King Solomon's Temple is given in the following words:

We read in the Holy Writings that it was decreed in the wisdom and Counsel of Deity aforetime, that a house should be built, erected to God, and dedicated to his holy name. We also learn from the same sacred source that David, King of Israel, desired to build the house, but that, in consequence of his reign having been one of many wars and much bloodshed, that distinguished privilege was denied him.
—California *Masonic Manual,* p. 247.[1]

In the *Book of Chronicles,* we do read indeed that David on one occasion called to him his son Solomon, and said:

'My son, as for me, it was in my mind to build an house unto the name of the Lord my God:

'But the word of the Lord came to me, saying, Thou hast shed blood abundantly, and hast made great wars: thou shalt not build an house unto my name, because thou hast shed much blood upon the earth in my sight.'
—*I Chronicles* 22:7,8.

The *Book of Chronicles,* however, does cite the various preparations that David had made, in materials and treasure, for the projected Temple of God:

And David commanded to gather together the strangers that were in the land of Israel; and he set masons to hew wrought stones to build the house of God.

And David prepared iron in abundance for the nails for the doors of the gates, and for the joinings; and brass in abundance without weight;

[1] To assist the reader in a clearer comparison of our current Masonic Lectures with the commentaries thereon, the former will invariably be printed in italics.

Also cedar trees in abundance: for the Zidonians and they of Tyre brought much cedar wood to David,[1] . . .

And David said to Solomon, . . .

Now, behold, in my trouble I have prepared for the house of the Lord an hundred thousand talents of gold, and a thousand thousand talents of silver; and of brass and iron without weight; for it is in abundance: timber also and stone have I prepared; and thou mayest add thereto.

Moreover there are workmen with thee in abundance, hewers and workers of stone and timber, and all manner of cunning men for every manner of work.

Of the gold, the silver, and the brass, and the iron, there is no number. Arise therefore, and be doing, and the Lord be with thee.

—*I Chron.* 22:2-16.

This is perhaps what the writers of the *Old Charges* had in mind when, as we have seen in the preceding chapter, they almost invariably credited David rather than Solomon with having 'begun' the Temple.

The analogous account in the *Book of Kings* merely contents itself with stating (in Solomon's letter to King Hiram of Tyre) that his father David had been too busy fighting wars and establishing his kingdom to build a house unto the Lord.

As to these wars, David's most conspicuous and best known military achievement, of course, was the subjugation of the Philistines; but he had also conquered the tribes of Moab, Ammon, Edom, and Aram, waging his wars vigorously and often employing stern measures.[2] But as a sober reason for not having built the Temple, biblical commentators have expressed the opinion that the passage in *Chronicles* must be an interpolation of somewhat later date, and not based on an on-the-spot report. In fact, they say that had David really desired to build the Temple, he could have done so. Later scribes, consequently, felt they had to explain the failure to do so

---

[1] The Cedars of Lebanon, which no doubt are the trees referred to here, are said to grow at an elevation of 6000 feet, but only seven of these world-famous trees are now believed to remain from that era, according to information said to have been gathered by the author of *Freemasonry and the Tabernacle and Temples of the Jews*, and when the new church at Montmartre was built some eighty-five years ago, 'the Maronite bishop sent to Paris planks of a Lebanon cedar said to have been one of Hiram's own seedlings' (p. 68).

[2] Cf. *I Chron.* 19–20.

7a   The Stevens reconstruction of the Solomonic Temple, from specifications prepared by W. F. Albright and G. Ernest Wright. *See page 85.*
Courtesy of American Schools of Oriental Research.

7b   Solomon and the Temple. Amiens Cathedral, south-western door, *c.* A.D. 1230. *See page 51.*

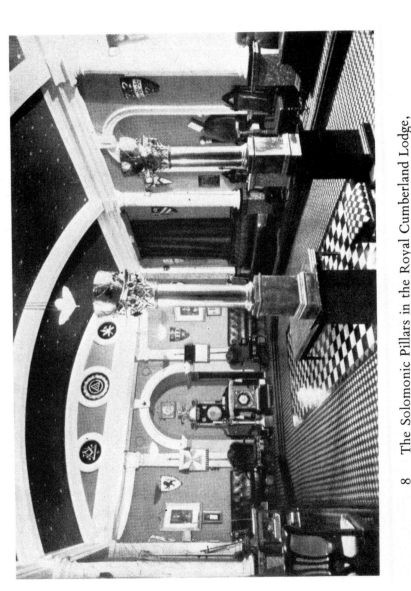

8   The Solomonic Pillars in the Royal Cumberland Lodge, No. 41, Bath, England. *See page 198.*

on the part of so pious a king; hence the attempted justification. On the other hand, Masonic tradition, unhampered by 'the higher criticism', has accepted the account of the Chronicler at face value.[1] And so we read in the *Graham MS.* (1726) the passage previously cited in the preceding chapter, wherein

> sollomon begun to Build the house of the Lord which his father david should have builded but was not admited to performe it because his hands was gultie of blood wars being on every side. . . .[2]

The much less elaborate account we find in the *Book of Kings* relative to the preparations for the Temple is in accord with the generally simpler and more realistic accounts usually found in these earlier Books of the Bible, as compared to the more embellished accounts in the later *Book of Chronicles*, generally credited to the Scribe Ezra, the date of writing being about 300 B.C. The two Books of *Kings*, on the other hand, were written closer to the actual period they cover—the estimates varying from two to as much as seven centuries earlier—and they are believed accordingly to be a more sober and more accurate portrayal of the historical events.[3]

As to the Books of *Chronicles*, *The Interpreter's Bible* points out that the Chronicler's principal purpose was to present a dramatic and impressive demonstration of God's will, rather than a simple historical account. What he had set out to depict was ideas and ideals, and for that end he did utilize records of the past but with 'complete freedom to suppress, modify, and inventively add to what he read'.[4]

Without this appreciation of the Chronicler's inward purpose, many of the details recounted by him would appear to be incredible, and this estimate of modern scholarship must be borne in mind throughout the present work, wherever we may have occasion to compare the parallel but not always identical accounts in *Kings* and in *Chronicles*.

---

[1] Cf. *Jew. Enc.*, xii, 99.
[2] *The Early Masonic Catechisms*, p. 88.
[3] Cf. Dr. Curtis, *International Critical Commentary*. New York, 1910, p. 14.
[4] *The Interpreter's* Bible, iii, pp. 341–343.

The Rev. W. Shaw Caldecott, however, has a higher estimate of the historical value of *Chronicles* as compared to the *Book of Kings*. His introductory section, 'The relative value, as history, of Kings & Chronicles', is worth reading— *Solomon's Temple, Its History and Its Structure*. Philadelphia, 1907.

But to continue with the Masonic account:

> *He [David] was not, however, left without hope, for God pro-*
> *mised him that out of his loins there should come a man who would*
> *be adequate to the performance of so great and glorious an under-*
> *taking.*
>
> —California Masonic Manual, p. 247.

As to God's promise, we read in the biblical record:

> And it came to pass that night, that the word of the Lord
> came unto Nathan, saying,
> Go and tell my servant David, Thus saith the Lord, . . .
> When thy days be fulfilled, and thou shalt sleep with thy
> fathers, I will set up thy seed after thee, which shall proceed out
> of thy bowels, and I will establish his kingdom.
>
> —II Samuel, 7: 4, 5, 12.

> . . . Thy son which shall come forth out of thy loins, he shall
> build the house for my name.
>
> —II Chron. 6:9.

> *That promise was verified in the person and character of Solomon,*
> *his son, who ascended the throne, and after David was gathered*
> *to his fathers, wielded the sceptre over Israel at a time when (as the*
> *great Jewish historian Josephus informs us) peace and tranquility*
> *pervaded the world, and all eyes seemed directed toward Jerusalem*
> *as if to witness the splendid display of the wisdom of Solomon.*
>
> —Masonic Manual, p. 247.

King Solomon, in fact, refers to this fulfilment of God's promise,
in the following words, when he later comes to dedicate the Temple:

> And the Lord hath performed his word that he spake, and
> [now] I am risen up in the room of David my father, and sit on
> the throne of Israel, as the Lord promised, and have built an
> house for the name of the Lord God of Israel.
>
> I Kings 8:20.

The *Dumfries No. 4* Catechism (*c.* 1710) accordingly here asks
the question:

> Q. what did yᵉ second man [do] when yᵉ first man died?
> A. he perfected ye work wᶜ [which] yᵉ first man Intended thus

king david y^t [that] intended to build ye temple but was prevented by death   but Solomon performed it.

The Early Masonic Catechisms, p. 57.

And a Jewish tradition has it that David once overheard the people grumble: 'How soon will the old man die, that his son may commence to build the Temple and we may visit the house of the Lord?'[1]

---

[1] *Jew. Enc.*, xii, 96.

VII

THE 'RECIPROCATIONS'

THE CORRESPONDENCE exchanged between King Solomon and King Hiram of Tyre, relative to the preparations for the building of the Temple, is expressed in the following terms:

About this time King Solomon received a congratulatory letter from Hiram, King of Tyre, desiring to participate, in a small degree at least, in the rich honours which then seemed to be clustering around his throne.

—Masonic Manual, p. 248.

And Hiram king of Tyre sent his servants unto Solomon; for he had heard that they had anointed him king in the room of his father: for Hiram was ever a lover of David.

—I Kings 5:1.

Huram said moreover, Blessed be the Lord God of Israel, that made heaven and earth, who hath given to David the king a wise son, endued with prudence and understanding, that might build an house for the Lord, and an house for his kingdom.

—II Chron. 2:12, 13, 16.

In his reciprocations with Hiram, of Tyre, King Solomon desired him to furnish a man well skilled in the arts and sciences, and his attention was directed to . . . etc.

—Masonic Manual, p. 248.

Send me now therefore a man cunning to work in gold, and in silver, and in brass, and in iron, and in purple, and crimson, and blue, and that can skill to grave with the cunning men that are with me in Judah and in Jerusalem . . .

—II Chron. 2:7.

And king Solomon sent and fetched Hiram out of Tyre.[1]

[1] Tyre—King Hiram's capital city—destroyed by the Moslems in the thirteenth century A.D., after it had been abandoned by the Crusaders. The site is now occupied by the insignificant little town of Sur; so called, no doubt, in memory of the ancient Assyrian name of Tyre, *Surru,* or the Phoenician *Sor.*

He was a widow's son of the tribe of Naphtali. . . .

—*I Kings* 7:13, 14.

Two versions of these 'reciprocations' between King Solomon and King Hiram of Tyre are given in the Bible, one in the First Book of *Kings*, and the other in the Second Book of *Chronicles*, both very similar in purport, but by no means identical, and with some actual interpolations and emendations inserted in the *Chronicles* version which do not appear in—or are even at variance with—the version in *Kings*. A comparison of the two versions is therefore of some interest, the principal differences being the following.

The letter from Solomon to Hiram, in *Chronicles*, is almost twice as long as the version in *Kings*, and the wording is nowhere identical at any point. In *Chronicles*, moreover, Solomon is made to request of Hiram: 'Send me now therefore a man,' etc., which is entirely absent in *Kings*. And to the promise from Solomon, couched in general terms, that 'unto thee will I give hire for thy servants according to all thou shalt appoint', as in *Kings*, the following more specific provision has been added by the Chronicler:

> And, behold, I will give to thy servants, the hewers that cut timber, twenty thousand measures of beaten wheat, and twenty thousand measures of barley, and twenty thousand baths of wine, and twenty thousand baths of oil.

In the reply sent by Hiram to King Solomon, the *Chronicles* version again is about two and a half times as long as in *Kings*. In *Chronicles*, Hiram King of Tyre thus describes the character of the man he was sending to King Solomon, in answer to his request:

> And now I have sent a cunning man, endued with understanding, of Huram my father's,
> The son of a woman of the daughters of Dan, and his father was a man of Tyre, skilful to work in gold, and in silver, in brass, in iron, in stone, and in timber, in purple, in blue, and in fine linen, and in crimson; also to grave any manner of graving, and to find out every device which shall be put to him, with thy cunning men, and with the cunning men of my lord David thy father.
> Now therefore the wheat, and the barley, the oil, and the wine, which my lord hath spoken of, let him send unto his servants:

And we will cut wood out of Lebanon, as much as thou shalt need: and we will bring it to thee in flotes by sea to Joppa; and thou shalt carry it up to Jerusalem.

None of these expanded details are to be found in *Kings*, and it is apparent that the Chronicler, writing some centuries later than the writer of the Book of *Kings*, while he may have had the *Kings* version before him, as stated by biblical scholars, did not find it incumbent upon him to follow it implicitly and in detail, but chose rather to embellish it with such oral traditions or written allusions as he may have additionally found at his disposal.

In this connection, it is interesting to note that our Masonic Lectures have made use of the more embellished account in *Chronicles* instead of confining themselves to the simpler version in *Kings*.

It is also curious to note in *Chronicles* the similarity between Solomon's request, as to the artificer that was to be sent to him out of Tyre, and King Hiram's response thereto:

> *King Solomon*: 'Send me now therefore a man cunning to work in gold, and in silver, and in brass, and in iron, and in purple, and crimson, and blue, and that can skill to grave with the cunning men that are with me in Judah and in Jerusalem. . . .'
>
> *King Hiram*: 'And now I have sent a cunning man, . . . skilful to work in gold, and in silver, in brass, in iron, in stone, and in timber, in purple, in blue, and in fine linen, and in crimson; also to grave any manner of graving' etc.

I have had occasion elsewhere to call attention to this curious similarity in wording, as if King Hiram 'just happened' to have available precisely the type of man that King Solomon wanted,[1] giving rise to the suspicion that perhaps these two accounts had been 'doctored up' to present this very similarity.

Commenting upon this suggestion, W. J. Atkinson has demonstrated a like and still more surprising similarity between the accomplishments attributed to our Hiram Abiff and those previously attributed in *Exodus* to two other builders, Bezaleel and Aholiab, known for their work on the construction of the Tabernacle in the Desert, and as can be seen from a consideration of *Exod.* 31:3–5, and 35:35.

[1] 'Further remarks on Hiram Abif', *AQC* vol. 77, p. 278.

Continuing the above account of the 'reciprocations', Josephus gives still another but essentially not very much different version, and adds that copies of the correspondence between the two kings were still extant in his own day, as noted in a preceding chapter. But there is generally not much credence among biblical commentators in his particular version of this correspondence, nor in the statement that he had himself seen the copies he refers to so confidently. As we have also noted in the same chapter, the six comparatively late versions of the *Old Charges* belonging to the Spencer Family give a version of the 'reciprocations' that has obviously been paraphrased from Josephus, rather than from the Bible. These versions of the Spencer Family are the *Fisher-Rosedale MS.* (*c.* 1725), the *Songhurst MS.* (*c.* 1725), the *Inigo Jones MS.* (*c.* 1726), the *Spencer* Print (1726), the *Cole* Print (1728), and the *Dodd* Print (1739), as listed by H. G. Rosedale, in his classification of the *Old Charges*, and where he treats of the Spencer Family under the alternative designation of the Dodd Family.[1] Rosedale presents a copy of the *Dodd* Print, and a comparison of Dodd's 'reciprocations' with the Josephus *Antiquities* (viii, 2:6, 7) can easily be made.

A further and somewhat different version of these 'reciprocations', again, is the one given by Eusebius, taken from a now-lost work by Eupolemus, a Hellenistic Jew who lived about 150 B.C. In this version, the letter from the King of Tyre to King Solomon is of particular Masonic interest, for it reads in part:

> . . . and I have sent to thee an architect, a man of Tyre from a Jewish mother from the tribe of David. He will tell thee whatsoever thou shalt enquire of all things under heaven, and whatsoever apperteineth to architecture for thee he will do.[2]

This constitutes the earliest reference so far found to our Hiram Abiff in the role of an architect, the biblical record itself being free of such reference. Eusebius (born about 270 A.D.) thus points to a very early architectural tradition with respect to Hiram Abiff, despite the biblical silence. 'Eusebius,' says the *Jewish Encyclopedia*, 'seems to have had a Jewish teacher, who instructed him in Hebrew,

---

[1] H. G. Rosedale, 'Some Fresh Material for classifying the "Old Charges" '. *AQC* xxxiii, 18, 22.
[2] *AQC* xliii, 166.

and through whom he became familiar with many haggadot and Jewish traditions.'[1]

A somewhat different translation of these Eusebius 'reciprocations' is offered in *Tales of King Solomon*, and is here given in full, because of its obvious Masonic interest:[2]

> Solomon to Hiram, King of Tyre, Sidon, and Phoenicia, his friend and his father's friend.
>
> Know that by grace of the great God I have taken possession of the kingdom of David my father, by whom also I was commanded to build a Temple to the Creator of heaven and earth. Now I beseech thee by this letter that thou wilt send me artisans and labourers from thy kingdom to serve me until I bring to an end this work dedicated to God, as I am commanded. I have sent to Galilee, to Samaria, to the Moabites, the Ammonites, and the Gileadites, bidding them provide each month all things that are necessary from their land, that is to say, each month ten thousand *cors* of corn and as many of wine; the oil and other things needful will come from Judea, and I have commanded Arabia to supply the animals for meat.
>
> Hiram to Solomon the great king, greeting!
>
> Blessed be God, the Creator of heaven and earth, who hath chosen so noble a man, the son of so noble a father. Thy letters have delighted my heart and I have rejoiced and given thanks to God that thou hast received the kingdom. I have sent thee eighty thousand Tyrians and Phoenicians, and amongst them is an architect, a man of Tyre whose mother is a Jewess of the tribe of David. He hath understanding in all manner of building, both in the theory and practice of the work. For the rest, it will be thy part to write to the governors of the districts, in order that they may be diligent to provide all that is necessary for so great a number of men.

Unfortunately for our Masonic Legend, however, and the specific architectural reference to H.A.B. in this version also, biblical commentators credit the authenticity of the Eusebian 'reciprocations' even less than they do those of Josephus. But the possible origin of the Masonic *tradition* relative to H.A.B.'s architectural accomplishments, as found in Eusebius, is of interest.

[1] *Jew. Enc.*, s.v. EUSEBIUS.
[2] St. John D. Seymour, *Tales of King Solomon*. London, 1924.

Josephus

A very brief discussion of Josephus (born 37 A.D.) and the place he occupies in our Masonic traditions may be of interest at this point. As previously indicated, we speak of him in a couple of places in our American Lectures as 'the great Jewish historian Josephus', (British working, generally, does not make any reference to him), and some citations from his works are used to embellish our Lectures. His influence on some of our *Old Charges* (without definite ascription) has already been demonstrated.

Our own opinion of his qualifications as an historian appears to follow the opinion generally held of him in early Christian times. The early Church Father Eusebius 'considers Josephus to have been the most learned man of his day; and Jerome calls him "the Greek Livy". The Byzantine chroniclers based their writings largely upon Josephus. . . . It cannot be denied that he possessed extraordinary literary talents. . . . '[1] From this it would appear that the more recent estimate that the writer in the *Cyclopedia of Biblical, Theological, and Ecclesiastical Literature* has made of him—stating that his history 'is, for the most part, only a loose and inaccurate paraphrase of the Old Testament narrative'—is too harsh. *The Jewish Encyclopedia*, on the contrary, supports a more tolerant view, stating that the errors of Josephus, whatever they were, merely reflected the errors of his time. His historical efforts, certainly, do not appear to have been strictly objective in purpose, being perhaps politically motivated, and specifically designed 'to counteract the current prejudice against the [Jewish] people and its institutions, and to exhibit both in a favourable light. To this end', it is said, 'he omitted things which might give ground for censure or ridicule, and embellished the narrative from legend and *midrash*' (scriptural exposition or exegesis).[2]

Thus the account that Josephus has given us of King Solomon's Temple (which is what we are here mostly concerned with), when compared with the simpler account in the Bible, may merely indicate the accretion of legendary material that had grown up in the intervening period, as Gerard Brett has shown.

Others, however, have not been so generous in their appraisal. Thus the architectural writer, James Fergusson, writing on *The*

[1] *Jew. Enc.*, s.v. JOSEPHUS.
[2] G. F. Moore, in *Encyclopedia Biblica*, art. 'Historical Literature'.

Temples of the Jews, thinks that 'Josephus so evidently exaggerates all the dimensions of Solomon's Temple—like the Book of Chronicles, by doubling them—and so frequently confounds what he knew of Herod's Temple with what he believed of Solomon's, that no reliance can be placed on his statements in this respect'.[1]

[1] Fergusson, *The Temples of the Jews*. London, 1878, p. 30.

VIII

The Temple and the Tabernacle

A CONSISTENT Masonic tradition exists to the effect that King Solomon's Temple was built upon plans earlier laid down in the Tabernacle of Moses in the desert. And every Masonic Lodge is said to be, allegorically, a representation of Solomon's Temple. 'This tabernacle [of Moses] was an exact model for King Solomon's Temple', and 'King Solomon's Temple, of which every Lodge is a representation' are familiar statements in our present-day Monitors, as they undoubtedly were in eighteenth-century England. A characteristic example of the latter is Finch's Catechism, *A Masonic Treatise*, wherein we read that

> Moses caused a *tent* or *tabernacle* to be erected in the wilderness . . . the model of that magnificent temple, built upon *Mount Moriah.* . . . [1]

This Tabernacle, Dr. Anderson had previously said in his 1723 *Book of Constitutions*, was 'a most beautiful Piece of Architecture (and prov'd afterwards the Model of *Solomon's* Temple) according to the Pattern that God had shewn to Moses in the Mount. . . . '[2]
'Thou hast commanded me,' similarly says the much earlier and apocryphal *Book of the Wisdom of Solomon* (ix, 8) 'to build a Temple in Thy Holy Mount, and an Altar in the city wherein Thou dwellest,

---

[1] *A Masonic Treatise*, with an Elucidation on the Religious and Moral Beauties of Freemasonry. Dedicated, by permission, to William Perfect, Provincial Grand Master for the County of Kent. By W. Finch, Canterbury, Second Edition, 1802. (The Catechism is mostly in cipher, but the passage given above is not.) The publication is said to represent a working used by Wm. Finch, and to some extent by others, around the turn of the century indicated. See the important paper by Col. F. M. Rickard, 'William Finch', in *AQC* lv.

[2] Anderson, *The Constitutions of the Free-Masons*, 1723. Facsimile Edition, 1923, p. 8.

a copy of the Holy Tabernacle which Thou didst before prepare from the beginning.'[1]

The location of the Temple

Mention has already been made of the *Dumfries No. 4 MS.* of *c.* 1710 and of its many references to details of King Solomon's Temple, so early in the development of our modern speculative science. The *Graham MS.* has also been mentioned, of approximately the same era, with its similar references to the Temple, though not nearly so great in number. This early Masonic interest in the details of the Temple we find to have been carried over into the Lectures of much of our eighteenth-century Freemasonry, especially towards the turn of the century into the nineteenth.

This is evidenced, for example, in the English set of Lectures known as *A Masonic Treatise*, which has just been referred to, and in it we find three entire 'Sections' comprising no less than 69 Questions and Answers given over to a very minute analysis and description of the Temple, its location, its architectural features, and its appurtenances.

In the United States, Webb also has given us a version of the tradition concerning the manner in which the 'mighty edifice' was erected, a tradition that is now found described partly in our present-day Lecture of the First Degree and partly in that of the Third. Curiously enough, however, the Webb version as originally presented is found, not in either of these Craft Lectures but in that on the Royal Arch—the 'Seventh Degree' in the Webb System. Here we begin by reading that

> *This famous fabric was situated on Mount Moriah, near the place where Abraham was about to offer up his son Isaac, and where David met and appeased the destroying Angel.*
>
> —Webb, *Freemason's Monitor*, 1797, p. 133.

Jeremy L. Cross, Grand Lecturer, and a pupil of Webb's, here finishes the sentence by saying, in his own Manual, ' . . . and where David met and appeased the destroying angel, who was visible over the *threshing floor of Ornan the Jebusite*'.[2]

---

[1] Cited by F. W. Farrar, Dean of Canterbury. *Solomon, his Life and Times.* New York (undated), p. 78.

[2] Cross, *The True Masonic Chart or Hieroglyphic Monitor.* New York, 1851. First published in 1819.

Samuel Lee, we find, had explained, in his *Orbis Miraculum* (1659), the reason for the locating of the Temple on Mount Moriah, this having been

> very famous for the intended offering of Isaac by his Father Abraham, and designed by God himself for this famous Temple, when the Angel appeared to King David (at the ceasing of that fearful Plague for numbring the People) by the Threshing floor of Araunah the Jebusite.

Similarly, John Bunyan had opened his *Solomon's Temple Spiritualiz'd* (1688) with the following words:

> The temple was built at Jerusalem, on Mount Moriah, in the thrashing floor of Aaron [Araunah, Ornan] the Jebusite; whereabout Abraham offered up Isaac; there where David met the angel of the Lord, when he came with his drawn sword in his hand, to cut off the people of Jerusalem, for the sin which David committed in his disorderly numbering the people.

But both of these writers may in turn have had their eye here on a *Targum* (the Aramaic version of the Old Testament), wherein we find:

> Solomon began to build the house of the sanctuary of the Lord at Jerusalem, in the place where Abraham . . . was about to offer his son Isaac for a burnt-offering; . . . and here the angel of the Lord appeared to David at which time David built an altar unto the Lord in the threshing-floor which he bought from Araunah the Jebusite.[1]

Following this old tradition, we find the Masonic *Dumfries No. 4 MS.* (*c.* 1710) declaring that

> david appointed ye foundation[2] of ye temple to be laid on a barn flore as you may read in ye holy bible Qr [where] it is called ye thrashing floor [of] araunah ye jebusit. . . .

but Webb and Cross follow the more detailed description of Lee and Bunyan and the *Targum*. They, in fact, may have been

---

[1] Cited in Clarke's *Commentary* to *II Chron.* 3:1.
[2] The laying of the Foundation to King Solomon's Temple (among other such ceremonies) has been discussed in brief by David Flather in his paper 'The Foundation Stone', *AQC* xlviii.

influenced by any one of the three, the wording being so closely similar.

Later eighteenth-century English working managed to retain this reference but in a somewhat oblique form, when it spoke of the 'holy ground' on which a Mason's Lodge is symbolically said to rest, by saying that this was in commemoration of the holy ground on which King Solomon's Temple was erected. And what particularly made this ground holy, says Finch's *Masonic Treatise*, as one example, was 'the Three Grand Offerings', two of which consisted of

> the ready compliance of Abraham to the Will of the Almighty in preparing his only son as a sacrifice to His command. . . . Secondly, for the many pious prayers of King David, when it pleased the Lord to stop the pestilence which then raged among his people, owing to his inadvertently having them numbered.

This explanatory material has in turn been carried forward into the present-day *Emulation* Lectures, in almost identical terms.[1]

All this alludes to two separate events in biblical history. The first of these is generally familiar:

> And it came to pass . . . that God did tempt Abraham, . . . and he said, Take now thy son, thine only son Isaac, whom thou lovest, and get thee into the land of Moriah. . . .
>
> —*Gen.* 22:2.

The 'land of Moriah' here is supposed to mean all the mountains of Jerusalem (Clarke's *Commentary*) and would therefore include Mount Moriah. It was there, on Mount Moriah, that Abraham is said to have offered up his son Isaac.

The second event referred to in the Webb account is not quite so well known, and the reason behind it is still less so. It has to do with an ancient superstition among the Jews, but prevalent among many primitive peoples, as Sir James Frazer has shown,[2] this superstition having to do with the practice of 'numbering' the people; that is, taking a census. And when David, disregarding this prevailing belief, did order such a census to be taken, 'God sent an angel unto Jerusalem to destroy it. . . . And the angel of the Lord

---

[1] *The Lectures of the Three Degrees in Craft Masonry*, 'Emulation' Working. Printed for A. Lewis. London, 1919, p. 29.

[2] Frazer, *Folk-lore in the Old Testament*. New York, 1927, pp. 307–313.

stood by the threshing-floor of Ornan the Jebusite',[1] thus identify-
ing the spot with the place elsewhere described as the locale of King
Solomon's Temple. But when David prayed that the anger of the
Lord be not brought down on the innocent people, but on himself
alone, since it was only he who had transgressed the law, 'the Lord
commanded the Angel; and he put up his sword again into the
sheath thereof'. Thus did 'David meet and appease the destroying
Angel'.

Then, as the Bible describes the event,

> Then Solomon began to build the house of the Lord at Jeru-
> salem in mount Moriah, where the Lord appeared unto David
> his father, in the place that David had prepared in the threshing-
> floor of Ornan the Jebusite.
>
> —*II Chron.* 3:1.

The Hastings *Dictionary of the Bible*[2] here points to the altar
of burnt-offering that stood before the Temple as a centre of
reference, and thinks that

> there is good reason for believing that the *sakhra* or rock under the
> dome of the [present-day] mosque of Omar is the spot where the
> altar in question stood. A very old tradition connects with this
> spot the incident in which Abraham prepared to offer Isaac, as
> also the threshing-floor of Araunah the Jebusite. It was on this
> threshing-floor that the destroying angel stood when Jehovah
> stopped him in his work of destroying the people. . . .

> German and French writers almost to a man, and the majority
> of English and American authorities, unite that the temple
> building proper stood west of the rock as advocated above. . . .[3]

The building commences

*It was begun in the fourth year of the reign of Solomon; the third
after the death of David; four hundred and eighty years after the
passage of the red sea, and on the second day of the month Zif,*

---

[1] *I Chron.* 21:15, 17, 27.

[2] Art. 'Temple'—one of the most detailed accounts of the Temple in the
current Dictionaries, Cyclopedias, and Commentaries on the Bible.

[3] An interesting photograph of the interior of this 'Dome of the Rock' is shown
in the *Jewish Encyclopedia* (vol. xii, p. 100), and showing what it calls there the
traditional site of the Holy of Holies in King Solomon's Temple.

being the second month of the sacred year . . . and . . . was finished, in all its parts, in little more than seven years.[1]
                                        —*Webb*, 1797, p. 133.

There are several biblical passages in support of the above statement in *The Freemason's Monitor*:

And it came to pass in the four hundred and eightieth year after the children of Israel were come out of the land of Egypt, in the fourth year of Solomon's reign over Israel, in the month Zif, which is the second month, that he began to build the house of the Lord. . . .
                                        —*I Kings* 6:1.

And he began to build in the second day of the second month. . . .
                                        —*II Chron.* 3:2.

And in the eleventh year . . . was the house finished throughout all the parts thereof. . . . So was he seven years in building it.
                                        —*I Kings* 6:1, 38.

It will be noted that Webb has combined the accounts in *Kings* and *Chronicles* to make a somewhat more complete and connected statement in his *Monitor*.

As to the precise time at which the Temple building was commenced, reckoned from the time of the Exodus, Professor J. McKee Adams thinks the base of reference used is entirely justified by the historical circumstances:

The greatest event in the life of Israel was the Exodus from the land of Egypt; practically all the prophets of the Old Testament revert to it in one form or another. It was not only securely fixed in the thought of the people, but, according to the clear statement in I Kings 6:1, its chronological setting was accurately defined and subsequently employed as a recognized point in Hebrew historical reference. The explicit statement that 480 years had intervened between the Exodus and the fourth year of Solomon's reign, when the Temple program was inaugurated, must therefore be accepted at its face value and with utmost confidence.[2]

---

[1] According to the Rev. W. Shaw Caldecott, the foundations were laid in 983 B.C. and the Temple completed in 977 B.C.—*Solomon's Temple*, etc., 1907.
[2] J. McKee Adams, *Ancient Records and the Bible*. Nashville, 1946, pp. 173–174.

The inauguration of the Temple therefore can be fixed, he thinks, at 966 B.C., in the month of May—assuming, of course, that we know the precise year in which Christ was born, about which, however, there appears to be much doubt in some quarters. Unfortunately, there is also some doubt as to the precise date of the Exodus, the figure 480 now being thought to be only a 'round number', based on the twelve generations known to have intervened between the Exodus and the building of the Temple, and multiplying twelve by forty, the average length of a generation. In accordance with the more widely-accepted chronology of Professor Albright, the Exodus may have occurred in the first half of the thirteenth century B.C., during the time of Ramses II (*c.* 1290–1224).[1] And the date of the commencement of the building, according to the writer in *The Interpreter's Dictionary of the Bible*, was 957 B.C.[2]

As to the month *Zif*, it was not till Solomon's time that the months of the year were designated by specific names; up to then, they were only designated numerically—for example, 'the second month'. The writer of *Kings* uses both types of designation. Josephus, many centuries later, calls it the month *Jur*,[3] and it is now known as *Iyyar*, the second month after *Nisan*. In earlier times, says Dr. Slotki, it was called *Ziv* (brightness), 'because it falls at the time of the year when the earth is "brightened" with blossoms and flowers'.[4]

> And Solomon's builders and Hiram's builders did hew them, and the stonesquarers: so they prepared timber and stones to build the house.
>
> —*I Kings* 5:18.

This statement is very similar to a paraphrased sentence now found in Webb's *Monitor*, probably composed by Webb himself, along with the description of the building of King Solomon's Temple, and the time and manner thereof, as cited in the preceding paragraphs. It is not to be found in Preston's *Illustrations of Masonry*, from which most of Webb's monitorial working was originally taken.

[1] *The Interpreter's Dictionary of the Bible*, vol. E–J, s.v. 'Exodus, Book of', p. 191.
[2] *Interpreter's Dictionary*, vol. R–Z, 'Temple, Jerusalem'.
[3] Josephus, *Antiquities*, viii, 3:1.
[4] Slotki, *Commentary on Kings*.

10

Then Huram the king of Tyre answered in writing, which he sent to Solomon, . . . [saying:]

And we will cut wood out of Lebanon, as much as thou shalt need: and we will bring it to thee in flotes by sea to Joppa; and thou shalt carry it up to Jerusalem.

—*II Chron.* 2:11, 16.

Finch's *Masonic Treatise* (1802) preserves this biblical tradition in the following form:

. . . the stones were hewn in the Quarry, there carved, marked, and numbered, the Timber was fell[ed] and prepared in the Forest of Lebanon, there carved, marked, and numbered also; from thence floated down to Joppa; from thence conveyed to Jerusalem, and there put together in this wonderful manner. . . .

The *Official Iowa Monitor* (1953 reprint), likewise, has preserved this in almost identical terms, reminiscent of other workings in the United States:

The stones were all hewed, squared and numbered in the quarries whence they were raised; the timbers felled and prepared in the forests of Lebanon, conveyed by sea in floats to Joppa, from thence by land to Jerusalem, where they were set up by wooden mauls prepared for the purpose. . . .

As to this, Clarke offers the following supporting commentary:

As the river *Adonis* was in the vicinity of the forest of Lebanon, and emptied itself into the Mediterranean Sea, near *Biblos*, Hiram could transport the timbers all squared, and not only cut to scantling, but cut so as to occupy the place intended for it in the building, without any further need of axe or saw. It might readily be sent down the coast on rafts and landed at *Joppa*, or Jamnia, just opposite to Jerusalem, at the distance of about twenty-five miles. . . . The materials had only to be put together when they arrived at Jerusalem.[1]

'The trees,' the Rev. F. W. Farrar tells us more specifically, in his very readable account of King Solomon's Temple, 'were sent down the heights of Lebanon by the process technically known as *schlittage*'—a procedure, he assures us, that is 'still much used in the

[1] Adam Clarke, *The Holy Bible*, with Commentary, ii, 401.

Vosges to carry trees down hill . . . and thence by road or river to the sea-shore. Huge rafts of the costly timber were thence floated by sea to Joppa, a hundred miles, and then with infinite toil were dragged about thirty-five miles up the steep and rocky roads to Jerusalem'.[1]

Joppa—the present-day Jaffa—is a sea-port some eighty miles down the Mediterranean coast from Tyre, and was the port of Jerusalem until superseded by the new city of Tel-Aviv. In addition to being a natural point of entry for building materials destined for Jerusalem, it would also be a natural point of departure for any miscreant (let us say) desiring to make his escape by sea out of the country. However, whether such a trip, by sea, into the interior of Africa—for example, Ethiopia, by way of the Nile—would have been practical from a seafaring man's standpoint is a question we need not enter into here. It is conceivable that in the eighteenth century, when such a trip could have been contemplated as a physical possibility, our knowledge of the relevant geographical details may not have been very profound.

(A current Sunday paper travel note tells us that 'it was from Jaffa that Jonah went out to be swallowed by the whale. Just beyond the little harbour is the rock where Andromeda was chained until rescued by Perseus and his winged horse.

'The Phoenician king, Hiram of Tyre, shipped cargoes of cedar logs to this port for the building of King Solomon's temple. The Romans sailed wheat ships to Jaffa 1000 years after that. St. Peter lodged here in Simon the Tanner's house and Napoleon captured the town in 1799.')

Our 'Temple' legends

One peculiar legend connected with the construction of King Solomon's Temple has already been mentioned, in connection with our study of the *Graham MS*.[2] Though more properly appropriated to the Mark Master Mason Degree, the legend is, however, referred to, after a fashion, in the Iowa *Companion to the Monitor*, which is, in effect, an unofficial extension of, and elaboration upon, the *Official Iowa Monitor*. Here we are told that

> The journey to the Middle Chamber is based upon a legend connected with the building of King Solomon's Temple. . . .

[1] F. W. Farrar, *Solomon, His Life and Times*, pp. 75–76.
[2] *Ante*, p. 116.

There were eighty thousand Fellow Crafts, who labored in the mountains and the quarries. When they had labored faithfully for six days, they were invested with certain mysterious signs, tokens, and words, by means of which they were able to pass the guards and gather in the Middle Chamber, where they received their wages. We now represent those Fellow Crafts of old and are following in their footsteps.[1]

The reader will recollect the earlier legends recounted in preceding chapters, having the same purport as the above, and particularly the one preserved by Dr. Oliver.[2]

Another legend, associated with the British version of the Mark Master Mason Degree, recounts the tradition that

two thousand Mark Men were employed in the building of King Solomon's Temple, under the direction or supervision of Stolkyn, each receiving a daily wage of nine shekels; and six hundred Mark Masters, under the direction of Ghiblim, each of whom received twenty-five shekels daily.[3]

Stolkyn, it might be stated, is the name found in one of the Scottish Rite Degrees as one of the Fellowcrafts ordered to go in search of the deserters from the Temple, after some well-known 'confusion in the Temple' had occurred.

Yet another legend connected with the Temple is to be found in an old Mark Master ritual still being regularly worked in some old Lodges in the West of England, despite its not being in accordance with the authorized ritual. In this version, the story is told of

the traditional division of the workmen at the building of King Solomon's Temple into eleven hundred Lodges, one hundred in each, composed of F.C. and E.A., the latter being under the superintendence of the former, who taught them their Craft. Over the whole presided 3,300 Menatschim, Overseers or Mark Master Masons, three to each Lodge, now represented by the Master and his two Wardens.

Further, each F.C. had a peculiar Mark known to his Overseers. With this he marked his work and without its production he could not receive wages, etc. etc.

[1] John T. Ames, P.G.M., *Companion to the Monitor.* Iowa Grand Lodge, 1951.
[2] *Ante*, p. 40.
[3] Bernard H. Springett, *The Mark Degree.* London, 1946, p. 15.

This Degree, like the three Craft Degrees, is stated to have been operative during the building of the Temple, and to have contributed in no small measure to the order and harmony which at that time prevailed among the workmen.

Indeed, without it so many different workmen of various nations and tribes must have been liable to continual confusion, whilst, with the arrangement and regularity it conferred, not only was each craftsman practically brought under the notice of the M.M.M., but every portion of the material for that stupendous structure was submitted to the nicest scrutiny and every faithful labourer received with punctuality the reward of his industry and skill.[1]

In like vein, we find William Preston making similar reference to the 'Harodim' or Overseers of King Solomon's Temple. He had, in 1787, created the 'Grand Chapter of Harodim', in London, as an unofficial 'Lodge of Instruction' attached to his Lodge of Antiquity No. 1, for the purpose of studying and carrying out the Lectures he had established for the Three Degrees. To give this Chapter of Harodim a traditional background, he made claim, in the Introduction to his *Pocket Manual* (1790), that it was in effect 'coeval with the building of Solomon's Temple and that it was established by the 3,300 eminent Masons who collaborated in its erection'.

These, and a number of other legends which could be cited as forming part of the explanatory content of our numerous Masonic Rites and Degrees, are merely brought forward to illustrate the manner in which King Solomon's Temple has been drawn upon in every possible way to provide the raw material out of which many valuable moral lessons have been elaborated, of which the 'fidelity' theme in the Third Degree is an outstanding—but by no means solitary—example. Needless to say, these legends themselves, valuable as they undoubtedly are from an ethical and spiritual standpoint, have little scriptural basis, if any, and practically no anterior Masonic history, for the most part, except in so far as they cover the same ground as the Craft Legends. The 'tumult' episode in the *Graham MS.*, previously noted, is an important exception.

Some of these Masonic legends are known to have had an ephemeral existence in our Lectures and then to have gone out of practice. A characteristic example is the legend that has to do with

[1] Springett, *The Mark Degree*, pp. 43–44.

the 'Foundation Stone'. Thus, Oliver makes mention of some 'continental fancies and innovations', as he calls them, justifiably, which he believes to have been extracted from the Jewish Talmud, and which came to be incorporated into our symbolical system and ritual. One of these traditions, he says,

> continued for a great length of time (to be) a cherished figment amongst us. It refers to the history of the Foundation Stone of Solomon's Temple, which was traced in the legend from Enoch through Noah, Abraham, and Solomon. . . . They described it (the Foundation Stone) as a double cube, every side, except the base on which it stood, being inscribed. The first face of the cube was said to have been engraved by Noah with an instrument of porphyry when the Ark was building; the second, by Abraham, with *the horn of the ram*—credat Judaeus!—which was substituted for his son on Mount Moriah! the third, with a porphyry tool by Moses; the fourth, by Joshua; and the fifth by Hiram Abiff, before it was deposited in its final bed at the north-east angle of the Temple.

Oliver very properly designates this so-called 'legend' as 'apocryphal'.[1]

As to the Word itself that is said in one of the Scottish Rite Degrees—'The Royal Arch of Solomon'—to have been inscribed on the Foundation Stone, the late H. C. Booth quotes from an old Northumbrian ritual:

> What are we to understand by the famous inscription of K.S. on the foundation stone of the Temple of J——?
> A Name that cannot be clearly comprehended, nor fully pronounced by the voice or tongue of man.[2]

The Rev. Geo. Oliver, D.D.

As in the case of Josephus, a few words may not be inappropriate at

[1] Rev. Geo. Oliver, D.D., *The Revelations of a Square*. Universal Masonic Library, New York, 1855. Vol. vii, pp. 70–71.

[2] Discussion on 'The Masonic Catechism', by Dr. Herbert Poole, *AQC* lx, 42. Dr. Oliver is said to have made reference to this matter in his lecture to the Witham Lodge, Lincoln, 1863. See *The Lectures of the Three Degrees in Craft Masonry*, printed for A. Lewis, London, 1886, pages xxl and xxll. My own copy of these Lectures is from a different edition, and I am consequently unable to comment.

this point with respect to that very prolific writer, who, with Dr. Anderson, is one of the most controversial among our accepted Masonic *literati*. Oliver had, and no doubt still has, his champions as well as his detractors, and among the former we may notice a serious student and one-time W.M. of Quatuor Coronati in 1900, T. B. Whytehead. 'Dr. Oliver, they tell us', he writes in the *Freemason* for 1884, 'was a wild enthusiast, a dreamer, and his works may be thrown on one side in these enlightened days as so much chaff in which the stray grains of wheat are so scarce as not to be worth looking for. I am afraid', he concludes, reflecting his own opinion, 'that those who make these assertions have either not read Oliver, or read him to very little purpose.'[1]

With this estimate I would be somewhat inclined to agree, but only with the proviso that we make a sharp distinction between two apparently watertight compartments in Dr. Oliver's mind—his philosophical and his historical compartment. In the former—with his wide and deep erudition concerning the ancient philosophies and universal symbolism and anthropology—he was a past-master; in the latter, he was a comparative tyro. It is a sad commentary on the progress of some men's minds that Dr. Oliver apparently knew more of what had transpired two thousand years before, in human culture and development, than he knew about his own immediately preceding century. But perhaps that is because more had been written about the former than about the latter, comparatively speaking, relative to matters of interest to Masonic thinking. A very similar anomaly is demonstrated in the case of C. W. Heckethorn's *The Secret Societies of all Ages and Countries* (in two volumes, London, 1875), a much respected work and often quoted in Masonic literature. Heckethorn's knowledge of the ancient secret societies was profound and extensive, but his ignorance of our modern 'secret society'—he himself almost obviously was not a Freemason— was deplorable.

To continue, now, with our Temple Legends, after this short but necessary digression; 'the construction of this grand edifice', Webb tells us, 'was attended with two remarkable circumstances. From Josephus we learn, that although seven years were occupied in building it, yet during the whole term it rained not in the day time,

[1] *Freemason*, Feb. 23, 1884. Cited in W. J. Hughan's *Origin of the English Rite of Freemasonry*. New and Rev. Edition, Leicester, 1909, p. 82.

that the workmen might not be obstructed in their labour. . . . '[1]

Here we come up against an embarrassing anachronism. For the passage referred to by Webb, and ascribed to Josephus, is not to be found in Josephus, *in connection with the building of King Solomon's Temple*. But in the account of the rebuilding of the *Third Temple*, under Herod, almost a thousand years later, we do find Josephus saying: 'It is also reported, that, during the time that the temple was building, it did not rain in the day time, but that the showers fell in the nights, so that the work was not hindered.'[2]

This erroneous passage of Webb's—erroneous, that is, in its faulty historical reference—is not to be found in the First Edition of 1797, and therefore is not in Preston's *Illustrations of Masonry*, from which Webb's First Edition was mostly taken. It is also not in Webb's Second Edition of 1802, and only appears for the first time in the Third Edition of 1805. It has not so far been found in any preceding Masonic work, and may therefore be a composition of Webb's own, based perhaps on faulty recollection of the works of Josephus, or on a story heard at second hand, in the absence of any opportunity for making a direct reference to the original.

This serious historical error has not been found in the English, Scottish or Irish workings, nor is it in any of the eighteenth-century English workings that have come to my notice. It would appear to be a pure Americanism, following upon Webb, but is not in universal use even in this country, some Jurisdictions having wisely eliminated it, perhaps because of the incorrect allusion.

It is interesting to note, however (though not in extenuation of the error mentioned), a somewhat similar tale of a miraculous occurrence associated with the workmen of King Solomon's Temple that has been left us by the Rabbis, who tell us that 'while they (the workmen) were engaged in its construction, none of them fell ill, or died, or met with any accident, or suffered from any disease of the eyes; their shoes or belts did not get lost. Neither spade nor shovel was broken, nor was any artificer's tool mislaid'.[3] It is just barely possible that, whoever brought the 'rained not in the daytime' episode into the story of King Solomon's Temple, may have dimly remembered the Rabbinic legend cited above, together with the

[1] Webb, *Freemason's Monitor*, 1805, p. 75.
[2] Josephus, *Antiquities*, Book XV, ch. xi, 7. I am indebted to Mr. Chas. Minetti, of Santa Rosa, California, for the discovery of this hitherto elusive passage.
[3] St. John D. Seymour, *Tales of King Solomon*. London, 1924, p. 134.

Josephus legend connected with the building of a Temple of Jerusalem, and may have unconsciously blended the two.

The second 'remarkable circumstance' alluded to by Webb in the Lecture quoted above will be treated in the chapter that is to follow, being 'remarkable' enough to warrant separate treatment.

Dedication of the Temple

This chapter on the building of King Solomon's Temple may fittingly close with a brief reference to its Dedication after its completion. This Dedication has not found reflection in any of our Craft Degrees, it is true, but it is an important celebration in the Royal Arch Chapter, in the United States at least, where one of the significant events that transpired on that occasion is recollected in one of its Degrees. The circumstances surrounding the Dedication are described in detail by the Rev. Caldecott in his *Solomon's Temple* (Philadelphia, 1907), soberly taken from the biblical record, but made specially readable. Similarly, the 'second Dedication'—at the end of the twenty-year building period which included the construction of the King's Palace and the other buildings in the area—is given special attention and is volubly described. It has been memorialized in the important annual celebration of the *Feast of Tishri* by the Ancient and Accepted Scottish Rite.[1] Similarly, the destruction of the Temple, and its rebuilding by Zerubbabel, are given due recognition in several Degrees of that Rite, and some elements associated with the Destruction also find significant recollection in the Holy Royal Arch.

[1] See my article, 'The "Feast of Tishri" in King Solomon's Time', in *The New Age*, Washington, D.C., Sept. 1967, pp. 21–23.

IX

'NO TOOL OF IRON'

THE SECOND of the 'two remarkable circumstances' referred to by Webb, and mentioned in the preceding chapter, has to do with a peculiar feature connected with the building of King Solomon's Temple, and, as has been intimated, deserves particular attention.

We read in the Holy Bible:

> And the house, when it was in building, was built of stone made ready before it was brought thither; so that there was neither hammer nor axe nor any tool of iron heard in the house, while it was in building.[1]
>
> —*I Kings* 6:7.

This feature is retained Masonically in our present-day monitorial working, which tells us that

> *From sacred history we also learn that there was not heard the sound of axe, hammer, or any tool of iron in the house while it was building. . . .*
>
> —Anderson, *Masonic Manual*, p. 249.

and which goes back to a Catechism at least as early as that represented by the *Graham MS.* (1726), where we read, as in the *Book of Kings*, that

> the House when it was in Building was build of ston made ready beffore it was brought theither so that there was nether hammer nor ax nor any tool off Iron heard in the house when it was in Building.

The peculiar spelling (peculiar even for that period) may perhaps suggest that this latter was something received 'from mouth to

---

[1] 'No hammers fell, no ponderous axes rung;
 Like some tall palm the mystic fabric sprung.
 Majestic silence!'—Reginald Heber (1783–1826), *Palestine*.

ear', and not merely something copied out of a written or printed text.

Late eighteenth-century English Lectures have invariably speculated on this absence of the use of iron tools in the building of King Solomon's Temple, and the reasons therefor. Thus, the Wooler Lectures, believed to be of North of England provenance, ask:

Q. Why were Metal Tools prohibited?
A. The better to show the ingenuity of the Craft in those days, for tho' the materials were prepared at so great a distance, when they were put together each part fitted with so exact a nicety that it seemed the work of the G.A. of the U. than that of mortal man.

Another set—the Lancashire Lectures, associated with the Lodge of Lights—gives, in addition to this explanation—a subsidiary reason why the noise of metal tool was not permitted in the building of the Temple:
—that nothing should be heard among the masons of Zion but harmony and peace.

Webb tried to retain this latter explanation in his monitorial Royal Arch Lecture, where he says:

The noise of the ax, the hammer, and every other tool of metal, was confined to the forests of Lebanon ... and the plains and quarries of Zeredathah, where the stones were raised, squared, marked and numbered; that nothing might be heard among the masons at Jerusalem, but harmony and peace.
—Webb, *Freemason's Monitor*, 1805, p. 164.

Webb's star pupil, Jeremy L. Cross (who later became Grand Lecturer for a number of Jurisdictions), changed the explanation of Webb, in his own Monitor, to conform to the explanation given in the Wooler Lectures, though perhaps not taken therefrom:

And when the building was finished, its several parts fitted with that exact nicety, that it had more the appearance of being the handy work of the Supreme Architect of the universe, than of human hands.
—Cross, *Masonic Chart*, 1820, p. 117.

Cornelius Moore has more recently made use of this explanation in his own monitorial working published under the title of *The Craftsman and Freemason's Guide* (Cincinnati, Third Edition, 1850), where he says, with some elaboration:

> *By the masonic art, and the wise regulations of Solomon, this famous fabric was erected without the sound of the axe, hammer, or any tool of iron; for the stones were all hewed, squared, and numbered in the quarries of Zeredathah, where they were raised; the timbers were felled and prepared in the forest of Lebanon, conveyed by sea in floats to Joppa, and from thence by land to Jerusalem; where the fabric was erected by the assistance of wooden instruments prepared for that purpose. And when the building was finished, its several parts fitted with such exact nicety, that it had more the appearance of being the handy work of the Supreme Architect of the Universe, than of human hands.*

This is found transcribed (with only one or two very minor changes) from the somewhat earlier work of Jeremy L. Cross just mentioned, the *True Masonic Chart or Hieroglyphic Monitor*, first published in 1819, and patterned on Webb's Royal Arch Lecture of a still earlier date.

Dr. Oliver cites an Arabic tradition to the same effect, giving Southey as his authority, 'in a passage quoted from the commentators on the Koran, which originated in the fact that the temple was built of stone and timber prepared in the quarries of Tyre and the forest of Lebanon, conveyed via Joppa to Jerusalem, and there put together by such a process, that nothing was heard among the workmen but harmony and peace, and that the stones had been prepared with such perfect accuracy, that when fitted together the joint could not be discovered.'[1] The wording, however, adheres so closely to that used in the Cross and Moore Monitors as to throw some shadow of suspicion on the accuracy of the Islamic quotation. The circumstance would bear further investigation.

A similar remark might be made in connection with a tale of the Queen of Sheba told by Charles A. Conover, in his paper on 'King Solomon's Temple', wherein

> Tradition informs us that when she first beheld this magnificent edifice, which glittered with gold, and seemed from the nice adjustment and exact accuracy of all its joints, to be composed

[1] Oliver, *Historical Landmarks*, ii, 178.

of a single piece of marble, she raised her eyes and hands in an attitude of admiration and exclaimed, 'Rabboni', signifying 'A Most Excellent Master had done this.'[1]

But this 'Masonic myth in the Most Excellent Master's Degree', as Mackey calls it, 'lacks the element of plausibility, inasmuch as the word (Rabboni) was not in use in the time of Solomon.'[2] The same anachronism, however, might be cited in connection with many if not most of our myths, since it is not in the character of a myth to be historically plausible.

As for our Craft Lectures themselves, and for the benefit of those interested in tracing the peregrinations of a tradition through its several variants in different times and places, I give below the complete Webb version, as found in the Royal Arch Lecture of 1797:

> *By the masonic art, and the wise regulations of Solomon, every part of the building, whether of stone, brick, timber or metal, was wrought and prepared before they were brought to Jerusalem; so that the only tools made use of in erecting the fabric, were wooden instruments prepared for that purpose. The noise of the ax, the hammer, and every other tool of metal, was confined to the forests of Lebanon, where the timber was procured, and to Mount Libanus, and the plains and quarries of Zeredathah, where the stones were raised, squared, marked and numbered; that nothing might be heard among the masons at Jerusalem, but harmony and peace.*

This was undoubtedly taken from English Craft Lectures of the late eighteenth century, as we find the tradition recounted in a Catechism of almost the same date as the above, in the set of Lancashire 'Lodge of Lights' Lectures, previously mentioned, and running as follows:

Q. Why were you . . . ?
A. First . . ., secondly, . . . thirdly, at the building of K.S.T. there was not heard the sound of any ax, hammer, or metal tool, throughout that whole building, . . . for the stones were hewn in the Quarry, there carved marked & numbered; the timber was felled and prepared in the Forest of Lebanon, there carved, marked and numbered also; from thence floated down to Joppa,

[1] *British Masonic Miscellany*, Dundee, vol. viii.
[2] Mackey, *Encyclopedia of Freemasonry*, s.v. RABBONI.

from thence conveyed to Jerusalem, and there put together in this wonderful manner with wooden mauls made for that purpose, . . . that nothing should be heard among the masons of Zion but harmony and peace; . . . yet when put together at Jerusalem, each part fitted with that perfect exactness as to make it resemble more the work of the Grand Architect of the Universe, than that of human skill.

The primary origin of the above is not far to seek. In Entick's 1756 edition of the *Book of Constitutions* originally prepared in its first two editions by Dr. Anderson, we find the following, relative to the building of the Temple:

> This magnificent work was begun on Monday the second day of the month Zif, which answers to the 21st of our April, being the second month of the sacred year; and was carried on with such speed, that it was finished in all its parts in little more than seven years, which happened on the eighth day of the month Bul, which answers to the 23rd of our October, being the seventh month of the sacred year, and the eleventh of King Solomon. What is still more astonishing is, that every piece of it, whether timber, stone, or metal, was brought ready cut, framed, and polished, to Jerusalem; so that no other tools were wanted or heard than what were necessary to join the several parts together. All the noise of axe, hammer, and saw was confined to Lebanon, the quarries and the plains of Zeredathah, that nothing might be heard among the masons of Sion save harmony and peace.

Dr. Oliver credits this last paragraph to Dr. Anderson himself; no doubt from memory, but certainly in error. For neither the 1723 nor the 1738 Anderson editions of the *Constitutions* carry anything like this elaborate description, and Anderson died the year following. For the record, and as a further illustration of the manner in which legends and traditions grow and expand and surround themselves with additional detail, I give below excerpts from the two Anderson editions:

> . . . the Eternal God's Temple at Jerusalem, begun and finish'd to the Amazement of all the World, in the short space of seven Years and six Months, by that wisest Man and most glorious King of Israel, the Prince of Peace and Architecture, SOLOMON

(the Son of David, who was refused that Honour for being a Man of Blood) by divine Direction, without the Noise of Workmens Tools, . . .

—1723 *Constitutions*, pp. 9–10.

. . . the Eternal's Temple at Jerusalem, built by that wisest mere Man and most glorious King of Israel, SOLOMON, (the Son of David, who was denied that Honour for being a Man of Blood) the Prince of Peace and Architecture, the GRAND MASTER MASON of his Day, who performed all by divine Direction, and without the Noise of Tools; all the Stones, Timbers, and Foundings being brought ready cut, fram'd and polish'd to Jerusalem.

It was founded in the 4th Year of SOLOMON, on the second Day of the second Month of the Year after the Exodus—480. . . .

—1738 *Constitutions*, p. 11.

The paragraph in question, wrongly credited by Oliver to Dr. Anderson, appears for the first time in the Entick edition of 1756, and there the trail ends. Where Entick may have got the composition of this story—beyond what is obviously out of *Kings* or *Chronicles*—is not definitely known. He may have composed it on his own authority, with the materials furnished him out of the two previous editions of Anderson, with perhaps some assistance from Josephus.

One thing is certain, that around the time of the transition from operative to speculative, there was already in existence a Masonic tradition that had to do with certain phases of King Solomon's Temple. And that some elements of this tradition were already at that time of an esoteric character is indicated by the statement Dr. Anderson makes, at the conclusion of his lengthy description of the building of the Temple—

But leaving what must not, and indeed cannot, be communicated by Writing, . . .

—1723 *Constitutions*, p. 13.

Why metal Tools were prohibited

In the late eighteenth century, practically all of the Lectures agree in another and still more curious formula respecting this prohibition of the use of metal tools. As stated in the Browne Lectures:

Q. Why were metal tools prohibited?
A. That the Temple might not be polluted.[1]

This prohibition of the use of metal tools, to prevent the Temple from being 'polluted', stems from the law laid down in *Exodus* 20:22, 25, where it is stated:

And the Lord said unto Moses, Thus thou shalt say unto the children of Israel, . . .
If thou wilt make me an altar of stone, thou shalt not build it of hewn stone: for if thou lift up thy tool upon it, thou hast polluted it.

The prohibition in *Exodus* does not, it is true, specifically refer to tools of *iron*, but Chief Rabbi J. H. Hertz, in his Commentary on the passage, states that the word commonly rendered 'tool' in the translations is literally 'sword' or 'iron instrument', and must be understood in that sense.[2] However, in the parallel injunction cited later in *Deuteronomy* 27:5–6, *iron* tools are specifically mentioned, and, in accordance with this prohibition, when Joshua had conquered Bethel and Ai, in his entry into the Promised Land, his first act of thanksgiving was to build an altar on Mt. Ebal—an altar, according to the description in the Revised Standard Version, 'of unhewn stones, upon which no man has lifted an iron tool . . .' (*Joshua* 8:30, 31). And, many centuries later, when Solomon's destroyed Temple came to be rebuilt after the Captivity, under Zerubbabel, an altar of unhewn stone was similarly made to replace the brazen altar previously used in King Solomon's time. Likewise, in the Third or Herod's Temple, an altar of burnt offering stood in front of the Porch, constructed of unhewn stones.[3]

For the greatest defilement was always considered to be that which was caused by the use of the iron tool; and in the work of

[1] *Browne's Masonic Master-Key* through the Three Degrees, by way of Polyglot. J. Browne, P.M. London, Second Edition, 1802. From Dr. Carl C. F. Krause's *Die drei ältesten Kunsturkunden der Freimaurerbrüderschaft* (The three oldest professional Documents of the Brotherhood of Freemasons) in the Iowa. Masonic Library, 1810. The Krause transliteration of the Browne work, which is mainly in cypher, is in both English and German. Dr. Krause's voluminous and scholarly annotations, throughout, are particularly worth-while.

Browne's publication is thought to have been popular at the time. See the paper by E. H. Cartwright, 'A Note on Browne's Master-Key', in *AQC* xlv.

[2] Hertz, *The Pentateuch and Haftorahs*, with Commentary; London, 1935.
[3] *Jewish Encyclopedia*, xii, 86, 97.

destruction it was an affront causing the deepest humiliation. 'A man,' sings the Psalmist, 'was famous according as he had lifted up axes upon the thick trees. But now,' he cries in anguish, 'they break down the carved work thereof at once with axes and hammers.'[1]

Accordingly, the Masonic tradition of a 'polluted temple', has deep biblical support. But the tradition, illustrated in the Browne Lectures, and others of the same era, has not been retained in American working, nor in present-day *Emulation* working in England, where the Bristol system appears to be the sole preserver of this older tradition, following the similar explanation in the English working, *The whole of the Lectures in Craft Masonry*, by G. Claret, 1845. It has also been faithfully preserved in the current Scottish Lecture, which elaborates upon the Browne catechism in a manner identical with Claret, and quotes the entire passage in *Exodus* upon which it is based, ending up with the explanation:

> King Solomon, conceiving this [Mosaic prohibition] to be a divine institution, peremptorily forbade the use of metal tools in that house which he was about to erect, and meant to dedicate solely to the service of the living God.

In the same manner did the Venerable Bede (seventh century) moralize the prohibition in *Exodus* by comparing it with the teaching in *Revelation*, to the effect that nothing common or unclean should enter the Holy City (Brett).

The 'Iron Taboo'

In pursuit of the origin for this prohibition expressed in *Exodus*, we do find, in fact, that there is evidence of the existence of an 'iron taboo' among the early Israelites which is of considerable anthropological interest. Among the Jews, this had led not only to the prohibition noted, but also—perhaps as a result—to the disparagement of all those who worked in iron, so that, in point of fact, the 'maker of idols' (believed to be the lowest gradation in the scale of human activity) came to be called, contemptuously, a *harash barzel*—a 'worker in iron' (*Isa.* xliv, 12). 'For the artificer sharpens the iron; he fashions *the idol* with an axe . . .' says the Septuagint version of this passage, the meaning of which is lost in the other translations.

It is, of course, possible—to go still further back—that the origin

[1] *Psalms*, 74:5, 6.

of this 'iron taboo', among the Jews at least, may in turn have had some connection with the hated Philistines, whom we remember so vividly from our Sunday-school days and the stories of Samson, and of David and Goliath, and who were the epitome, to the Jews of that day, of everything detestable—religiously, politically, and militarily.

The Philistines were a non-Semitic and warlike people who had invaded the country from the North—some say from Crete—and are said by archaeologists to have introduced the knowledge and use of iron into Palestine, and to have thus ushered in the Iron Age, but only for their own exclusive benefit. These Philistines had in fact managed to maintain a rigid control over their monopoly in the working of iron, and thus secured a strangle-hold on the life and economy of the Jewish people, through the latter's dependence upon the Philistines for every tool and implement of peace as well as every article of war. By the time of Elijah (ninth century B.C.), it is said that the Jews were already in possession of iron sickles, with which at least twice as much grain could be reaped in a given time as compared to the primitive wooden sickles lined with flint that they had heretofore used; and the carpenter similarly had iron tools of all kinds, axes and adzes and bucksaws, chisels, gouges, and sledge-hammers (Albright, Gerstang). Yet it had been a plaint in Israel, in the early days of the Philistine monopoly, that 'there was no smith found throughout all the land of Israel: for the Philistines said, Lest the Hebrews make them swords or spears:

'But all the Israelites went down to the Philistines, to sharpen every man his share, and his coulter, and his axe, and his mattock. . . .

'So it came to pass in the day of battle, that there was neither sword nor spear found in the hand of any of the people that were with Saul and Jonathan. . . .' (*I Sam.* 13:19-22).

It is thus an interesting speculation whether it was the natural hatred for the Philistines (whose yoke was not finally overthrown till the time of David), with their death-grip over the weapons of war and the implements of peace and livelihood, that may have had something to do with this adoption of the 'iron taboo' by the Israelites, so that the 'worker in iron' had become in time synonymous with the 'maker of idols', as has been mentioned, and the lifting up of an iron tool upon a sacred object had become tantamount to defiling it, and thus making it unfit for its consecrated purpose; and so that, in fact, King Solomon's Temple, which was to be erected to God, and dedicated to His Holy Name, had necessarily to be built without the sound of axe, hammer, or any other tool of iron while it was in building.

But the Jews are not alone in the possession of this 'iron taboo' at one time, as Dr. Jacob Singer has shown. It is also found among the Ancient Greeks and Romans, the Sabines, and the Hottentots.[1]

The Interpreter's Bible, commenting on this taboo on the basis of primitive animism, describes the earliest sacrificial altar as having been literally the 'place of slaughter', the place where sacrifices were offered to the god believed to inhabit it. And, later, 'when the development of shrines into permanent stone buildings took place, all stone brought onto the site would thereby be made sacred, so that whatever squaring and shaping of the stone was done would have to be done before transport'. In this manner, too, the peculiar method of preparation said to have been used at the building of King Solomon's Temple becomes explainable.

Turning, now, from the purely symbolical and religious aspects of the question to those of more practical import, Rodk. H. Baxter, writing on 'The Architectural Style of King Solomon's Temple', raises the question of how the prohibition against the use of iron tools is to be reconciled with the statement in the Bible that the nails used in the construction of the Temple weighed fifty shekels of gold. 'Could they,' he asks, 'possibly have been driven with some tool *not* made of iron?' The latter, certainly, it might be offered in reply, is not beyond the bounds of probability. In the Solomonic era, the Jews were hardly out of the Bronze Age.[2]

The Rabbinical Tradition

Most of the Rabbis have been inclined to take the prohibition in *Exodus* quite literally, but they explain the reason for it symbolically, on the basis of the use of iron in weapons of war. The views of Rashi and Nachmanides (eleventh and thirteenth centuries respectively) are typical in this respect: 'The tool, forged of iron,' they say, 'is a symbol of destruction, whereas the altar prolongs life. The altar is a symbol of reconciliation between God and man, but the tool of iron is a symbol of severance and strangement.'[3]

[1] Jacob Singer, *Taboo in the Hebrew Scriptures*. Chicago, 1928, p. 61.
[2] See Baxter, *AQC* xxxiii, 114–134. In this well-illustrated paper, Baxter discusses the various attempts that had been made by architectural writers to arrive at some realistic conception of the appearance of this famous Temple, and provides a list and a commentary upon some sixteen works on the subject.
[3] *The Soncino Chumash*, 1947.

But Rabbinical attempts at explanation are also not without fanciful speculation at times. Thus it is said by one Rabbi that the building of King Solomon's Temple was entirely miraculous, from start to finish, the Temple having in fact built itself by its own inherent power. For, says this Rabbi, that must be the precise meaning of the phrase, 'The House, when it was in building. . . .' In proof of his interpretation, he points out that 'it is not written, "*which they built*" but "*when it was in building*"; that is,' he explains, further, 'of itself it built itself.' And the explanation, thinks this pilpulistic Rabbi, is still further proven by an additional phrase (as rendered in the Masoretic Text): 'Out of stone made ready at the quarry. . . .' 'That is to say,' he goes on to explain, 'the stones broke themselves off, and flew thither, and laid themselves upon the structure.'[1]

This 'explanation' is not without parallel in Rabbinical lore generally, where we find Solomon even enjoying the assistance of angels and demons in the work of building the Temple. *The Testament of Solomon*, said to be of about the fourth century of our era, tells many such tales.[2] Arabic legends are to the same effect, surprisingly, and there it is stated that it was the *Jinns*, whom Solomon had been able to overcome by his magic power, who worked silently in the building of the Temple—Solomon having been, according to their own traditions, a Muslim.

Josephus, however, thought that he had found a more rational explanation than the Rabbis had proposed. Writing at a time when the intellectual atmosphere was permeated by Graeco-Roman scepticism, he strove to make this incident of the supposedly-miraculous construction of the Temple—like other quasi-miraculous events recorded in the history of the Jewish people—more palatable to his sophisticated Roman friends and patrons; and he explains the building of Solomon's Temple:

Now the whole structure of the temple was made, with great skill, of polished stones, and those laid together so very harmoniously and smoothly, that there appeared to the spectators no signs of any hammer, or other instrument of architecture, but as if, without any use of them, the entire materials had naturally

---

[1] St. John D. Seymour, *Tales of King Solomon*, p. 124.
[2] An English translation of the *Testament* is to be found in the *Jewish Quarterly Review* for Oct. 1898.

united themselves together, that the agreement of one part with another seemed rather to have been natural, than to have arisen from the force of tools upon them.[1]

But the Wooler Lectures, it will have been noted—and those explanations that appear to have been derived therefrom, down to our own time, retaining the opposite tradition—express this appearance of perfection not in terms of natural but of supernatural causes.

The Legend of the Shamir

'The general opinion of the Rabbis,' says the *Jewish Encyclopedia*, on this subject of the construction of the Temple, 'is that Solomon hewed the stones by means of the *Shamir*, a worm whose mere touch cleft rocks.'[2] This miraculous *Shamir* is said to have been especially created from the beginning of the world for this 'operative' purpose, and ceased to exist after the Temple was completed. According to one legend, 'when Solomon asked the Rabbis how he could build the Temple without using tools of iron,' in order to conform, obviously, to the Deuteronomic injunction, 'they called his attention to the *shamir* with which Moses had engraved the names of the tribes on the breastplate of the high priest. . . .'[3] And in Arabic literature there is a very similar legend concerning a stone which cut stone without noise, and which King Solomon is said to have used in the building of his Temple.

Similarly, Ranulf Higden (*c.* 1300–1363 A.D.) cites the legend of the stone-splitting worm (which he calls Thamir) in his *Polychronicon*, but gives little detail.[4]

John Yarker has reproduced at some length this Rabbinic Legend of the *Shamir*.[5] Some versions, taken from both Jewish and Arabic literature, are also to be found in *Tales of King Solomon*, in the

---

[1] Josephus, *Antiquities*, VIII, 3:~.
[2] *Jewish Encyclopedia*, s.v. SOLOMON.
[3] *Op. cit.*, s.v. SHAMIR.
[4] A very rare manuscript copy of his work—so frequently cited in the *Cooke MS.*—is in the Huntingdon Library at Pasadena, California, together with a reprint, in Latin and English translation, published in 1869, under the title *Polychronicon Ranulphi Higden*. H. L. Haywood has an interesting chapter on this *Polychronicon*, with numerous excerpts, in his *More about Masonry*; Chicago, 1948.
[5] Yarker, *AQC*, xxi, 264.

collection of St. John D. Seymour. 'The "Old York Lecture", as Dr. Geo. Oliver terms it in nearly every volume in which he quotes the ritual,' Yarker reminds us, 'told us that the secret which was lost by the joint compact of three G.M.'s was that of "the *insect* Shermah" [obviously a corruption or variant of *Shamir*] used to give a very high polish to the stones.' And in a paper on 'The Old York Rite and Ancient Masonry Generally',[1] Yarker again refers to the operative secret of the *Shermah* as representing 'that which was lost'.

Similarly, in a collection of ritualistic and monitorial material under the designation *Wooler*, to which reference has already been made, and which has some points of resemblance to what Yarker has here laid out as 'the Old York Lectures', we find the following explanatory material in a Lecture on the Third Degree. As a reward to the workmen after the completion of the Temple, we are told, those of the highest degree (said to have been that of the 'Super-excellent') 'were to receive the Grand Secrets relative to the Noble in- Sh- which was that which constituted the secrets of the 3 Grand Masters and [for] which H.A.B.' etc. etc. 'In- Sh-' is obviously intended to indicate the 'insect Shermah [or Shamir],' and the abbreviations used are no doubt intended to indicate the erstwhile esoteric (or supposedly esoteric) character of the information imparted; but the context in which this 'Lecture' is set is so involved, and incrusted with such a profusion of irrelevant detail, as to throw serious suspicion on the genuineness of the working.

The ritualistic basis, if not the details, of this alleged working may however be factual, nevertheless, and in *Miscellanea Latomorum*, Dr. W. W. Westcott gives an excerpt from an 'old ritual' which has reference to this very matter of the 'secret' of the insect *Shamir* and the three G.M.'s. The following excerpt may not be without curious interest:

Question: What was the real secret. . . . ?

Answer: Not the s. t. w.[2] of . . . as erroneously [?] asserted, but the wonderful properties of that noble insect the S...A [Sherma?], which cut and shaped all the sacred utensils and holy vessels, etc., in King Solomon's Temple, etc. . . . In truth, they

[1] Yarker, *Miscellanea*, Allied Masonic Degrees, vol. iv, 1948.
[2] No doubt 'signs, tokens, and words' is intended.

illegally conspired to extort from H.A.B. the said secret of the S...a, the wonderful creature that could cut stones.[1]

At any rate, we find that the Masonic tradition of the Shamir, or Sherma, is no longer prevalent in any British or American working, if indeed it ever was, to any appreciable extent.

[1] W. W. Westcott, *Miscellanea Latomorum*, xxviii, No. 5, 1944.

X

THE BUILDERS OF THE TEMPLE

HAVING DISCUSSED the building of the Temple, we now come by natural progression to a consideration of the builders who actually took part in its erection.

Webb tells us, in his Third Degree Lecture in the *Freemason's Monitor*·

> *There were employed in its building three grand masters; three thousand and three hundred masters, or overseers of the work; eighty thousand fellow crafts; and seventy thousand entered apprentices, or bearers of burthens. All these were classed and arranged in such a manner by the wisdom of Solomon, that neither envy, discord nor confusion were suffered to interrupt that universal peace and tranquility, which pervaded the world at this important period.*
>
> —1805 Edition, p. 76.

The *California Manual* slightly changes this last phrase to the more limited 'peace and goodfellowship which prevailed among the workers', as to which, however, the biblical account is silent—as it is, also (and understandably so) in regard to the 'three grand masters'. The *Manual* further identifies the fellow crafts, in the Webb account, as 'hewers on the mountains and in the quarries'.

The above account generally follows the account in *I Kings*:

> And Solomon had three score and ten thousand that bare burdens, and fourscore thousand hewers in the mountains;
>
> Beside the chief of Solomon's officers which were over the work, three thousand and three hundred, which ruled over the people that wrought in the work.
>
> —*I Kings* 5:15, 16.

In the parallel version given in *II Chronicles*, we read, not of three thousand *three* hundred overseers, but of three thousand *six* hundred (2:18). Here, again, except for this discrepancy, the account in *Chronicles* agrees with that in *Kings*.

Dr. Anderson, in his 1723 edition of the *Book of Constitutions*, follows the account in *Chronicles* rather than that in *Kings*, and attempts a rather lame explanation of the discrepancy in the number of overseers. Mackey thinks it may be only due to a copyist's error, but Cook's *Commentary* thinks there is no real discrepancy at all, if we take the entire account into consideration. For, in *I Kings*, we find 3300 mentioned in 5:16 and an additional 550 in 9:23, or 3850 'chief officers' in all. *II Chronicles*, on the other hand, gives 3600 in 2:18 but only 250 in 8:10, thus again making 3850 in all. Consequently, the apparent discrepancy turns out to be only a matter of arrangement and classification. On the other hand, the Septuagint version confuses the question still further by rendering the verse in *Kings* (*III Kings* 5:17, in the Septuagint arrangement) as 'three thousand six hundred masters,' thus obliterating any apparent discrepancy between *Kings* and *Chronicles* in the modern versions.

A somewhat different manner of harmonizing the *Kings* and *Chronicles* version was the one attempted Masonically in the Finch Lectures (1802), where we read:

Q. Who were the 3600, and what was their employ?

A. 3,300 were overseers in the work and expert Master-masons, the other 300 were the principle Rulers over the whole,

following one of the suggested explanations previously thrown out in a foot-note by Dr. Anderson. But earlier still, at least one of our early Masonic Catechisms also appears to have this tradition of the 300 Rulers. In the *Dumfries No. 4 MS.* (*c.* 1710), we find the following:

And Solomon his son performed ye temple yt [that] his father had begun and divers massons of severall lands gathered together so yt yr [there] was eighty thousand & 3 hundred of ym [them] w^c [which] was Qualified and made over seers of ye worke.
—*Early Masonic Catechisms*, p. 49.

Of course, the '3 hundred' could be a copyist's error for [3 thousand] 3 hundred'; or it could even be—though less likely—'3 [thousand 6] hundred.' Such copyist's errors and omissions in our *Old Charges* and *Catechisms*, and early Masonic works generally, have been found elsewhere. Thus, in the *Henery Heade MS.* (1675), as we have had occasion to note, we apparently find that

'Solomon had four thousand' Masons only (*AQC* xxi), where 'four *score* thousand' must have been meant. And in Hutchinson's *The Spirit of Masonry* (1775), we find him quoting erroneously from the *Second Book of Chronicles* to the effect that Solomon 'set three hundred and ten thousand of them to be bearers of burdens', where obviously 'three *score* and ten thousand' was meant.

The tradition relative to the builders of the Temple, as it finds itself reflected in our various *Old Charges*, is very much confused, and has already been treated at great length. The *Cooke MS.* (*c.* 1410–20)—the first of the *Old Charges* to contain the Legend of the Temple—merely states that 'Solomon had four score thousand Masons at his work', and here Mackey attempts to explain the omission of any reference to the 'bearers of burthens' by saying that they were only common labourers, who therefore, in the opinion of the operative Masons of the fourteenth century, could not have been members of the Craft, while the 'overseers of the work' were obviously looked upon as only officers of the Court, and therefore similarly not to be considered in any enumeration of the Masonic Craft proper.

The account given in the later versions of the *Old Charges*—those belonging to the Dodd or Spencer Family, mentioned in a previous chapter—is somewhat more elaborate than that found in the older versions, and demonstrates the growth of the tradition. Here we find Hiram Abif mentioned by name for the first time, instead of by the 'substitute names' found in the earlier versions, or by no name at all. The story of Hiram Abif will be told in greater detail in the last two chapters; here we cite only the account of the building of the Temple as given in the Dodd or Spencer Family of *Old Charges* (*c.* 1725 to 1739):[1]

> Solomon, King David's Son, to finish the Temple that his Father had begun, sent for Masons, into diverse Countries, and gathered them together; so that he had Fourscore thousand Workmen, that were Workers of Stone, and were all named Masons; and he chose three Thousand of them to be Masters and Governors of his Work.
>
> And Hiram King of Tyre, sent his Servants unto Solomon, for he was ever a Lover of King David; and he sent Solomon Timber and Workmen to help forward the Building of the

[1] *AQC* xxxiii, 23.

Temple. And he sent one that was named Hiram Abif (*I Kings* 7, 14) a Widow's Son of the Tribe of Naphtali. He was a Master,[1] of all his Masons, Carvers, Ingravers, and Workmen, and Casters of Brass, and all other Metals, that were used about the Temple.

King Solomon confirmed both the Charges and Manners that his Father had given to Masons, thus was the worthy Craft of Masonry confirmed in Jerusalem, and many other kingdoms, and he finished the Temple Anno Mundi 3000.

It would be profitable, at this point, to compare this more elaborate account with the very bare one given in the earliest version as given in the *Cooke MS.*, to observe the growth of the tradition.[2]

The account given in the above later version of the *Old Charges* may seem to be contradictory in one further particular, in addition to the discrepancies previously noted, in that the 'Masters and Governors' of the work, to the tune of three thousand, are here said to be taken *from among* the eighty thousand 'Masons', whereas the biblical version puts 'Solomon's officers' as being *in addition to* the eighty thousand.

It is to be noted that neither Dr. Anderson nor the *Old Charges* take into consideration the levy of thirty thousand men, under Adoniram, whom Solomon sent into Lebanon, 'by courses'—i.e., in shifts—obviously for the timber for which that region was justly famous (*I Kings* 5:13, 14), but Mackey remarks at this point, again, that these were wood-cutters only, and as such—like the 'bearers of burthens' and the officer 'overseers'—would not be recognized by the mediaeval stonemasons as brother-members of the Craft. '. . . He had fourscore thousand workers of stone,' says my version of *Dowland's MS.*, 'who were all named Masons.' The title was a distinction, in the eyes of our operative brethren; it was not lightly shared.

Curiously enough, no specific mention is made, in either version of the Bible, of any of the workers and artificers who must have been used on the site of the building itself, to rear 'the mighty edifice'. Presumably, some of the 70,000 'bearers of burdens' would be used here to carry and raise the stone and timber and other materials of construction, and some of the 'overseers' would be in charge here also, but no specific workers or skilled artisans of any

---

[1] Some versions say 'Master of Geometry'.
[2] See Chapter V, *ante*.

kind are mentioned—except one, of course, who wrought all the brass work for the Temple. In the Bible we merely read:

> And Solomon's builders and Hiram's builders did hew them, and the stone-squarers: so they prepared timber and stones to build the house.
>
> —*I Kings* 5:18.

For 'stone-squarers', Clarke's *Commentary* points out, the marginal reading is 'Giblites, *haggiblim*' in the original Hebrew; i.e., 'the Giblim', or men of Gebal, a Phoenician city not far from the coast—the modern Jebeil, about twenty miles north of Beiruth, and some sixty-five miles north of the ancient city of Tyre. In the Greek period, Gebal was known as Byblus. 'These men of Gebal,' Dr. Slotki thinks, in his Commentary, 'must have been famed as skilled stone-masons.'

The memory of these *Giblim* has been preserved Masonically in at least one of the eighteenth-century Catechisms, *The Grand Mystery of Free-masons Discover'd* (1724), where we find:

Q. Give me the *Jerusalem* Word.
A. *Giblin* [*sic*]

It is similarly found in *The Wilkinson MS.*, an Entered Apprentice catechism thought to be *circa* 1727:

Q. Whats the Name of a Mason
A. Giblin

Prichard's *Masonry Dissected* (1730), whose 'Enter'd 'Prentice's Degree' has numerous similarities with the *Wilkinson* working, omits the above reference, and it is no longer to be found in present-day Craft Masonry. But the word has significance for the Installation Ceremony in England, and is to be found in the United States (and perhaps elsewhere) in the Past Master Degree as a preparation for the Royal Arch.

The learned commentary on this word, given partly below, by the editors of *The Wilkinson MS.*, is of interest:

> In a footnote on p. 16 of his *Constitutions* of 1723, Anderson writes of 'Men of Hewing called also . . . *Ghiblim*, Stone-Squarers and Sculpturers' giving I Kings 5:18. [A.V.] as the reference. The Hebrew word 'Giblim', which 'stone-squarers'

is intended to represent in that verse, would not appear to have any etymological association with either stones or stone-cutters. No corresponding translation occurs in the Septuagint or in the Vulgate; nor is it found in the Genevan Bible (1560) or in the Douai (Roman Catholic) English version (1582). The first version in which the hybrid [stone-squarers] occurs is apparently the Bishops' Bible (1568). In the Revised Version (1884) the Hebrew word is given as a proper name—'Gebalites'. . . . In Kings the marginal note to 'stone-squarers' reads 'or Giblites'. . . .

Jewish commentators regard it as an historical fact that the town of Gebal contained a gild of stoneworkers. The neighbourhood was a rocky one, and would afford opportunity for local people to become experts in the hewing and dressing of stone. Jewish commentators think that I Kings 5.18. indicates that as the builders of Solomon and Hiram of Tyre did the *wood*-work in connection with the Temple, the Giblites did the *stone*-work; hence the *explanatory translation* of 'Giblim' as 'stone-squarers'. In a word, they think that 'stone-squarers' is a legitimate *interpretation* of the word Giblites, based on what is accepted as an historical fact, but it is not a literal translation. . . .[1]

In simpler language, A. W. Adams explains the translation of the Hebrew word *haggiblim* in the Bible into 'stone-squarers' in this fashion:

The old translators knew that Giblim meant men of Gebal, but as they thought it impossible that 'strangers should be permitted to participate in the holy work of building the Temple,' they looked about for another meaning. They supposed that the Giblim were in their day famed for their skill in masonry, that all good masons, whatever their nationality, came to be called Giblim, so that the word became a synonym of masons or stone-squarers.[2]

Of course, a subsidiary difficulty inevitably emerges from the above supposition that strangers would not have been permitted to participate in the work of the Temple, in view of the men known to have been sent down from Tyre, according to the biblical record itself.

[1] *The Wilkinson Manuscript*, Transcribed and Edited by Douglas Knoop, G. P. Jones, and Douglas Hamer. Sheffield, 1946, p. 39.
[2] A. W. Adams, *The Story of the Two Hirams*. Birmingham, 1931, p. 20.

Morton Deutsch, however, in a recently published work, *From Whence Came You?*—a sufficiently impressive title—thinks that this word Giblim may also be derived from the Ghibellines, said to have been an important political party in twelfth- and thirteenth-century continental Europe, and perhaps having some Crusader connection with the 'Knights of The Temple of Solomon' and the 'Knights of the Holy St. John of Jerusalem', and thus coming into Masonry through its imagined connection with those Crusaders.[1] But this seems to me to be reaching out too far afield for a meaning, when a simpler and much more reliable explanation is so much closer to hand. The number of similar phonetic—but otherwise meaningless—coincidences in Masonic lore is legion.

Our present-day Masonic traditions, it must be noted, generally fail to provide for any specific enumeration of the artisans who must have been at work on the site of the Temple, beyond the division into the 'hewers in the mountains and the quarries', the 'bearers of burdens' and their 'overseers'. But Calcott—in *A Candid Disquisition*, etc., 1769, one of the earliest works designed to demonstrate the origin, nature, and purpose of the Masonic institution —attempted to remedy this deficiency by sub-dividing at least the eighty thousand fellow-crafts—our present-day 'hewers in the mountains and the quarries'—into three separate classes:

1. *Ghiblim*, Stone Squarers, Polishers and Sculptors
2. *Ish Chotzeb*, Hewers
3. *Benai*, Setters or Layers—'being able and ingenious Fellow Crafts'.

This may have been only a personal interpretation, based, perhaps, on Dr. Anderson's attempt in a similar direction. In a footnote to his 1723 *Constitutions*, Anderson speaks of the '80,000 *Ish Chotzeb*, Men of Hewing, called also *Ghiblim*, Stone-Cutters and Sculpturers; and also *Bonai*, Builders in Stone, part of which belong'd to Solomon, and part to Hiram, King of Tyre, I Kings v. 18', the Hebrew words being those used in the Bible to describe various types of workmen. Anderson, too, may have voiced only a personal interpretation in this instance, or he may have been simply recording once more one of the 'traditions of old Masons, who talk much of these things'.

Calcott, on his part, cites in addition the 300 *Harodim*, Rulers or Masters—as in the Finch Lectures, mentioned earlier; 3300

[1] Morton Deutsch, *From Whence Came You?* New York, 1958, pp. 141–142.

Menatzchim or Overseers; and 70,000 who were 'the remains of the old Canaanites', and who correspond to our 'bearers of burdens'.[1]

All these classes and sub-classes appear to be enumerated in a very detailed Lecture appearing in Finch's *Masonic Treatise* (1802), to which reference has already been made on several occasions:

Q. How many Israelites were employed in this building for the worship of God.

A. 30,000, besides 3,600 overseers, and 150,000 Bondsmen.

Q. What did the 30,000 consist of,

A. The Levy of Jerusalem.

Q. Who was appointed the superintendent,

A. The noble Prince Adoniram.

Q. Who were the 150,000,

A. The remains of the old Canaanites.

Q. What was their employ,

A. To prepare the materials for the building, except the inferior workmen, who were the bearers of burthen.

Q. Who were the 3,600, and what was their employ,

A. 3,300 were overseers in the work and expert Master-masons, the other 300 were the principle Rulers over the whole.

The present-day *Emulation* Lectures make an almost similar count, as in the following enumeration, but they leave out the 30,000 wood-cutters forming the 'levy of Jerusalem':

Q. Name the number in each class.

A. There were three hundred Rulers, three thousand three hundred Overseers, and eighty thousand Craftsmen. The Rulers and Overseers were all skilled Craftsmen, or men of science. . . .

Q. Were there any others employed in the building?

A. There were seventy thousand others employed, consisting of men of burden and hewers of stone, . . . so that the total number of men employed in the building, was one hundred and fifty-three thousand six hundred.

On the other hand, *Henderson's MS.*, which purports to be Prestonian in origin, does count the 30,000 wood-cutters, but leaves out the 70,000 Bearers of Burdens, in accordance with the *Old Charges* practice, and 'it is said that there were 300 Rulers, 3600

[1] Cf. Moore, *New Masonic Trestle Board*, Pt. II, p. 7.

overseers, and 80,000 craftsmen', thus adding the 300 to the 3600 (instead of to the 3300).

In this instance, we find that Webb does not follow Preston. In fact, it can be said that the tradition generally retained in the American Lectures leaves out all mention of the 300 *Harodim* or Rulers, at the top of the classification, and the 30,000 wood-cutters in the forest of Lebanon, at the bottom. It enumerates, specifically, only the 'bearers of burdens', the 'hewers on the mountains and in the quarries', the 'overseers of the work', and, of course, the 'three Grand Masters', as members of the Craft supposed to have taken part in the erection of King Solomon's Temple.

Now, who were these men who took part, physically, in the work —not counting, of course, the 'three Grand Masters'? Were they all Israelites? Or partly Israelites and partly Phoenicians? Or of other origin? And were they freemen or slaves? Here the biblical record and the Masonic traditions are both more confused than ever, and we get no very clear picture from either one or the other.

'It has been suggested', says Gordon Hills in his excellent discussion of Rodk. H. Baxter's paper on "The Architectural Style of King Solomon's Temple", 'that all along building operations had been distasteful to the Israelites, from their association with Egyptian bondage, and that it was upon the subject races in the Holy Land that the labour of such operations devolved. The account of King Solomon's organization of the work seems somewhat to bear this out. There is a difference drawn', Gordon Hills points out, 'between those *bondsmen* who worked as bearers of burdens and hewers in the quarries, who were survivors of those nations Israel was not able to destroy utterly, and the levies of *freemen* of the nation. It is particularly to be noted that *of the Children of Israel* were the *chief officers* that Solomon appointed.'[1]

But the various professional biblical commentators are of not much help in a definitive solution of the question, since they differ among themselves as to the exact meaning of Holy Writ in this connection. Some of the biblical verses touching on the question we have already cited; others will here be cited along with them, to bring them into focus in one continuous context:

And Solomon sent to Hiram, saying . . .

Now therefore command thou that they hew me cedar trees out

[1] Gordon Hills, *AQC* xxxiii, p. 126.

of Lebanon; . . . for thou knowest that there is not among us any
that can skill to hew timber like unto the Sidonians. . . . And my
servants shall be with thy servants. . . .

—I Kings 5:2, 6.

And king Solomon raised a levy out of all Israel; and the levy
was thirty thousand men.

And he sent them to Lebanon: . . . and Adoniram was over the
levy.

—I Kings 5:13, 14.

And Solomon's builders and Hiram's builders did hew them,
and the stone-squarers: so they prepared timber and stones to
build the house.

—I Kings 5:18.

The account in *Chronicles* follows generally the information laid
down in *Kings*, but with this important addition:

And Solomon numbered all the strangers that were in the land
of Israel, . . . and they were found an hundred and fifty thousand
and three thousand and six hundred.

And he set three score and ten thousand of them to be bearers
of burdens, and four score thousand to be hewers in the mountain, and three thousand and six hundred overseers to set the
people a work.

—II Chron. 2:17, 18.

In the *Kings* account, as we have seen, the total number comes
to 153,300 in place of 153,600 enumerated in *Chronicles* (brought
about by the 3,300 and 3,600 that were counted to be 'overseers'
in the two versions), but, apart from this apparent discrepancy,
which is immaterial to our present discussion, the *Chronicles*
account makes them all out to be 'strangers' in the land—not
Israelites. These 'strangers', says Cook's *Commentary*, were 'the
descendants of those Canaanites whom the children of Israel did
not drive out', as it is said in *I Kings* 9:21, 22: 'Their children that
were left after them in the land, whom the children of Israel also
were not able utterly to destroy, upon those did Solomon levy a
tribute of bondservice unto this day. But of the children of Israel
did Solomon make no bondsmen. . . . ' The latter were subject to
the levy, says Garstang in comment on this passage, but retained

12

their civil status as free men, while the aboriginal inhabitants temporarily became slaves.[1]

But a totally different view is that held by Dr. Curtis, in his *Critical Commentary on Chronicles*, and he thinks that 'the historical fact seems to have been that Solomon made a levy upon pure Israelites to carry out his building operations. A later writer, taking exception to the reduction of Israelites to practical slavery, made the levy consist of non-Israelites. The Chronicler, following this later view, represents the levy as consisting of sojourners . . . (*gerim*) . . . foreigners who for one reason or another left their native clans and attached themselves to the Hebrews'.[2]

Dean Farrar concurs in this view. These 'seventy thousand burden-bearers and eighty thousand quarrymen . . . according to the Chronicler, were bondslaves from the unextirpated remnants of the Canaanite races. They were in fact the helots of Palestine'.[3]

The Finch Lectures, it will have been noted, preserved this tradition of the 150,000 'bondsmen, the remains of the old Canaanites'.

This question of 'freedom' versus 'bondage', in King Solomon's time, may profitably be compared to the many references to the 'impressment' of British masons in mediaeval times, by King and Church, in the writings of Knoop and Jones.[4]

Just as there is no agreement among the biblical commentators as to whether the workers at the Temple were bond or free, so is there no agreement among them as to what relative part the men of Solomon (whether Israelites or Canaanites) and the men of Hiram of Tyre played in the work. 'As the text stands', comments the *Encyclopedia Biblica*, 'Solomon asks Hiram for help in the hewing of timber'—"*for thou knowest that there is not among us any that can skill to hew timber like unto the Sidonians*" (this being the name by which the Phoenicians were generally called, as we have seen). 'It is in the hewing of stone that Solomon's labourers are represented as taking a prominent part.' The *Cyclopedia of Biblical Literature*, on the other hand, in agreement with Moffat's Translation, makes

---

[1] John Garstang, *The Heritage of Solomon*, p. 369.

[2] Dr. Ed. L. Curtis, *The International Critical Commentary*, *Chronicles*. New York, 1910, pp. 255–256.

[3] Rev. F. W. Farrar, *Solomon, his Life and Times*, p. 76.

[4] See especially under 'Impressment of Masons', in *The Mediaeval Mason*, by Knoop and Jones. Manchester, 1933, pp. 90 *et seq.*

the 80,000 to have been 'hewers of wood in the mountains', and not hewers of stone, as generally understood. The various versions of the Bible, in fact, are themselves not all too specific in this respect, except the Douay Version (Roman Catholic), which unequivocally refers to the 'eighty thousand to hew stones in the mountain', together with the Greek Septuagint, which similarly calls them 'hewers of stone'. The Jewish Masoretic Text of both *Kings* and *Chronicles* refers only to 'hewers in the mountains', without further ascription, but Dr. Slotki understands this to refer to 'hewers of stone'. 'The Mountains', says this commentator, 'are assumed to be the hill-country of Canaan which yields a fine quality of lime-stone . . . eminently suitable for building purposes'. It is this latter and perhaps more correct interpretation of the 80,000 as 'hewers of stone in the mountains' that has been followed in the Masonic tradition.

As to the total number of workers cited in our traditions—153,300 or 153,600, according to which biblical text is followed—this is in general agreement with the findings of biblical scholars. Th. H. Robinson's *History of Israel* offers an estimate that 'the total of men employed for the twenty years during which Solomon's building operations were in progress must have been between 150,000 and 200,000 men'; and John Garstang reaches a similar conclusion independently,[1] which, however, is at variance with the writer in *The Interpreter's Dictionary of the Bible*, who thinks that the numbers of workers given in *I Kings* 5:13, 15 'appears to be a later exaggeration'.[2]

Of this number, the figure 80,000 is continually referred to, in the Bible, in the *Commentaries* upon it, and in the Masonic traditions. One account that is of particular interest with respect to these 80,000, has come down to us from Eusebius, an ecclesiastical historian of the third and fourth centuries A.D., whom we have had previous occasion to mention. In this account, the Pharaoh of Egypt, whose daughter King Solomon married (along with a few others), sent with his daughter, as dowry, a number of builders, to the tune of eighty thousand. This numerical coincidence with the 'fourscore thousand hewers in the mountain' mentioned in the Bible is curious, if inconclusive. This number of 80,000 Egyptian work-men, furthermore, is said in one Commentary to be in addition to

---

[1] John Garstang, *Heritage of Solomon*, p. 368.
[2] *Inter. Dict.*, vol. R-Z, p. 535.

the 80,000 that are supposed to have come from Tyre; and, according to still another commentator, this tradition preserved by Eusebius 'may have some foundation in spite of its exaggerated numbers. . . .'[1] Could the account in general be corroborated, the several features in King Solomon's Temple which some writers have compared with analogous features in Egyptian architecture would be capable of easy explanation.[2]

The two Royal Grand Masters

One final item concerning these Builders of the Temple, with specific reference to two of the Grand Masters concerned therein, and under whose auspices that mighty edifice was erected, will now be noticed.

There is a tradition in some quarters to the effect that Hiram, King of Tyre, made an engagement with King Solomon to pay the Craft their wages, if any be due, that none might go away dissatisfied. But this appears to be an error, if we are to follow biblical testimony; for the scriptural account, in both *Kings* and *Chronicles*, gives us the exact opposite:

> And Solomon sent to Hiram, saying . . .
> . . . Unto thee will I give hire for thy servants according to all that thou shalt appoint. . . .
>
> —*I Kings* 5:2, 6.

> And Solomon sent to Huram the king of Tyre, saying . . .
> And, behold, I will give to thy servants, the hewers that cut timber, twenty thousand measures of beaten wheat, and twenty thousand measures of barley, and twenty thousand baths of wine, and twenty thousand baths of oil.[3]
>
> —*II Chron.* 2:3, 10.

It would appear, therefore, that it was King Solomon who had made an engagement with King Hiram to pay the Craft their wages, and not the reverse.

---

[1] *Cyclopedia of Biblical, Theological, and Ecclesiastical Literature*, s.v. SOLOMON p. 865. New York, 1894.

[2] This account of the Egyptian workmen may in fact be the origin of the tradition preserved in the *Old Charges* relative to the Masons that Solomon is said to have secured from 'diverse countries'.

[3] A 'measure' or *cor* is about eleven bushels. A 'bath', among the ancient Hebrews, was a liquid measure equivalent to about eight gallons (Slotki).

Incidentally, we also see here the probable origin of our tradition pertaining to the 'Corn, Wine, and Oil' that was used as currency with which to pay the wages of the workers at the building of King Solomon's Temple, and now symbolically treated.

In Cabalistic literature there is a legend further associating the two kings, but this time not in connection with the building of the Temple. It is there said that Solomon had ordered a demon to convey Hiram, King of Tyre, down to the seven compartments of hell, so that, on his return, he could reveal to Solomon all that he had seen in the nether world[1]—an attempt, perhaps, at a quasi-magical explanation of some of King Solomon's proverbial 'wisdom'. In Josephus, too, we read of the wagers that Solomon and Hiram of Tyre used to engage in, to see which one could outdo the other in solving the riddles and problems they sent to each other, reference to which is made in another portion of the present work.[2]

Some Phoenician historians link the two kings in still another way. In this account, Hiram of Tyre is said to have given his daughter to King Solomon in marriage.[3] Still another Phoenician account has it that King Solomon presented the King of Tyre with a duplicate of his own temple, which was subsequently erected at Tyre.[4]

As to the personality and character of King Hiram himself, it is curious to note the remark made in Clarke's Commentary on *I Kings* 5:7 to the effect that 'from this, and indeed from every part of Hiram's conduct, it is evident that he was a worshipper of the true God'—overlooking, apparently, the temples King Hiram is said to have reared to Herakles and Astarte, in the account of Menander preserved by Josephus.[5] But this remark of Clarke's may be no more realistic, in fact, than the opposite belief entertained by the Arabs to the effect that King Solomon had been a follower of the Moslem religion.

However, the relationship between the two kingdoms of which Solomon and Hiram were the crowned heads may nevertheless go further than mere geographical propinquity. The discovery of the cuneiform *Ras Shamra Tablets*, about a hundred and sixty miles

---

[1] *Jewish Encyclopedia*, s.v. SOLOMON.

[2] Josephus, *Antiquities*, Bk. VIII, 5:3. *Against Apion*, Bk. I, 17.

[3] *Cyclopedia of Biblical Literature*, etc. New York, 1894, vol. 9, p. 865.

[4] *Historians History of the World*, II, ch. iii; cited by Newton, *The Builders*, p. 75.

[5] Josephus, *Against Apion*, I, 18.

north of Tyre, and said to date from the period 1400 B.C., appears to show some remarkable similarities between the ritual of the dwellers in that region and that of the worshippers of Yahweh. 'The explanation of this parallelism,' says Dr. J. McKee Adams, commenting on the phenomenon, 'doubtless lies partly in the fact that the Phoenicians and Israelites belonged to the same Semitic race, and inherited the same ritual and religious customs.'[1] The Tablets, it is said, reveal, in fact, unexpected similarities in ritual, sacrifice, feast, and other religious observances, and disclose such Old Testament names as El, Elohim, and probably Yahweh. Thus, the essential religious difference between Solomon, King of Israel, and Hiram, King of Tyre—when thrown realistically against the background of their actual social and religious environment *circa* 1000 B.C.—may not be as violent a contrast as now appears to us from the vantage point of three thousand years later; the two kings may in reality have been closer in religious feeling than we have been wont to assume.

---

[1] J. McKee Adams, *Ancient Records and the Bible*. Nashville, 1946, pp. 93, 153.

XI

THE THREE GRADES

THE CLASSIFICATION of the Craftsmen into the three grades that we find today in the Webb *Monitor*[1] is primarily due, no doubt, to Dr. Anderson who, in his 1723 *Constitutions*, departed somewhat from the rather simple and unimposing account found in the *Cooke MS.* and in the *Old Charges* that followed it, but went directly to the account in *II Chronicles*, with its 'bearers of burdens', and 'hewers in the mountain', and 'overseers'. But he now gave them a distinctly Masonic designation. To the 'bearers of burdens', he gave the name of 'Entered Apprentices'; the 'hewers in the mountain' he called 'Fellowcrafts'; and the 'overseers of the work' became 'Master Masons'. Thus all three classifications now came to be blanketed into Craft membership, according to the version of the Legend elaborated by him.

In the Second or 1738 edition of the *Constitutions*, Dr. Anderson goes a step further. Now he tells us that

Solomon partitioned the Fellow Crafts into certain Lodges with a Master and Wardens in each; that they might receive commands in a regular manner, might take care of their tools and jewels, might be paid every week, and be duly fed and clothed, etc., and the Fellow Crafts took care of their succession by educating Entered Apprentices.

'*All these*,' Webb further tells us, in his still more elaborate version of the story, '*were classed and arranged in such a manner by the wisdom of Solomon, that neither envy, discord nor confusion were suffered to interrupt that universal peace and tranquility, which pervaded the world at this important period.*'

Some Jurisdictions elaborate upon this Legend in an interesting manner. In Holland, for example, the 'Bro. Orator' delivers himself of the following Lecture to the Candidate, during the course of the ceremony of Raising:

[1] Webb, *Freemason's Monitor*, 1805, p. 76.

When Solomon wished to fulfil his determination to build his Temple, he had need of an outstanding Architect to superintend the work, and properly organize all things. The King of Tyre, Hiram, was a friend of Solomon, and, in order to give proof of his friendship, sent him the Master Builder H.A.B.

He, amongst other regulations, directed that the workmen be divided into three grades, according to their ability. He made them Apprentices, Fellows and Masters. The wages of each were different, as is only just. The Masters received more than the Fellows, and the Fellows more than the Apprentices. H.A. stipulated that the Apprentices should receive their wages at the Column J., the Fellows at the Column B., and the Masters in the Middle Chamber.

Where several thousands were working on the building of the Temple, it was not possible to know each one personally, H.A. therefore gave a different word of recognition to each grade.

This rule had the best results, each was paid in proportion to his merit.[1]

In this version of the Legend it is H.A.B. who organizes the workmen, and not King Solomon, as in the generally accepted tradition. The different places of payment for each Grade are also worthy of notice.

Other Masonic writers have taken a hand at elaborating upon our traditions in this matter of King Solomon's Temple. Some of these have already been referred to. According to Hutchinson, King Solomon not only carried out the work he has generally been credited with, but also, in a Masonic sense, organized the workers in a particular manner; he

gave them particular signs and secret tokens, by which each rank should be distinguished, in order that the whole might proceed with propriety, and without confusion; he selected those of most enlightened minds and comprehensive understandings—religious men, piously zealous in good works—as masters to superintend the workmen; men skilful in geometry and proportions, who had been initiated and proved in the mystical learning of the ancient sages; those he made overseers of the work; [and] the whole was conducted with that degree of holy reverence, that even the noise

[1] C. C. Binns, 'The Ritual of Raising, Grand Orient of the Netherlands'. *Transactions*, Leicester Lodge of Research No. 2429, 1953–4, p. 51.

of a tool or instrument was not permitted to disturb the sacred silence on Moriah, sanctified by the presence of the Almighty, and by his miraculous works.[1]

And all this, with an air of gravity and of historical simplicity, as if the records of the time had come to life, and the account was being read from the description of a personal witness.

Dr. Oliver—from whose edition of *The Spirit of Masonry* this excerpt is taken—adds an editorial footnote to this legendary tale to the effect that

> an ancient masonic tradition relates that our G. M. King Solomon, struck with the harmony produced by the admirable arrangements which had been adopted amongst the workmen, conceived the idea of forming an universal bond of brotherly love, which should unite all nations in the pursuits of virtue and science. For this purpose, he admitted to his system those illustrious sages who visited Jerusalem from every part of the globe, and allowed them to participate in his mysteries. And hence, when they returned home, they diffused Freemasonry over the whole face of the earth.

This so-called 'tradition'—which has not been met with elsewhere in this particular form—illustrates the notion of the origin of Freemasonry at the time of the building of the Temple which we discussed in detail in our second chapter—but is probably as apocryphal as the legendary connection between the Masonic institution and that of the crusading Knights Templar.

In another one of his works—*The Antiquities of Free-Masonry*, 1823—Oliver goes into a great deal of detail concerning the number of lodges that met in the quarries and in the forest of Lebanon. And, in accordance with another alleged tradition, he discusses the nine classes of Masons—from Entered Apprentice to Super-Excellent, each with its own Grand Master. But all this may be only an idle tale, whatever its source, having no other purpose than to embellish an already over-burdened legend.

As to Dr. Anderson's account, written closer to the days of the operative Masons, his authority for the amplified version he gives us, according to his own statement, as we have seen, is 'the traditions of old Masons, who talk much of these things'. But 'if such a

[1] William Hutchinson, *The Spirit of Masonry*, 1775. Oliver Edition, p. 97.

tradition ever existed', Mackey wrote in comment—and his remarks can be made to apply to many of the other versions as well—'it is now lost, for it can not be found in any of the old manuscripts which are the record of the Masonic traditions'.[1] In the intervening period, no new evidence seems to have come to light, despite the rediscovery of many manuscripts that were not known in Mackey's time. Still, this does not rule out the possibility that some such tradition, in the historical records of the mediaeval Masons, may yet be brought forward some day in support of some of these Legends. We do know of the wilful destruction of some valuable records by a few overzealous brethren, about the time of the first formation of Grand Lodge—perhaps for the very reason that they contained some traditions or allusions that were considered sacred by those brethren. And we do know of the Great Fire of London in 1666, which must have wreaked much havoc in this as in other directions. In addition, we also know of several *Old Charges* that are specifically referred to in various records but which have since dropped out of sight and are now no longer to be seen. And finally, we have the prime example of the profoundly significant *Graham MS.*, which for the first time gives us an indirect allusion to at least one form of what has now come to be known as the Hiramic Tradition, which, in the minds of some students, appeared to be of Grand-Lodge-era fabrication, because it showed no evidence of prior existence. This *Graham MS.*—which is inscribed with a date that *appears* to read 1726, but has been taken by some as perhaps cryptically meaning 1672—was completely unknown to the modern world of Masonic scholarship till it was rediscovered, as recently as 1936.[2] With all these valid considerations before us, the cautious student becomes rather chary of dubbing any tradition as 'fabricated', merely because no documentary evidence exists at the present time in support of it.

But to get back to the Builders themselves, we are told in the now-current Legend of King Solomon's Temple of the three kinds of Lodges that met in the Temple, and the number of Masons of each Grade that composed each of these Lodges as a minimum number. One *Monitor* designates the number as follows:

[1] Mackey, *History of Freemasonry*, i, 158.
[2] This *Graham MS.* has been briefly referred to on several previous occasions in the present work, but it is more fully discussed, in respect of the Hiramic Tradition, in our concluding chapter.

Seven constitute a Lodge of Entered Apprentices—one Master Mason, and six Entered Apprentices. They usually meet[1] on the Ground Floor of King Solomon's Temple.

Five constitute a Lodge of Fellow Crafts—two Master Masons and three Fellow Crafts. They usually meet in the Middle Chamber of King Solomon's Temple.

Three constitute a Lodge of Master Masons—three Master Masons. They meet in the Sanctum Sanctorum, or Holy of Holies of King Solomon's Temple.

This numerical tradition is based, no doubt, on a tradition of at least a seventeenth-century vintage, for we find in several of the early Masonic Catechisms this designation of a 'just and perfect Lodge' as consisting of not less than a certain specified number of Masons—just as, in the old Hebrew traditions (still practised), and from which our own Masonic custom may have been taken, no 'congregation' can meet for prayer or other ritualistic observance, unless there be at least a *minyan* of ten men.

The completely operative *Schaw Statutes* of 1598 list the rules and regulations of the Mason Craft in Scotland of that period, and are signed by 'William Schaw, Maistir of Wark' (comparable to the Office of Surveyor-General to which Sir Christopher Wren was appointed by the Crown in the Southern kingdom some seventy years later, and perhaps corresponding to the Office of Grand Master Mason by which name that Office is now known in Scotland, among our speculative Masons). Among these operative statutes of sixteenth-century Scotland is one item which reads:

> na maister or fallow of craft be ressauit [received] nor admittit w'out the number of sex maisteris and twa enterit prenteissis[2]

With the transition to speculative Masonry, we find in the *Sloane MS*. No. 3329 (said to be written down about 1700, but of early seventeenth-century dating as to the language employed):

Q. where were you made a Mason
A. in a just and perfect or just and Lawfull Lodge
Q. what is a just and perfect or just and Lawfull Lodge
A. a just and perfect Lodge is two Interprintices two fellow

---

[1] 'Used to meet' would no doubt be more correct, as an expression of the Legend.
[2] D. Murray Lyon, *History of the Lodge of Edinburgh* (*Mary's Chapel*) *No. 1*; London, 1900, p. 10.

craftes and two Masters more or fewer the more the merrier the fewer the Better Chear but if need require five will serve that is two Interprintices two fellow Craftes and one Master on the highest hill or lowest Valley of the world without the crow of a Cock or the bark of a Dogg.[1]

The minimum number composing the various Grades was not always and everywhere the same, as the above would indicate. In *A Mason's Examination* (1723), we find that a 'just and perfect Lodge' consisted of 'a Master, two Wardens, four Fellows, five Apprentices'; in *A Mason's Confession* (Scottish, *c.* 1727), it is 'Five fellow-crafts, and seven entered prentices'; *The Mystery of Free-Masonry* (1730) repeats the list of 1723 but leaves out the 'five Apprentices', while the Scottish *Graham MS.* is less specific as to the classifications, merely requiring 'any od number from 3 to 13'—a formula repeated in the *Essex MS.*, of about 1750.

From about 1730 we find things beginning to be somewhat better organized in this respect. *Masonry Dissected* (1730) gives 'Seven or more' for the 'Enter'd 'Prentice's Degree', and these are made to consist of 'one Master, two Wardens, two Fellow-Crafts and two Enter'd 'Prentices' (the English Masons having by now adopted the originally Scottish designation of Entered Apprentice), while, in this same 1730 publication, five are said to 'make a Lodge', and these are supposed to consist of at least 'one Master, two Wardens, one Fellow-Craft, one Enter'd 'Prentice'.[2] And, in the 'Master's Part':

Q. What makes a Perfect Lodge of Masters?
A. Three.

As to the Three Grades that are said by Dr. Anderson to have held separate Lodges in King Solomon's time and Temple, it is necessary to bear in mind a point we have already stressed, to the effect that—in the words of Lionel Vibert—'Master and Fellow Craft were convertible terms as far as any question of degrees was concerned, implying only one ceremony', at the time of the publication of the 1723 *Constitutions*.[3] And, prior to that time, in the old

[1] *Early Masonic Catechisms*, p. 41.
[2] This last enumeration, while found in Prichard's 'Enter'd 'Prentice's Degree', may have more properly belonged to the 'Fellow-Craft's', but perhaps got misplaced in the recorder's memory.
[3] *AQC* xxxvi, 60.

operative days, the two terms represented only one Grade, as far as proficiency was concerned. Consequently, the tradition relative to the three separate Grades supposed to have been in existence in King Solomon's time could only have been evolved at a time when the three separate Degrees were already recognized and practised—in other words, some time after the 1723 *Constitutions* had been published. As a matter of fact, we do not find any Andersonian reference to the Three Grades tradition until the 1738 edition. This alleged tradition relative to King Solomon's time must therefore have been evolved—Mackey would probably have used the harsher term 'invented'—some time between these two periods.

The question impinges upon the more general problem of Anderson's reliability in such matters as we have been discussing here. He was neither by vocation nor by avocation an historian, and the pressures playing upon him in those early days—either self-imposed or imposed upon him by his fraternal colleagues—may not have given him sufficient time or opportunity 'to digest the old records into a better method' with any amount of historical accuracy. It is therefore understandable that he could not have emerged as a Macaulay or a Gibbon in matters of Masonic history, and it is consequently conceded on all sides that as a Masonic historian, Anderson is not to be trusted. But it is not with matters of history that we are here immediately concerned, but with matters of tradition. The question, to put it bluntly, is simply this. Did Anderson in fact invent out of whole cloth some of the 'traditions' he claimed to have collected from the written traditions of the Free Masons of many ages, amplified with the oral traditions that had come down to his own day, and found among the 'old Masons, who talk much of these things'? Did he in fact try to palm off on his brethren some invented and fabricated so-called 'traditions' which were, in point of fact, not genuine traditions at all but creations of his own fertile imagination? And are we consequently saddled today, and perhaps for all time in the foreseeable future, with a body of 'traditions' some of which, at least, have been artificially manufactured?

Mackey, as has already been brought out, definitely thought so with respect to at least one specific 'tradition'. And others have thought that the Hiramic Legend was similarly an invention of Dr. Anderson's. The vital importance that this particular Legend enjoys in the Masonic system certainly emphasizes the need for students to examine carefully the history and development of that system, seen now as an institution of legends and allegories and moral teachings and a philosophy, and not merely as a political organization with its obviously indispensable constitutions and edicts and by-laws.

This question of Dr. Anderson and his general veracity in the matter of the collection and dissemination of traditions has accordingly agitated the minds of many students. Rodk. H. Baxter, for one, has expressed the opinion that 'it is hardly consistent with the nature of his sacred calling that a Presbyterian divine should be capable of direct mendacity',[1] but this perhaps is only begging the question. After all, some ministers of all faiths and denominations— like the members of other professions—*have* been known at times to be mendacious, and the question is not one that can be settled on general principles alone.

But it is worthy of note that on at least two specific charges which have threatened to discredit the memory and reputation of Dr. Anderson, more recent findings have served to remove the stain from his character.

One of these charges is the serious matter of his having allegedly tampered with the Minute Book of Grand Lodge, which at one time had been entrusted to him for the purpose of extracting information to be incorporated into the second edition of his *Constitutions*. On this alleged tampering, W. J. Songhurst expressed himself rather severely, but J. E. S. Tuckett thinks there is good reason to believe that these alterations in the Minute Book may have been authorized.[2]

The second but less consequential matter that has reflected on the character of Dr. Anderson is his claim to the degree of D.D., previously believed to have been self-invested, as no record had been found to substantiate his claim. In fact, there had existed a good deal of general uncertainty and speculation concerning Dr. Anderson's entire career, his Masonic origin and connections, and other personal details of his life, until the appearance of an important and exhaustive paper by A. L. Miller, P.M. of the Lodge of Aberdeen, on 'The connection of Dr. James Anderson, of the "Constitutions", with Aberdeen and Aberdeen University',[3] in which certain newspaper accounts dated 1731 are shown to have now been found that support Dr. Anderson's right to the title.

[1] *AQC* xxxvi, 69.
[2] *AQC* xxxvi, 78.
[3] *AQC* xxxvi.

It is therefore thought not unreasonable to hope that other evidences may yet some time be found that will still further clear the character of this much-maligned man. Tuckett himself thinks that, all in all, the various charges against Anderson's character are 'not proven'.

The 'Overseers of the Work'

There is one further point with regard to these 'overseers of the work' that we have mentioned which is not frequently touched upon, but which illustrates a confusion in our traditions that is generally ignored but in which there appears to be some internal inconsistency and self-contradiction. Here we have to talk with a certain amount of circumspection, but the 'intelligent craftsman' will have no difficulty in giving it the proper meaning.

We are told, in one place, that at the building of King Solomon's Temple there were three Grand Masters under whose auspices the Temple was erected, and apparently the Lodge of Master Masons that is supposed to have existed at that time consisted of only these three and no more. In fact, it could not possibly have consisted of more than these three, if the Hiramic Legend as we now have it is to have any consistency. The 'word', which only these three are supposed to have known, would have been equally well known to the other Master Masons, had there been any others.

But now, what of these 'overseers of the work' that we have been talking about? Were they, too, not Master Masons? Anderson says that they were, and Webb confirms it. This is further corroborated when the newly-inducted Master Mason is now told of the tradition concerning the manner in which the Apron was worn at the building of the Temple, by each of the Three Grades of Mason—the Entered Apprentice, or 'bearer of burden'; the Fellow Craft, or 'hewer on the mountain and in the quarries'; and the Master, or 'overseer of the work'. Here, then, we have an obvious contradiction. Three Master Masons only, in one phase of the Legend; but 3303 (or 3603, depending upon which biblical version you take), in another. No attempt has ever been made, as far as I know, to reconcile this particular inconsistency. Nor can it ever be reconciled. We have here, apparently, two entirely separate and independent strands of tradition, originally disconnected and separately disseminated, and therefore not originally possessing any essential necessity for mutual consistency. And when the two strands were finally brought into one quasi-historical account, their inconsistency and self-contradiction was apparently never noticed; or, if noticed, was conveniently ignored.

There is one comment that can be made at this point, however, on the subject of traditions and inconsistencies, generally. A work of literary creation—a novel or a play, for example—can easily be made self-consistent if proper care is taken in choosing and marshalling the characters and events portrayed therein, these things being under the control of the creative writer. But a genuine Tradition, a Legend—when its initial letter thus deserves to be capitalized—does not come into being that way. It is not 'created' by the brain or the pen of any one person. It comes into being in some mysterious manner, we often don't know how, and there it is; self-created, apparently, and acknowledging no author or fabricator as its sire. It knows not its father and is, for once, proud of it. And when that Tradition or Legend begins to betray signs of self-contradiction— when such self-contradiction could easily have been forestalled by a skilful creator of tales—that very self-contradiction attests to the genuineness of the Tradition, and to the validity of the Legend. On the other hand, a so-called 'tradition' or 'legend' that is perfect in every detail, rounded out and coherent in all its aspects, becomes rightfully suspect because of this very perfection—tell-tale evidence of an obvious fabrication artificially created for a specific purpose.

There is one further point, in connection with these Legends and Traditions, especially as they appear in the *Old Charges*, and in so far as they are contradictory to historical or scriptural accounts. H. L. Haywood brings this point out in an article on 'The Legend of the Craft'. There were no histories or scholarly encyclopedias in the Middle Ages, he reminds us. A learned man would instead collect writings of any and every sort, and compile them into what was often called a 'Polychronicon'; that is, a miscellaneous collection of all sorts of information, including historical details of various eras. One of these 'Polychronicons' was the one by the Benedictine monk Ranulf Higden (*c.* 1300–1363 A.D.), previously mentioned; undoubtedly there were others. 'The author of the original version of the *Old Charges* drew his own data from such a *polychronicon*,' Haywood continues; 'we know this to be true because he told us so. This means that his paragraphs about Noah, Cain, Abel, Tubalcain, the Tower of Babel, David, Solomon, and the Temple [of Solomon], were copied not from the Bible, but from that *polychronicon*. This fact is all-important to a student of Freemasonry because it explains why . . . so many of the biblical elements in the Ritual are not found in the Bible itself. The biblical elements came into the Craft at second-hand and along a roundabout route, not directly. . . .'[1] Hence the many discrepancies between our Legend of the Craft and biblical history.

---

[1] H. L. Haywood, *Freemasonry and the Bible*, 1947, p. 15.

PART III
ARCHITECTURAL DETAILS

XII

SOME DETAILS OF THE TEMPLE

1. The Twin Pillars

HAVING TO some extent disposed of the circumstances surrounding the building of King Solomon's Temple, and the Builders themselves (except in the case of one prominent one, who will be left for special consideration in our concluding chapters), we can now devote some time to the architectural and ornamental features of the Temple itself, as they make their appearance both in Masonic tradition and the biblical account, embellished, as before, with rabbinic legend and exposition, and with present-day biblical commentary and criticism. Here, again, we will note some corroboration, and some discrepancies between Masonic tradition and the Scriptures, and even some inconsistency between several Books of the Bible themselves, and between various versions and translations; also some anachronisms and improbabilities, all of which we will here at least endeavour to understand, even when we are unable to justify.

Our first purely architectural reference to the details of the Temple will be to the Twin Pillars in the Porch, certainly our most prominent present-day relic of the Temple.

The Pillars in our Lodge Rooms

These Twin Pillars are now, as they have been for a long time, familiar features in many Lodge Rooms, but their use is not uniform, either in this country or elsewhere. Oliver, in the preceding century, wrote, relative to English practice, of 'the two pillars which are usually disposed in front of the Master's chair'.[1] But in the present century, writes the late J. R. Dashwood, 'every Lodge seems to do something different! Some have the Pillars on either side of the Master's Chair, some at the entrance, some have them on the front of the Master's Pedestal.' (Thus, two Pillars, marked J and B, can be seen on both sides of the Master's Pedestal in Shakespeare

[1] Geo. Oliver, *Historical Landmarks*, ii., 204.

Lodge No. 426, Spilsby).[1] 'Bristol has them in front of the Senior Warden. ... In the majority of cases they are not represented at all!'[2]

Bernard E. Jones similarly speaks of some Lodges in England 'which perpetuate the old style by still having pillars standing on the floor', and we still 'find the large pillars in some old lodges at Exeter, Newton Abbot, Gloucester, Cardiff, Penarth, etc., [and] in the Danish lodges, and even in a lodge at Ottawa, Canada. In the last of these there is a central altar, between which and the Senior Warden's chair in the south [sic] are two tall wooden pillars right out on the floor.'[3] This last detail is of particular interest (if 'south' is not an error for 'west', and if 'Senior' is not an error for 'Junior'). In George Washington's old Lodge at Alexandria, Virginia—as can still be seen in the full-size replica of the Lodge Room preserved in the Museum of the George Washington Masonic Memorial in that city—the Two Pillars are found on both sides of the Junior Warden's Pedestal in the South; in memory, perhaps, of our first J.G.W. (according to one version of the Legend) who originally fashioned them.

'The earliest descriptions of the lay-out of the lodge in the 1700's,' says Harry Carr, the present-day Secretary and Editor of Quatuor Coronati, and still speaking of the practice in England, 'show both Wardens seated in the west, facing the Master. The two pillars are generally near them, forming a kind of portal, so that the candidates passed between them on their admission, a custom which exists in many lodges to this day.'[4]

This use of the Two Pillars is also common in the United States, where they are generally placed in the North-west entrance, for the same purpose, but in Bristol, today, they are found in front of the Senior Warden's station in the West, somewhat comparable to their position in the England of the 1700's. An example of the Pillars in precisely this position, in front of the Senior Warden's station, is shown in the illustration of the present-day English Lodge Room, in Royal Cumberland Lodge, No. 41, Bath. They are of brass,

---

[1] *AQC* x, 44.
[2] From a private letter. J. R. Dashwood was, until his death a few years ago, Secretary of Quatuor Coronati Lodge No. 2076, London, and Editor of its Transactions.
[3] Bernard E. Jones, *The Freemason's Guide and Compendium*, p. 357.
[4] H. Carr, 'Pillars and Globes, Columns and Candlesticks', *AQC* lxxv, 206.

stand 5 ft. 9 inches in height, and are said to date from the late eighteenth century.[1]

In the middle of the eighteenth century, the Two Pillars seem to have been physically represented, in England, by the small Senior and Junior Wardens' Columns, set apparently on their respective pedestals. The publication *Jachin and Boaz* (1762) has the following foot-note in explanation:

> The senior and junior wardens' columns are about twenty-five inches long, and represent the columns that support the porch of Solomon's temple; the senior's is called JACHIN, and signifies strength, the junior's BOAZ, and signifies to establish in the Lord. See the first book of Kings, chap. vii.

Curiously enough, the very similar publication *The Three Distinct Knocks* (1768, first published in 1760), carries an almost identical statement, except that it is the Senior's Pillar that is called Boaz, signifying Strength, while the Junior's is called Jachin, signifying 'to establish'.[2] The reason for the reversal may be appreciated when we remember one of the prime contentions between the Grand Lodge of the Antients versus that of the Moderns.

In America, and undoubtedly elsewhere as well, these small columns now stand on the Senior and Junior Wardens' pedestals, merely as symbols of their respective stations, and their previous eighteenth-century connection with the Pillars Jachin and Boaz is completely forgotten.

The Pillars in Solomon's Porch

Architecturally and Masonically speaking, the most important feature of King Solomon's Temple was without doubt this pair of Pillars in the Porch. The amount of space devoted to a minute description of these Pillars in the Bible also is a fair indication of their previous religious importance.

These Pillars are believed by a few students (e.g., Fergusson, in Smith's *Dictionary of the Bible*) to have been structural members, with an entablature supporting the roof; or, as in another attempt by Fergusson, as supporting a transverse pair of screens.[3] Most commentators, however—lay, clerical, and Masonic—accept them to

---

[1] *Op. cit.*, 207.

[2] H. Carr, *op. cit.*, p. 206.

[3] James Fergusson, F.R.S., *The Temples of the Jews*. London, 1878. Fergusson devotes a considerable amount of space in this work to discussing his own

have been free-standing columns, and purely ornamental, or emblematic, just as they are depicted on our Tracing Boards, or represented in furniture in our Lodge Rooms. Dr. Immanuel Benzinger, for example, writing in Cheyne and Black's *Encyclopedia Biblica* (article 'Temple'), gives satisfactory reasons for the general belief that they were free-standing, and were symbolical in character; being, in fact, 'symbols of the deity'. And 'an almost overwhelming body of opinion', similarly, says Professor W. F. Stinespring, 'favors the free-standing hypothesis'.[1] As against this wide non-Masonic support of the Masonic tradition, it is curious to note Mackey's defence of the Fergussonian hypothesis to the effect that the Two Pillars were not free-standing but supported the roof.[2]

These Pillars of Solomon may perhaps have been set up more specifically in imitation of the Obelisks that have been found at the gateways to Egyptian Temples—the pair of Obelisks at the entrance to the Temple at Karnak being very impressive in this connection.[3] Or, perhaps, they may have been copied from Tyre, the home of the workman who wrought them, and where Herodotus some time later reported to have seen two similar pillars standing before the Temple of Hercules—'one of pure gold, the other of emerald', as has previously been mentioned. But, whether copied from one or the other, the wide prevalence of Twin Pillars of one form or another, in the ecclesiastical architecture of the Mid-East of the period, has been commented upon by many writers; e.g., R. B. Y. Scott of the United Theological College of Montreal, who writes on 'The Pillars Jachin and Boaz' in the *Journal of Biblical Literature*.[4] He mentions particularly two such pillars found at the entrance to the temple at Byblos (later known as Gebal, as we have already noted; the home of the Gibblites, the 'stone-squarers' of King Solomon's Temple).

In Syria, excavations of the Oriental Institute of the University of Chicago at Tell Tainat 'have uncovered the small chapel of the

---

conception of the construction and appearance of these remarkable columns, but a detailed account of his views is beyond our present scope. See, however, pp. 33–34 and 156–159 in the work cited.

[1] *The Interpreter's Dictionary of the Bible*, 1962, vol. R–Z, p. 541.

[2] Mackey, *Encyclopedia of Freemasonry*, ii, 779.

[3] See the photographs in Adams, *Ancient Records and the Bible*, p. 96.

[4] *Op. cit.*, vol. 58, pp. 143–149. See also his article 'Jachin and Boaz' in *The Interpreter's Dictionary of the Bible*, vol. E–J.

eighth century kings of that city', as we have had occasion to note.[1] The illustration previously seen clearly shows two pillars in the porch of the Syrian temple, standing free, and apparently purely ornamental or symbolical, rather than architecturally functional. 'There is now adequate evidence', says Dr. G. Ernest Wright, 'that this type of construction was quite common in Phoenicia.'[2]

As to the Egyptian Obelisks, the best known is perhaps the pair that Tethmosis III is said to have erected at Heliopolis (City of the Sun), in the fifteenth century B.C., and which Augustus Caesar later removed to the Caesareum at Alexandria, one of them now adorning the Thames Embankment in London, and the other— both are commonly referred to as 'Cleopatra's Needle'—in Central Park, New York.

That the Twin Pillars of King Solomon must have had some interest for the operative Masons of the Middle Ages is perhaps indicated by the two pillars that Benjamin of Tudela is reported to have seen in the twelfth century, in the Church of S. Giovanni a Porta Latina in Rome, each with the name 'Solomon, son of David' engraved upon it (Brett). There is also the more recently seen two pillars originally set up in the façade of the eleventh century Wurtzburg Cathedral (later found inside the building, flanking a Gothic doorway leading to a small vaulted chamber, perhaps in allusion to Solomon's Porch). These were erected, Lionel Vibert thought, by some Comacine builder, and perhaps intended as a piece of symbolism. Perhaps also, he says further, as an afterthought, it may even have had something to do with their passwords. Incidentally, the names of these pillars were here found inscribed, according to the late R. J. Meekren, as IAC HION and BOO Z, each in two separated syllables;[3] and it is similarly given with an 'I' in place of a 'J' in a Catechism of 1724, *The Grand Mystery*.[4]

The Twin Pillars in the Bible

The biblical description of the Solomonic Pillars, according to the version in *Chronicles*, is as follows:

[1] See *ante*, p. 83.
[2] G. Ernest Wright, 'Solomon's Temple Resurrected'. *The Biblical Archaeologist*, May 1941.
[3] *AQC* lxvi, 102.
[4] *Early Masonic Catechisms*, p. 72. The now anglicized 'J' is universally represented in Hebrew by the sound 'Y'; e.g., Jerusalem—*Yerushalayim*.

And Huram finished [!] the work that he was to make for King Solomon for the house of God;

To wit, the two pillars, and the pommels, and the chapiters which were on the top of the two pillars, and the two wreaths to cover the two pommels of the chapiters which were on the top of the pillars;

And four hundred pomegranates on the two wreaths; two rows of pomegranates on each wreath, to cover the two pommels of the chapiters which were upon the pillars. . . .

In the plain of Jordan did the king cast them, in the clay ground between Succoth and Zeredathah.

—II Chron. 4:11–17.

Also he made before the house two pillars of thirty and five cubits high, and the chapiter that was on the top of each of them was five cubits.

And he made chains, as in the oracle, and put them on the heads of the pillars; and made an hundred pomegranates, and put them on the chains.

And he reared up the pillars before the temple, one on the right hand, and the other on the left; and called the name of that on the right hand Jachin, and the name of that on the left Boaz.

—II Chron. 3:15–17.

But in the much earlier account of *Kings* it is said, partly:

For he cast two pillars of brass, of eighteen cubits high apiece: and a line of twelve cubits did compass either of them about. . . .

And nets of checker work, and wreaths of chain work, for the chapiters which were upon the top of the pillars; seven for the one chapiter, and seven for the other chapiter. . . .

And the chapiters that were upon the top of the pillars were of lily work in the porch, four cubits.

And the chapiters upon the two pillars had pomegranates also above, over against the belly which was by the network: and the pomegranates were two hundred in rows round about upon the other chapiter.

—I Kings 7:15–20.

The height of the one pillar was eighteen cubits, and the

chapter upon it was brass: and the height of the chapiter three
cubits. . . .

—*II Kings* 25:17.

As to this brass-work, Gordon Hills reminds us, in his excellent
discussion of Rodk. H. Baxter's paper on 'The Architectural Style
of King Solomon's Temple', that, in the words of James Fergusson:

this was the bronze age of architecture. Homer tells us of the
brazen house of Alcinous. The treasuries at Mycenae were
covered internally with brazen plates, and in Etruscan tombs of
this age, metal was far more essentially the material of decoration
than carving in stone, or any other of the modes so frequently
adopted. The altar of the Temple was of brass, and the molten
sea supported by twelve brazen oxen. The bases, the lavers, and
all the objects and implements in metal work were in reality what
made the Temple so celebrated. . . .[1]

The location of the Pillars

There has been a good deal of speculation among Masonic and non-
Masonic commentators alike, as to whether the designation of the
Pillars as 'right' and 'left' is from the viewpoint of a person entering
or leaving the Temple. But the question is generally clouded by a
presupposition, and this has frequently precluded any clear thinking
on the subject.

The presupposition in question is in connection with the subsidiary question of Orientation (which will be more fully discussed
under its own heading). Thus, on the presupposition that the Temple
entrance faced East—for which, it is true, there are good but not
incontrovertible arguments—many commentators have come to the
conclusion that the Pillars in the Porch were situated in the position
shown in the accompanying diagram (Fig. 4).

Such an arrangement is arrived at on the basis of equating the
word 'right' with the geographical position 'south', and 'left' with
'north'. For this, also, there are good and sufficient reasons. 'It is
well known,' says Joseph Young, 'that in ancient times, the Hebrews
referred to what we term the four cardinal points of the compass,
from the position of a man looking towards the rising sun. . . . So
that when speaking locally, it is evident that the Right hand and

[1] Cited in *AQC* xxxiii, 126–127.

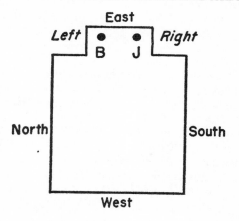

The Pillars in the Porch
Fig. 4

the South are synonymous terms.'[1] This view of the Cardinal Points is borne out by the *Encyclopedia Biblica*, which states that 'east was called "the front"; the west, "the back part"; the south, "the right"; and the north, "the left".'[2] It is, again, confirmed by Dr. Kaufman in the *Jewish Encyclopedia*.[3]

On the basis of the above view, the position of the Two Pillars in the above diagram must be assumed to be, in the biblical description, from the standpoint of the worshipper *leaving* the Temple, and approaching the Pillars from the inside.

But this attempted solution of the problem, in my opinion, is highly artificial. The first view of a building is always from the outside, not the inside. Consequently, any *first* description of a building or of any of its external features (as these Pillars must be assumed to be), must similarly be assumed to be from the standpoint of an observer approaching or viewing the building for the first time, and this must necessarily be from the outside. Therefore, any discussion of these Two Pillars from the standpoint of a worshipper *leaving* the Temple is unrealistic, for, before he can leave it, he must first have entered it.

[1] Jos. Young, 'The Temples of Solomon', *British Masonic Miscellany*, ix, 54.
[2] *Enc. Bib.*, s.v. 'Earth (Four Quarters)'.
[3] *Jew. Enc.*, s.v. 'East'.

A curious contradiction in this respect occurs in the Iowa *Companion to the Monitor*, previously mentioned (not to be confused with the *Official Iowa Monitor*). Here the author tells us, speaking of these Two Pillars, that, 'looking out from the Temple toward the east, the one called Jachin was on the right or south side and represented the pillar of cloud; the one called Boaz was on the left or north side and represented the pillar of fire.' This would therefore be seen to conform to our Fig. 4. But the statement is contradicted by the following, in the same work:

> In our journey from the quarries to the Middle Chamber, we are now within the precincts of the Temple, and before us is the beautiful arched gateway which leads to the inner court. Passing through this gateway, we come to the porch and the entrance of the Temple, where you observe two brazen pillars, one on the right hand, the other on the left, called Jachin and Boaz.

This can now no longer be seen to conform to the diagram in Fig. 4, where the Temple is made to face East, as in the customarily accepted orientation. But the description of the imaginary journey does conform to the diagram in Fig. 5, where, however, the two pillars are now found to be in a reversed position as compared to their location (by name) in Fig. 4. But to bring this about, we had to make the Temple face *West*.

On the other hand, Thos. N. Cranstoun-Day, writing specifically on 'The Two Great Pillars', favours the arrangement as in Fig. 4, but his basic assumption is found to be incorrect. 'All versions [of the Bible]', he says, 'agree that the pillars were set up in those positions on the right and left of the porch, or vestibule, *which faced the east.* . . .'[1] [italics added]. In this, as regards the portion italicized, he is incorrect. *None* of the biblical descriptions of the Temple unequivocally show it to be facing east (except Ezekiel's visionary or idealized temple; see below, the section on Orientation). Furthermore, the example the author of the article gives—comparing the Temple with a ship at sea, where 'starboard' (right) and 'port' (left) conform to the position of an observer standing on deck and looking towards the bows—is again highly artificial, when compared to the situation on land. The two examples, in fact, are incompatible, and not to be compared with one another, and no conclusions ought to be drawn from such an unnatural analogy. A ship at sea is a

[1] *AQC* lxxviii, 230.

self-contained entity, with all its personnel being normally on board; whereas an edifice on land can only be seen *in toto* from the outside. It has in fact been frequently pointed out by biblical commentators that the Temple of Solomon (particularly because of its small size) was never designed to contain numerous worshippers, but only the comparatively few officiating priests; the worshippers themselves being expected to congregate in the Temple Court, from whence they would only be able to see the Pillars from the outside.

Both these considerations impel one strongly to the view that

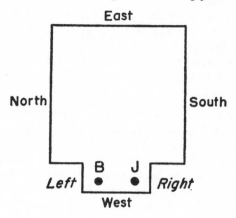

The Pillars in the Porch
Fig. 5

the biblical description of the location of the Two Pillars by name is from the standpoint of an external, not an internal, observer; and 'right' and 'left' must consequently be taken to refer to an observer facing the Entrance or Porch of the Temple as in the accompanying diagram (Fig. 5). But this necessarily makes the Temple face West, not East, as has been indicated—a situation not entirely impossible, as we shall soon see.

But Norman Rogers does not agree with this. 'There is no other position possible than to view the pillars from inside the porch.'[1] This, in a sense, is quite true, but only on the presupposition that the Temple faced East. But it becomes no longer true when we

[1] *AQC* lxviii, 85.

approach the problem free from any such presupposition. Here, in Fig. 5, we in fact see the possibility which Norman Rogers denies, and without actually negating any of the indications given in the Bible—once we admit the theoretical possibility that the Temple may have faced West, which, in fact, the Bible never explicitly denies. For this, see the section on 'Orientation', below.

An interesting illustration of the correct approach to this question, as suggested here, is afforded us in the current novel *Solomon and Sheba*, by Jay Williams (New York, 1959), all the more interesting because it is 'natural', unbiased, and presumably without prepossessions of any kind whatsoever, ecclesiastical, Masonic, or otherwise. In describing the Dedication of the Temple, and of the proceedings leading up to the Dedication ceremony, the author says:

'And thus, at last, they came into the forecourt of the Temple, and up to the doors of the House of God.

'At the portals stood two columns, made by Huram-abi, of cast bronze six times the height of a man from their bases to their great capitals, decorated with lilies and with pomegranates. That upon the right was called Jachin, that on the left was named Boaz. . . .'[1] This clearly conforms to our Fig. 5, not Fig. 4.

Josephus clarifies the situation sufficiently well when he amplifies the biblical description by saying:

'The one of these pillars he set at the entrance of the porch on the right hand, and called it *Jachin*; and the other at the left hand, and called it *Booz*.'[2]

The addition of the one word 'entrance' would seem to put the matter beyond doubt. One normally 'enters' a porch for the first time from the outside. Here, again, Fig. 5 is indicated.

We similarly find the learned Dr. John Lightfoot, writing in 1684 on 'A Prospect of the Temple', describing the location of the Two Pillars thus: '. . . on your right hand and on your left, as soon as ever you were stepped within the Porch,' presumably coming in from the outside.[3] In our own time, comparatively, Dr. Mackey has supported this view of Lightfoot's, and on the same basis, when he speaks of Jachin and Boaz (in that order), as being, one of them, 'on the right, and the other on the left, as soon as the visitor stepped

---

[1] Jay Williams, *Solomon and Sheba*, pp. 67, 68.
[2] Josephus, *Antiquities*, Bk. VIII, ch. iii, 4, p. 245.
[3] *The Works of the Reverend and Learned John Lightfoot, D.D.* Vol. i, London, 1684, p. 1076.

within the porch.'[1] Here, again—if one may be permitted to be-
labour the point once more—a visitor first steps within a porch
from the outside, before he can step into it again, from the inside,
when going out.

It is quite possible, of course, that each of these writers—from
Josephus to Mackey—who seem to favour this 'approach from the
outside' principle, in fixing the position of Jachin and Boaz, respectively, would be shocked to find that this at the same time neces-
sitates seeing the Porch as facing West, not East; but there it is,
and 'figures' don't lie.

It will be noticed that the position of each of the Pillars, in Fig. 5,
is reversed with respect to the Temple itself, as compared to Fig. 4,
while still retaining 'right' and 'left' as in the biblical description.
Interestingly enough, this Fig. 5 is precisely the position of the
Two Pillars in many Masonic Lodge Rooms today, when they are
situated at the North-west entrance, on the way to the Masonic East.

As if to cinch the matter, Masonically, we find, in *The Grand
Mystery of Free-Masons Discover'd*, a Catechism dated 1724, once
before alluded to, the following Question and Answer:

Q. in what Part of the Temple was the [first] Lodge kept?
A. In Solomon's Porch at the West-End of the Temple,
where the two Pillars were set up.

There is, also, one curious allusion in Josephus which has
apparently not been sufficiently well understood,[2] and which has a
direct bearing on this problem. After describing the setting up of
the Two Pillars by 'an artificer out of Tyre, whose name was
Hiram', Josephus goes on to describe the construction and location
of the ten lavers, by saying:

and he set five of the lavers on the left side of the temple, which was
that side towards the north wind, and as many on the right side,
towards the south, but looking towards the east.[3]

---

[1] Mackey, *Lexicon of Freemasonry*, p. 356. The current *Encylcopedia of Freemasonry*, also by Mackey, but revised by Clegg, cites Lightfoot as in the *Lexicon*,
but omits the important corroborating opinion of Mackey himself. *S.v.* 'Pillars
of the Porch'.

Mackey's earlier *Lexicon* devotes seven pages to an exhaustive discussion of
this important subject. His revised *Encyclopedia* is only about half as long.
[2] Cf. Bernard E. Jones, *Freemasons' Guide and Compendium*, p. 358.
[3] Josephus, *Antiquities*, Bk. VIII, ch. 3, 6, p. 246.

Now, the laver, says Mackey, is 'a large brazen vessel for washing placed in the court of the Jewish tabernacle, where the officiating priest cleansed his hands and feet, and as well the entrails of victims'.[1] To be effective for this purpose, it must consequently have been located in front of the Temple; it could not possibly have been in the back. But such an arrangement, to conform to the Josephian statement, is only possible in Fig. 5; it is physically impossible in Fig. 4—unless one would be viewing the Temple *from behind*, for which there is no earthly reason.

But Whiston, in a footnote, in attempting to clarify this description of Josephus, succeeds only in confusing the language when he says that 'by the right hand he (Josephus) means what is against our left, when we suppose ourselves going up from the east gate of the courts towards the tabernacle or temple themselves, and so vice versa; . . .'

And there is, finally, the biblical description in *II Chronicles* ch. 3 of the setting up of the Two Pillars:

The Temple has now been finished, and a description has been given of all its internal arrangements, its accessories and appurtenances; its dimensions are also given, as of a finished edifice; the 'most holy house', the Holy of Holies, is described, with its cherubims, and the vails. Then, *and only then*, at the very end of the chapter, does the Chronicler come to the Two Pillars:

And he reared up the pillars before the temple, one on the right hand, and the other on the left; and called the name of that on the right hand Ja-chin, and the name of that on the left Boaz.

Can it now be doubted that this *rearing up* was done from the outside of a finished Temple, and that the terms 'right' and 'left' can only be considered from that standpoint?[2]

18 or *35* cubits?

These two Pillars we have been discussing are interesting to us not only 'for their intrinsic value', in connection with our Lectures, but particularly so because of certain confusions, discrepancies, and anachronisms that are associated with them, in the attempted resolution of which we manage to come in contact with a rich literature

[1] Mackey, *Encyclopedia*, s.v. LAVER, BRAZEN.
[2] For an opposite viewpoint, however, see J. E. S. Tuckett, 'The Left Hand Pillar', in *Miscellanea Latomorum*, vol. X, May 1926, pp. 129–132.

on the subject, some of which, in fact, we have already had occasion to examine.

Several sets of discrepancies—or apparent discrepancies—with respect to the Pillars are to be noticed at the outset in the biblical account itself. The first of these is in regard to their height, which is given as 18 cubits in *Kings*, and 35 cubits in *Chronicles*.

The length of a cubit in this instance is generally taken to be a foot and a half, but the exact figure is immaterial to our present discussion. It may be noted, however, that there were, in fact, a number of different 'cubits' used at different times and for different kinds of measurement.[1] Canon J. W. Horsley uses the ratio 5 cubits equals 6 ft., which he claims to be in accordance with 'comparatively recent discoveries as to the origin and value of the systems of measurement adopted by Solomon'.[2] And the Rev. W. Shaw Caldecott devotes a chapter to the discussion in his *Solomon's Temple*, making the 'building cubit' equivalent to $1\frac{1}{5}$ ft., or 14.4 ins. The more recent *Interpreter's Dictionary of the Bible* (1962) thinks it was the 'royal cubit' that was used in the building of the Temple, and makes this equivalent to 20.9 ins.[3]

Confining our discussion, now, to the pillars in terms of the cubit itself, whatever its equivalent in our present system of measurement may be, we find that our Masonic lectures, here and abroad, have varied in their fidelity to either of the two accounts in the Bible relative to the height of the Pillars, some using the 35 cubit figure, and some, 18. This is true even as between the various Jurisdictions in the United States, as we shall soon see. The practice in England, also, has varied. *Henderson's MS.*, which purports to refer to a working as of Preston's time (late eighteenth and early nineteenth centuries), gives 18 cubits, but some of the other contemporary English workings—Finch's *Masonic Treatise*, and Browne's *Masonic Master-Key*— give 35. Present-day *Emulation* working, on the other hand, follows Preston (almost), while Preston's American contemporary, Webb, does not, if we are to judge from 'Barney's Notes', said to be a record, in single-letter cypher, of the original Webb work.

Much fruitless ingenuity has been expended by both Masonic and non-Masonic writers in trying to account for this obvious discrepancy in the biblical account, and it is curious to observe the twist-

[1] *Jew. Enc.*, s.v. 'Weights and Measures: The Cubit', xii, 483.
[2] *AQC* xxi, 6.
[3] *Interpreter's Dic. of the Bible*, vol. R–Z, p. 535.

ings and turnings of the commentators as they try this way and that to reconcile the irreconcilable. Others, on the other hand—like Clarke's *Commentary*, and *The Interpreter's Bible*—finding the problem perhaps insoluble, in fact, have ignored the discrepancy altogether, preferring to look the other way.

The question of the actual height of these Pillars has been generally held by Masonic writers to be of antiquarian interest only— as if to say, 'so what?'—but in 1903 the Grand Lodge of Iowa boldly set about making an investigation as to the relative accuracy of the two accounts in this respect, J. W. Barry being appointed to look into the matter. His report is accordingly given at some length —but perhaps with more heat than light—in the Grand Lodge Proceedings for the year 1904 (pp. 168–194). His conclusion, to the effect that all architectural writers without exception who have investigated the subject, so far as he could learn, subscribe to a height of 18 cubits, is probably beyond question, but the manner in which he attempts to bolster the argument from his own findings of archaeological and architectural evidence is open to criticism. This is especially so in his attempted exposition to the effect that these Pillars were in reality structural members supporting an entablature, and not merely free-standing decorative or emblematical columns as is now generally accepted.

Barry's most constructive contribution to the discussion, however, is the poll which he took of the various American Jurisdictions (and one Canadian) with respect to the question of Masonic usage in their own area, only four Jurisdictions not deigning to reply, for reasons of their own. Of the forty-four who did, fourteen (including one from 'Indian Territory', now part of the Grand Lodge of Oklahoma), stated that they used the 18 cubit figure, while 27 used 35; one, curiously enough, used 30.[1] Four Jurisdictions indicated that the height was either not given or not regulated in their Lectures, while one declined giving any information on the grounds of an alleged impropriety. It is interesting to note that—as a result,

[1] This unusual figure for the height of the Pillar is also found in the discussion of Canon Horsley on the subject, apparently on the authority of a then-recently published work by the Rev. W. Shaw Caldecott on Solomon's Temple, which has been drawn upon on occasion in the present work. Cf. J. W. Horsley, 'New light on the Old Pillars which stood in front of the Porch of Solomon's Temple', *AQC* xxi, 6.

On the whole, Canon Horsley's paper is a particularly unsatisfactory study of the Two Pillars, and the 'new light' is but little better than the old.

no doubt, of this investigation—Barry's own Jurisdiction of Iowa, which at the time had been using the 35 cubit figure, later changed its monitorial instruction to 18. But in its Proceedings for 1904, (p. 169), it is explained that 18 was the height of one pillar; 35, the height of the two combined, without further elucidation.

Attempted Explanations

The most ingenious (or apparently so) of the attempted solutions of the discrepancy between *Kings* and *Chronicles* is this 'explanation' —made by biblical scholars also—that in one case the height of only one pillar is given; in the other case, the height of the two pillars is taken together (making, however, thirty-*six* cubits). To take up the slack, a subsidiary 'explanation' is then attempted. Both Irish and *Emulation* working in England cut the Gordian Knot by giving the height of each pillar as $17\frac{1}{2}$ cubits, making 35 for the two combined. This would appear to follow a suggestion thrown out by a marginal note in the Geneva Bible (first printed in 1560) which has this to say, relative to the height of the Pillars:

> Euery one was eighteene cubits long, but the halfe cubite could not be seene, for it was hid in the roundnesse of the chapiter, and therefore he giueth to euery one but 17 and a halfe.

It was apparently in accordance with this theory that Dr. Dodd, in his Commentary on the Bible (1765) expressed the view that the given height of 35 cubits referred 'to the height of both of them together, . . .'[1] and this is the view that Dr. Mackey appears to favour, following, no doubt, his mentor Dr. Oliver.[2] The Commentary to *Chronicles*, by Dr. I. W. Slotki (London, 1952), similarly states that 'Jewish commentators explain that the two pillars were cast in one piece having a length of thirty-five cubits'—as if the difficulty of casting them in two lengths of $17\frac{1}{2}$ cubits each (about 27 feet), four inches thick, and six feet in diameter, were not enough! 'Then it was cut in two,' Dr. Slotki goes on to say, 'and each pillar supplied with an attachment on top, half a cubit in width, to hold the *capital* which adorned it. In this', say the commentators, 'the two verses are harmonized.' [!]

[1] *AQC* xxi, 11.
[2] Cf. Oliver, *The Book of the Lodge*, vol. i, of the Universal Masonic Library; Lodgeton, Kentucky, 1856, p. 92. And Mackey, *Encyclopedia of Freemasonry*, ii, 779–780. But why the Two Pillars have to be taken 'combined', no one has yet been able to explain.

As against such a hypothesis, however, Cook's *Commentary* expresses the view that 'the height of 35 cubits . . . is not to be accounted for by any theory of duplication, . . .' a theory that must especially be discounted when we consider the Greek Septuagint version of Jeremiah 52:21. Here, in fact, we find the unequivocal statement: 'And as for the pillars, the height of one pillar was thirty-five cubits, . . .' which clearly refers to each of the pillars separately, as they might have been seen in Jeremiah's time, lying on the ground, after the destruction of the Temple by Nebuchadnezzar; and not the two pillars combined, as they might possibly (but not probably) have been seen at the time of their casting.

But the most telling argument against this theory of duplication, it seems to me, is the very phrasing of the biblical statement itself. 'Also he made before the house,' it says, 'two pillars of thirty and five cubits high.' *Before the house*, where the Two Pillars stood as separate entities; not 'in the plain of Jordan', as the biblical account could easily have said, where the Two Pillars might conceivably have been thought to have been cast in a single piece, before being cut apart.

The 'explanation' attempted by Fergusson in Smith's *Dictionary of the Bible* (1893) is even more curious. 'The apparent discrepancies (18 and 35 cubits high),' he says, 'arise from including or excluding the ornament which united the shaft to the chapiter, etc.' but the argument fails to harmonize itself, leaving 8 cubits to be accounted for, in the figure given in *Kings*. Here Cook's *Commentary* makes the suggestion that, if we could imagine the Pillar to have a stone pedestal of 8 cubits, this would satisfactorily save the situation. But a pedestal of any size whatever is not called for in the biblical description.

An explanation of somewhat similar import appears to have been taken up a few years after Fergusson's, in the work on Solomon's Temple by the Rev. W. Shaw Caldecott, previously mentioned. Caldecott also starts out with a Pillar of 18 cubits in height, but adds to it a base of 3 cubits, a capital of 5 cubits, and a 'supra-capital' of 4 cubits, or a total of 30 cubits in all—still leaving ten to be accounted for, to harmonize *Kings* with *Chronicles*. Later, in a Table of Measurements of the Two Pillars, he mentions in addition the 'Height, including steps, bases and capitals' as being 35 cubits, in accordance with *II Chron.* 3:15—but the latter verse, as a matter of fact, says nothing whatever relative to the imaginary 'steps' and 'bases'; and the combined height of column and capital, in *Chronicles*, is actually 40 cubits, not 35.

Caldecott makes a valiant attempt to show that, as a matter of fact, 'there would seem to be no incongruity between the two accounts [of *Kings* and *Chronicles*]; rather, they are supplementary to one another,' but his proposed reconciliation appears to me to be far from convincing.[1]

As against this Caldecott denial—and others of a like nature—that there is any discrepancy whatever, the Variorum Teacher's Bible, we are told, has a note to the effect that the reading in *Chronicles* 'is corrupt translation'.[2]

This perhaps may have to do with such an explanation as that which Cook appears to favour most—supported by a few biblical scholars he mentions—to the effect that there has actually been a corruption in the numbers given in the two passages in question, brought about by the resemblance between the Hebrew characters for 18 and 35. These are, he points out, *yod hé* and *lamed hé*, respectively. A badly written *yod*—or, let us say, a *yod* that had been disfigured by time—could, in manuscript, be conceivably mistaken for a *lamed*; a partly obliterated *lamed* could still more easily be mistaken for a *yod*. This, perhaps, is the explanation for the Septuagint rendering of *Jer.* 52:21 as 'thirty-five', when the A.V., the R.S.V., and the English translation of the Masoretic Text give the same word in *Jeremiah* as 'eighteen cubits' for the height of each Pillar. Curtis, on the other hand, does not think this could be the right explanation,[3] 'because we have no evidence of the use of such signs in ancient Hebrew' as Cook refers to—but, then, how else can we explain the 'thirty-five' in the Septuagint of *Jeremiah*?

The second discrepancy to be noted, in the description of the Pillars, but this time a minor one, is in regard to the height of the chapiters on top of the pillars, given in *II Kings* 25:17 as three cubits, while five cubits is given in both *I Kings* and *II Chronicles*. Here we apparently have to do merely with a copyist's error. Ignoring this, Masonic accounts have invariably used the five cubit figure. In the work of the Rev. Caldecott's, previously mentioned, this 'chapiter of three cubits' is thought to be actually a base at

---

[1] Caldecott, *Solomon's Temple*, pp. 244, 346. These arguments of Caldecott's have also been cited in *AQC* xxi, 10.

[2] *AQC* lxxviii, 230.

[3] *International Critical Commentary on Chronicles*, p. 328.

bottom, rather than a chapiter at top, but Wm. Wonnacott thought that 'the argument for this is weak, almost puerile'—a conclusion with which we can heartily concur. As against this, the German archaeologist Jahn thought the apparent discrepancy could possibly be due to a diminution in height brought about by some repair to the Temple at some time (*Upham's Trans.*, 1827), but here again there appear to be some cogent reasons against such a supposition.[1] Dr. John Lightfoot, whose 'Prospect of the Temple' has already been drawn upon, thought that the 'three cubits' of the Chapiter is 'well answered by the Jews, that the lowest two cubits of the Chapiter were plain, and without any graving or imbroidering', and so were not reckoned as part of the 'imbroidered' Chapiter proper,[2] but more modern commentators, as stated, simply ascribe the 'three cubits' to an error in copying.

The Pomegranates

Still another point to be considered is in regard to the number of pomegranates on the chapiters or capitals of the Pillars—these important decorations being 'emblems of fertility', according to a commentator in *The Interpreter's Bible*, 'because of the extraordinary number of pips which they contain'.

II Chronicles gives two wreaths on each chapiter, and two rows of pomegranates on each wreath, with apparently two hundred pomegranates in each row, or four hundred on each Pillar. But the same Book of the Bible, in an earlier chapter, speaks of 'chains', with a hundred pomegranates on each chain. This would require two chains in each row, to make it agree with the above.

The *Emulation* and Irish Lectures give 'two rows of Pomegranates on each Chapiter, one hundred in a row', or two hundred on each Pillar, which is exactly one-half of the quantity given in *II Chronicles*. Perhaps for this reason, the Scotch Lectures specify only the number of pomegranates per row, but leave the number of rows unspecified. This little detail, specifying the precise number of pomegranates, has not been carried over into the Webb Lectures.

Were the Pillars 'hollow'?

The Masonic tradition that the Two Pillars were 'made hollow' is a further departure from *Kings* and *Chronicles* in practically all the

[1] Samuel Lawrence, P.G.M., *Practical Masonic Lectures*. Atlanta, Ga., 1874.
[2] Lightfoot, Collected *Works*, etc., p. 1074.

versions of the Bible. The Revised Standard Version, and Moffatt's Translation, have the description: 'It was hollow, and its thickness was four fingers,'[1] but this detail is omitted in the King James Authorized Version, in the Greek Septuagint, in the Roman Catholic Douay Version, and the Hebrew Masoretic Text. *The Interpreter's Bible* gives both the A.V. and the R.S.V., side by side, one with the 'hollow' and the other without, but offers no comment on the difference.

While not following, generally, the version in *Kings* and *Chronicles*, the Masonic tradition is in harmony with the account in *Jeremiah* in this matter of the hollow Pillars, ostensibly describing the Pillars as they might have been seen at the time of Nebuchadnezzar's destruction of the Temple, perhaps with the Pillars lying despoiled on the ground (*Jer.* 52:21). So it is, at least, in all the better-known translations of *Jeremiah* except the Greek Septuagint, which leaves out the 'hollow'. Josephus, in Whiston's translation, says that 'Hiram made two [hollow] pillars', the bracketed word perhaps indicating an editorial interpolation; based, perhaps, on *Jeremiah*. In this connection, however, it is necessary to point out that biblical critics look upon Chapter 52 in *Jeremiah* as a late addition, 'an appendix to the book of Jeremiah added in order to show how some of his prophecies were fulfilled', and apparently not written by Jeremiah himself.[2] This would therefore tend to minimize if not destroy the evidential value of the verse in question.

From a foundryman's standpoint, the Pillars may have been cast by necessity only four fingers or 'an handsbreadth' in thickness, in order to reduce their weight, and would thus have been made hollow; but the brass must have been poured around a central core of sand or clay, which would then have had to be laboriously scooped out, as an aid to transport and erection. The brass itself, based on the 18 cubit height, would have been about 27 tons,[3] and, as against the comparative ease or difficulty of transporting and erecting these Pillars, with or without the central core, we may bear in mind the pair of Obelisks in front of the Temple at Karnak, previously

---

[1] It is also said of the Molten Sea that it was 'an hand breadth thick' (*I Kings* vii, 26), a phrase we now apply to the Twin Pillars. It appears that the Babylonians, as well, used the 'palm' as a unit of measurement, equal to about $3\frac{1}{2}$ ins (Caldecott, *Solomon's Temple*, p. 219).

[2] *Interpreter's Bible*, v, 790.

[3] Jos. Young, 'The Temple of Solomon', *British Masonic Miscellany*, ix, 59.

mentioned, and erected some centuries before Solomon's Pillars, and which are said to be almost 98 ft. in height, and to weigh 350 tons each.

On the other hand we are told that, according to Smith's *Greek and Roman Antiquities*, 'the art of casting metal with a core that could be removed was not known until the fifth or sixth centuries B.C.'[1] or four or five centuries after the building of King Solomon's Temple.

An imaginative account of the casting of the Solomonic Pillars is given in *Craft Unions of Ancient and Modern Times*, by John P. Frey, President of the Metal Trades Department of the American Federation of Labor (Washington, 1945), but the author makes no comment on the 'hollow' feature.

The Pillars are said to have been cast 'in the plain of Jordan, . . . in the clay ground between Succoth and Zeredathah' (*II Chron.* 4:17), along with all the other vessels and utensils of brass and articles of furniture for the Temple mentioned in the Chronicle. 'Zeredathah', as given in *Chronicles*, is given as 'Zarthan' in *Kings*, and some Masonic Lectures have accordingly used the one version, while others have used the other. It is thought by some commentators that the name Zarthan, used at the time of the writing of the *Book of Kings*, may have changed somewhat in the Chronicler's time, some centuries later. In the translation from the Jewish Masoretic Text, the difference in the name at these two different periods is not quite so marked; it is 'Zarethan' in *Kings*, and 'Zeredah' in *Chronicles*.[2]

These localities, Succoth and Zeredathah, are on either side of the Jordan: Succoth, on the east bank, being usually identified with the present *Tell Deir 'Alla*, about a mile north of the River Jabbok; while Zeredah, or Zeredathah, is identified by Curtis as being probably the modern *ed Damieh* on the west bank, twenty-four miles from the mouth of the Jordan.[3] While no archaeological remains of a Solomonic foundry appear to have been uncovered in this region, Dr. W. F. Albright calls attention to Nelson Glueck's excavation, in 1938, of some copper refineries at Ezion-geber, at the northern end of the Gulf of Akabah, and which was undoubtedly a great smelting plant in its time, and may therefore have furnished the raw material

---

[1] W. H. Riley, 'The Pillars in Freemasonry'. *British Masonic Miscellany*, viii, 36.

[2] *The Holy Bible*, Jewish Publication Society, Philadelphia, Pa.

[3] *International Critical Commentary*, Curtis, p. 334.

for the foundries further to the north.[1] This discovery has been dealt with very extensively in a preceding chapter.

The Revised Standard Version (1946-1952) and Moffatt's Translation (1913), which show the 'hollow' feature, are of course much too recent to have been of any influence on the Masonic tradition of the hollow pillars—a tradition which is found in rituals as far back, at least, as the beginning of the nineteenth century, as exemplified, for instance, in the Finch *Masonic Treatise* (1802). The relevant portion of the Catechism has it:

    25. Where [were] they hollow or solid,
        Hollow.
    26. Why so,
        The better to serve as Archives to Masonry, and to hold the Constitutional Rolls.

The explanation has been preserved in *Emulation*, thus further accentuating the long-prevalent and seemingly eternal belief in the organized state of Freemasonry at the time of the building of the Temple, with its 'constitutional rolls' and other imagined evidences of corporate status. This reflects a tradition faithfully and quite literally preserved in Lodge La Césarée No. 590—an English Lodge in St. Helier working in French, where it is said that 'when the warrant is to be shown to the candidate it is produced from the interior of an ornate pillar'—an obvious reminder of this Legend of the Hollow Pillars.[2]

The late H. L. Haywood has justified this Masonic tradition on the basis of archaeology, the use of a hollow pillar as a store-house for clay or paper records promulgating the laws to be observed being an ancient Babylonian practice. Such a pillar, he says, was called in that ancient Semitic language a *jachin*. Similarly, another such Babylonian pillar, also 'made hollow', and containing rules of deportment and behaviour, as well as the etiquette governing rites and ceremonies, was called a *boaz*.[3] Unfortunately, he gives no references, and the archaeological note is not repeated in any of his more detailed works, particularly his Third Volume supplement to Mackey's *Encyclopedia of Freemasonry*—which may perhaps justify us in not taking this appetizing titbit of Masonic information too

---

[1] W. F. Albright, *The Archaeology of Palestine*, 1949, pp. 127–128.
[2] Lionel Vibert, *Freemasonry before the Existence of Grand Lodges*. London, p. 136.
[3] Grand Lodge of Iowa *Bulletin*, June 1958.

seriously, until it is capable of being checked and verified. I am personally inclined to agree with Bernard E. Jones when he says, in connection with the general question of the 'archives' theory, that 'the alleged reason for casting these great pillars in hollow form—that they should serve as archives to masonry—does not carry conviction'.[1]

This Legend of the Hollow Pillars and their use as a repository has been elaborated upon in the 'old ritual' that has been cited from Dr. Westcott's writings on one or two occasions, in connection with the Legend of the *Shamir*, also previously mentioned. Here it is stated that the secret of the magical *Shamir* 'and the history of its properties was carefully preserved among the ancient records in the hollow archives of masonry, the Two Pillars, and this was the place where all their valuable records and writings were deposited'. It is possible, of course, that Westcott here had reference to the two Antediluvian Pillars (of which more anon) and not the Pillars of Solomon, but, in any case, this alleged legend that he cites has not been heard of elsewhere.

From an anthropological point of view, the phallic significance of these Hollow Pillars will no doubt have impressed itself upon the reader, following the suggestion of Drs. Curtis and Madsen to the effect that these pillars were only a survival of the ancient stone pillars, the *Mazzeboth*,[2] these being originally phallic emblems, as the writer in the *Jewish Encyclopedia* frankly admits. In this connection, the illustration of a Phoenician 'mazzebah' shown therein furnishes convincing evidence.[3] As if in still further confirmation, J. S. M. Ward tells us that, at Heirapolis (the modern Membij), 'there were two large phalli, thirty fathoms high, which stood at the door of the temple of Astarte, and that twice every year a man . . . climbed to the summit *from the inside* [italics added], where he was supposed to hold converse with the Gods, to ensure the prosperity and fertility of the land. In reality he dramatically represented the process of fertilisation. . . .' And he makes the further comparison that, in the case of the similarly phallic Solomonic Pillars, these 'two pillars with their globes . . . and even the ornate chapiters with their detailed carving [the pomegranates], conveying the idea of fertility, are nothing more than the remains of the prepuce (the

---

[1] Bernard E. Jones, *Freemasons' Guide and Compendium*, p. 359.

[2] *Mazzebah*—'a stone monument set up as a memorial or as an object of worship'.

[3] *Jew. Enc.*, s.v .'Temple of Solomon' and 'Stone and Stone-worship'.

rest being removed in circumcision) artistically disguised.' (Even the 'lily-work' adorning the capital, as an emblem of purity, may not be out of place in this symbolism.) 'Here, then,' says Ward, 'we see not only the true nature of the two pillars in the porch of King Solomon's temple, but also the reason why they were made hollow. The explanation, that this was to enable them to serve as archives, was no doubt invented after the original object had been forgotten.'[1]

In final comment on the word 'hollow', it may be worthwhile to point out a possible source of confusion, having to do with an incorrect use of the word, in the early Masonic Catechisms. This occurs in a 1711 Catechism, the *Trinity College, Dublin, MS.*, where it is stated:

'The Enterprentice's sign is sinues, the word Boaz or its hollow.'[2]

This use of the word 'hollow' (which might have been more correctly written in the context *'it's* hollow', or 'it is hollow') appears to be a mistaken reference to the left-hand Solomonic Pillar, but only through a misunderstanding on the part of the writer of the MS., who evidently thought that the word 'Boaz' had something to do with the now-obsolete and like-sounding word 'bose' or 'boss'—and which does, or did at one time, mean 'hollow'.[3] This is correctly indicated in another Catechism, *A Masons Confession* (? 1727), which makes the curious statement:

> If one should come to a mason working at a stone, and say, 'That stone lies boss,' the prentice is taught to answer, 'It is not so boss but it may be filled up again'; or, 'It is not so boss as your head would be if your harns [brains] were out.'[4]

Another Catechism, the *Sloane MS.* No. 3329 (*c.* 1700) gives a somewhat analogous indication of one of their signs of recognition as of that operative period—as the above is obviously also intended to have been:

> If he takes one of their tooles or his own Staff and Strike(s)

---

[1] J. S. M. Ward, *Who was Hiram Abiff?* London, 1925, pp. 35, 36. The story of the phallic ceremony at Heirapolis, Ward indicates, is on the authority of Lucian's *De dea Syria* (2nd century A.D.). Cf. N.M. Penzer, *The Ocean of Story*, i, 275.

[2] Knoop, Jones, and Hamer, *The Early Masonic Catechisms*, p. 64.

[3] The Oxford Dictionary gives, among numerous other definitions, and derivations, this definition for the word 'boss'. 'Hollow, empty'.

[4] Knoop, Jones, and Hamer, *The Early Masonic Catechisms*, p. 97.

saftly on the wall or worke saying this is bose or hollow—he will answer it is solid. . . .[1]

The meaning of the Twin Pillars

There has been a good deal of speculation on all sides as to the possible meaning and significance of the names given in the Bible to these Two Pillars, and the suggestedly phallic origin of the Pillars does not by any means exhaust the controversy that has been turned upon the question, mostly in a more orthodox direction. First comes the problem as to why they were given any names at all; and secondly, the puzzle of their possible meanings.

As to the first question, it appears to have been the custom among the ancient Mid-Eastern peoples to give names to sacred objects. Thus, Dr. Eberhard Schrader tells us that the Babylonians, in common with the nations roundabout, 'had this custom of bestowing significant and, to some extent, sacred names upon buildings'.[2] Similarly, it is stated in *Exodus* 17:15 that, in celebration of the Israelites' victory over the Amalekites, 'Moses built an altar and called the name of it *Adonai-nissi* (the Lord is my banner).' Thus we establish the fact that the Two Pillars were not merely articles of architectural adornment or function but must have been sacred objects, because of the peculiar names given to them.

And as to the second question, their meaning has been interpreted both etymologically and symbolically. In the Greek translation of the Bible, the Septuagint, the two names in *Chronicles* are rendered by the words meaning 'strength', and 'right'. The Venerable Bede (seventh century) refers to them as 'J., that is, firmness', and 'B., that is, in strength'.[3] The Geneva Bible, which is the one said to have been in use in England from 1560 till late in the seventeenth century, translates Jachin as 'To establish', and Boaz as 'In strength', but Lionel Vibert thinks this is not quite accurate, and should be, instead, 'He will establish' and 'In him is strength', respectively.[4]

All this, whatever the variants, may be taken to refer to the passage in *II Samuel* 7:5, 16, where God says to the Prophet Nathan in a dream:

[1] *Op. cit.*, p. 40.
[2] Eberhard Schrader, *The Cuneiform Inscriptions and the Old Testament*. London, 1885, i, 174.
[3] Gerard Brett, 'King Solomon'. *AQC* lxvi, 94–95.
[4] Lionel Vibert, *Freemasonry before the Existence of Grand Lodges*. London, p. 134.

'Go and tell my servant David, Thus saith the Lord. . . .
'Thine house and thy kingdom shall be established for ever. . . . '

Dr. Mackey speaks of the Two Pillars as memorials of God's repeated promises of support to His people Israel, since Jachin, he thinks, is derived from *Jah*, which means 'Jehovah', while *achin*, which means 'to establish', signifies that 'God will establish His house of Israel'. Boaz, similarly, is compounded, he says, of *B*, which means 'in', and *oaz*, which means 'strength', the whole signifying 'in strength shall it be established'.[1]

Hutchinson, in like manner, thought that Solomon had raised up these Two Pillars as a memorial 'of the promises made by the Lord unto his father David, and which were repeated unto him in a vision, in which the voice of God proclaimed (*I Kings* 9:5), "I will establish the throne of thy kingdom upon Israel for ever." '[2] And in the almost contemporaneous *Henderson's MS.* of William Preston, as an example of the Lecture material delivered in his time, we find him describing his symbolical journey across the Porch of the Temple with the following words: 'At the entrance of the porch, were two great pillars named the one Boaz, denoting strength, and the other Jachin, meaning to establish, the words conjointly signifying stability, for God said, in strength will I establish this mine house.'[3]

This habit of moralizing the names of these Two Pillars is not a Masonic invention, however. The Puritan Divine, Samuel Lee, exhibited it in his seventeenth-century work, previously mentioned, where he moralizes in like manner upon the Pillars to a considerable extent. These Pillars were set up, he says in his allegorical description of Solomon's Temple, 'to note that it was God that gave him the power and dominion over all those Nations, and had fulfilled his promise made to Moses and to his people Israel'.[4] 'The Tops of the Pillars were curiously adorned: to shew that those who persist to the last constantly shall be crowned. The

---

[1] A. G. Mackey, *The Lexicon of Freemasonry*. Philadelphia, 1867, pp. 355–356. See also his *Encyclopedia of Freemasonry*, s.v. 'Pillars of the Porch'.
[2] William Hutchinson, *The Spirit of Masonry*, c. 1775. Oliver Ed., Lodgeton, Ky, 1856, p. 96. Vol. 2 of the Universal Masonic Library.
[3] From a typescript copy in the Grand Lodge Library, London. It will be noticed that, here too, the visitor describes himself as approaching the Pillars *from the outside*. See *ante*, Fig. 5, p. 206.
[4] Samuel Lee, *Orbis Miraculum*, etc., 1659, pp. 280, 281.

Lilly work (symbolized) the Emblem of Innocency: Pomegranates, of Fruitfulnesse, there being many grains in one Apple: their Crown shall declare their Glory. . . . '

In line with the previously-mentioned custom among the ancient Hebrews of giving significant names to sacred objects, modern biblical scholars are generally agreed that the names of these two Pillars must be enigmatical. Furthermore, 'they must have a religious significance', says T. K. Cheyne. 'The pillars . . . have names because they are sacred objects. . . . ' Searching for the possible significance of these obviously enigmatical names, and 'looking next at the Psalm which Solomon is said to have sung on the completion of the temple, we notice that two of the striking phrases in it are . . . for the "establishment" of the sun in his glorious mansion in the sky, and . . . for the "high house" or temple in which Yahwé was to dwell for ever'.[1]

Drs. Curtis and Madsen think the names are simply appellations —by indirect allusion—of the deity. 'These pillars were in Solomon's Temple,' they say, 'because they were a usual feature of Semitic temples, symbols of the deity.'[2]

'But why *two* pillars,' asks T. K. Davies, 'if but one deity is thus represented? Among the Semites and other primitive peoples,' he answers, 'gods went in pairs, male and female, as Baal and Ashtoreth, Osiris and Isis, etc. Possibly the two pillars stood for male and female, the active and passive principle in nature.'[3]

The Rev. C. J. Ball, a well-known Masonic and biblical scholar, suggests that 'as the two pillars in the great Temple of Tyre were twin symbols of Melkart, the god of Tyre, so, in all probability the two pillars set up by the Tyrian Master [H.A.B.], before the Temple of Jerusalem, were intended as symbols of Jahoah, the God of Israel. Their very names', he points out, 'bear out this inference', and 'the names of "*The* Two Pillars"—the Hebrew text has the definite article—are themselves, strictly speaking, designations of Jahoah, or, as we say, Jehovah. Boaz probably denotes "He in Whom is strength" . . . which is a natural epithet', he thinks, 'of the Strength of Israel, the Rock of Ages'.[4]

[1] *Encyclopedia Biblica*, s.v. 'Jachin and Boaz'. New York, 1889–1903.
[2] E. L. Curtis and A. L. Madsen, *Commentary on the Books of Chronicles*. New York, 1919, p. 329.
[3] Hastings *Dictionary of the Bible*, s.v. BOAZ.
[4] *AQC* v, 138–139.

As emblems of Deity, Clarke, too, believes the names to be emblematical, and quotes in support the following from a *Targum*:

> The name of that on the right hand was *Jachin*, because the kingdom of the house of David was *established*; and the name of the left was *Boaz*, from the name of *Boaz* the patriarch, of the family of Judah, from whom all the kings of the house of Judah have descended.[1]

The latter explanation of the name of Boaz has been retained in *Emulation*, as well as in Scottish and Irish working, but has been considered unsatisfactory by some because of the fact that there appears to have been nothing in the life or character of the patriarch so named to entitle him to have his name immortalized by a Solomonic pillar. There is a similar objection, and for analogous reasons, to the explanation sometimes given for the Pillar Jachin being so named in commemoration of one of the ancient Israelites of that name. Probably the best philological explanation of these two names is still the one given in the *Jewish Encyclopedia*:

'Jachin' ('He [or 'It'] shall establish') and
'Boaz' ('In him [or 'it'] is strength')[2]

—which recalls the analogous explanation in the Geneva Bible and in Bede.

R. B. Y. Scott, however—in his paper on Jachin and Boaz— suggests that these names are actually the initial words of two complete sentences, a practice for which he says there appears to be both biblical and extra-biblical precedent. Thus, he cites Gressman's statement to the effect that 'in Babylonia it was customary to give certain pillars a whole sentence as name', and Scott himself suggests that the Pillars of Solomon may have had some special significance for the covenant and the coronation ceremonies, similar to that which the stone of Scone has for the coronation of a British king. As to the former, we read, regarding Josiah (II Kings 23:3): 'And the king stood by a pillar, and made a covenant before the Lord. . . .' And as to the latter, we also read (*II Kings* 11:14) of the coronation of King Joash: 'And when she [Athaliah] looked, behold, the king stood by a pillar, as the manner was. . . .'

This last is supported by the Rev. Caldecott, who cites some

---

[1] Adam Clarke, *The Holy Bible*, London. Commentary to *II Chron.* 3:17. *Targum*: The Aramaic version of the Jewish Scriptures.
[2] *Jew. Enc.*, s.v. PILLAR.

additional verses in explanation of the meaning of the word *Jachin*: He will establish—*I Chron.* 17:11, 22:10, and 28:7; *Ps.* 89:4. 'The raising and naming of this pillar,' he says, 'was, therefore, a kind of votive offering,' and 'every separate sovereign, at his coronation, stood beside this pillar, and afresh took upon himself the obligations implied.'[1]

Following up these thoughts, and Gressman's suggestion, Scott looks to the language of the dynastic oracles and the accession Psalms for some hint as to the possible nature of the pillar inscriptions in their originally complete form, and offers for this purpose an examination of *II Samuel* 7:8–17, and especially verses 12, 13 and 16. Considering all the circumstances, and equating 'Jachin' with 'Yahweh', as an emblematical equivalent for the deity [compare Dr. Curtis's remarks, above, to the same effect], he thinks that 'there is sufficient evidence to justify the opinion that the pillar on the South side of the temple porch derived its name from the initial word of an inscription upon it in some such words as these: "He (*Yahweh*) will establish the throne of David, and his kingdom to his seed forever." ' The name *Boaz*, on the other hand, he finds to be not quite so easily explainable, unless the Masoretic Points are changed to read *Booz*, as in the Septuagint and in the Vulgate. In this case, some suggestions readily present themselves; for example 21:2a (slightly adapted): *B*e*oz yahweh yismah melek*, 'in the strength of Yahweh shall the king rejoice'.[2]

The Rev. Caldecott, however, finds here again no difficulty in this name: 'The pillar on the left, Boaz, was that by which stood every High Priest at the moment of his consecration. Boaz "In it is strength", was a perpetual reminder to him, as he passed and repassed it, that his "strength" lay in the favour of Jehovah and in the keeping of His law.

'Thus were the highest dignitaries in Church and State, with many befitting accessories [namely, the Twin Pillars] . . . set apart for the service of Jehovah and His people.'[3]

In this connection, and in respect of the original development of the Masonic formula interpreting these names, it is interesting to note that in 1765 Dr. Dodd credited the authors of the *Universal History* with the similar suggestion that the words 'Jachin' and

[1] Caldecott, *Solomon's Temple*, pp. 251–252.
[2] R. B. Y. Scott, *Jl. of Biblical Literature*, 58: 146–148.
[3] Caldecott, *loc. cit.*

15

'Boaz' were the initial words of two complete inscriptions on the base of the Two Pillars, which have now come to be known by their initial words only, just as the Books of Moses are called by the first words used in each of the books of the Bible.[1] Similarly, Bernard E. Jones, perhaps following this line of reasoning, thinks that 'each pillar may possibly have [originally] borne its name inscribed on it, so that the approaching worshipper would read the name in the form of a sentence, "He in Whom strength is, may He establish [this house]." '[2]

As to this word *Boaz*—a point of difficulty for some commentators —we find a suggestion from another Masonic scholar, the Rev. Morris Rosenbaum, to the effect that 'its first syllable implies that the house of God is the embodiment of religious strength and the source of the nation's temporal power; and the second syllable [implies] that "in God is all strength", somewhat analogous to the Divine name denoted by the Hebrew word *shaddai*, Almighty'. 'The pillars,' says Slotki's Commentary likewise, 'thus bore testimony to the might of God and to Israel's trust in His constant help.'

Emulation similarly gives a partly cryptic rendering combining the meaning of the Two Pillars into one running sentence, but the Lewis compilation adds in a footnote: 'but a passage of Scripture is not to be found exactly in support of the reading given'—a remark that could be made with equal justice with respect to the somewhat similar reading given in some American Lectures.[3]

Some investigators, it may be noted in passing, have gone somewhat far afield in their search for a possible rendering of the names of these Pillars. Thus, Sir John Cockburn, P.D.G.M. of South Australia, thought there might be a corruption of language involved in these names (as sometimes does happen), and that the original names attached to these Two Pillars were the Greek names Iacchus and Boue. 'Iacchus, or Bacchus, was the God of Youth and of the procreative powers, who in some of the Grecian mysteries was slain

[1] Cited by Canon Horsley, 'New Light on the Pillars of Solomon's Temple', *AQC* xxi, 12.

[2] Bernard E. Jones, *Freemasons' Guide and Compendium*, p. 358.

[3] The *Official Iowa Monitor*, however, merely says: 'The word Boaz denotes strength, the word Jachin, establishment. Together they allude to the promise of God to David that he would establish his kingdom in strength.' It may be noted that the *Emulation* reading, like the one given in some American Jurisdictions, is only an elaboration of the Preston rendering. See *ante*, p. 222.

and rose again. Boue means the primaeval chaos, the dark womb of time, and so the womb of all mothers'—thus bringing us back, by another channel, to the phallic significance of these Pillars. But the theory, plausible as it seems, has met with little or no support, and I have not found it elsewhere.[1]

Other symbologists have been equally imaginative in equating the names of our Pillars with those of other cultures. The Chinese Society of Heaven and Earth, J. S. M. Ward tells us, 'had a chop, or badge . . . and among other Chinese characters written upon it is the word "Keh", which means "a pillar", and has the further meaning of "to establish firmly".'[2]

Albert Churchward (not the Churchward of the 'Land of Mu' series) similarly points us in the other direction—towards Egypt—where, 'at the principal entrance of the Temples there were always Two Pillars. One was the Pillar of Set and the other was the Pillar of Horus . . . one was called Tatt, the other Tattu. . . . Tatt, which, in Egyptian, means "In strength", and Tattu which means, in Egyptian, "To establish".'[3]

But it would take a linguist to assess the value and correctness of these various suggestions.

A quite different line of reasoning is that taken by Dr. Leroy Waterman, and is only cited here as an indication that a symbolical interpretation of the Twin Pillars—of whatever kind—is by no means universal. Writing on 'The damaged "blue-prints" of the Temple of Solomon' (a complete misnomer as far as the title is concerned), he expresses the opinion that the meaning of these Pillars, 'whether religious or secular, remains obscure', but he does venture the surprising suggestion that the Temple of Solomon as a whole was not originally designed to be a temple at all, but 'could have been appropriately called the house of the treasury' (since it is known, from the biblical record, that treasures were stored therein). He accordingly thinks that the 'lofty light-giving cressets for use at night before the royal treasury'—which is what he and some other commentators think the Two Pillars supported—'would have had a very pertinent function, free from any religious flavor. . . . These things,' he finally concludes, somewhat strangely, especially in view

[1] Cited in 'The Pillars of Freemasonry', by N. W. J. Haydon, Associate Editor of *The Builder*, St. Louis, Mo., April 1926.

[2] J. S. M. Ward, *Freemasonry and the Ancient Gods*. London, 1921, p. 60.

[3] Albert Churchward, *The Arcana of Freemasonry*. London, 1915, ch. I and VI.

of the Dedication ceremony that followed the completion of the edifice, 'appear to make Solomon innocent of any religious motives in building his "treasure house".'[1]

Much of the rest of Dr. Waterman's curious commentary is equally controversial and questionable, and Dr. Wright's criticism of it is very much to the point.[2]

Further Masonic interpretations

As to the allusions to these Twin Pillars of Solomon in Masonic tradition, there is no reference to them to be found in the *Old Charges* of the operative Masons, as has been indicated, where only a quite different pair—the Antediluvian Pillars—are consistently mentioned. It has accordingly been thought that the Solomonic Pillars came into Masonry, not through the English operative traditions, but through the Scottish ceremonies associated with the now obsolete institution, the 'Mason Word', as Douglas Knoop has shown. This, Dr. Poole thinks, indicates that the two degrees which he believes were conferred around about that time were what have been called 'Pillar Degrees'.[3]

In the pre-Grand Lodge *Dumfries No. 4 MS.* (*c.* 1710), we find these two Solomonic Pillars moralized upon, after the manner of Samuel Lee and John Bunyan, in typically Christian fashion, as was the Masonic custom of the time, though perhaps nowhere so strongly exemplified as in the *Dumfries*. And in some of the later Catechisms we find explanations along some such lines as the two following:[4]

I. Q. How many Pillars?
   A. Two; Iachin and Boaz.
   Q. What do they represent?
   A. A Strength and Stability of the Church in all Ages.
   —*Grand Mystery of Free-Masons Discover'd*, 1724.

II. JACHIN signifies Strength and BOAZ beautiful. and had reference to the two Sons of Abraham. One to the Free Woman and another to the Bond. And also to the two Covenants. One of Works. and one of Free Grace.
   —*The Whole Institution of Masonry*, 1724.

[1] *Jl. of Near Eastern Studies*, ii, 293–294.
[2] *Ibid.*, vol. 7, p. 53.
[3] *AQC* lxi, 134.
[4] From Knoop, Jones, and Hamer, *Early Masonic Catechisms*.

It is curious to note in this connection the meanings given to these Pillars in the publication *Jachin and Boaz* (1762), which has already been cited, but without comment. It refers these Pillars to the S.W.'s and J.W.'s Columns, and says, in a footnote:

> The senior's is called JACHIN, and signifies strength, the junior's BOAZ, and signifies to establish in the Lord. See the first book of Kings, chap. vii.

The biblical reference, of course, only gives the names of these Pillars, but not their meanings; and these meanings, it must be noted, are completely but incorrectly reversed in the publication referred to. The parallel publication *Hiram* (1765), gives their meanings correctly, however, in the course of an editorial comment:

> The Senior and Junior Wardens Columns, which they carry in their Hands, are generally a Foot and an Half long, and represent the Columns or Portico at the Entrance of the Temple of Solomon, called JACHIN and BOAZ; the Junior's is called *JACHIN*, which signifies, *To establish in the Lord*; and the Senior's *BOAZ*, which denotes STRENGTH.

It will be remembered that in 1739, the Grand Lodge of England (later to become known as the 'Moderns') made a significant change in the order of two words, with their corresponding meanings. The latter of the two publications cited above, conforming to this change, retains the meanings along with the words to which they apply; the author of the former publication, however (in the edition I have examined), while conforming to the change as well, confuses the situation by only reversing the words but failing to similarly reverse the meaning.

Mackey's *Encyclopedia of Freemasonry* (perhaps following Oliver) credits Hutchinson (*c.* 1775) with having first introduced the symbolism of the Pillars into the Masonic system. But it can beseen, from the above, that the earlier workings cited preceded Hutchinson in this, and in fact went back to the *Early Masonic Catechisms* of at least half a century earlier still.

Coming down to more modern times, we find that in the English *Emulation* Lectures, as well as in Irish and Scottish working, these Pillars are said to have been set up as a memorial of the Pillar of Cloud and the Pillar of Fire which aided the Israelites in their flight from Egypt at the Exodus. In the first-mentioned working, the 'Explanation of the Second Tracing Board' has the following:

> They were set up as a memorial to the Children of Israel of that miraculous pillar of fire and cloud, which had two wonderful effects: the fire gave light to the Israelites during their escape from their Egyptian bondage, and the cloud proved darkness to Pharaoh and his followers when they attempted to overtake them. King Solomon ordered them to be placed at the entrance of the Temple, as the most proper and conspicuous situation for the Children of Israel to have the happy deliverance of their fore-fathers continually before their eyes, in going to and returning from Divine worship.[1]

This explanation is derived from the earlier eighteenth-century working, as in the Catechism in Finch's *Masonic Treatise* (1802), which is virtually similar in wording; and the Lancashire 'Lodge of Lights' working that has previously been referred to, as of *c.* 1799, does likewise. However, E. W. Donovan, writing on 'Some Notes on the Pillars', thinks that the symbolism of the Pillar of Fire and of Cloud 'does not seem to be looked upon with any favour by the more serious investigators' in present-day England, and this explanation has not been followed, to any considerable extent, in the American Lectures. C. W. Moore, however, did attempt at one time to retain the British explanation of the Pillar of Cloud and of Fire, in his *New Masonic Trestle Board* (Boston, 1868), in the following words:

> They [the Two Pillars in the Porch] are supposed to have been placed there as a memorial to the children of Israel, of the happy deliverance of their forefathers from Egyptian bondage, and in commemoration of the miraculous pillars of fire and cloud, etc. etc.

virtually as in *Emulation*. An identical paragraph has also been pre-served in the Sickels Monitor, *General Ahiman Rezon and Free-mason's Guide* (New York, 1904). Currently, in the 'Companion to the [Iowa] Monitor', which has already been mentioned, we find the correlative explanation of the Two Pillars, 'in commemoration of the pillar of cloud and the pillar of fire which guided the Israelites through the wilderness', but the explanation is not found in the *Official Iowa Monitor*.

[1] *The Perfect Ceremonies of Craft Masonry*. A. Lewis, London, 1926, pp. 91–92.

The analogy, it might be stated, is an incorrect one, though it appears to have been current in non-Masonic circles as well, as Dr. Dodd takes the trouble to refute it.[1] Dr. Oliver ascribes the symbolism to Abarbinel,[2] also known as Abravanel, a fifteenth-century Jewish biblical commentator and exegete.

The reason the analogy is here considered to be incorrect— 'inexact' might perhaps be a better term—is the fact that there were in reality not two separate pillars (one of Fire, and one of Cloud) but one pillar only: a pillar of cloud by day which turned fiery at night (cf. *Exodus* 14:20).

In the *Wooler* Lectures, at least some parts of which are believed to represent late eighteenth-century working in the North of England, there is a long quasi-historical account of the supposed origin of these two Pillars in the Porch, said to have been set up in memory of two others with precisely the same names, supporting an arch and forming a sort of gate-way, and originally erected by 'the Noble and Godly Boaz', Great-grandfather to King David. It was under this gate and its two Pillars (so the story goes) that Solomon asked to be anointed King; it was there that he was married to the daughter of the King of Egypt; it was there that the Lord God appeared to him in a dream and offered to grant him any wish he might have, whereupon he chose Wisdom; it was there that he had his first interview with Hiram, King of Tyre and with Hiram Abiff. 'On this memorable ground,' finally, 'he received the famous and learned Queen of Sheba when she came from her own country to visit the King and view the glorious T– of Jerusalem. Thus we trace the origin of those two famous pillars so necessary to be known by the fraternity.'

This latter embellishment of the Legend of the Two Pillars has not been carried over into present-day British or American Masonry; nor, for that matter, has it been found in any other eighteenth-century working that has come to my attention.

The *Emulation* 'Explanation of the Second Tracing Board', previously mentioned, combines and interpolates some of the information given in the Bible on the Two Pillars, and says in part:

The height of those pillars was 17 cubits and a half each, their circumference 12, their diameter 4; they were formed hollow, the

---

[1] Dodd, *Commentary on the Bible*, 1765. Cited by Canon Horsley, *AQC* xxi, 11.
[2] Geo. Oliver, *Dictionary of Symbolic Masonry*, s.v. 'Pillars of the Porch'.

better to serve as archives to Masonry, for therein were deposited the constitutional rolls. Being formed hollow, the outer rim or shell was four inches or a hand's-breadth in thickness. They were made of molten brass, and were cast in the plain of Jordan, in the clay ground between Succoth and Zeredathah, where King Solomon ordered those and all his holy vessels to be cast. The superintendent of the casting was H. A. Those pillars were adorned with two chapiters, each 5 cubits high; the chapiters were enriched with net-work, lily-work, and pomegranates; net-work, from the connection of its meshes, denotes unity; lily-work, from its whiteness, peace; and pomegranates, from the exuberance of their seed, denote plenty. There were two rows of pomegranates on each chapiter, one hundred in a row. Those pillars were further adorned with two spherical balls, on which were delineated maps of the celestial and terrestrial globes, pointing out 'Masonry universal'. They were considered finished when the network or canopy was thrown over them.[1]

In America, the *Official Iowa Monitor* (1922), to mention only one working, expresses itself in almost identical terms.

It is worth-while comparing the above symbolism with Samuel Lee's earlier attempt in this direction (1659): 'The Lilly work, [symbolizes] the Emblem of Innocency: Pomegranates, of Fruitfulness, there being many grains in one Apple.'

It is curious to note, however, that the Rev. Caldecott thinks that the reference in the Bible to 'pomegranates' (the fruit) is incorrect, and that the representation in brass on these Twin Pillars was rather that of pomegranate *blossoms*, thus destroying, of course, the oft-imputed symbolism. However, just what justification there is for this unusual rendering is not brought out, and the references he does give cite only the usual 'pomegranate', and say nothing of flowers.[2]

The Antediluvian Pillars

'They were formed hollow,' we have seen said in *Emulation*, describing the Twin Pillars of Solomon, 'the better to serve as archives to Masonry, for therein were deposited the constitutional rolls.'

'They were cast hollow,' similarly says the *Official Iowa Monitor*, as an example of American working, 'the better to serve as safe repositories for the archives of Masonry against all conflagrations and inundations.'

[1] *The Perfect Ceremonies of Craft Masonry*. A Lewis, London, 1926, pp. 91–92.
[2] Cf. Caldecott, *Solomon's Temple*, p. 255.

This last addendum—'conflagrations and inundations'—points up a possible confusion that may have existed at one time in the minds of some of our speculative ancestors; a confusion between these Twin Pillars of Solomon and quite another set of Twin Pillars—the Pillars of Seth, sometimes spoken of as the Pillars of Enoch, or the Pillars of Noah, and now generally referred to, simply, as the Antediluvian Pillars. 'Some call them Seth's Pillars,' says Dr. Anderson, in his 1738 *Constitutions*, 'but the old Masons always call'd them Enoch's Pillars,[1] and firmly believ'd this Tradition,' as preserved and handed down by the operative Masons.

Unlike our Solomonic Pillars, which do not find mention in the *Old Charges*, these Antediluvian Pillars do find mention therein. In the *Cooke MS.*, they are referred to as the two pillars erected by Jabal, brother of Jubal and of Tubal Cain. One of these pillars was of marble, a material that 'would never burn', as is there stated; and the other was of *Laterus*, or brick, a material that 'would not sink in water', as also there stated, but incorrectly (though they may have known of 'a porous brick-like material that was lighter than water). In any case, both these materials were considered to be of such a character that the Antediluvian Pillars were thereby supposedly made indestructible by either 'conflagration' or 'inundation', to use the now-current phrase.

For these three sons of Lamech had foreknowledge 'that God would take vengeance for sin, either by fire or water; and they had great care how they might do to save the Sciences that they had there found, and therefore they wrote their Sciences in the two Pillars of stone; and some men say that they wrote in the stones all the Seven Sciences'—veritable 'archives', one might say, of an earlier day—successfully restored to mankind in due course (so the story goes) when 'a great clerk that men called Pythagoras found the one, and Hermes the Philosopher found the other; and they taught forth the Sciences that they found therein written'.[2]

The story of these two Antediluvian Pillars in the *Cooke MS.* was probably suggested by Higden's *Polychronicon* (fourteenth century), where we read (as transliterated by H. L. Haywood):

[1] E. W. Donovan thinks that the Legend of the Pillars of Enoch is now preserved Masonically in the Royal Order of Scotland and probably nowhere else.—*British Masonic Miscellany*, viii, 73.
[2] *The Cooke MS, of c. 1420*. A Modernised Version. Q. C. Pamphlet No. 5. Quatuor Coronati Lodge No. 2076, London, 1949, p. 11.

The time men knew, so Adam had said, that they should be destroyed by fire or by water, therefore the books that they had made by great travail and study would be destroyed. They enclosed them in two great pillars of marble and of tile. In a pillar of marble for water, and in a pillar of tile for fire, in order to save them for the help of mankind.

This story in the *Polychronicon*[1] Higden had in turn obtained from Josephus, as he frankly acknowledges; and the Josephus account, in turn, no doubt represents a tradition handed down by the Rabbis, as an accretion to the biblical lore of the period, since we know it is not found in the Bible itself. But in both the Josephus and Higden versions,[2] as we see from the above, it is Adam who foresaw the destruction of humanity and the possible loss of all knowledge, and it is the children of Adam's third son Seth who erect the Two Pillars destined to preserve the knowledge of the past—hence the occasional reference to these Pillars as 'the Pillars of Seth'. In the *Cooke MS.*, on the other hand, and in the succeeding versions of the *Old Charges* that have derived from it, it is the three sons of Lamech—Jabal, Jubal, and Tubal Cain—who decide to erect the Pillars, but the basic nature of the legend remains the same, and especially the attempt to save the accumulated knowledge of mankind against possible loss by either fire or water.

This somewhat altered but essentially similar Legend found in the *Cooke MS.* is decidedly Masonic in origin, since it is found nowhere else, and was probably introduced into the Masonic tradition, Douglas Knoop thought, sometime in the second half of the fourteenth century. Dr. Poole even saw some archaeological evidence that is perhaps a quarter to half a century earlier still, and he calls attention—apparently for the first time in Masonic circles—to the Hitchin Tile, 'found at the restoration of Hitchin Church (Herts.), embedded in a portion of the wall, which seems to have been built very early in the fourteenth century and not disturbed'. 'It is not impossible,' he says, 'that the two pillars shown at the sides

[1] This fourteenth-century work was written in Latin, and some 118 manuscript copies of this Latin text are in existence, it is said. About 1425 A.D., John Trevisa made a Middle English translation of this, in a 674-page MS. that has only recently been re-discovered, at an auction sale, and acquired in 1965 by the Huntington Library at Pasadena, Calif., which also is the proud possessor of Higden's original holograph MS. as well.

[2] Cf. Josephus, *Antiquities*, Bk. I, ii:3.

[of the illustration] give it a definitely Masonic significance . . . its date, *c*. 1300–1320. . . . '[1]

Knoop and Jones state that this Legend of Lamech and the Pillars comes from a separate Jewish tradition,[2] but they give no references and I have been unable to trace it in any Jewish context, other than the Josephus reference previously given, which, however, speaks instead of the children of Seth.

This Legend of the Antediluvian Pillars appears, in one form or another, over a wide area of space and time. It has been found in Berosus, the Babylonian priest (*c*. 330–250 B.C.) who gave us the Chaldean account of the Deluge; and another version—this time with two *sets* of Pillars, seven of brass and seven of brick, on which were inscribed the whole of the seven liberal arts, also against a threatened judgment of God—has been ascribed to Zoroaster,[3] and 'of all our traditions', Pick and Knight say, no doubt with some justification, 'this has the longest pedigree. . . .'[4]

The story of the Antediluvian Pillars is presented for consideration at this point because of its basic similarity—in some respects at least—to our present-day account of the Solomonic Pillars, occasioning a possibility of confusion between the two. That such a confusion may have existed in the minds of Masons from the earliest speculative times is indicated by the *Dumfries No. 4 MS.* (*c*. 1710), where these two entirely different sets of Pillars are spoken of almost in the same breath:

'Q where [was] the noble art or science [of masonry] found when it was lost

A it was found in two pillers of stone the one would not sink and the other would not burn'

This is *immediately* followed by the following:

'Solomon set up twoo notable Names yt [that] on yᵉ Right hand called Jachine yt is in it yr [there] is strength. . . .'

—and so forth.

---

[1] *AQC* lxi, 133. See the illustration opposite p. 133.
[2] Knoop and Jones, *The Genesis of Freemasonry*, pp. 67–70. Cf. also W. J. Williams, 'The Antediluvian Pillars in Prose and Verse', *AQC* li, 100–125.

In regard to the Hitchin Tile, the peculiar posture of the figure between the two pillars is certainly very suggestive, if not a sheer coincidence.
[3] Knoop and Jones, *loc. cit.*
[4] Pick and Knight, *The Pocket History of Freemasonry*. New York, 1953, p. 31.

However, this confusion is not entirely Masonic in origin. Early in 1596 one Thomas Nashe appears to have laboured under a similar confusion, for he is found to have written a phrase which included the following: ' . . . die ere we can set up brazen pillars for our names and sciences to preserve them from the deluge of ignorance',[1] —thus obviously confusing the brazen pillars (of Solomon) with the brick and marble pillars (of Seth, Enoch, or Noah).

Be that as it may, and as far as the Masonic tradition is concerned, the Legend of the Solomonic Pillars came in time to be universally adopted into the Masonic system, while the older Legend of the Antediluvian Pillars came to be forgotten, as far as our formal Lectures were concerned. *But not quite.* Two of the most prominent and indispensable features of the story of the Antediluvian Pillars managed to get themselves retained in Masonic memory, but are now found to be superimposed upon and associated with the Pillars of Solomon instead. These two characteristics are: the inscription upon the Antediluvian Pillars of the Seven Liberal Arts and Sciences, now transformed into the 'archives' of Masonry, as in the English Lectures, for which reason these Pillars are said to have been made hollow; and, secondly, their capacity to resist fire and flood, now similarly ascribed to the Solomonic Pillars, as in the American Lectures. As we have seen, the *Iowa Monitor* in fact fuses the two explanations into one, by saying that 'they were cast hollow, the better to serve as safe repositories for the archives of Masonry against all conflagrations and inundations'. As Knoop and Jones have suggested, this perhaps 'represents an attempt to harmonize the two different pillar legends',[2] but the attempt was perhaps unconscious and inadvertent. 'The voice is the voice of Jacob, but the hands are the hands of Esau.'

Dr. Herbert Poole, however, is of the opinion that there may actually have been some earlier ritualistic connection with the Antediluvian Pillars in the Masonic tradition, similar to that which we today have in connection with the Solomonic Pillars. In evidence, he points especially to the *Thistle MS.*, a 1756 version of the *Old Charges*, wherein the scribe shows some reluctance to write certain words in full. Thus, in his reference to these two Antediluvian Pillars, he writes: 'Therefore they engraved them upon 2 p——

[1] *AQC* li, 118.
[3] *AQC* lv, 297.

&c.' And 'Hermorian [that is, Hermes] . . . found the afforsaid p—— &c . . . with the siences written thereon. . . . '[1]

Dr. Poole accordingly thinks that this cryptic and apparently esoteric reference to these earlier Pillars rather implies that the later Solomonic Pillars are 'descended ritually' from the original pair which, in their time, 'played a more important part than we have imagined in the early ritual, and that the story of *their* loss has perhaps had some share in the selection of our third degree legend'.[2] In supporting this conclusion of Dr. Poole's, J. E. S. Tuckett thinks that there is a still further indication pointing to a formerly *ritual* significance in the story of Lamech's family. This occurs in the survival of a certain password, having to do with that family, but having no other ostensible reason for its selection than the suggested ritual connection with the family, and, through it, with the Antediluvian Pillars.[3]

H. L. Haywood goes a step further. He thinks the earliest eighteenth-century Lodges in England may have simultaneously had two sets of Pillars—the Antediluvian Pillars of the *Old Charges*, and the Solomonic Pillars of the speculatives. 'Whether the former was dropped out, or the two became coalesced, it is impossible to know.'[4] Knoop and Jones, however, are more certain. Solomon's Pillars, they think, 'came into masonry . . . through the Scottish ceremonies associated with the Mason Word. . . . The masonic tradition that the pillars set up by Solomon were made hollow, the better to serve as archives for masonry, doubtless represents an attempt to harmonize the two different pillar legends.'[5]

As to the first portion of the above statement, Douglas Knoop, in his Prestonian Lecture on 'The Mason Word', reminds us that 'the Rev. Robert Kirk, Minister of Aberfoyle, writing in 1691, says the Mason Word "is like a Rabbinical Tradition, in way of comment on Jachin and Boaz, the two Pillars erected in Solomon's Temple. . . ."'[6]

---

[1] It is just barely possible, of course, that the scribe merely confused the Antediluvian Pillars with the Solomonic, and took them to be esoteric for that reason.
[2] *AQC* xxxv, 56.
[3] *AQC* xxxvi, 191.
[4] *Encyclopedia of Freemasonry*, iii, 1336, S.v. 'Pillars, Two Great'.
[5] *AQC* lv, 297.
[6] See *The Collected Prestonian Lectures*, 1925–1960, London; and Knoop and Jones, *The Genesis of Freemasonry*, 1947, p. 217. The Prestonian Lecture referred to is reproduced in Knoop and Jones, *The Scottish Mason and the Mason Word*, Manchester, 1939.

Harry Carr thinks this entry of the Solomonic Pillars into the Masonic tradition, in place of the Antediluvian, took place some time between about 1500 and 1630.[1]

ii. The Two Globes

In addition to the pomegranates, with their chains and wreaths, and the lily-work, the Pillars of Solomon are also said in our Lectures to have been 'adorned with Two Spherical Balls', delineated with 'Maps of the Celestial and Terrestrial Globes', as stated in the *Emulation* Lectures, and in comparable terms in some American Monitors. This is supposed to have taken place at an historical period when, as is now well known, the world was generally ignorant of the spherical character of the earth. 'The spherical form,' says the *Encyclopedia Britannica*, 'is undoubtedly a discovery of Pythagoras,' who lived five hundred years *after* King Solomon. The Jews of Solomon's time, like the Babylonians, believed instead in the flat shape of the earth.

Thus, the placing of the Two Globes on the top of our Two Pillars is an historical anachronism, but it is a somewhat late development in Masonic practice, as it is not found in some of the early Tracing Boards, especially in French practice; and even the present-day Dutch Tracing Board does not appear to follow it.[2] Similarly, a Certificate issued by the Lodge 'Zur Hoffnung', of Berne, Switzerland, and dated 1804, depicts two Pillars marked J & B but without any superimposed Globes.[3] In the '*Trahi*, one of the early French exposures . . . the Apprentice Plan'—a Tracing Board, in effect—'contains illustrations of the two pillars, marked J. and B., both conventional Corinthian pillars, with *flat tops*'.[4]

The Globes in English Lodge Rooms

As to present-day practice in English Lodges, 'at the top of many old pillars', says Bernard E. Jones, 'is to be found a terrestrial globe'. But this historical anachronism appears not to have been

[1] H. Carr, 'Pillars and Globes, Columns and Candlesticks', *AQC* lxxv, p. 205.
[2] *Royal Arch Mason* Magazine, Trenton, Mo., March, 1959, p. 138.
[3] *AQC* lxvii, 64.
[4] Harry Carr, *AQC* lxxv, 207.

practised by the 'Antients', whose vituperative first Grand Secretary, Laurence Dermott, attributed the custom to the ignorance of the 'Moderns'.[1]

Accordingly, we find in the old Lodge records, evidence of the Globes having been used as individual pieces of furniture, free from association with the Pillars. In the Minutes of Apollo Lodge No. 301, at Alcester, we find under date of 1794, an item of expense in the amount of two guineas for 'Globes', kept perhaps on a Trestle-Board, along with other symbolical emblems; as is, in fact, indicated in the illustration in the 1784 *Book of Constitutions*.[2] This is confirmed by Dr. Oliver, who tells us that, in the eighteenth century, the brethren used to have a long table down the centre of the room in their Lodge Halls, around which the 'work' was conducted —the 'Table Lodge'—and that on these tables were disposed a pair of 18-in. globes, along with other symbols of the Craft. These tables were not generally done away with till the Union in 1813.[3]

The Globes also used to be kept, sometimes, on the floor. An 1812 Lodge Cloth of the French Prisoners' Lodge at Ashby, now in the possession of the Royal Sussex Lodge at Burton-on-Trent, shows two Globes each in their respective floor-mounted receptacles.[4] In 1829, an inventory of the Lodge of Probity No. 61, Halifax (founded in 1738), showed one item reading: 'Box with Globes and Stands'. And 'All Souls Lodge, No. 170 (founded in 1767), had until 1888 a handsome pair of globes, each mounted on a tripod base, clearly of eighteenth century style, similarly placed left and right of the W.M.'[5]

But this more ancient custom of treating these Globes as individual pieces of emblematic furniture dies hard, and Phoenix Lodge No. 94, Sunderland (founded in 1755), still had, at the time of writing (*c.* 1962), 'a pair of eighteenth-century globes, each mounted on three legs, standing left and right of the Master's pedestal'. Similarly, 'the Lodge of Peace and Unity, No. 314, Preston (founded in 1797), in a recent sketch of its lodge-room, shows a pair of globes

[1] Bernard E. Jones, *The Freemasons' Guide and Compendium*, p. 357.

[2] Reproduced in *AQC* xxix, opposite p. 260. See also some of the Tracing Boards in Dring's 'Evolution and Development of the Tracing or Lodge Board', *op. cit.*

[3] Geo. Oliver, *The Book of the Lodge*, vol. I of the Universal Masonic Library, pp. 98–99.

[4] *AQC* lxiv, opp. p. 80.

[5] H. Carr, 'Pillars and Globes, Columns and Candlesticks', *AQC* lxxv, 207–208.

on low, three-legged stands, placed on the floor of the lodge, left and right, a yard or two in front of the S.W.' And, 'among the unique collection of lodge equipment known as the "Bath Furniture" is a pair of globes, each about 24-in. high, and the minutes show that they were presented to the Royal Cumberland Lodge in 1805'.[1] Summarizing the situation, F. L. Pick says, 'pairs of globes are still to be seen in many North-country Lodge Rooms', in continuation of the ancient practice.[2]

The meaning of the Globes

These Globes, now generally found on top of the Pillars, are perhaps in mistaken allusion to the 'pommels' in the *Chronicles* description of the Pillar Chapiters, which were believed to have been spherical or at least ovoid in shape. Rabbi Solomon, commenting on *I Kings* 7:16, uses the word *pomel*, in reference to the chapiters, and this has been described as an architectural term which 'denotes generally any ornament of a globular form'.[3] Thus, 'in some Masonic instructions it is said that "the pillars were surmounted by two pomels or globes".'[4]

The Rev. Castells says that the placing of the Globes on the Pillars was a 'matter of tradition, which the Kabbalists handed down to the Freemasons', but unfortunately gives no references—perhaps because there were none to give. But in Randle Holme's manuscript of his *Academie of Armory*, published in 1688 (Randle Holme, in the days before official speculative Masonry, was a distinguished 'Accepted' or non-operative Mason), there appears a sketch of a Coat of Arms belonging to the operative Masons which shows two pillars, each surmounted with a circular figure that could easily be taken for a globe. The fact that this Masons' Coat of Arms showed the two pillars, in the seventeenth century, says the Rev. Castells, 'means that the Freemasons of that time had the symbol of the twin Pillars'.[5] But it may only mean, in fact, that the operative Masons had a physical *emblem* of two pillars; whether they also had the philosophical *symbolism* now associated with our Solomonic Pillars,

[1] Ibid.

[2] F. L. Pick, *AQC* lv (1942), 62.

[3] Parker, *Glossary of Architecture*, p. 365. Cited by Mackey.

[4] Mackey, *Encyclopedia of Freemasonry*, s.v. GLOBE.

[5] F. de P. Castells, *English Freemasonry* in its period of transition. London, 1931, p. 203.

or any other symbolism, for that matter—which is something entirely different—has not been conclusively proven, and would make an interesting subject of investigation. And, bearing in mind the Antediluvian Pillars of Enoch, which are the only ones alluded to in the operative *Old Charges*, it may well be that the two pillars in the operative Coat of Arms are not Solomonic at all.

But to return to the question of the Spherical Balls, after this slight digression into Kabalism and Freemasonry, we find that in Fuller's *Pisgah Sight of Palestine* (1650), there is a Plate with a number of designs, one of them showing two pillars surmounted with spherical balls, and one of these appear to show the lines of longitude and latitude found on globular maps.[1]

And here we are tempted to digress once again.

Discussing this feature of Dr. Fuller's exposition, W. J. Williams calls attention to the friendship between Thos. Fuller and his contemporary Elias Ashmole, another one of our prominent non-operative 'Accepted' Masons of the seventeenth century, and an antiquary in his own right.[2] Williams thinks that 'it almost necessarily follows that he (Elias Ashmole) would have been acquainted with his friend Fuller's account of Solomon's Temple. It is not an extravagant inference', he says further, 'that he would have called the attention of other members of the craft to the writings of Fuller and their bearing upon operative and traditional Freemasonry with the result that certain features found in Fuller's book have now a place in our ritual.' And, 'it is not at all unlikely,' he concludes, 'that the compilers of our Ritual had his (Fuller's) book before them and used it as part of their materials. . . .'[3]

It is more likely, however, that Elias Ashmole and Thos. Fuller are a bit early for such ritualistic developments as those found, for instance, in the *Dumfries No. 4 MS.* (*c.* 1710), with its numerous 'Questions concerning the Temple' (see *ante*). Nevertheless, the suggestion of W. J. Williams might be borne in mind in future investigations on the subject.

To return once again to our Pillars and Globes:

In Lee's *Orbis Miraculum* (1659), we see an illustration of these

---

[1] Thos. Fuller, *A Pisgah Sight of Palestine*. London, 1869 (first published in 1650). Plate facing p. 331.
[2] See my 'Elias Ashmole'. *AQC* 78, pp. 83–86. Also the Review of *Elias Ashmole*, by Dr. C. H. Josten, written by H. Carr, *AQC* 79, pp. 240–248.
[3] *AQC* xxxiii, 131, 132.

16

Pillars, with the characteristic 'pomels or balls', but this time ovoid in shape.[1] A similar woodcut of a pillar but with a spherical 'ball' or 'globe' is to be found in the illustrations of some of our early Bibles. All this perhaps goes back to the woodcut found in the Geneva Bible of 1560, with its marginal note on the 'chapiter or round ball vpon the pillar of five cubites height. . . .'[2]

The imagined connection between the 'Globes Terrestrial and Celestial' and the Two Pillars is still further indicated in a non-Masonic work published in 1598, consisting of an English translation of a French poem *La Sepmaine*, by du Bartas, under the English title *Divine Weekes and Workes*, and describing the early scriptural history of the world. In this poem there is a section on 'The Columnes,' but these are the Antediluvian Pillars, called here the Pillars of Seth, after the story in Josephus. But what is of particular interest is the illustration on the title-page. Here we see two pairs of Columns (representing the *quadrivium* of the Liberal Arts and Sciences: Arithmetic, Geometry, Astronomy, and Music). Over each pair we find an abacus; and over each abacus is a Globe—one of them clearly and unmistakably representing a map of the heavens; the other, a map of the earth.[3]

Another suggestion comes to us from the 'globes above the pyramids in the Title-page of the 1640 edition of Bacon's *Advancement of Learning*'—that perennial 'origin of Freemasonry'—one of them, again, being marked 'Mundus Visibilis', and the other, 'Mundus Intellectvalis'.[4] The rather close similarity of phrasing with the *Emulation* 'celestial and terrestrial globes' is somewhat striking, certainly, but hardly conclusive, except for the suggestion of borrowing.

Still further, R. B. Y. Scott tells us that Hollis indicates some existing connection between our Solomonic Pillars and the Obelisks of Egypt, 'early forms of which were surmounted by a disc or sphere [commemorating the sun], like the bowls or globes at the top of the Jerusalem pillars.'[5]

Thus, our late eighteenth-century or early nineteenth-century Masons may have had good pretext (if no good reason) for taking

[1] See also *AQC* xii, opposite p. 137.
[2] See also *AQC* lxi, opposite p. 133.
[3] See W. J. Williams, 'The Antediluvian Pillars', *AQC* li, 108.
[4] *AQC* lx, 92.
[5] *Jl. of Biblical Literature*, vol. 58.

the Globes off their Lodge Floors or Trestle Boards and placing them anachronistically upon the pre-Copernican Pillars, for all good Masons to ask in future time, 'How come?' But it may be remarked, finally, somewhat in extenuation of our 'ancient brethren', that the Hebrew word *gulloth*, translated 'pommels' in the Authorized Version, is translated 'bowls' in the Revised, and perhaps in earlier versions as well. Hence, perhaps, the word 'balls' in our Lectures, through an understandable phonetic error—sometime, somewhere —by way of mouth-to-ear.

But the attempted justification in Mackey's *Encyclopedia*, as worded (perhaps carelessly), is inexcusable. 'For being globular,' he says, 'or nearly so, they may be justly said to have represented the celestial and terrestrial spheres.'[1] They *may* have done so, after Copernicus, and perhaps even after Pythagoras—but they could obviously not have done so in Solomonic times.

Still, all in all, there seems to be a decided connection between our Two Globes, now generally found atop the Two Pillars, and the Solomonic Pillars themselves. In fact, says Mackey's *Encyclopedia* categorically, elsewhere, 'the Masonic globes were really the *chapiters* described in the Book of Kings',[2] and this is the usual belief. In view of this, it is somewhat difficult to understand the precise sense of the statement by Pick and Knight that 'the theory that they represent the chapiters of the two Pillars is decidedly far-fetched'.[3] (That is the difficulty with titbits, whether literary or gastronomical; they can never give the satisfaction of a well-rounded meal.)

It is possible that these two statements are not as mutually-contradictory as they appear. What Mackey surely must have meant was that 'the Masonic globes *represent* the chapiters described in the Book of Kings', since the Hebrew word *pomel* clearly indicates their globular character; and what Pick and Knight must have meant was that our present-day 'globes celestial and terrestrial' could not have represented those chapiters in King Solomon's time, though they undoubtedly may be considered to do so today. Thus rectified, perhaps even Mackey's preceding statement, which we found to be so inexcusable, can now be understood and justified.

Commenting on the fact that 'there is no mention in the Bible of

[1] Mackey, *Encyclopedia of Freemasonry*, s.v. PILLARS, II, 781.

[2] Mackey, *Encyclopedia of Freemasonry*, s.v. GLOBES.

[3] Pick and Knight, *The Freemason's Pocket Reference Book*. London, 2nd Editio n 1955, p. 113.

the "globes",' J. S. M. Ward speculates that 'in reality these were domes, not true globes, and the fact that they indicated a phallic significance was not overlooked by the Hebrew revisers who deleted all reference to them. Nevertheless,' he thinks, 'the masonic tradition has retained them, and therein is undoubtedly correct.'[1]

However, in regard to the last conclusion, Ward is undoubtedly in error, since the placing of the globes atop the Pillars was not an original piece of Masonic symbolism, but a decidedly later addition, as we have already seen.

There is a real contradiction, of course, in the interpretation by Mackey to the effect that 'the Masonic globes were really the *chapiters* described in the Book of Kings', and the *Emulation* 'Explanation of the Second Tracing Board' (see *ante*) wherein, *in addition to* the chapiters, the Pillars are said to have been 'further adorned with two spherical balls'. And perhaps this is what caused Pick and Knight to make the remark they did.

iii. Of Columns and Pilasters

To continue now with yet another set of Pillars connected with King Solomon's Temple, we read in our Lectures that

> *This famous fabric was supported by fourteen hundred and fifty-three columns, and two thousand nine hundred and six pilasters; all hewn from the finest Parian marble.*

—Webb, 1805, p. 76.

This obviously has its basis in Dr. Anderson's first *Book of Constitutions*, wherein he speaks of 'the 1453 Columns of Parian Marble, with twice as many Pilasters', among other fantastic details, all designed as a 'Prospect to transcend our Imagination' in respect of an edifice that 'was justly esteem'd by far the finest Piece of Masonry upon Earth before or since, and the chief Wonder of the World. . . .'[2]

All this of course is entirely in line with the fabulous character once attributed to King Solomon's Temple, as exemplified in the various Models and drawings of the Temple that have been made

[1] J. S. M. Ward, *Who was Hiram Abiff?* pp. 35, 36.
[2] Anderson, *Book of Constitutions*, 1723, p. 13.

from time to time, most of which exhibit it in a profusion of rich detail and extravagance in size which goes far beyond the relatively simple description in the *First Book of Kings*, wherein we read, instead:

> And the house which king Solomon built for the Lord, the length thereof was threescore cubits, and the breadth thereof twenty cubits, and the height thereof thirty cubits.
>
> *—I Kings* 6:2.

There is comparable restraint in the biblical description of the Temple's other features, accessories, and decorations.

As contrasted with these extremely elaborate Models of the Temple that have been mentioned,[1] one of the latest—the Howland-Garber Model, made under the supervision of Professor Paul Leslie Garber of the Department of Bible at Agnes Scott College, Decatur, Georgia[2]—is a more sober and realistic reconstruction. This Model, taken principally from the simpler description in the *Books of Kings*, is therefore at variance with the Hudson Model in the Museum of the Grand Lodge of California, as well as the very similar Model that was exhibited at the New York World's Fair, in 1964–65, in the Masonic Pavilion, these latter two being based on the more elaborate description in the *Book of Chronicles*.

But all of these attempted reconstructions, Dr. G. E. Wright tells us, 'must be taken with a liberal supply of salt. The plain fact is that no vestige of the Temple has ever been found—[as we have indeed seen in a previous chapter]—and we must place our confidence *only* in a reconstruction derived from the combination of a careful and comparative study of the relevant archaeological discoveries with the Old Testament record.' This, he believes, is now possible of achievement, and the Howland-Garber Model is the result.[3] Later, Dr. Wright seems to have favoured still another attempt at reconstruction—the Stevens-Wright Model—referred to, also, in a previous chapter.

'The Temple,' says Professor Garber, 'was essentially a house of

[1] See, for example, the elaborate model said to have been constructed for the Palestine Exploration Society, and shown opposite p. 1026 of Mackey's *Encyclopedia of Freemasonry*, vol. ii.

[2] Paul L. Garber, 'Reconstructing Solomon's Temple', *The Biblical Archaeologist*, Feb. 1951; and *Archaeology*, vol. 5, No. 3, 1952.

[3] G. E. Wright, 'Solomon's Temple Resurrected', *The Biblical Archaeologist*, May 1941.

two rooms arranged lengthwise ... The larger room, called the Holy Place (*Hekal*), was 60 ft. long, 30 ft. wide and 45 ft. high. The inner room, called the Holy of Holies (*Debir*), was a cube 30 ft. by 30 ft. by 30 ft.', which would make the Floor Plan of the Temple proper to be a rectangle of only about 90 by 30 ft. Thus, as to the alleged number of Pilasters and Columns in the Anderson and Webb account, this is physically impossible. But, as stated above, the exaggeration is altogether in line with the fabulous conception our 'ancient brethren'—and exuberant non-Masonic writers as well—entertained with respect to the size and magnificence of their favourite Temple. Our more modern architectural writer, Fergusson, in his attempted restoration of King Solomon's Temple, allows for only four columns in the sanctuary, and ten in the hall, which again is a more sober and realistic estimate.[1]

As regards the Parian marble said to have been used in the construction of the Temple, the *Jewish Encyclopedia* tells us generally that 'the Hebrews in olden times were not acquainted with the use of marble as a building stone'. And, although 'marble stones' are mentioned among the materials 'stock-piled' by King David against the future building of the Temple by his son Solomon,[2] 'the correctness of the text has been doubted.'[3] Josephus speaks only of 'white stone'. Furthermore, King Solomon's commercial exploits are known to have brought him 'gold from Ophir, cedar-wood from Lebanon, probably also copper from Cyprus, and tin from Spain and Cornwall' and purple from Tyre;[4] and, from the lands washed by the Indian ocean, 'gold and silver and precious stones, nard, aloes, sandle-wood, almug-trees, and ivory'—but no marble, Parian or otherwise. Instead, 'The material of which the house and its appendages were built,' says Hastings's *Dictionary of the Bible*, 'was the white hard limestone which abounds in the country, and which can be polished like marble; indeed it is a kind of marble.'[5] Perhaps, in fact, it is from this resemblance to marble that the tradition may have originated.

The *Testament of Solomon*[6] does mention the use of marble in

---

[1] Smith's *Dictionary of the Bible*, vol. 3, p. 1458.
[2] *I Chron.* 29: 2; it is not mentioned in the *Kings* version.
[3] *Jewish Encyclopedia*, s.v. MARBLE.
[4] *Cyclopedia of Biblical Literature*, s.v. SOLOMON.
[5] *Op. cit.*, s.v. TEMPLE.
[6] Windle, *AQC* xiv.

the building of the Temple, but this has been determined to be a relatively late work, perhaps third or fourth century of our own era, and is besides a fanciful work of folk-lore and oriental magic and not to be taken seriously, but it may well have helped perpetuate a legend. The operative Masons, apparently, did have a definite tradition as to the use of marble in the construction of King Solomon's Temple. This is indicated in the *Dumfries No. 4 MS.*, where the 'white marble' is not only mentioned but also properly moralized upon, in true 'speculative' fashion. And in view of the fact that a similar tradition is found among the post-biblical Rabbis, who also ascribed the use of marble in the construction of the Temple,[1] the operative Masons may perhaps be forgiven their own tradition.

As to the specific designation 'Parian', this is now found— together with the fanciful number of columns and pilasters—only in Anderson's *Book of Constitutions*, and has not been found any earlier. But Anderson, perhaps, may have found this to have been 'according to the Traditions of old Masons, who talk much of these Things', as he suggests in his second edition.

'Parian' apparently takes its name from the Isle of Paros, off the coast of Greece, which supplied some of the finest marble known to the Ancient Greeks, and was used in the finest Grecian statuary. The Parthenon, at Athens, and the Hall of the Mysteries, at Eleusis, had tiles made of Parian Marble, no doubt because of its translucent quality; and the entire Temple of Vesta, at Tivoli, outside Rome, was built of this material, as were most of the Temples of Ancient Greece. The ascription of Parian Marble to the columns and pilasters of King Solomon's Temple is thus only another demonstration of the veneration that Masons have always had for that 'famous fabric', and their resulting attempt to endow it with every form of excellence and beauty.[2]

From the biblical record we find that the pillars supporting the Temple—whatever their number—were actually made from the almug tree—

> And the king made of the almug trees pillars for the house of the Lord. . . .
>
> —*I Kings* 10:12.

---

[1] *Jewish Encyclopedia*, xii, 96.
[2] For further details, see my article, 'What is Parian Marble?' *The Royal Arch Mason* Magazine, Sept. 1956.

These almug trees were imported by King Hiram's merchant fleet from the mysterious land of Ophir, as the immediately preceding verse tells us; a region, however, whose even approximate location has been very much in dispute. It has been assigned to the most various and distant points of the compass, including such far-apart places as Armenia, Spain, South Africa, India, Ceylon, the West Indies, and Peru. Dr. Carl Peters was certain it referred to Africa, which is at least phonetically plausible,[1] but 'the most probable view', says the *Jewish Encyclopedia*, 'is that Ophir was situated in Arabia'.[2] From Ophir, also, came much of Solomon's gold and precious jewels (*I Kings* 10:11), and the novelist H. Rider Haggard has accordingly made Africa the locale for his *King Solomon's Mines*.

iv. The Mosaic Pavement

'The Mosaic pavement,' says Webb, 'is a representation of the ground floor of king Solomon's Temple. . . .' (1805, p. 41).

This, at first blush, appears to be a pure Americanism. English working does not appear to connect it so definitely with the Temple of Solomon; but, as stated more soberly in the First *Emulation* Lecture, as well as in the Irish and Scottish Lectures, the Mosaic Pavement is merely 'the beautiful flooring of the Lodge', without further ascription.

There is some indication in very early eighteenth-century English working, however, that this piece of 'Furniture' of a Freemason's Lodge (as it was then called) may have had some connection in their minds with the Temple of Solomon. In one particular place—the oft-quoted *Dumfries No. 4 MS.*—'Mosaic' may even have been mistakenly considered as an adjective referring to Moses—the 'Pavement of Moses,' so to speak. This is perhaps suggested in the following Charge:

You shall serve the true god and carefully keep his precepts in generall particularlie the Ten words delivered to Moses on

[1] Robert W. Bowers, *Freemasonry and the Tabernacle and Temples of the Jews*, p. 70.
[2] *Jewish Encyclopedia*, s.v. OPHIR.

mount Sinai As you have them explained in full on ye pavement
of the Temple. . . .

Dr. Oliver apparently considered the Pavement in that light, and
he refers it originally to the Tabernacle of Moses, which is said by
him to have had such a Pavement; 'which method of paving has,
from this circumstance,' says Oliver, 'been termed *Mosaic*.' But the
etymology, it must be said, is as doubtful as the archaeology is false.

In another place—Prichard's *Masonry Dissected*, 1730—there
seems to be an indication that the Mosaic Pavement was considered
to be both the flooring of a Lodge as well as that of King Solomon's
Temple.

As to the first:

Q. Have you any Furniture in your Lodge?
A. Yes.
Q. What is it?
A. Mosaic Pavement, the Ground Floor of the Lodge, Blazing
Star in the Centre, and Indented Tarsel the Border round
about it.

And as to the second, the following Questions were asked and
answered in the course of a discussion of King Solomon's Temple:

Q. What are the Master-Jewels?
A. The Porch, Dormer and Square Pavement.
Q. Explain them.
A. The Porch the Entring into the *Sanctum Sanctorum*, the
Dormer the Windows or Lights within, the Square Pavement the
Ground Flooring.

Despite the somewhat enigmatical form of the third 'Jewel',
there can be no doubt that it refers to King Solomon's Temple just
as the two other 'Jewels' certainly do. This is clearly indicated in the
current Third *Emulation* Lecture, where we find the last 'Jewel'
(here called an 'Ornament') defined as 'the Square pavement for
the High Priest to walk on', this office obviously referring to the
Temple of Solomon.

The ascription of a Mosaic Pavement as an architectural feature
of the Temple is of course unhistorical, and there is no biblical or
archaeological sanction for the current version in American working. Architecturally, mosaic pavements are more likely to be of

Graeco-Roman than of ancient Hebrew origin. Thus, speaking of the Third or Herod's Temple, *The Jewish Encyclopedia* states that 'the open space beyond the cloisters was paved with various kinds of stone, probably forming a mosaic'. But, if so, this was already in the days of Vitruvius, and in the hey-day of Roman architecture, when mosaic pavements (as has been ascertained from the ruins at Pompeii and other locations) were generally well known.

The Jewish Museum of Art, in New York City, similarly displays an embroidery, used as a covering for the Ark of the Covenant, whose design is said to be 'based upon a part of the mosaic floor of the ancient synagogue of Beth Alpha (sixth century of the Christian Era)'. The mosaic design is mostly in the form of a picture, but at the bottom is an exact representation of a typical Masonic 'Mosaic Pavement' with black and white squares inside a square border. But this is already at the end of the Roman period, sixteen hundred years after King Solomon's time.

A recent work on *Roman Painting*, by Amedeo Maiuri (Geneva, 1953), shows a villa of the Mysteries at Pompeii, with the characteristic Mosaic Pavement composed of a black-and-white diamond-shaped pattern, as in some of our Tracing Boards, and the Roman practice of constructing mosaic floors of various types is described in great detail in *The Remains of Ancient Rome*[1] and similar works. I have myself seen, in the Museum of Rome, located amid the ruins of the old Baths of Diocletian, a relic which consists of a rectangular slab 20 ft. × 15 ft., originally part of a house, and said to have been unearthed in a small town to the south of Rome, as the result of some street work done around 1949. It shows a mosaic of black and white squares, surrounded, interestingly enough, by a decorated border.

It is possible that it was designs such as the above, bolstered by similar designs found in Jewish temples and synagogues, that gave rise to the notion that the floor of King Solomon's Temple—like King Herod's, built on the same site—may have previously also taken the form of a 'Mosaic Pavement'. In the Bible, the palace of the Persian king Ahasuerus in Shushan, about 500 B.C., is described as possessing bed-chambers with 'a pavement of red, and blue, and white, and black, marble' (*Esther*, 1:6), but no comparable description is given anywhere of King Solomon's time and place.

As for the Tabernacle of Moses, Dr. Oliver says (but on what

[1] J. Henry Middleton, *The Remains of Ancient Rome*. London, 1892, pp. 80–82.

authority is not stated) that 'the floor of this most holy place was composed of square stones of an equal size, and placed alternately black and white. . . .'[1] But, from the fact that this Tabernacle was intended as an easily movable structure, to be used during Israel's wanderings in the desert, the supposed presence of stones of any kind in the flooring is to be greatly questioned.

And as for the Temple of Solomon itself, it is said that the king 'covered the floor of the house with planks of fir . . . overlaid with gold' (*I Kings* 6:15, 30). But the Hastings *Dictionary of the Bible* says more soberly, and perhaps more realistically: 'The floor of the house was probably made of hewn stone . . . covered with cypress wood. . . .' Dr. Oliver, however, feels certain that a mosaic pavement 'must have been under the planks of fir',[2] but that is carrying unsupported speculation to a fantastic degree of improbability.

It is possible that the Masonic tradition of the supposed Mosaic Pavement in King Solomon's Temple may be due to a literal rendering of the Latin Vulgate corresponding to *II Chronicles* 3:6—

Stravit quoque pavimentum templi pretiosissimo marmore, decore multo; porro aurum erat probatissimum

—which the Douay Version translates into

He paved also the floor of the temple with the most precious marble of great beauty[3]

but which the Authorized Version renders in an entirely different manner:

And he garnished the house with precious stones for beauty: and the gold was gold of Parvaim[4]

—but with no suggestion, this time, of a 'Mosaic Pavement'. The English translation of the Masoretic Text agrees with the Authorized Version in this respect, and even the *Septuagint* is quite similar. Clarke's *Commentary* thinks this verse refers only to the use of 'precious stones, in the ordinary sense, i.e. gems, which it is supposed were used in the ornamentation of the walls here and there'.[5]

[1] Geo. Oliver, *The Antiquities of Free-Masonry*, 1856, p. 189.

[2] Geo. Oliver, *Historical Landmarks*, II, 190.

[3] *The Holy Bible*, Catholic Book Publishing Co., New York, 1949.

[4] *II Chronicles* in the A.V. is here found to correspond to *II Paralipomenon* in the Douay Version, the latter following the Greek designation of the Book in the *Septuagint*.

[5] Note: 'walls'; not 'pavement'.

The Rev. Caldecott discusses this question of the floor of King Solomon's Temple, like the other commentators, but no mosaic work is mentioned.[1]

v. Orientation of the Temple

The Orientation of Masonic Lodges—wherein the Master's Chair is always considered to be 'in the East'—is one of the most deeply rooted of our traditions, and the consequent Orientation of the Lodge itself is one of the few elements that has persisted practically unchanged throughout the course of our earliest *Catechisms* of the seventeenth and eighteenth centuries, down to the present day, and universally diffused throughout the Masonic world.

The reference is always (explicitly or inferentially) to King Solomon's Temple as the origin for the Masonic practice, though the Tabernacle is also brought in, as the *ultimate* origin, in turn, for the Solomonic practice. The *Edinburgh Register House MS.* (1696) expresses it thus:

> Q. How stands your lodge
> An. east and west as the temple of Jerusalem.

A quaint but unconvincing reason is given in *Dumfries No. 4 MS.* (*c.* 1710) for this traditional Orientation, viz., that it might conform to the position of the Ark containing the two Tables of stone found on the threshing floor that formed the foundation for King Solomon's Temple. Something very similar is given in Finch's *Masonic Treatise* (1802) as one of the 'three grand reasons' for our Orientation. Here it is said that

> Moses caused a tent or tabernacle to be erected in the wilderness, which tent or tabernacle contained the Ark of the covenant, wherein was deposited the two tables of stone, containing the Law of God, which was given to Moses upon Mount Sinai; this tent or tabernacle was the m[odel] of that magnificent temple, built upon Mount Moriah, by that wise and learned Prince K S, whose regal splendour and unparalleled lustre, far transcends our ideas. This is the t[hird] l[ast] and grand r[eason] which

[1] Caldecott, *Solomon's Temple*, p. 236.

Masons have why all C[hristian] C[hurches] and places of d[ivine] w[orship] as well as Masons' well formed regular constituted Lodges, are or ought so to be.

An almost identical primary reference to the Tabernacle of Moses, with a secondary reference to the Temple of Solomon, is found in present-day *Emulation*. And something very similar, again, is found in our present-day American Lectures, though absent in Webb's work, despite the fact that the Prestonian *Henderson's MS.* does carry the same three explanations for the situation of the Lodge due East and West as now found in *Emulation*.

A further reference to East and West is found in the eighteenth century Lectures as given in Finch, in connection with the question:

How blows the wind?
Favourably, due East and West. . . .
Why due East?
In commemoration of that miraculous wind which wrought the happy deliverance of the antient Jews from their Egyptian bondage, and proved the fatal overthrow of Pharaoh and his host, in his attempt to follow them.

The California *Masonic Manual* combines the above explanations in the following manner:

Lodges are situated due East and West, because Moses, after having been instrumental in conducting the children of Israel through the Red Sea, when pursued by Pharaoh and his hosts, by Divine command erected a tabernacle which he placed due East and West, to commemorate the miraculous east wind by which their mighty deliverance was wrought. This tabernacle was an exact model for King Solomon's Temple, for which reason all Masonic Lodges are, or should be, situated due East and West.

—Anderson, p. 232.

Almost identical wording is found in several other American Monitors from the second half of the nineteenth century to the present, an obvious attempt to bring our monitorial working in line with the older English tradition. It is equally obvious, from the above, that our present explanation for the Orientation, in the American Monitors, is a combination of two originally separate explanations, which are still kept entirely separate in *Emulation*.

The connection between King Solomon's Temple and the Tabernacle of Moses, mentioned in our Lectures, is well authenticated in the Apocryphal *Book of Wisdom* (ix, 8), wherein Solomon acknowledges to God his having been commanded 'to build a Temple in Thy Holy Mount, and an altar in the city wherein thou dwellest, a resemblance of the Holy Tabernacle which thou hast prepared from the beginning'. Smith's *Dictionary of the Bible* accordingly states that 'the Temple of Solomon was nothing more nor less than an exact repetition of that earlier Temple [the Tabernacle of Moses], differing only in being erected of more durable materials, and with exactly double the dimensions of its prototype, . . .' and most biblical commentators agree with this view.

As to the Orientation of the Tabernacle, this may be a reasonable inference from *Exodus* 27:12, 13, where the breadth of the Tabernacle is spoken of as being along the 'west side' and the 'east side', from which it would necessarily follow that its length (and therefore its 'orientation') would be along an East-West axis. Josephus, accordingly, says that, 'as to the tabernacle itself, Moses placed it in the middle of that court, with its front to the east'.[1] Modern commentators, again, generally agree.

And as regards the 'miraculous east wind by which their mighty deliverance was wrought', it is said that

> Moses stretched out his hand over the sea; and the Lord caused the sea to go back by a strong east wind all that night, and made the sea dry land, and the waters were divided.
>
> —*Exodus* 14:21.

But nowhere in the Holy Bible is it specifically stated that the Tabernacle was placed due East and West *in commemoration* of that 'miraculous east wind'. This interpretation is purely Masonic. As expressed in the *Graham MS.* (1726): 'the East winde dryed up the sea before the children of Israell so was the temple of the Lord builded'—a phrase repeated in somewhat better English in the *Essex MS.* of about 1750:

Q. Why does Churches stand East & West
A. Because the East wind dryed up the Sea before the Children of Israel.

Our Masonic tradition, as we have seen, gives several reasons for

[1] Josephus, *Antiquities*, III, 6:3.

the Orientation of Masonic Lodges, but only two of them concern us here. The *Dumfries No. 4 MS*. (*c.* 1710) expresses this as follows:

Q. wᶜ [which] way stands your lodge
A. East & West because all holy churches & temples stands yᵗ [that] way and particularlie yᵉ temple of jerusalem

As far as 'all holy churches & temples' are concerned, this appears to be a generally well-accepted principle of ecclesiastical architecture, though not invariably carried out in practice. But as to the 'temple of jerusalem,' specifically, we are not so certain. Ezekiel does say, it is true, that 'the forefront of the house stood towards the east' (*Ezek.* 47:1), but it is generally agreed among biblical scholars that he was speaking of an idealized vision of the Temple, not of the physical edifice itself that he might have seen, before its destruction.[1] And while Josephus does say (as he does with reference to the Tabernacle, as we have just seen) that 'its front was to the east,' this may have been only in repetition of Ezekiel. Among the more modern investigators, Prof. Paul L. Garber, who has already been mentioned in connection with his Model of the Temple, uses the more cautious phrase, with regard to the Temple: 'The entrance, which may have faced East, . . .' which leads to the obvious implication that, perhaps, it did not. It is only fair to add, however, that this Orientation, with the entrance to the East, is generally accepted by all biblical commentators, perhaps from ecclesiastical rather than archaeological considerations. 'There seems little reason to doubt,' says the *Interpreter's Dictionary of the Bible*, 'that the Solomonic structure had a similar orientation [to Ezekiel's temple], facing the sunrise. Solar elements in the religions round about caused many temples to be so oriented, and . . . Solomon's Phoenician architects would have followed current practices.'[2]

But in the midst of all this uncertainty regarding the actual 'situation' of King Solomon's Temple, it may be remarked that, just as in the case of the 'Parian marble', and the fantastic number of 'columns and pilasters', the ascription of an orientation due East and West to the Temple of Jerusalem is but another attempt on the

---

[1] 'The vision of a Temple which the prophet Ezekiel saw while residing on the banks of the Chebar in Babylonia in the 25th year of the Captivity . . . is not a description of a Temple that ever was built. . . .'—James Fergusson, in Smith's *Dictionary of the Bible*, vol. 3, p. 1460.
[2] *Op. cit.*, vol. R–Z, p. 539.

part of our 'ancient brethren' to see every manner of perfection in their ideal 'house', but having its origin, perhaps, in their first-hand knowledge of the principles of ecclesiastical architecture in their own time.

In this respect, the Rev. Covey-Crump goes even further, and he thinks that 'considerations apparently of heliacal reflection had much to do with the alignment of temples in ancient times, both in Egypt and other countries; and therefore, it may reasonably be regarded as an old operative secret . . . connected with the Building fraternities from whom so much of our symbolism has been derived.'[1]

My own theory is that this principle of Orientation—whether or not it was connected with a secret of heliacal reflection—goes back to the Operatives' knowledge of Graeco-Roman architecture in Classical times, as laid down in the principles of Vitruvius, a knowledge of whose work, *On Architecture*, 27 B.C., appears to have been in evidence among them. For it was Vitruvius who formulated the principle that

> the sacred temples of the immortal gods . . . are so to be appointed . . . that those who come to the altar to sacrifice or make offerings may look towards the eastern Heaven. . . . For all the altars of the gods should look to the east. . . .[2]

—I. 231.

It is to be noted that the Orientation of the Tabernacle of Moses and of the Temple of Solomon, in the Masonic tradition, is only in a *direction* or along an axis that is East-and-West, without specifically designating the entrance as having faced either East or West. In this connection we might bear in mind the relative position of the Two Pillars in the Porch, and their designation 'left' and 'right', as given in the Authorized Version, and corresponding to the more specific designation 'north' and 'south', as given in the Revised Standard Version, and the question whether these designations are to be taken from the standpoint of the worshipper leaving the Temple, or entering it. This has already been discussed in the section on the Two Pillars, and if the argument that the description in

[1] Covey-Crump, 'The Orientation of Masonic Lodges', *AQC* xxxv.
[2] But if the worshippers, standing before their altars, faced East, then it follows that the entrance to the temple faced West, as it is my contention that King Solomon's Temple did likewise, and for analogous reasons.

the Bible is given from the latter position be valid, then the Temple of Solomon must be seen as having faced West.

This suggested arrangement has the additional advantage of necessarily locating the Holy of Holies in the East, the farthest from the Western entrance, and it also makes our modern Masonic Lodges—with the Master's Pedestal and the Letter 'G' in the East, and the Twin Pillars (in such Lodges as use them) in the West— correspond exactly to the 'situation' of King Solomon's Temple. But the entire question, of course, may still be largely considered to be in the realm of speculation.

As far as Masonic practice is concerned, we see this reflected as far back at least as the Catechism in the *Graham MS*. (1726), where we read:

Q. How do you administer these words [i.e., the prayers]
A. kneeling bairhead fface towards the east.

In explanation of this Orientation, Dr. Oliver is, for once, soberly factual when he says that it is 'in allusion to the course of the sun, which rises in the east, gains its meridian in the south, and sets in the west'.[1]

---

[1] Geo. Oliver, *Historical Landmarks*, ii, 210.

PART IV

THE BUILDER OF THE TEMPLE

XIII

THE ARCHITECT OF THE WORK

W^{E NOW} finally arrive at a study connected with the traditional chief of the builders of the Temple, largely left out of the general discussion in the preceding sections of this work. The importance and complexity of the subject causes it to deserve and in fact necessitate special treatment, and to this we will now turn our attention in the concluding two chapters of this work.

'There is no character in the annals of Freemasonry,' says Mackey's *Encyclopedia*, truly, 'whose life is so dependent on tradition as the celebrated architect of King Solomon's Temple,' and one can find no argument with this estimate of the importance of tradition—as opposed to history—in any appreciation of the character of Hiram Abiff. 'To fill up the space between his life and his death, we are necessarily compelled to resort to those oral legends which have been handed down from the ancient Freemasons to their successors,' the myth having, by constant repetition, finally assumed the formal appearance of a truthful narrative. This, Mackey goes on to say, has been the case with the myths of all nations. It is doubly important for us, however, to make the attempt to disentangle the mythical from the truly historical, as represented in the biblical account, our only original source in this respect. This is mainly true of much of our legendary history, and it is more true of the Hiramic than of any other Legend connected with the Masonic symbolism and philosophy.

The investigation that students have undertaken, in respect of the Hiramic Tradition, has mainly followed three paths of inquiry.

First: To what extent, and in what manner, is the traditional personality and accomplishments of Hiram Abiff, and the events of his life and death, borne out by the scriptural account?

Second: To what sources can we reasonably attribute the non-scriptural legends and traditions that have grown up around this personality?

Third: Did the Hiramic Legend form part of the tradition carried down to speculative times by the operative Masons of old? If so, how did it originate, and how did it manifest itself among the Operatives?

And lastly: What relation does it bear—in myth and symbolism and philosophical interpretation—to other similar myths of old, or to historical events of one kind or another, and what derivative or imitative connection may there possibly be between them?

The greatest amount of Masonic thought has perhaps been devoted to the last phase of the inquiry—in many cases, unfortunately, because of the easy opportunity it has afforded for unhampered speculation—but it is precisely this aspect of the question to which a definite answer is the most difficult. All that will be attempted, in the final chapter of this work, will be a collection of opinions relative to the possible origin of the Hiramic myth, from various sources more or less responsible and worthy of consideration, and from these the individual reader will have to form his own conclusions.

The personality of Hiram Abiff

A good deal of study has been devoted by a large number of competent Masonic students to the question of the personality and accomplishments of the person who has been credited, according to our traditions, with the design and superintendence of King Solomon's Temple and the creation of its magnificent utensils and religious appurtenances. A significant number of papers in *Ars Quatuor Coronatorum*, and the Transactions of other Research Lodges around the world, as well as articles in Masonic magazines, attest to this general interest in the archaeological aspect of the problem, especially as it may find reflection in the *Old Charges*, the *Early Catechisms*, and other Masonic documents of old. Mackey offers an important chapter on 'The Legend of Hiram Abif' in the second volume of his extremely readable *History of Freemasonry*, and in the first volume of his *Encyclopedia of Freemasonry*, while the first officially sanctioned publication of our very first Grand Lodge— Dr. Anderson's *Book of Constitutions*, 1723—devotes a similarly significant amount of attention to the name, personality, and accomplishments of this biblical and Masonic character, with some added commentary, in the second or 1738 edition, on his tragic end. The Rev. W. W. Covey-Crump has written more recently, and more fully, on *The Hiramic Tradition*, in its several aspects, while Rev. J. S. M. Ward has similarly devoted a larger work to a discussion of the question.[1] Both Mackey's and Waite's Encyclopedias of Free-masonry, of course, give an adequate amount of space to the subject, from various aspects, and practically every general Masonic exposition—e.g., Knoop and Jones's *The Genesis of Freemasonry* (1947) and Bernard E. Jones's *Freemasons' Guide and Compendium* (1950)—do likewise. This suggestive though very fragmentary bibliography merely high-lights but barely scratches the surface of the Hiramic literature, and is only given for the purpose of starting the interested reader along the paths of an intriguing and almost inexhaustible line of exploration on his own account. It is also given because only the barest essentials of the Hiramic question can be discussed here, and only certain aspects can be considered to be germane to the general topic with which we are here concerned, namely, the Builder of King Solomon's Temple, in terms of sacred history and the Masonic tradition.

Tribal lineage of Hiram Abiff

The Rev. C. J. Ball, a Hebraist of recognized reputation, writing on 'The Proper Names of Masonic Tradition; a Philological Study', thinks it is the Hebrew expression *Huram abiv* (*II Chron.* 4:16) that gave rise to the Masonic expression *Hiram Abiff*, or *Abif*, while the difference in the Hebrew text between the 'Hiram' of *Kings* and the 'Huram' of *Chronicles* is only the difference between the characters *yod* and *waw*, and perhaps due to a copyist's error,[2] these two Hebrew characters being, in fact, quite similar.

As to H.A.B.'s birth and antecedents: In the *Book of Kings* he is described as 'a widow's son of the tribe of Naphtali', while in the *Book of Chronicles* his mother is said to be 'of the daughters of Dan, and his father was [i.e., had been] a man of Tyre. . . .'

The apparent discrepancy between the tribes of Naphtali and of Dan, in this description, is easily resolved by most commentators on the assumption that the father had been of the tribe of Naphtali, but residing in Tyre, while the mother had been of the tribe of Dan[3] —both tribes having their domicile, be it noted, in the northern part of the country and in the environs of the Phoenician city of

[1] J. S. M. Ward, *Who was Hiram Abiff?* London, 1925. Perhaps the most controversial, but certainly not one of our most noteworthy efforts in this direction.
[2] *AQC* v, 137–138.
[3] Cf. Dr. I. W. Slotki, *Kings*, Hebrew Text and English Translation, with Commentary. And *Chronicles*, by the same author. London, 1950. See *I King* 7:14 and *II Chron.* 2:13.

Tyre. This was clearly understood by Dr. Oliver, who wrote: 'His father was an Hebrew residing at Tyre, and therefore in respect of country is termed a man of Tyre; but as regards family, he was of the tribe of Naphtali. On the mother's side he [Hiram Abiff] was a Danite.'[1] In another work, Oliver attempts again to reconcile the apparently contradictory statements with regard to H.A.B.'s antecedents by saying that 'his mother was a native of the city of Dan, in the tribe of Naphtali . . .' and that there was, consequently, no contradiction.[2]

Despite apparently logical considerations, most Christian commentators on the Bible appear to be of the opinion that the father was in fact a Phoenician, and that the son, at best, was a Jew only on the mother's side. As against this, Josephus makes his mother to be of the tribe of Naphtali as well, while his father was of 'Ur, of the stock of the Israelites',[3] which the *Jewish Encyclopedia* thinks may have arisen through a confusion between 'Hiram' and 'Bezaleel', the builder of the Tabernacle of Moses in the Desert, who was the son of Uri, and who, like his fellow-craftsman Hiram, 'was said to be highly gifted as a workman, showing great skill and originality in engraving precious metals and stones and in wood-carving'— precisely the attributes and accomplishments that are related of Hiram.[4] As for the latter, Cheyne and Black, who discuss the etymology of the name of Hiram Abiff in detail, point out in their *Encyclopedia Biblica* that *I Kings* ch. 7, in fact, 'leaves it open to the reader to suppose that his father, as well as his mother, may have been Israelitish'. There is also the suggestion of Bishop Patrick, cited by Mackey, to the effect that Hiram's Tyrian 'father' may have been in reality his stepfather, whom his mother had married, and who brought him up, being called 'father' merely as a title of courtesy, or perhaps even as a result of adoption. Jewish commentators have generally been satisfied to accept Hiram as a full-blooded Israelite,[5] while Freemasonry has, by implication at least,

[1] Oliver, *Historical Landmarks of Freemasonry* (1843). 1908 edition, ii, 180.
[2] Oliver, *The Antiquities of Freemasonry*, p. 223.
[3] Josephus, *Antiquities*, VIII, 3:4.
[4] *Jewish Encyclopedia*, s.v. HIRAM and BEZALEL. Compare *I Kings* 7:14 with *Exod.* 31:3, 4; and *II Chron.* 2:13, 14 with *Exod.* 31:5, 6 and 35:35, as suggested by W. J. Atkinson.
[5] Cf. Slotki, *Commentary on II Chronicles*, 2:13. His *Commentary on I Kings*, 7:14 is similarly to the effect that Hiram's father belonged to the tribe of Naphtali, while his mother was of the tribe of Dan.

generally agreed with the Jewish interpretation, for on no other basis can we justify some of the events and activities associated with the Hiramic Drama.

The name of the Master Builder

As to the references in the *Old Charges* concerning King Solomon's 'master mason', under whatever name, it is to be noted that he is almost invariably made to be the 'son' of Hiram King of Tyre, except in the later versions. This has already been pointed out, as in the following example from the *Cooke MS.*: 'Solomon had four score thousand Masons at his work; and the King's son of Tyre [i.e., the son of the King of Tyre] was his Master Mason.'

Only one or two Masonic commentators who have come to my attention appear to have offered any answer whatever to the question why, in the majority of these *Old Charges*, the master mason who held sway at the building of King Solomon's Temple is there called the son of the King of Tyre. Lyon appears to have even considered this master mason to be, for this reason, an entirely different individual from Hiram Abiff, for, in a footnote, having reference to the *Atcheson Haven MS.* of 1666, he says that, in it, 'Aymon, son of the Tyrean monarch, is made to take the place which in other versions is assigned to Hiram Abiff'.[1] But this does not represent a quite accurate view. Aymon is not an individual substituted for Hiram Abiff—if this is what Lyon really meant, which is by no means certain; it is only the *name* which has been substituted. Aymon (and all the other substituted names in the *Old Charges*) *is*, in fact, Hiram Abiff under another name, and his being made out to be the son of the King of Tyre is, it seems to me—as it has seemed to Dr. Poole[2]—only due to the mistranslation prevalent among the English and Scottish Bibles in use at the time, wherein the *abiv* in the original Hebrew was translated 'his father'—and *taken literally*.[3]

But, then, what *is* the true meaning of the *Ab*, *Abi*, *Abiv*, found in the Bible, apart from their Masonic connection? Literally interpreted, it is true, *Ab* does mean 'father'; *Abi*, 'my father'; *Abiv*, 'of his father', or 'his father's'. But critical commentators point out

[1] D. Murray Lyon, *History of the Lodge of Edinburgh (Mary's Chapel) No. 1.* London, 1900, p. 118.
[2] Cf. *AQC* lxi, 133.
[3] Cf. Mackey's *Encyclopedia of Freemasonry*, s.v. ABIF.

that the literal interpretation is not the only one possible, and that a subsidiary interpretation is more consonant with the textual material. 'In Hebrew,' Mackey explains, 'the word *ab*, or *father*, is often used as a title of respect. . . . Thus, Doctor Clarke, commenting . . . on the very passage in which this word *Abif* is used, he says: "אב *father*, is often used in Hebrew to signify *master, inventor, chief operator*".'

Numerous commentators have followed a similar line of interpretation, with variants on the title suggested by the Hebrew term, all more or less to the same effect. To Chas. C. Torrey, of Yale University, in an article 'Concerning Hiram ("Huram-abi"), the Phoenician Craftsman', the word *Ab* means 'trusted counsellor'.[1] M'Clintock & Strong's *Cyclopedia of Biblical Literature* similarly gives it the meaning of 'counsellor, i.e., *foreman*, or *master-workman*'. The Rev. C. J. Ball, writing on 'The Proper Names of Masonic Tradition', agrees with the above, and points out that this is in accordance with 'a well-known Hebrew usage . . . just as Joseph is said to have become a "father" to Pharaoh (*II Chron.* ii. 13, 14; cf. *Gen.* xlv. 8)'.[2] The Masoretic Text of *The Holy Bible*, published by the Jewish Publication Society, accordingly gives the name in *II Chron.* ii, 12 the meaning of 'master craftsman'. Dr. Slotki does likewise.[3]

It is curious to note that Dr. James Anderson, writing his first *Book of Constitutions*, 1723, did have, in fact, a very similar alternative interpretation in mind, but he seems to have preferred the more literal.[4]

All this, in some students' minds, suggests the thought that the basic personality of the Hiramic Myth can indeed be found in the Bible itself, in his true Masonic character, when correctly interpreted, and as the central *dramatis persona* of the Hiramic Drama, and that there is therefore nothing inherently impossible in the idea having occurred to the operative Masons of the Middle Ages, this to have become elaborated by them out of the simple and restricted materials found in the Bible story.

One idea that has appealed to some arises from the curious confusion between the biblical name Hiram and the equally biblical

[1] *Jl. of Biblical Literature*, 31 (1912), pp. 151–155.
[2] *AQC* v, 136.
[3] Slotki, *Chronicles*. Soncino Press, 1952.
[4] Facsimile Reproduction, London, 1923, footnote p. 11.

name Adoniram, whose literal signification, in the split form *Adon Iram*, is 'the Lord Hiram'. This Adoniram was master of Solomon's workmen on Mount Lebanon (*I Kings* 5:14), and got stoned to death by the mob, in the reign of Solomon's son Rehoboam, as an unwelcome tax-collector (*I Kings* 12:18). Here, then, we have at least two distinct circumstances now found in the Hiramic Legend, and the identification of these two essentially distinct personalities—credited, in its origin, to Louis de Travenol (*Catechisme des Francs Maçons*, 1744), writing under the pseudonym Leonard Gabanon[1]—has accordingly been taken up into the French working. A whole Rite has, in fact, been developed on the basis of this personality of Adoniram. And in the ritual as originally worked in the German language in Pilgrim Lodge No. 238, London, the 'traditional history' is called 'The Life of the Father', and deals with Adoniram, or Adoram (an alternative form), the Candidate being told that 'the story of the "Life of our Father" has been handed down since ancient times from father to son and that the greatest part of it can be found in the Talmud'.[2]

The craftsmanship of Hiram Abiff

As to the craft and accomplishments of our Hiram Abiff, there is a good deal of misunderstanding and much needless speculation. In *Kings*, he is spoken of simply as 'a worker in brass'—an accomplishment well evidenced by his making—aside from numerous smaller ornaments and utensils—the two huge and splendidly adorned Brazen Pillars in the entrance to the Porch of the Temple, and the still more marvellous Brazen Sea or Laver outside, some fifteen feet in diameter and half as deep, containing some sixteen thousand gallons in volume, and resting on twelve brazen oxen, 'three facing north, three west, three south, and three east'. But in the *Book of Chronicles*, said to have been written some centuries later, we already find him endowed with additional capacities and skills—the accumulation, no doubt, of legendary accretion—as he is described in the letter from the King of Tyre to his fellow-monarch in Israel: 'skilful to work in gold and in silver, in brass, in iron, in

[1] Mackey's *Encyclopedia*, i, 23, *s.v.* ADONHIRAMITE FREEMASONRY.
[2] A manuscript of this old Zinnendorf Ritual is in the Manchester Research Lodge Library. It was worked from 1779 to 1846, when the Lodge changed its working to the Schroeder Ritual.—F. Bernhart, 'Pilgrim Lodge No. 238'. *Transactions*, Manchester Assn. for Masonic Research, xlix.

stone and in timber, in purple, in blue and in fine linen and in crimson', etc. But nowhere do we yet find him described as a builder or architect—the central presupposition in the Masonic tradition.

Mackey thinks that it is the *Cooke MS*. (*c.* 1410) that appears to be originally guilty of recording this latter phase of the legend, which has been perpetuated in Masonic tradition ever since. The error (from the purely biblical standpoint) of making Hiram an operative master-mason, says Mackey, is repeated in Anderson's *Book of Constitutions* (1723), where he is now elevated to the rank of 'Master of Work' or general superintendent, for the first time. Here, Anderson speaks of Hiram as 'the most accomplish'd Mason upon Earth', and as 'the divinely inspired Workman', excelling by far the performances of Aholiab and Bezaleel and who, in their time, were 'also universally capable of all sorts of Masonry'. But in the 1738 edition, Anderson elevates Hiram still further, to the rank of 'Deputy Grand Master' in the absence of King Solomon, and 'Senior Grand Warden' in his presence, and 'principal Surveyor and Master of Work' besides, adding, in a footnote, some additional attributes gleaned from the scriptural account.

This is then still further elaborated in Entick's 1756 edition of the *Constitutions*, in the following words:

> This inspired Master was, without question, the most cunning, skilful, and curious workman that ever lived; whose abilities were not confined to building only, but extended to all kinds of work, whether in gold, silver, brass or iron; whether in linen, tapestry or embroidery; whether considered as architect, statuary, founder or designer, separately or together, he equally excelled. From his designs and under his direction, all the rich and splendid furniture of the Temple and its several appendages were begun, carried on, and finished.[1]

'This character has adhered to him in all subsequent times,' says Mackey in comment, 'and the unwritten Legend of the present day represents him as the "Chief Builder of the Temple", the "Operative Grand Master", and the "Skilful Architect" by whose elaborate designs on his trestle-board the Craft were guided in their labors and the edifice was constructed'.[2] In this form of the Legend he

[1] Mackey, *Encyclopedia of Freemasonry*, i, 456.
[2] Mackey, *History of Freemasonry*, ii, 429.

finally comes to be elevated to the rank of Grand Master on a level with the two Kings of Israel and of Tyre.

Numerous details now begin to surround the legendary personality of this erstwhile metal-worker, some of them in harmonious development of the central Masonic theme, but some of them of doubtful authenticity and of questionable symbolical or allegorical value, while others are clearly out-and-out fabrications created for the occasion. Some of these legends have managed to insinuate themselves into the Craft working. Others, not finding a suitable setting in the Craft Degrees, have found their way into the so-called Higher Degrees of one Discipline or another; either in current working, or in Rites that have now become more or less obsolete. All this but attests to the wealth of traditional detail that has grown up surrounding this legendary figure through the ages, as in the parallel case of King Solomon previously referred to. And, as also in the case of King Solomon, some of these legendary details are of non-Masonic origin—as, for example, in the operatic librettos we have already examined in connection with King Solomon and the Queen of Sheba—while some go back to the rabbinic tales of pre-Christian times.

Mackey's Theory of the Smith

In trying to solve the riddle of how it was that the Masons of the Middle Ages should have incorporated into their *Legend of the Craft* the idea that a simple worker in metal—in plain words, a smith—could have been the chief builder at the Temple, Mackey allows himself to indulge in a considerable amount of speculation, in the course of which he evolves an elaborate theory of the Smith on the basis of the prevalent veneration held for that type of craftsman in the Middle Ages. It was the Smith, as a worker in metals, Mackey reminds us, who fabricated shields and swords for warriors, armour for the knights of old, and jewelry for queens and noble ladies of the court, and who thus became the central and important figure, so to speak, in the economy and in the popular estimation of the feudal society of earlier times. Around such an important character, accordingly, numerous legends were certain to develop, Mackey thinks, and a myth that has the metal-worker as its central figure is therefore found among the traditions of the earliest peoples, from Scandinavia in the North to the southern limit of the Latin race; as well as in the mythology and folk-lore of Assyria, of India, of

Greece, and of Rome. Thus the Greeks had their Hephaestus, 'the mighty workman, the immortal smith who forged the weapons of the gods'; the Romans, their Vulcan, related etymologically to the biblical Tubal Cain, the 'sharpener of every instrument in brass and iron', according to the Vulgate, and the founder of 'the Smith Craft of gold and silver, iron and copper and steel', according to the Masonic *Legend of the Craft*.

Hence the myth of a wonderfully cunning artist was found everywhere, and the *Legend of the Smith* became the common property of all the Scandinavian and Teutonic nations, and was so impressive a character that it continued to exist down to mediaeval times, and traces of it have extended to the superstitions of the present day. May we not justly look to its influence for the prominence given by the old Masonic legendists to the Master Smith of King Hiram among the workmen of Solomon?...

The idea that of all handicrafts smith-craft was the greatest was unwittingly retained by the Masons when they elevated the skilful smith of Tyre, the 'cunning' worker in brass, to the highest place as a builder in their Temple legend.[1]

This overly elaborate theory of the Smith, however—plausible as it no doubt sounded in Mackey's time—becomes entirely superfluous now when we consider the fact (apparently unknown to him) that the ascription of architectural qualifications to Hiram was *not* an invention, pure and simple, of the Masonic legend-makers of the Middle Ages (as Mackey apparently thought it was), but is of far older origin. Gerard Brett calls our attention to the fact that both Clement (second century) and Eusebius (fourth century) refer to Hiram as an architect rather than as a bronzecaster,[2] and as to Eusebius, his own prior source appears to have been Eupolemus, the Hellenistic Jewish writer of about 150 B.C., whose version of the 'Reciprocations' we have already given. In this connection, Bernard E. Jones is no doubt on safe ground when he expresses the conviction that, 'as the writings of these two ancient authors (Clement and Eusebius) have endured to this day and are known to scholars, there must have been, all through the mediaeval period, some learned men well aware that, in the early centuries A.D., Hiram had had a place in an architect tradition.

[1] Mackey, *History of Freemasonry*, ii, 421–428.
[2] *AQC* lxvi, 95.

'It is therefore possible, even not unlikely,' he concludes, 'that a legend persisted in some quarters, all through the centuries, that Hiram was more than Solomon's metal founder—that he was, indeed his "principal architect". . . .' And while some of us, he says, may have previously tended to ascribe the transformation of a (biblical) metal-founder into a (Masonic) master-builder as the work of some editor unafraid to take liberties with his original material, we may perhaps have done an injustice, he now thinks, to this unknown 'fabricator' of the Masonic legend.[1]

It is interesting to note that modern biblical scholars generally—outside of the Masonic field—are also satisfied to accept the architectural imputation that has become the central core of the Masonic tradition, despite the lack of clear scriptural corroboration. Thus, Smith's *Dictionary of the Bible* speaks of Hiram as we do, as 'the chief architect of the Temple'. Hastings's *Dictionary of the Bible* does likewise, while Professor Paul Leslie Garber, the designer of one of the more authentic modern models of the Temple, based on 'the latest findings of textual study and the relevant data from biblical archaeology', writes on 'The Jerusalem Temple which Hiram of Tyre designed and constructed', referring, of course, not to the King, but to the 'widow's son of the tribe of Naphtali'.[2] Professor G. Ernest Wright, editor of the periodical above cited, while discussing this model of Professor Garber's from the archaeological standpoint, incidentally refers to the labour furnished by King Solomon in erecting the Temple, while Hiram King of Tyre 'furnished the architects and artisans to draw up the plans and direct the work', having obviously the 'chief architect' in mind as one of the number.

Furthermore, Cook's *Commentary* attempts to interpret the phrase '*to find every device*', in the letter from King Hiram of Tyre (see *ante*), by pointing to the Septuagint version which gives in that place the Greek word *architektonesai*, 'to act as chief artificer', 'to be the director of works'. Thus, says Cook, extra-Masonically, 'there can be no doubt that the "devices" intended are plans or designs connected with art, which Huram could invent on any

[1] *AQC* lxvi, 99.
Dr. Geo. Oliver, with his exuberant imagination, even makes H.A.B. to have been the builder of Tadmor, or Palmyra, but on what authority, is not stated.—*Antiquities of Freemasonry*, p. 223.
[2] P. L. Garber, *The Biblical Archaeologist*, Feb. 1951.

subject that was "put to him",' thus ascribing, indirectly, an 'architect tradition' in respect of Hiram to a period as early as the writing of the pre-Christian Septuagint version of the Bible. And, as to the several other artistic accomplishments ascribed to Hiram or Huram in the *Chronicles* version of the 'Reciprocations', 'the combination of all this artistic skill in one man seems strange to our modern notions', says Cook, 'but the history of art furnishes numerous instances of versatility almost as great'.

On the other hand, the simpler account in the earlier *Book of Kings*, where he is only described as being 'cunning to work all works in brass', when compared with the more elaborate description in the much later *Book of Chronicles*, may only indicate the accretion of legend and tradition that had grown up around the personality of Hiram in the intervening period, among the ancient Jews themselves, as has been said of the writings of Josephus in a similar connection. *The Jewish Encyclopedia*, however, thinks that even from the account in *Chronicles*, which it apparently takes literally, Hiram 'seems to have superintended all the work of the Temple' (*s.v.* HIRAM).

Who WAS Hiram Abiff?

A number of Masonic writers have taken a hand at evaluating the personality of the reputed 'principal architect', and seeking for the origin of the Hiramic tradition, though J. S. M. Ward is the only one who has given the subject any very extensive treatment. His work, however, is of more interest for its anthropological and mythological detail rather than for any real light it might throw on the question, his main theme appearing to be that Hiram Abiff was 'one of the Priest-kings of Tyre, the living incarnation of Adonis, who was offered up as a Consecration Sacrifice at the completion of the great Temple at Jerusalem . . . in order that the new Temple might stand firm for ever'.[1] At one point, he makes him the father of Hiram King of Tyre himself, but his argument is never closely reasoned (aside from the reference to the 'Consecration Sacrifice' which, as a general practice, seems to be well-founded).[2] For the most part, his treatment seems to be a mythological tempest in a Masonic teapot—the tea, it might be remarked, being extremely weak.

[1] J. S. M. Ward, *Who was Hiram Abiff?* pp. 172, 175.
[2] See G. W. Speth's *Builders' Rites and Ceremonies: The Folk Lore of Masonry.* Q.C. Pamphlet No. 1, Quatuor Coronati Lodge No. 2076, 1951.

The Rev. W. W. Covey-Crump's *Hiramic Tradition* (London, 1934) hews much closer to the line of historical fact, generally, wherever history manages to obtrude itself, but he, too, indulges in some fanciful speculations where it does not. Thus, when we are told that 'King Solomon sent and fetched Hiram out of Tyre', Covey-Crump has 'no hesitation in contending that the Hiram who was thus sent for was none other than the King of Tyre himself'—contrary to our general reading, and contrary, moreover, to our conception of oriental kingly dignity.

Covey-Crump in this manner makes one Hiram out of the conventionally-accepted two Hirams—the King and the artisan—while A. S. MacBride, on the other hand, travels in the opposite direction, and tries to make a case for no less than 'Four Hirams of Tyre', two of them, father and son, being engaged in the work of King Solomon's Temple, the first having died while the work was in progress, leaving his son to finish the task. It is the first, he says, whose death we commemorate, and it is the second who survived and eventually returned to Tyre alive.[1]

Newton, and other reputable writers—all of them apparently following Oliver—credit Josephus originally with the statement that Hiram Abiff lived to a ripe old age and eventually died in his home-city of Tyre,[2] a statement which Newton gives out 'as a fact', without stating how this important fact had been arrived at. I have so far been unable to find the precise statement in Josephus to which Newton apparently refers with so much assurance, and several correspondents whose assistance I have drawn upon have likewise come up with a negative answer. One of these, who has patiently gone through his entire *Josephus*, categorically states that there is no such statement in the work.

Oliver, I find, similarly says in his *Freemason's Treasury*: 'Why, it is well known[!] that the celebrated artist (HAB) was living at Tyre many years after the Temple was completed,'[3] but he, too, fails to indicate the basis for this 'well known' fact of his.

Wm. A Paine tells us, on the other hand (again following Dr.

[1] *The Builder*, 1917, p. 113.

J. S. M. Ward goes one better than A. S. MacBride by making *five* Hirams out of the original two, but his argument hardly deserves the effort of serious refutation. Cf. Ward, *Who was Hiram Abiff?* Ch. ii.

[2] Joseph Fort Newton, *The Builders*. Cedar Rapids, Iowa, 1916, p. 77. (Not to be confused with the periodical, *The Builder*).

[3] Oliver, *Freemason's Treasury*. London, 1863, p. 291.

Oliver, no doubt), that it is Abdemon who is said by Josephus to have 'returned to Tyre, where he died at a good old age',[1] and while it is further stated that Abdemon is *supposed* to be a pseudonym for Hiram Abiff, the grounds for this supposition are not given. Josephus, it is true, does refer to a certain Tyrian by the name of Abdemon, when quoting from certain non-Jewish historians, writing of the Solomonic era, but a careful examination of the works of Josephus (as we shall presently carry out) fails to disclose the basis for these two statements of Paine's.

What Oliver does say (and this must be the basis for the Paine allegation) is that 'H.A.B. not only lived to finish all the work, in whatever capacity he might have been engaged [and here Oliver does give several references to *I Kings* and *II Chronicles* in support of his obviously correct statement—*so far*], but also, according to the testimony of Josephus, who calls him ABDEMON, he returned to Tyre and died there at a good old age.'[2]

The statement that Josephus himself identifies Hiram Abiff with Abdemon, in so many words, or even by inference, can be categorically stated to be incorrect, as he does not do so. As a matter of fact, when he does have occasion to refer to H.A.B., he does not fail to call Hiram by name.[3] The further statement, in another work of Oliver's, to the effect that 'this Abdemonus was another name of Hiram Abiff, according to Dius and Menander'[4] is also without foundation. Josephus does quote from these two historians, Dius and Menander, in connection with the relationship between Solomon, King of Israel, and Hiram, King of Tyre, and mentions, incidentally, 'Abdemon, a man of Tyre', but there is no hint anywhere of any connection between this 'artificer out of Tyre, whose name was Hiram' and 'Abdemon, a man of Tyre', other than their place of origin.

This story of Abdemon, *in Josephus*, is precisely as follows:
' . . . The king of Tyre sent sophisms and enigmatical sayings to Solomon, and desired he would solve them. . . . Now so sagacious and understanding was Solomon, that none of these problems were

[1] *The Builder*, iii, 138.
[2] Oliver, *op. cit.*, p. 300.
[3] Example: 'Now Solomon sent for an artificer out of Tyre, whose name was Hiram . . .' (Josephus, *Antiquities*, Bk. VIII, ch. iii, par. 4). Josephus obviously would have had no reason to call him Hiram in one place and Abdemon in another, without going into the reasons for the change.
[4] Oliver, *The Antiquities of Freemasonry*, p. 223.

too hard for him; but he conquered them all by his reasonings . . . '
But Hiram, King of Tyre, was not so successful. For we read
[Josephus now quotes Dius, from the latter's History of the
Phoenicians], that Solomon, in turn 'sent riddles to Hiram [the
King] . . . and when he was not able to solve the riddles, . . . he
afterward did solve the proposed riddles by means of Abdemon, a
man of Tyre. . . . '[1]

*This is absolutely all that Josephus has to say with respect to
Abdemon*, as a reference to his Index will disclose.

Just how this imagined identification between H.A.B. and Abdemon could have come about, in Oliver's mind, is somewhat of an
enigma. It may be that, since Hiram Abiff is stated to have been 'a
cunning man, endued with understanding, . . . skilful . . . to find
out every device which shall be put to him' (*II Chron.* 2:13, 14),
and since Abdemon is similarly described by Josephus to have
been capable of solving the riddles proposed by Solomon, the two
came to be confused as necessarily one and the same.But to ascribe
this identification to Josephus himself is entirely unwarranted. And
Newton, Paine, MacBride, *et al.*, are even less pardonable for their
uncritical acceptance of Oliver's statement at second hand, when a
simple reference to the original and easily available Josephus
record could have set matters straight.

As to the statement that Hiram 'returned to Tyre and died there
at a good old age', the only possible solution that could be offered,
as far as Josephus is concerned, is the story said to have been
preserved by Eusebius, and credited to Eupolemus, to the effect
that 'Solomon sent back the Egyptians and Phoenicians each to his
own country and gave to each man ten shekels of gold'.[2] Now,
since no exception is made in this statement concerning the Phoenician Hiram, the widow's son, and since there is otherwise no
record of his having died, it could be assumed that the latter is
supposed to be included in the Eupolemus account. Josephus does
mention this Eupolemus, but in quite a different connection, and it
is just barely possible that whoever happened to remember this
story of Eupolemus's, and vaguely remembered at the same time
seeing the name in Josephus, could have put two and two together

[1] Josephus, *Antiquities*, Bk. VIII, ch. v, p. 251. (The page reference is to the
Whiston translation, Philadelphia edition.) The story is repeated in Josephus,
Against Apion, Bk. I, p. 866, where he quotes from both Dius and Menander.
[2] See Covey-Crump, *The Hiramic Tradition*, p. 68.

and made it come out six. Ever since, the story has been going around in various publications that, 'according to Josephus', Hiram returned to Tyre after the completion of the Temple and lived to a ripe old age. A similar confusion and false ascription to Josephus has already been noticed in connection with the 'did not rain in the day-time' story.

Another theory regarding the origin of the story generally ascribed to Josephus regarding the return to Tyre is the one proposed by H. C. de Lafontaine, who thinks it may have originated instead with the French Masonic writer Ragon, who is said to have stated, in his *Orthodoxie Maçonnique*, that Hiram, after the completion of the Temple, 'probably returned to Tyre'.[1] Be that as it may, the belief that the chief architect did not in fact die as commonly portrayed has managed to work its way into at least one ritual, as Arthur E. Waite tells us, a ritual 'fortunately obscure and long since ceased from working—in which the story is emptied of all symbolical significance because the Master does not die but, being healed of his hurts, retires into a distant region and ends his days in peace'.[2]

This statement of Waite's may possibly have reference to the Rite of Mizraim, practised for a time in France and Italy, but now extinct. Here, 'Hiram is said to have returned to his family, after the completion of the Temple, and to have passed the remainder of his days in peace and opulence'.[3] Mackey, who gives us this account, does not say in which of Mizraim's ninety Degrees the above version of the legend is found, but in *The Rite of Mizraim*: 'Apprentice, Fellowcraft, Master', published by the Grand College of Rites of the U.S.A. (1955), the Legend of Hiram Abiff is given as in our traditional form, with only minor variations. If it is indeed the Rite of Mizraim that Waite has reference to, it could possibly be in one of the remaining eighty-seven Degrees, much as the Ancient and Accepted Scottish Rite has embellished the Hiram Legend in some of its additional Degrees, after carrying out the Third Degree in the traditional fashion.

As to Covey-Crump's theory that Hiram Abiff is identical with the personage Hiram, King of Tyre, we find a paper by him on

[1] 'The Hiramic Legend'. *British Masonic Miscellany*, x, 18.
[2] Arthur E. Waite, *Emblematic Freemasonry* and the evolution of its deeper issues. Philadelphia, 1925, p. 188.
[3] Mackey, *Encyclopedia of Freemasonry*, ii, 673.

'Scriptural Evidence concerning Hiram',[1] which is much to the same tenor as his book-length work, but his main thesis, we may note, met with unqualified—and no doubt well-deserved—scepticism among his confrères in that Lodge of Research, and no student since 1930 has come forward to defend his views.

But the opposite theory that *two* Hirams, father and son, were involved in the biblical account of the artificer (as stated by MacBride)—and not one Hiram only (according to the general reading)—was earlier developed by Rev. Morris Rosenbaum and Professor Marks, in a paper on 'Hiram Abif'.[2] It was their opinion as well that, while the majority of readers find no visible reference in the Bible to the death of Hiram Abif, 'some (indirect) reference to the disappearance of our illustrious Grand Master does exist in the Holy Scriptures'. This they attempt to demonstrate on the assumption of there having been, in fact, two Hirams, father and son; one of them descended from the tribe of Dan, while the other was of the tribe of Naphtali. Thus do they attempt to explain the apparently varying accounts as to H.A.B.'s antecedents as given in *Kings* and in *Chronicles*—a variance that has been otherwise explained on more satisfactory grounds, as we have already seen. The father, a brass-smith only, is said in the Rosenbaum-Marks account to have made the pots and other temple utensils, while the son, an all-around craftsman, made the Two Pillars. It was the latter, they assert, who was the 'widow's son of the tribe of Naphtali', having become a 'widow's son', in fact, by the death of the father. But it is the father himself, they insist, whose death we commemorate.

On this basis, they say, Hiram Abif (a name they translate literally as 'Hiram his father') must have died while the temple was being erected, and it must have been for this reason that it is later said that 'King Solomon sent and fetched him [the son, they say] out of Tyre', ostensibly to complete the work his father's death had left unfinished.

This theory of two separate and distinct but related Hirams is credited by Rev. Dr. A. Cohen, P.M., to a still earlier non-Masonic writer, the Jewish commentator Meir Loeb Malbim (1809-1879).[3] However, the anomaly in a father and son allegedly having the

[1] *AQC* xliii.
[2] *Transactions*, Leicester Lodge of Research, 1903.
[3] A. W. Adams, *The Story of the Two Hirams*. Birmingham, England, 1931. Foreword by Dr. A. Cohen.

same name—in an Oriental country where such practices are generally eschewed—has not been explained, a point which Covey-Crump was not slow to pick up.[1] John Kitto, in his *Cyclopedia of Biblical Literature*, discounts such a possibility emphatically, 'in an age when no example occurs of the father's name being given to his son',[2] and the comment in the *Jewish Encyclopedia* is even more far-reaching. 'Before the Exile,' it says—and this is precisely the period we are considering—'children seem never to have been named after their relatives, not even in the royal family.'[3] This avoidance of giving the son the same name as the father is still observed in present-day orthodox Jewish tradition and practice, and even among those who follow the tradition without being strictly orthodox in the religious sense.

But the 'theory of the two Hirams' seems to receive additional support, in the view of Rabbi Rosenbaum and Professor Marks, from the circumstance that, in *II Chron.* 4:11, the Hebrew text gives the name as both *Huram* and *Hiram* in the same verse, thus indicating to these two writers that two different artificers are here meant. But, as against this, it is to be noted that the parallel passage in *I Kings* 7:40 gives the name as *Hiram* in both instances.[4] And we may profitably remember in this connection the comment by the Rev. C. J. Ball, who pointed out that the difference between *Hiram* and *Huram*, in the Hebrew text, is only the difference between a *yod* and a *waw*, and could be due to a copyist's error.[5]

It must be emphasized, moreover, that no satisfactory explanation has so far been offered for the circumstance of Hiram Abiff's death not being *clearly* alluded to in the Bible, instead of inferentially only. The attempt of Rosenbaum and Marks to ascribe this to the alleged 'fact' that the death was a 'Masonic secret' falls strangely on our ears these days when the non-historical theory of the 'origin' of our institution from the building of King Solomon's Temple has been pretty well demolished. Referring to a Jewish legend to the effect that, in reward for his participation in the erection of the Temple, Hiram never tasted death, but was taken

[1] Covey-Crump, *The Hiramic Tradition*, p. 31.
[2] Cited in Mackey's *Encyclopedia*, i, 24, *s.v.* ADONIRAM.
[3] *Jewish Encyclopedia*, *s.v.* NAMES (PERSONAL).
[4] In addition, Slotki, ignoring the two Hebrew forms of the name in *Chronicles*, pointed out by Rosenbaum and Marks, translates them *both* as 'Huram'.
[5] *AQC* v, 138.

up alive into Paradise, Rosenbaum and Marks believe that this legend may, in fact, have been the origin of our Hiramic Tradition.[1] 'The Israelites,' they say, 'being unacquainted with the facts of his murder, the knowledge of which was confined to only a few, accounted for his mysterious disappearance by stating that he had been received alive into Paradise.' These investigators consequently feel that, 'since the Bible . . . does, more or less indirectly, inform us of the death of Hiram Abif, we should be convinced that the legend of the third degree is something more than a legend, that it is historically true, and that they who assert that the biblical records are entirely silent upon this point, have themselves not yet seen the light'.[2]

Well!

With death—even violent and treacherous death—such a common experience in those almost-barbarous times, as in our own, this omission of a clear report of the death of Hiram Abiff, in *Kings*, *Chronicles*, *Ezekiel*, *Jeremiah*, and *Josephus*, and even in the legends of the rabbis, makes the story of the two Hirams extremely controversial and suspect, and it is high time, in my opinion, that it be consigned to the forgotten limbo of exploded theories.[3]

---

[1] This rabbinic legend is apparently the same one mentioned by Covey-Crump as having been 'recorded in a work called *Pesik Rabbati* (vi. 25, a, in Friedman's edition, 1880), . . . which was, I believe, compiled some time in the fourth century. . . .'—*The Hiramic Tradition*, p. 67.

[2] 'Hiram Abif'. The paper has been reprinted in *AQC* lxxvi, 220–224.

[3] See my article 'Further Remarks on Hiram Abif', in refutation of Rabbi Rosenbaum's theory, in *AQC* lxxvii, 274–278.

XIV

ORIGIN OF THE HIRAMIC MYTH

IT IS highly significant that as early as 1730—only a few years after
the formation of our first Grand Lodge and the official beginning
of speculative Masonry—attempts were already being made to
account for the Hiramic Legend and to seek for its meaning and
origin in the literature of the ancient past. In the anonymous
Defence of Masonry, believed by some to have been written by Martin
Clare, a prominent Mason of his time, as a counterblast to Samuel
Prichard's 1730 publication of his *Masonry Dissected*, we find the
attempt made to compare some Masonic practices, symbols, and
legends—as of that period—with similar occurrences and thoughts
among the ancients. Among these are some details of the Hiramic
Drama.[1]

'The Accident, by which the Body of Master *Hiram* was found
after his Death,' says the anonymous author, 'seems to allude in
some Circumstances to a beautiful Passage in the sixth Book of
Virgil. *Anchises* had been dead for some Time, and *Aeneas* his Son
professed so much Duty to his departed Father, that he consulted
with the *Cumaean Sybil*, whether it were possible for him to descend
into the Shades below, in order to speak with him. The Prophetess
encouraged him to go, but told him he could not succeed unless
he went into a certain Place and pluck'd a golden *Bough* or *Shrub*,
which he should carry in his Hand, and by that means obtain
Directions where he should find his Father.

'*Anchises*, the great Preserver of the *Trojan* Name,' comments the
same writer, 'could not have been discovered but by the help of a
Bough which was pluck'd *with great Ease* from the Tree; nor it
seems could *Hiram, the Grand-Master* of *Masonry*, have been

---

[1] R. F. Gould was among the supporters of the Martin Clare authorship of this
work, but the question has never been positively settled. Cf. W. Wonnacott's
paper on 'Martin Clare and the *Defence of Masonry* (1730)' in *AQC* xxviii, and
the Notes by Knoop, Jones, and Hamer, in *Early Masonic Catechisms*, p.
160.

found but by the Direction of a *Shrub*, which (says the *Dissector*) *came easily up.*'

Again, 'the principal Cause of *Aeneas*'s Descent into the Shades', continues the writer, seeking for still another analogy, 'was to enquire of his Father the Secrets of the Fates, which should some time be fulfilled among his Posterity. The Occasion of the Brethren's searching so diligently for their Master was, it seems, to receive from him the *secret Word of Masonry*, which should be deliver'd down as a Test to their *Fraternity* to After-Ages. . . .

'But,' says the writer again, 'there is another Story in *Virgil*, that stands in a nearer Relation to the Case of *Hiram*, and the Accident by which he is said to have been discovered; which is this':—and he proceeds to tell the story of Priamus, King of Troy, who had sent his son Polydorus to the King of Thrace with a great sum of money; but the Thracians, for the sake of the money, killed the son and privately buried him. '*Aeneas* coming into the Country, and accidentally plucking up a *Shrub* that was near him *on the Side of a Hill*, discovered the *murdered* Body of *Polydorus*. . . .

'The Agreement between these two Relations is so exact,' the writer confidently adds, in conclusion, 'that there wants no further Illustration.'[1]

This example is given, not to concur in the ascription of the Hiramic myth to either story of Virgil's, but rather to illustrate the manner in which, since the time of the above *Defence*, innumerable attempts have continued to be made, in all possible directions (and some impossible and improbable ones) to trace the origin of this most important of Masonic myths, the Hiramic, and especially to ascertain the approximate date of its first appearance in the Masonic system of symbology and dramatics, as well as the circumstances surrounding that first appearance.

Some have contented themselves to search in the literature, like our anonymous author had done, for some indication of origin or some suggestion, veiled or overt; while others, thinking this to be a somewhat barren and almost-hopeless task, have resorted to speculation pure and simple, based only on what each one considered to be a reasonable deduction from the few known facts. Others have gone

[1] Reproduced in *The Early Masonic Catechisms*, by Knoop, Jones and Hamer. Manchester University Press, 1943, pp. 172–174. This work, long out of print, has been reprinted by Quatuor Coronati Lodge No. 2076 (1963), and is a *must* for all students.

still further, attempting to cut the Gordian Knot by a direct reference to the Ancient Mysteries, with which our Myth does indeed have so much in common, but without giving any serious thought to historic continuity or the physical possibility or impossibility of direct transmission.

But this attempt to refer the Hiramic Myth to the Ancient Mysteries is found to have more to do with interpretation, allegory, and symbolism, all of which lie in a somewhat different dimension from our present historical study, and this will therefore be largely ignored as being outside our immediate scope and purpose. But as an example of the median course, we may take note of the opinion of an important American writer, H. L. Haywood, in the chapter on 'The Hiramic Legend', in his excellent work on *Symbolical Masonry* (Kingsport, Tennessee, 1923), towards the end of which he says:

'To me it seems reasonable to believe that the core of the drama came down from Solomon's day; that it was preserved until mediaeval times by Jewish, and especially Kabbalistic, literature; that it found a place among the traditions of the old builders because it was so intimately related to the story of the Temple, around which so much of their symbolism revolved; that it was inherited by seventeenth-century Masons, in crude form, and along with the mass of other traditions; that it was elaborated and given its literary form by the early framers of the Ritual; and that it was adopted by them because it embodied so wonderfully the idea at the centre of the Third Degree.' To all this he adds, candidly enough, 'this theory can not be proved by documentary evidence, but it is the opinion toward which the *drift* of all our data seems to lead one'.

With those who are satisfied to follow such drifts and general indications—and there are many among our most sincere and devoted Brethren—there can be no quarrel, but to those others who would seek for something more substantial in the way of evidence we will now address ourselves.

The literary evidence

Dr. George Oliver, trying to follow the written evidence, comes to the (for him) surprising conclusion that the Hiramic Myth was only a product of the first Grand Lodge period, and thinks it may even have been the concoction of Dr. James Anderson.[1] From the

[1] Geo. Oliver, *Freemason's Treasury*. London, 1863, pp. 309–310.

numerous variations that we actually find in the Working Tools used in various Jurisdictions, as part of the Hiramic Drama, and the various gates of the Temple at which they are said to have been used, as well as the different names of the three assassins involved in the affair, Oliver argues that 'if the Third had been an old and firmly established degree at the revival of Masonry in the eighteenth century', such variations in the Drama would scarcely have happened. (But 'variations', it would seem, on the contrary, are as natural and inevitable a product of genuine legend as they are of biological heredity.) Before 1717, Oliver says, further, 'the subject was never ventilated', and hence, he thinks, 'the wilderness of criticism on the subject in the eighteenth century constitutes a cogent evidence that it was a new creation'. But this criticism he speaks of appears to have been mainly in the realm of speculation with regard to its symbolism and interpretation, and it is hardly conceivable that any such speculation could have taken place in the days of the purely operative Masons, before the speculatives had come on the scene.

So on both counts Dr. Oliver seems to be in error with respect to the novelty of the Hiramic Legend, and more recent Masonic scholarship is found to be almost unanimously opposed to him.

It is true that such an important critic as Dr. W. Begemann, the great classifier of the *Old Charges*, agrees with Dr. Oliver's belief in the comparatively late creation of the Hiramic Legend, though on other grounds. He points in evidence to the *Spencer MS.*, as an example of these *Old Charges*, in which the double name of Hiram Abif appears to have been introduced for the first time. He consequently comes to the conclusion that the original MS. from which the *Spencer MS.* was compiled 'was fabricated about 1725', and 'the arbitrary insertion of Hiram *Abif* seems to have been the chief purpose of the compiler, in order to maintain the antiquity of the Hiramic legend (the Third Degree having been introduced in 1724).' But he does not think that the perpetrator of this alleged antiquity was Dr. Anderson, as Dr. Oliver and some others have thought, although he does point to the introduction, for the first time, in Anderson's *Constitutions* of 1723, of the double name 'Hiram Abif', which he claims was unknown to Masonic tradition before that time.[1]

Unfortunately, Dr. Begemann chooses to ignore the long list of

[1] Dr. W. Begemann, *AQC* i, pp. 202, 206–208.

'substitute names' by which the artificer of the Temple was certainly known in practically all of the preceding *Old Charges*. The esoteric significance of these 'substitute names', and the purpose for which they were used, in place of the real one, has been ably and more recently analysed and demonstrated by J. E. S. Tuckett, as we shall presently see, and this would now seem to vitiate to a large extent the criticism that Dr. Begemann had expressed as to the 'alleged' antiquity of the Hiramic Legend.

Historical indications

In the Discussion of Professor S. P. Johnston's paper on 'Seventeenth-Century Descriptions of Solomon's Temple', Chetwode Crawley has so excellently summarized in a few words the many historical possibilities—and impossibilities—involved in the question of the Hiramic Legend that I do not hesitate to quote his exact words, although I am not fully in agreement with all his ideas.

'The Hiramic Legend,' he begins by saying, 'is so prominent in the speculative Freemasonry of to-day that we find it hard to conceive a time when it did not form part of our Ritual. . . .

'If we may apply the ordinary canons that govern historical investigation, it would seem that the choice of such a stage for the setting of a Builder's Legend could only be made in Christian times. . . . Some speculators have, indeed, suggested that such a Legend might have come to the *Collegia Fabrorum*[1] in the interval between the building of King Solomon's Temple and the Birth of Christ. But there is not a shadow of probability, much less a tittle of evidence to support the speculation. . . . The gap caused by the Dark Ages, the gap of five centuries between the cessation of Architecture in the West and the resuscitation of the art by the Cathedral builders after the eleventh century, cannot be bridged over, consistently with our present knowledge. [But] the Cathedral-builders were occupied with the transmission of Geometrical methods that enabled them to conquer the intricate mechanical and mathematical problems involved in the construction of the marvels of architecture they have bequeathed to us. Thus the Geometry derived from classical sources tinged their inner work, and a

---

[1] One of the divisions of the *Roman Collegia*, said to have been instituted by Numa Pompilius about 700 B.C. Cf. A. G. Mackey, *History of Freemasonry*, ii, pp. 474–475.

Hebrew Legend would have been incongruous.[1] . . . Very cogent evidence would have to be presented before any student acquainted with the anti-Jewish prejudices of the time could give credence to the acceptance of a Hebrew hero in our Craft Assemblies at any period during the Middle Ages.'[2]

'Thirdly, King Solomon's Temple may have presented itself to the authors of the Revival of 1717 as a fitting *mise en scène* for the embodiment of the highest moral truths. . . . But it is incredible that the Legend should have been introduced by them as a pure innovation. The introduction of incomparably smaller innovations in the same generation raised such a storm that the Craft in England was split in twain for many a year. . . . Here, again, the historical circumstances seem to show that the Revival of 1717 was not the epoch of which we are in search.

' . . . There remains a fourth epoch which has hardly yet emerged from the realm of pure conjecture. The suggestion has been made that the Legend may have been brought home by Craftsmen who had accompanied the Crusaders to lands where such a Legend may have been current. . . . But the hobby was ridden so hard in the hope of establishing some connection with the Knight Templars, that all men nowadays fight shy of it. . . .

'The subject is not ripe for judicial decision. . . . Still, it would not come wholly as a surprise if it should turn out the planting of the Legend in a Hebrew environment was due to English Craftsmen, amongst whom the leaven of Lollardism was working.'[3]

In the Discussion of the same paper of Prof. Johnston's, W. H. Rylands took occasion to cite a statement of the architectural writer James Fergusson (author of the article 'Temple' in Smith's *Dictionary of the Bible*) to the effect that 'throughout the middle ages it [Solomon's Temple] influenced to a considerable degree the forms of Christian Churches, and its peculiarities were the watchwords and rallying points of all associations of builders'. Now, says Rylands, following the argument to an obviously logical conclusion, if 'the Temple and its builder were subjects of admiration, imitation,

---

[1] This is not necessarily true. But as a personal opinion it may stand alongside other such opinions.

[2] This also is not quite true, as the almost enthusiastic acceptance of King Solomon as the hero of an enormous body of legend, by an otherwise anti-Jewish society, readily demonstrates.

[3] *AQC* xii, p. 143.

and it may be emulation, with the Master Masons of the middle ages, we need not look far for the origin of the connexion between the Temple and its builder, and the legend of the speculative Masons'. And he adds a confirmation of the view we have just seen expressed by Dr. Chetwode Crawley as to the necessarily earlier-than-1717 age of that legend, *contra* Begemann and Oliver. 'The legend,' says Rylands, 'may have been adopted at any period, but I cannot think that it was within the power of the newly "revived" Grand Lodge to at once make any radical change in the Masonry it inherited.'[1]

Reverting again to the Discussion of Prof. Johnston's paper, and to Dr. Chetwode Crawley's suggestion as to the period of the Crusades, G. W. Speth offers the confirmatory thought that he himself can see no epoch more likely for the incorporation of the Hiramic Legend into mediaeval Masonry than that of the return from the Crusades, contrary to the opinion that Chetwode Crawley himself had expressed. 'The Knights of the Cross', Speth reminds us, 'were enthusiastic builders: the remains of their churches dot the Holy Land to this day. The European builders [of these churches] must, in the nature of things, have acquired large numbers of native workmen to assist them, and among these the Temple legend, *if it existed* [my italics] would certainly be known. The builders on their return would have brought the legend with them, and it would have been adopted all the more readily as it was in perfect accord with the traditions, aye, even the practices, of that age in England. And possibly the first echo we have of its existence is, as already pointed out, in the Matthew Cooke MS. This is only a theory', he admits, but, he thinks, 'a plausible one.'[2]

As to the seventeenth-century literature respecting King Solomon's Temple which had developed so much interest in the Discussion, Prof. Johnston had found that 'in the seventeenth century, the description of Solomon's Temple excited a very considerable amount of attention and interest, but that in the writings that appeared, there was little if anything of special Masonic importance. . . . It shows that the legends were not taken wholesale into our system from an outside source of current knowledge, and leaves us with the alternative that this characteristic of our Craft was either part and parcel of the ancient teaching, or that it was an

[1] *AQC* xii, 146.
[2] *AQC* xii, 148.

addition made at or about the beginning of modern Masonry.'[1]

A similar scholarly paper on 'King Solomon' by Gerard Brett comes to a like conclusion. '. . . There are no traces of it [the Hiramic Legend] in mediaeval literature, and its absence where so much else is present is highly significant.'[2] What he obviously means by 'highly significant' points in the direction of the first alternative offered by Prof. Johnston, namely, that the Legend must have been 'part and parcel of the ancient teaching'. In fact, says R. J. Meekren, 'it seems too much to believe that such a Legend, coupled with such a Ritual, . . . could have been devised by eighteenth-century scholars, or even evolved by sixteenth-century craftsmen.'[3]

'The Master Builder'
in the Constitutions and Catechisms

One of the difficulties encountered in any attempt to push the Hiramic Legend back to a time antecedent to its more or less overt reference in Anderson's 1723 *Book of Constitutions* is the well-known fact that the name of Hiram or Hiram Abiff is not openly mentioned in any of the earliest *Old Charges* or *Manuscript Constitutions* but only in those belonging to the relatively late group of MSS. Among these latter is the *Cama MS.* (1700–1725), the *Dumfries No. 4 MS.* (*c.* 1710), the *Spencer MS.* (1726), and the *Inigo Jones*. This last-mentioned MS., it is true, is found inscribed with the date 1607, but with what appears to be a brush stroke rather than with the fine pen used in the rest of the MS., thus giving the suggestion of a later interpolation. In spite of this, the early dating has been accepted by some as genuine, and this has led to no little confusion, but the inscription is now thought by most reputable students to be false. From internal evidence, says Tuckett, the MS. 'could not have been written until after 1655', and, says Gould, 'must really have been compiled about 1723–25'.[4]

As to the *Book of Constitutions*, the first edition of 1723 gives us,

[1] Prof. Swift P. Johnston, 'Seventeenth Century Descriptions of Solomon's Temple', *AQC* xii.

[2] *AQC* lxvi, p. 89.

[3] R. J. Meekren, 'The Origin of the Legend of the Third Degree'. *The Builder*, June 1923.

[4] R. F. Gould, *A Concise History of Freemasonry*. London, 1903, p. 218. A facsimile of the title-page with the 1607 inscription can be seen in *QCA* (Reprints of Quatuor Coronati Lodge) vol. vi.

on two succeeding pages, a very long footnote by way of commentary on several passages in *Kings* and *Chronicles* where the name of Hiram (Abiff) is mentioned, in an endeavour to elucidate the meaning of the name, in its several significations, as well as to ascertain the tribal affiliation of the person so named, and his importance in the Solomonic scheme.

The existence of this long footnote, and the necessity (at least in the mind of Dr. Anderson, and, presumably, in that of his readers) for its interpolation, has led to a good deal of speculation, *pro* and *contra* the frequently-alleged antiquity of the Hiramic Tradition. On the one hand, the fact that this name came to be so suddenly sprung for the first time, so to speak, upon the official Masonic world in 1723 has caused some (R. F. Gould, for example)[1] to conjecture that the whole Hiramic myth was, in fact, an invention of the period in question, and not a genuine tradition carried over from a more or less remote past. But on the other hand, there have been those, like G. W. Speth (the first Secretary of Quatuor Coronati Lodge of Research, in London, and editor of its Transactions, and a reputed scholar on his own account), who have argued that this long footnote indicated, quite to the contrary, that Hiram Abiff 'was a character of special importance to the Fraternity, and his peculiar name required explanation. He must, therefore,' Speth continues, 'have been known to the Craft at that time, although not mentioned by name in any of our earliest MS. Constitutions,' the so-called *Old Charges*. 'To argue otherwise,' he points out, 'is equivalent to the assertion that Anderson deliberately introduced an unfamiliar name, not found even in the then current Scriptures, for the sole purpose of explaining and commenting on it in an unusually long note: an act of sublime pedantry with which I am not prepared to credit him.'[2] J. E. S. Tuckett has accordingly expressed the opinion that the account of H.A.B. in the 1723 *Book of Constitutions* was certainly an indication, at the very least—even if this indication does not amount to absolute proof—that 'the Legend of the III° was already (1723) a part of Masonic Tradition'.[3]

As still another indication, Tuckett calls attention—in an important paper on 'The Hiramic Legend and the Revival of 1717'—to the Catechism appearing in a 1723 newspaper, subsequently titled

[1] Cf. *AQC* i, p. 36.
[2] *AQC* xi, 58.
[3] *AQC* xxxii, 49.

by Gould *A Mason's Examination*, and which refers to 'the Master's Part' (the name by which the Degree of Master Mason was called at that period) and to a blind-folded Candidate's 'Ceremony of—' (not otherwise identified, but which Tuckett thinks refers cryptically to the 'raising'), after which 'the word *Maughbin* is whisper'd by the youngest Mason to the next, and so on, till it comes to the Master, who whispers it to the entered Mason, who must have his Face in due Order to receive it,' the Points of Fellowship being also specifically mentioned (six, in this case).[1] Tuckett consequently thinks that, 'remembering Brother Gould's judgment as to the antiquity of the text of this Catechism,'[2] and 'admitting freely that the demonstration is not absolute, it is nevertheless claimed that there is the strongest possible reason, short of actual documentary proof, for believing that not only the Hiramic Legend but also its Masonic Application belong to the pre-Grand Lodge period of our Order.'

'To sum up and conclude,' he says, 'the matter may be conveniently stated thus—on Philological grounds, the Hiramic Legend is declared to be older than 1717. . . . "The Master's Part" in a printed document of date 1723, but of which the text is much earlier, included [presumably] the Hiramic Legend of the Death of the Builder. There was a "Master's Part" before 1717.'[3]

The 'Philological grounds' to which Tuckett has reference has to do with an important paper by the Rev. C. J. Ball (said to have been one of our best Hebraists), entitled 'The Proper Names of Masonic Tradition: A Philological Study.'[4] The most significant part of the paper, for our present purpose, could not be printed, unfortunately, but we have the testimony of R. F. Gould himself to the effect that the presentation in Lodge settled 'beyond dispute . . . that what we now call the [Legend of the] Third Degree, existed

---

[1] The complete Catechism is reproduced in Knoop, Jones and Hamer's collection, *The Early Masonic Catechisms*, pp. 65–69.

[2] '. . . The catechism of 1723 contains a reading which is several years older than the printed copy . . . Its whole tenor betrays an *operative* origin. . . .' R. F. Gould, *History of Freemasonry*, iii, 114. (Page references to Gould's longer *History* are to the 1905 Pacific Coast Yorston Edition in five volumes.)

[3] J. E. S. Tuckett, Somerset Masters Lodge No. 3746 *Transactions*, 1921. (I have added the word 'presumably' because the demonstration, in my estimation, is not quite as positive as Tuckett would make it out to be.) Tuckett's important paper can also be found cited in part in Mackey's *Encyclopedia of Freemasonry*, 1946 Ed., ii, 654.

[4] *AQC* v, 136–141.

before the era of Grand Lodge. . . .'[1] G. W. Speth expressed himself even more definitely and to the same purpose.[2]

In the main, Dr. Poole is found to have agreed with Tuckett's exposition, as detailed above, but he appears to have come to his own conclusion from a somewhat different direction, which perhaps adds to the weight and value of his opinion. Analysing the Masonic Catechisms of the two decades preceding the formation of Grand Lodge, he infers from the words and signs found therein that 'at the end of the seventeenth century there was a particular interest in Hiram, the Master Craftsman of King Solomon's Temple, and in the manner of his death. . . . Both the word and the "points of fellowship" associated with it (especially in the *Trinity College Dublin MS.*) [1711] suggest very strongly that this third degree was concerned with Hiram. . . .'[3]

Like Tuckett, with his 1723 *Mason's Examination*, Harry Carr calls our attention to the fact that only some four years or so after the 1723 *Book of Constitutions* had come out, and some three years before Prichard's *Masonry Dissected*, '*The Wilkinson MS.* (which may be dated about 1727) also has a Hiram question which indicated the existence *in Masonic usage* of a Hiramic legend at that time.'[4]

Attention has also been called by some writers to the fact that, at the Installation of the Duke of Montagu as Grand Master in 1721, we are told that he 'immediately call'd forth (without naming him before) as it were carelessly, John Beal, M.D. as his *Deputy Grand Master*, whom Brother *Payne* invested, and install'd him in *Hiram Abiff's* Chair on the *Grand Master's Left Hand*'.[5] If, in fact, this represents a true and accurate account of the actual proceedings, this casual reference to 'Hiram Abiff's Chair' betokens a familiarity with the place this personage must have enjoyed in the Masonic scheme as early as 1721 that is not always appreciated.

It must be pointed out, however, that the argument loses some

---

[1] R. F. Gould, *Concise History*, p. 306.
[2] *AQC* xi, 59.
[3] H. Poole, 'The Substance of Pre-Grand Lodge Freemasonry'. *AQC* lxi, 132, 134.
[4] The passage in question is as follows:
   Q. What is the form of your Lodge
   A. An Oblong Square
   Q. Why so
   A. the Manner of our Great Master Hirams grave.
The Wilkinson Manuscript, ed. by Knoop, Jones and Hamer, 1946, p. 26.
[5] *The New Book of Constitutions*, by James Anderson, D.D., 1738. *QCA* vii, 113.

of its force when we recollect that this report was not made till 1738. By that time, the use of the term may have become well established, and its reported use as of 1721 may have been only an unconscious trick of memory. The Minutes of Grand Lodge do not commence till June 24, 1723. Despite this, G. W. Speth was of the opinion that 'the statement, nevertheless, comes down to us on evidence of great weight', and that the reference to Hiram Abiff in the Installation Ceremony mentioned above 'goes far to prove that the Hiramic Legend was well known in its entirety long before we hear of a Master Mason's degree. . . .'[1]

Antiquity of the Hiramic Tradition

Speth has applied himself to this question of the antiquity of the Hiramic Tradition from still another angle. In his scholarly *Builders' Rites and Ceremonies: The Folk Lore of Masonry*,[2] he has shown the widespread prevalence of a traditional belief among builders of all ages and climes in the necessity for a 'foundation-sacrifice' or a 'completion-sacrifice' to ensure the stability of any important edifice. And, says he, 'whether the actual immolation took place or not, the tradition of it was so ingrained that almost every important edifice was connected with some tragic legend. In the majority of cases, the alleged victim was either the builder, architect, or an apprentice.' And why, asks Speth pertinently, should Solomon's Temple, of all buildings, lack such a tradition? 'Is it not highly probable,' he argues, elsewhere, 'so probable as to practically amount to a certainty, that the masons would have preserved a similar legend in connection with the Temple of Jerusalem?'[3]

Another argument in favour of the pre-Grand Lodge antiquity of the Hiramic Legend—and perhaps even of the ceremony associated with it—comes from the pen of Lionel Vibert, and was expressed by him in his 1925 Prestonian Lecture on 'The Development of the Trigradal System'. 'We are often told,' he reminds us, 'that both legend and degree were constructed in the early years of Grand Lodge, presumably therefore in or before 1721. But it is to me, at all events, difficult of acceptance that so drastic an innovation —for such it would assuredly have been—was not only permitted but was endorsed by the Antients when, in 1751, they came to

[1] *AQC* ii, 80.
[2] Quatuor Coronati Pamphlet No. 1, 1951.
[3] *AQC* xi, 59.

restore the old system and remove the alterations introduced by the Premier Grand Lodge. . . .' Vibert then goes on to give some reasons for believing it 'difficult to avoid the conclusion that there was not merely a murder legend among the Craft in this country from a very early date, but that for two centuries at least [that is, in the sixteenth and seventeenth centuries] it had been definitely a Hiramic Legend', when 'the scribes who copied the various versions of our Old Charges had scruples as to writing the name of Hiram the builder, and substituted Anon or Amon or the like for it . . . I think we can assert unhesitatingly,' he concludes, 'that the Master's Part, and therefore the Hiramic Legend, antedates the Grand Lodge era.'[1]

R. J. Meekren has similarly expressed himself as saying, in a series of articles on 'Historical Notes on the Masonic Ritual', that 'the chief reason for believing in the antiquity of the Master's grade, . . . is the fact that it is a psychological impossibility that it could have been invented in the eighteenth century.'[2] And H. L. Haywood has stated that 'the internal evidence indicates that it is much older than the Eighteenth Century. In its spirit and feeling and action it is far more Mediaeval than modern.'[3]

Arguments such as these, however—cogent as they may appear to be on the surface, and reputable as their proponents undoubtedly are—have failed to convey complete conviction in the opinion of some, because of the absence of positive proof of the existence of the legend in question, as far as the mediaeval masons were concerned. This lack of conviction has been aided and abetted by the total absence, above referred to, of any mention even of the name of Hiram Abiff in any except the latest of our *Old Charges*. Thus R. F. Gould, in his 1903 *Concise History*, reasons that, 'if Hiram Abif had either figured in the ceremonial or the traditions of the Craft at a period anterior to the eighteenth century, the Manuscript Constitutions of corresponding date would not maintain, as they do, such a uniform and unbroken silence with respect to the existence (legendary or otherwise) of such a leading character in the later history and symbolism of the Craft.'[4]

[1] *The Collected Prestonian Lectures*, 1925–1960, pp. 39, 42.
[2] *The Philalethes Magazine*, Dec. 1949, p. 4.
[3] A. G. Mackey, *Encyclopedia of Freemasonry*, iii, 1210.
[4] R. F. Gould, *Concise History*, p. 219. Gould, apparently, did not realize the obvious contradiction between this negative view and his previously-noted opinion relative to the pre-Grand Lodge antiquity of the Third Degree. See p. 289, *ante*.

Others, however, arguing from the same well-established facts, have come to a diametrically opposite conclusion. They base this conclusion, in fact, upon the very *absence* of direct reference to the *name* of Hiram Abiff (except, as stated, in the comparatively late Spencer Family of MSS.), while on the other hand there is the ever-present account of the 'master mason' *himself*, in the flesh, in all the *Old Charges* beginning with the *Cooke MS.*, our second oldest, dated about 1410 A.D. However, as we have seen,[1] this 'master mason' is almost always referred to in these *Old Charges* by a 'substitute name' such as Aynon, Amon, Hynon, Dynon, and other variants; while in at least two cases—the *Langdale MS.* (late seventeenth century) and the *Antiquity MS.* (1686)—the name is left entirely blank.[2] All this, they think, bespeaks a certain mystery connected with the personality of this 'master mason', to the point where even his name would be held to be too esoteric to be given in its correct form; or, as in the case of the *Langdale* and the *Antiquity*, in any form at all.

Thus, 'it has often been suggested', says Dr. Poole, with obvious approval, 'that the form "Aymon" (or variant), which could hardly have been the result of a copying error, was used as a disguise for Hiram, as this name had some esoteric significance attached to it.'[3] 'It certainly is difficult to derive Aynon from Hiram philologically,' says G. W. Speth, arguing along similar lines, 'especially if we remember that a mere reference to any Bible would have instantly given the correct name. Why then this persistence in setting out a false one? Is it intentional? and does it point to a mystery?'[4] Lionel Vibert, in fact, thinks that it does, and that the name itself may have been a password, and had perhaps come to be associated at a very early date with some narrative or parable.[5]

The 'substitute names' of Hiram Abiff

J. E. S. Tuckett has given this subject of the 'substitute names' the most explicit elaboration, in a highly significant and well-received

[1] Ch. V.
[2] E.g.: From the *Antiquity MS.*: '. . . and he had a son called . . . that was Master of Geomitrie and was cheife Master of all his Masons. . . .' etc.—W. J. Hughan, *The Old Charges of British Freemasons*. London, 1872, p. 65. A similar blank space occurs later in the MS.
[3] *AQC* lxi, 133.
[4] *AQC* xii, 147.
[5] Lionel Vibert, *The Story of the Craft*. London, p. 76.

paper on 'The Old Charges and the Chief Master Mason',[1] wherein he analyses in detail these 'substitute names' that we find in the *Old Charges*, and traces them to their possible or probable Hebrew roots and derivatives.

Analysing them thus, he finds that these 'substitute names' were not arbitrarily chosen, neither were they corruptions of genuine names, but have significances in themselves that are definitely suggestive.

These 'substitute names' used in the *Old Charges* for Solomon's Master Mason, Tuckett tells us, fall into two classes. The first class contains the most numerous examples, wherein we find such variants as *Amnon, Aymen, Aaman, A Man*, etc. Tuckett calls attention to the name *Amnon*, for example, which in Hebrew signifies *faithful* or *faithful one*.[2] Similarly, *Amon* is rendered *a master workman* in the Revised Version, while *Aman* (*Song of Solomon*, 7:1–2) is translated *a cunning workman* in both the Revised and Authorized Versions of the Bible. Several Hebrew-English Lexicons give different variants of this word the rendering of *artificer, architect, artist*.[3]

Equally suggestive, says Tuckett, is the second class of 'substitute names', found only in two of the *Old Charges*: the *Stanley* and the *Carson MSS.*, both of 1677. These do not employ the *Aman* variant, but give the King's Master Mason the completely different 'substitute name' of *Apleo* instead. This, Tuckett thinks, may have some connection with a Hebrew-Arabic root APL, signifying *to*

[1] *AQC* xxxvi, 179–192.

[2] I might, in addition, here cite the *Jewish Encyclopedia* (New York, 1901) which mentions the name of *Amnon* (s.v.), the eldest son of King David and Ahinoam, and whose name the Encyclopedia translates as 'Steadfast'.

[3] But a curious commentary on the power of coincidence, however, is afforded us in a note by Lionel Vibert, in his suggestion of the possibly accidental connection between the 'Aymon' in some of the *Old Charges* and the Aymon of the Charlemagne Ballad Cycle. 'The story of the Four Sons of Aymon', Vibert tells us, 'was one of the first works printed in England by Caxton. . . . In that story Renaud, the eldest son, is stated to have worked as a mason at the building of Cologne cathedral, where he was slain with a mason's hammer by certain of his fellows who were jealous of his superior strength.'—*Freemasonry before the Era of Grand Lodges*, p. 138. For the full story, see *AQC* xxxviii, 94.

Many Masonic speculations have been wrecked on similarly accidental verbal coincidences, yet Covey-Crump thinks the story might conceivably have given colour to the Hiramic Tradition in either Freemasonry or the French Compagnonnage.—*The Hiramic Tradition*, London, 1934, p. 68.

disappear, and with some derivatives all connected with *darkness* (cf. *Amos* 5:20).

Considering all these various substitutions given in the *Old Charges* for the real name of Hiram Abiff 'the widow's son of the tribe of Naphtali', Tuckett demonstrates that all these variants, when conjoined, describe the actual *person* (whose true *name*, however, is not given) as

> A cunning master workman, entrusted, found true and faithful, THE MASTER, (whose name was the) Secret to be concealed, i.e., not to be communicated (except to those qualified.)

A collateral line of reasoning with respect to the possible antiquity of the Hiramic Tradition centres itself around the various translations of the Bible in so far as they do or do not disclose the double name *Hiram Abiff* (or *Abi*, *Abiv*, *Abif*). The *double* name, as in the original Hebrew, is first found (among the translated versions) in Luther's German Bible, 1534. Then, in England, in the Coverdale Bible, 1535; the Matthew Bible, 1537; the Taverner Bible, 1539. But the frantic destruction of Protestant Bibles which raged during the influence of the Roman Church, in the time of Henry VIII and of Mary is said to have 'conferred upon *all* the editions of the Coverdale, Matthew, and Taverner Bibles the halo of extreme rarity', so that from 1551, the date of the second edition of the Taverner Bible, the double name of Hiram Abif 'disappeared entirely so far as the English Bible is concerned', and thus faded from the consciousness of the British Bible-reading public. In the meantime the name had continued to be used in Masonic circles, it is believed, but as a secret name; and was represented in the exoteric *Old Charges* only by means of a substituted Hebrew title or description which nevertheless correctly indicated the character of the person so represented. The true name eventually reappeared publicly and suddenly in Anderson's footnote of 1723, but, since it could not have then come from *current* knowledge of the English Bible, Tuckett argues that it could only have been handed down by oral Masonic tradition. And the obvious content of that tradition, he suggests, may have been in connection with the Hiramic Drama.

Ivor Grantham has expressed a very similar view, and in very emphatic terms.[1]

Now, the original from which *Dowland's MS.* is believed to have

[1] *AQC* lxxii, 37.

been copied, and the first of the *Old Charges* (in our present collection) to have carried a substitute name, is ascribed by Wm. J. Hughan to a date of about 1550 A.D.,[1] and the operative Masons are known to have used these *Old Charges* for the purpose of reading them out at the admission of Apprentices, and perhaps also at the 'passing' of a Fellowcraft, as we have seen.[2] We are thus left with the quite plausible surmise that these operative Masons, from about 1550, and conceivably even earlier, may have been well aware of the imputed esoteric non-biblical character of the Chief Master Mason who officiated at the building of King Solomon's Temple, but which they wished to commemorate for some reason of their own. They, however, effectively concealed this esoteric character and this commemorative reason under a number of substitute names—so effectively, in fact, that it was not till their comparatively recent 'decoding' by Tuckett that we have been able to demonstrate some 'secret' associated in their minds with that artisan, though the exact nature of that 'secret' has so far not come to light. We may reasonably infer, however—considering, once again, the inherent conservatism and tradition-mindedness of our institution—that it was of a nature similar to, and perhaps even identical with, the present one.

The birth and growth of a Legend

We may now briefly take note of some of the legends that have gradually encrusted themselves in the Masonic tradition around the personality of Hiram Abiff.

The earliest public utterance of this kind, in the first edition of Anderson's *Book of Constitutions*, 1723, is simple enough. In the course of a discussion of the building of King Solomon's Temple, and the aid given to the King of Israel by Hiram, King of Tyre, Anderson adds:

'But above all, he sent his Namesake HIRAM, or *Huram*, the most accomplish'd Mason upon Earth.'[3]

Anderson then indulges in a lengthy footnote on the name and antecedents of this *le Huram Abhi*, mentioned in the Second *Book*

---

[1] See *ante*, p. 100.
[2] See *ante*, pp. 90, 91.
[3] *The Constitutions of Freemasons*, 1723. Bernard Quaritch Facsimile Edition, 1923, p. 11.

of Chronicles, the significance of which we have already had occasion to examine.

But in the second edition of the *Constitutions*, 1738, Anderson now sees fit to embellish the previously simple account:

> 'But above all, he sent his Name sake HIRAM ABBIF, the most accomplish'd Designer and Operator upon Earth, who in *Solomon's* Absence fill'd the Chair as *Deputy* Grand Master, and in his Presence was the *Senior* Grand Warden, or principal Surveyor and *Master* of *Work*.'[1]

Anderson here goes into the same lengthy dissertation on the name of Hiram Abiff, in a footnote, as in the first edition, but follows this with a description of the division of the Craft in Solomon's time into Masters, Wardens, Fellow Crafts, and Enter'd Prentices, 'according to the *Traditions* of old Masons, who talk much of these Things', as he explains in a marginal notation.

The Temple, he then goes on to say, 'was finish'd in the short space of 7 Years and 6 Months, to the Amazement of all the World; when the *Cape-Stone* was celebrated by the *Fraternity* with great joy. But their Joy was soon interrupted by the sudden Death of their dear Master HIRAM ABBIF, whom they decently interr'd in the *Lodge* near the *Temple* according to antient Usage.'

And finally, after a paragraph citing the mourning over the death of Hiram Abiff, and the subsequent Dedication and Consecration of the Temple, Anderson adds in his Second Edition—just as he had done in his First, immediately after a description of some of the architectural features of the Temple, together with its Dedication and Consecration—the short but highly significant phrase that has been so much commented upon by almost every writer on the subject:

> 'But leaving what must not, and indeed what cannot be committed to Writing. . . .'

This further embellishment of the Legend, in 1738, is believed by some to have been prompted by the appearance, in 1730, of Samuel Prichard's *Masonry Dissected*, giving one alleged version of the Hiramic Myth. Tuckett, commenting on this last phrase of Anderson's, just cited, says, with obvious justification, 'it is absurd to suppose that these matters which may not be *written* . . . are no more than details of the plan and equipment of the Temple. There

[1] *The New Book of Constitutions*, 1738. *QCA* vii, p. 12.

is no valid reason to doubt that the [Andersonian] reference is to the Hiramic Legend of the Death of the Builder.'[1] And, it might be added, if this Legend had been invented out of hand around about that period, as has been claimed by some writers, any such exhortation to secrecy as Anderson expressed here would have been found ridiculous in the extreme by the Freemasons of the time and would have been laughed out of court.

To continue with the growth of the Legend.

In the course of the planning of the design of the Temple, and on the trestle-board used by Hiram Abiff for that purpose, made of wood and coated with wax, as was the custom, says Mackey, Hiram 'inscribed his plans with a pen or stylus of steel, which an old tradition, preserved by Oliver, says was found upon him when he was raised, and ordered by King Solomon to be deposited in the centre of his monument. The same tradition informs us that the first time he used this stylus for any of the purposes of the Temple was on the morning that the foundation stone of the building was laid, when he drew the celebrated diagram known as the forty-seventh problem of Euclid, and which gained a prize that Solomon had offered on that occasion.'[2]

This latter detail may possibly have reference to a legend found in a sheet appearing under the title *Freemasons Hewreka and Guide*, sub-headed 'The Origin of the Masonic L——s', and which may be a Finch publication (which would therefore place it at about the beginning of the nineteenth century), and containing the following:

'. . . Solomon, King of Israel, sent to Hiram, King of Tyre, for men and materials to carry on the Temple of Jerusalem; when *Hiram Abiff* was sent with the strongest recommendation imaginable. This noble recommendation of King Hiram was soon after amply verified, in the admirable discovery he made to King Solomon, on the morning the foundation stone of the Temple was laid; which discovery has ever since been considered by Freemasons his amazing HEUREKA. This procured him the distinguishing mark of King Solomon's approbation, in appointing him *Grand Architect of Jerusalem.*'

This passage is preceded by a description of the filial duty displayed by Hiram Abiff on previous occasions, in freely relinquishing

---

[1] J. E. S. Tuckett, 'The Hiramic Legend and the Revival of 1717', *Transactions*, Somerset Masters Lodge No. 3746 (1921).

[2] Mackey's *Encyclopedia of Freemasonry*, i, 457.

honours bestowed upon him by the King of Tyre, in order to attend to his aged and ailing father, and, later, his widowed and ailing mother. All this, in an attempt to establish the source of our English 'Lewis' tradition:

'When the workmen were about to quit Jerusalem, at the finishing of the Temple, he [King Solomon] strongly recommended them to prefer a man for his *filial duty*, who was *free* and otherwise qualified, to any other person, however dignified by birth or fortune; and at all initiations, to take precedence of every other person; and if such a man was the *son of a Mason*, with good natural capacity, he might receive the honours of masonry three years under the common age of maturity. This recommendation of King Solomon was to serve them and us, as a perpetual memorial of their worthy and inspired Grand Master Hiram Abiff.'[1]

So far, of course, there is no hint of tragedy of any sort, other than the simple though untimely demise of the Grand Architect previously recounted. Frequent reference has been made to the 1730 publication of Prichard's *Masonry Dissected* as the supposedly first appearance in print of some details of the Hiramic Legend, as given at the end of our Chapter V.

But some of these details are already found to have been common knowledge around the year 1728, when John Coustos is said to have made some reference to his Masonic experiences in London, in his painfully forced disclosures to the Portuguese Inquisition in 1743, as we have already noted.[2] This is laid out for us in the following terms:

He [John Coustos] further said:

That the first institution and origin from which were derived . . . the signs of the Masters, come from the time when Solomon built his sumptuous Temple, whereby for the better administration of the work, and distinguishing between Officers and Apprentices labouring therein, he, Solomon, made the separation of signs above described, which were initiated by a Master named Hiram, who was next in government to Solomon, and to whom alone was revealed the Sign which pertained to him as Master,

---

[1] *AQC* viii, 27, 32, 162. (For the tradition connecting Hiram Abiff with a theme of filial devotion, as given in the *Hewreka and Guide*, see Bernard E. Jones, *Freemasons' Guide and Compendium*. London, 1950, p. 314.)

[2] See *ante*, p. 61.

in order thus to be differentiated from the other and inferior officers who worked in the same undertaking. And some of the Officers or Apprentices perceiving this, and desiring to learn the secret sign which he had, three of the said Officers arranged amongst themselves that, upon the first occasion on which he next came to the Temple to give the customary orders, they would compel him to reveal the said Sign, guarding for this purpose the three doors of the said Temple which faced the East, the West, and the South; and when the said Master was come, he was first asked by the Officer at one of the doors for the said Sign, to which he replied that he could not divulge it since he was forbidden to do so; and that they, having already been a long time in the service, would in due course attain and discover that position they desired; whereupon the Officer struck him upon the head with a wooden cudgel; and the Master seeking to escape by the remaining doors, the others likewise gave him other blows, one with a wooden crowbar, and the other with a hammer, also of wood; so that with the last blow he fell dead; and in order that the said Officers might conceal what has just been described they buried him in a distant spot where he might not be discovered.

After three days King Solomon having noticed his absence enquired for him, and seeing that he did not appear, he appointed fifteen of the said Officers to use all possible diligence in discovering what had happened to the said Master.

And fifteen days having gone by in this search one of the said Officers came to that spot, and being much fatigued with the journey he sat down on the grass there, and there inadvertently clutching hold of a small bush in that place he noted on reflection that he had pulled it very easily out of the ground, the earth appearing to have been disturbed in such a way that it was clear it had been well dug over in that spot a few days before; and becoming more curious to know what was there he discovered the body of the Master which had been buried there.

On giving an account of all this to the king, Solomon caused a command to be given to the Officers and Apprentices that they divest themselves of everything which was of silver, or any other metal, and that, wearing their Aprons tied to their waists, as their custom now is, and gloves on their hands, they should go to the said place and disinter the body; and that the first thing they should do was to take hold of the hand thereof by making the very signs which are still used by the Officers and Apprentices today.

And setting forth on their errand they arranged between themselves that if on the body of the Master, or in his pockets, they did not find the means of ascertaining what the signs were which pertained to him in his capacity as Master, they would follow the course of using the first word and sign which they used to each other after they had used those normally employed as Officers and Apprentices; and all being arranged in this manner they came to the place where the body lay; and making first the Sign of the Apprentices, which is to lay hold of the joint of the finger next the thumb, it became severed due to its rottenness; and making the second Sign, which is to lay hold of the joint of the principal finger, seeking thus to raise up the body, it also became detached in the same manner, whereby they saw clearly that it was necessary to lay hold of the wrist, and thus raising him upright, the first word which he who raised him uttered was in fact 'Mag Binach' which means in our language that 'it did stink'; and so it came to pass that from that time onwards the sign of the Master was this last action of laying hold of the wrist, and the said words; and for this reason they still today observe the same insignias, ceremonies and signs as have already been stated above.

And they took the body of the Master to the King, who ordered it to be buried, being accompanied by the Officers and Apprentices with the same insignias as stated earlier: and upon his sepulchre there was ordered to be engraved the following = Here lies Hiram, Grand Master Architect of the Freemasons.[1]

The legend surrounding the death of Hiram Abiff also finds itself elaborated upon by Dr. Geo. Oliver, a century or so after Dr. Anderson's comparatively simple account in his *Book of Constitutions*, but based, perhaps, on some of the 'Traditions of old Masons, who talk much of these things', as Anderson indicates with respect to his own account:

We have an old tradition, delivered down orally, that it was the duty of Hiram Abiff, to superintend the workmen; and . . . at

---

[1] From Doc. No. 13, dated 21 March, 1743, Confession. Dr. S. Vatcher, 'John Coustos and the Portuguese Inquisition', *AQC* 1968, vol. 81.

The reader will no doubt feel that such an involved legend, as of 1728, must have an antiquity well before the Grand Lodge period, and could not have been developed in the short dozen years since 1717.

the opening of the day, when the sun was rising in the East, it was his constant custom, before the commencement of labour, to enter the temple and offer up his prayers to Jehovah for a blessing on his work. And in like manner, when the sun set in the West, and the labours of the day were closed, and the workmen had departed, he returned his thanks to the Great Architect of the Universe for the harmonious protection of the day. Not content with this devout expression of his feelings morning and evening, he always went into the temple at the hour of high twelve, when the men were called from labour to refreshment to inspect the progress of the work, to draw fresh designs upon the tracing board, if such were necessary, and to perform other scientific labours, never forgetting to consecrate his duties by solemn prayer. These religious customs were faithfully performed for the first six years, in the secret recesses of his Lodge, and for the last year in the precincts of the Most Holy Place. At length, on the very day appointed for celebrating the cape stone of the building, he retired, as usual, according to our traditions, at the hour of high twelve, and did not return alive.[1]

Various elaborations of the Legend, in an ever increasing crescendo, had of course appeared in the interim, the first of these being the account in Prichard's *Masonry Dissected* (1730). Some thirty years later, three well-known publications—*The Three Distinct Knocks* (1760), *Jachin and Boaz* (1762), and *Hiram* (1764)—furnish, in almost identical terms, some additional details which had only been indicated, but not elaborated upon, in Prichard. *Jachin and Boaz*, for example, mentions 'the custom of *Hiram*, at twelve at noon, as soon as the men were called off to refresh themselves, to go into the *Sanctum Sanctorum*, or holy of holies, to pay his devotion to the true and living God', as in the tradition preserved by Oliver, and as briefly indicated in Prichard. The East, West, and South Gates of the Temple are now specifically designated, and Hiram's meeting with the three ruffians is described in great detail, where Prichard had only indicated the occurrence in a few words. The Working Tools are also now given as being a Twenty-four inch Gauge, a Square, and a Gavel or Setting Maul, in place of Prichard's 'Setting Maul, Setting Tool, and Setting Beadle', indicating some

---

[1] Geo. Oliver, *The Antiquities of Free-Masonry*. Universal Masonic Library, vol. iv, Lodgeton, Kentucky, 1856, pp. 228–229, footnote.

further development in the Legend. Twelve recanting Fellowcrafts are said to go in search of the slain Master, in place of 'Fifteen Loving Brothers' chosen by King Solomon. And it is now explained that 'there were only three in the world to whom it [the key-word] was known; and unless they were present, it could not be delivered. *Hiram* being dead, it was consequently lost'. The exclamations from 'the cliff of a rock' are given, and the details of the ruffians' execution are described.

Not long afterwards, the Legend takes on a still greater elaboration. This is indicated in a foolscap diary for the year 1867, but purporting to be a copy made by John Turk from material 'carefully revised by Brother William Preston Esq 1816', as is stated in the title page. The 'Traditional History', as presented by P. R. James, in his paper on 'The Lectures of English Craft Freemasonry', and no doubt paraphrased by him, is partly as follows:[1]

HAB was appointed Superintendent of the Work. The assassins posted themselves at the S., E. and W. gates and the search was carried out by 15 Brethren selected from the three classes of workmen. Fifteen days were spent in fruitless search— the loose shrub—acacia (casia)—substitute secrets. The murderers, who were Tyrians, failed to leave for Tyre because the winds were contrary and were found in a cave. HKT was informed and a trial took place in K.S.'s Ministry of Justice. After some hesitation the first assassin fell on his left knee, confessed and was sentenced to the penalty in the OB. of the First Degree; the second fell on his right knee and was sentenced to the penalty in the OB. of the Second Degree; the third fell on both knees, confessed at once and was set aside to await the King's pleasure. This was all reported to K.S. who ordered another trial. There the sentences were repeated except that the third assassin was awarded the penalty in the OB. of the Third Degree and all were carried out at the furthest extremity of the coast. The 15 Brethren who recovered the body were convened in Chapter to record these events and from this are derived the various Degrees of our Institution. There follows what is much like the modern Lecture on the T.B.

Still further details are indicated in a set of Lectures sometimes referred to (perhaps incorrectly) as the Lancashire Working;

[1] *AQC*, vol. 79, p. 145.

sometimes, more specifically (but perhaps just as incorrectly) as the Lodge of Lights Working.[1] A transcript of this is to be found in the John Yarker Notebook in the Iowa Masonic Library, and is one of our important documents. It is found annotated:

'Copied from an old M.S. book with clasps—watermark of the paper "Durham & Co.—1799"—& bearing on the first leaf the name "John Smith" in pencil, formerly belonging the Lodge of St. John meeting in Manchester, & afterwards removed to Warrington & united with the Lodge of Lights, meeting at Warrington.

'Lent to the writer of this by Bro. H. B. White P. M. Lodge of Lights. . . .

Faithfully copied by John Yarker, Jr. 1865. from the original which is beautifully written.'

R. J. Meekren refers to this working in his paper on 'The Age of the Master's Part', citing two similar copies Yarker had made in 1888 for Quatuor Coronati Lodge No. 2076, and for the Grand Lodge Library, both of London.[2] Still another transcript is in the New York Grand Lodge Library, perhaps made from the one in Iowa. Meekren mentions that the so-called Lancashire Lectures are very much like Finch's *Masonic Treatise* and Browne's *Master Key*, and are of the 'Modern' type, and 'much resemble the post-Union catechisms'.

In the matter of the Hiramic Legend, as regards these post-Union catechisms, and taking the *Emulation* Lectures as an example, there are some interesting elaborations that we find in *Lancashire* that are absent from the somewhat curtailed details in *Emulation*, and some of the details that are given in both are entirely different; for example, the three Gates of the Temple, and the Working Tools employed, indicating perhaps a difference in some of the details preserved in different parts of the country. Two Words are indicated in *Emulation* (probably arranged to satisfy both of the Grand Lodges that joined in the Union of 1813), while in *Lancashire* only one is given.

In the latter working, the three ruffians come to be suspected of their crime as a result of the additional fact that 'at the building of the T. it was the usual custom for E.A.P.'s to mess 7 in a mess, the F. Crafts 5; at that time there were 3 F. Crafts missing from

---

[1] For a discussion of these designations, see P. R. James in *AQC* vol. 79, pp. 152–154.
[2] *AQC* lxxii, 52.

their messes at noon, likewise their Lodging at night', which corroborated the information provided by the recanting brethren. To apprehend the ruffians, King Solomon ordered that 'an embargo should be laid on all vessels & floats', and he further 'placed guards in all frontier towns, with a strong injunction that none should quit his dominions without his previous knowledge'. In their search for the ruffians, one group of Fellow-crafts 'was to go down to Joppa where the materials were landed for the building & enquire if any such men had been there, at the same time to describe them. They received for answer there had, but owing to the embargo they could not obtain a passage they therefore returned into the interior part of the country. Those 3 Br. then returned likewise & on passing by the mouth of a cave by the seaside, they heard the following exclamations: Oh! that etc. etc.[1] They knowing by their voices, that they were men of Tyre & by their exclamations that they were the same they were in pursuit of, they therefore rushed in & bound the same, they then bound them & brot them before K.S.' The examination of the three ruffians is now given in great detail:

Q. How did A.[2] appear?

A. He as paying homage to his King, fell down on his left k.., & on being questioned as to the punishment of those who had been the horrid murderers of our Master H. he not thinking there was sufficient evidence to convict him boldly answered he ought to have etc; but being closely questioned by K.S. guilt flew in his face & he confessed the fact, whereby he was ordered out to the ministers of justice there to await his further pleasure.

Q. How did O.[2] appear?

A. In nearly the same manner as the first, he falling down on his right k . . , [etc. as before].

Q. How did M.[2] appear?

A. In a more humiliating posture he paying due homage on both knees, [etc. as before].

Q. After the examination & confession of those guilty assassins how did K.S. then proceed?

A. Ks. being in alliance with H.K.T. sent an embassy to

[1] In another working that will shortly be mentioned, under the designation *Vancouver*, these exclamations are repeated three times: 'oh! that etc.—oh! that etc.—oh! that etc'.

[2] The names of the three ruffians are here indicated only by their terminal letters—A, O, & M.

acquaint him that 3 of his subjects had been the horrid perpetrators of the death of HAB., he likewise sent him a schedule of their examination, guilt, & confession, & wished to know how they were to be disposed of.

Q. What was H's answer?

A. That he might consult his own pleasure, but in his opinion, the punishment they had prescribed for others ought to be executed on them.

Q. Was that done & where?

A. It was, down at Joppa as near to the extremity of the 2 countries as possible, they being deemed the outcasts of both & worthy of neither.

Q. Where did K.S. order the body of HAB to be buried?

A. In the L. near the T, which was done with magnificent funeral honours, H.S. [K.S.?] & all the Craft lamenting the untimely death & irreparable loss of so worthy & excellent a Master M.

I have made reference to another working under the name of the *Vancouver MS*. This is now in possession of Western Gate Lodge No. 44, B.C.R., Vancouver, B.C. In the matter of the Hiramic Legend, which is all we are concerned with at the moment, the wording is perhaps 99% a verbatim replica of the *Lancashire*, but in other respects there are important differences between the two workings, indicating that each represents an independent development of its traditions. This tends to make the similarity in the details of the Hiramic section all the more striking. But one very curious interpolation must be mentioned. In the *Vancouver MS.* we find the following:

Q. What did they then [do] with it?

A. Took it to the brow of a hill called Calvary, and there very indecently interred it.

Lancashire, which is generally even more strongly Christian than the *Vancouver*, or any other working with which we are familiar, omits the mention of Calvary.

One further reference and we are done.

In both the *Vancouver* and the *Lancashire*, we find the ruffians referred to, as stated, by their terminal letters only: A, O, and M. This circumstance appears to have led to the theory—I believe it can be safely credited to Albert Pike—that 'the true word of a

Master Mason' had some surprising connection with the mystic word of the Hindus and Buddhists—OM, AUM, or, alternatively, AOM—now found preserved, it is said, in the names of the three ruffians, 'where it remained for centuries, its presence unsuspected'.

Possible origins of the Hiramic Myth

Much ingenuity, as I have said, has been expended in trying to trace the possible and probable origin of this Hiramic Myth.

'According to Masonic legend,' the *Jewish Encyclopedia* informs us—to start with a non-Masonic suggestion—'he (Hiram) was killed by three workmen just at the completion of the Temple; and there is a mystery about his death as represented in the Masonic rites. This may possibly trace back to the rabbinic legend that while all the workmen were killed so that they should not build another temple devoted to idolatry, Hiram himself was raised to heaven like Enoch.'[1]

Another possible tie-in with the biblical tradition centres itself in a confusion between the name Hiram and that of Adoniram, referred to in some Continental Rites as *Adonhiram*, and translated literally as 'the Lord Hiram', since 'Adon' means 'Lord'. Now, Adoniram also appears in the Bible under the name Adoram, believed to be one and the same, and he is said to have been 'over the tribute', that is, head of the tax collectors (*II Sam.* 20:24). Again, under this name Adoram (*I Kings* 12:18), or Hadoram (*II Chron.* 10:18), this tax collector is said to have been stoned to death while in the performance of his duties. In the story of the building of King Solomon's Temple, Adoniram is also said to have been 'over the levy' of those who were sent into the mountains of Lebanon to cut down the timber needed for the Temple (*I Kings* 5:14). Out of this nest of confusion, it is easy to see how many of the Masonic 'legends' could have become concocted.[2]

We will now turn our attention to some of the many theories that have been advanced to account for the Hiramic Myth.

But first we must clear away some of the 'rubbish in the temple', by considering and disposing of those theories that appear to have led nowhere.

[1] *Jew. Enc.*, s.v. FREEMASONRY.
[2] Cf. Mackey's *Encyclopedia of Freemasonry*, s.v. ADONHIRAMITE FREE-MASONRY, *et seq.*

False Alarms and Blind Alleys

A 'discovery' that seems to have created quite a good bit of excitement at one time was made about 1877–79 by Prof. T. Hayter Lewis, and presented in the form of a short note in the first volume of the *Transactions* of Quatuor Coronati under the title of 'An early version of the Hiramic Legend'. He describes this discovery as the outcome 'of some casual observations made some seven years since' at University College, in the course of a conversation with Prof. Marks. The discussion centred itself in an Arabic MS., written in Hebrew characters, which Dr. Marks thought could be of the fourteenth century, and the excerpt that seems to have attracted his attention was the following phrase:

MOCH מאח
We have found מצאנו
Our Master אדנו
Hiram חירם

—the word MOCH[1] forming a key-word, as it were, leading to an acrostic which ran to the last three lines given above.

Upon following up this conversation some seven years later, for the purpose of making the above report, Dr. Marks offered the explanation that 'to the best of my belief I found the book containing it at the Bodleian Library . . . and if I mistake not, it was an introduction or preface to the Sunnah', an oral exposition of the Koran. Prof. Hayter Lewis adds, by way of comment, that 'I have since been informed that a MS. which seems to be of the character of that referred to by Dr. Marks, is said to have been in the Cambridge University Library, and, very possibly, may be the actual one to which he refers'.[2]

It is obvious that this discovery, if corroborated, would be of first-rate importance in substantiating the antiquity of the Hiramic Legend, and indicating its probable source. Commenting on this report, in fact, the then Worshipful Master of Quatuor Coronati, Sir Charles Warren (one time President of the Palestine Exploration Fund), expressed the opinion (somewhat prematurely, I think) that 'we had here a clue to its [the Hiramic Legend's] real origin which,

[1] This is given elsewhere in the same report as MACH, but may be of no significance, as the *Aleph* in the Hebrew alphabet is pronounced as a short 'O' by Ashkenazic Jews and as a broad 'A' by the Sephardic.
[2] *AQC* i, 34–37.

according to his views, could be neither recent, nor Western, nor Jewish, but probably very ancient and derived from the Phoenicians'. Some years later, however, John Yarker was in a position to contribute a more positive solution of the question. Being present at a lecture in Liverpool delivered by G. W. Speth, at which time this alleged discovery by Prof. Hayter Lewis was brought up, Yarker was informed by a brother who had been received into the Dervish Sect in Morocco that a similar salutation phrase was in use among the Dervishes, and was translated thus: 'We have found in our Lord (Allah) *Cherim*' or *Kerim*, that is, rest—a not far cry from the acrostic quoted by Prof. Marks, from memory, after the passage of some seven years. 'I, myself, entertain no doubt', said Yarker in comment, 'that it was this phrase which Professor Marks saw, and, being a non-mason, misinterpreted.'[1]

W. J. Hughan, commenting on this very same 'discovery' some dozen years still later, had occasion to state that 'the Hebrew reference was quite familiar to me, in a slightly altered form, long before the reading of the paper by the lamented Professor T. Hayter Lewis, and was supposed to explain the esoteric portion of the Third Degree, but to my mind entirely failed to do so'.[2] However, he also failed to state at the time just what this 'slightly altered form' of the reference consisted in, and we are thus left dangling in an atmosphere of fruitless and somewhat frustrating speculation.

As a final postcript to this episode, it might be added that search was nevertheless made for the original manuscript that Prof. Marks thought he had seen, the search being conducted in the most likely places that had been suggested—the Bodleian Library and various other libraries at Oxford, as well as the University Library at Cambridge, in the latter of which the Rev. Covey-Crump says he himself took a hand, but all to no avail, although he himself did not agree with Yarker's interpretation.[3]

The alleged 'discovery', therefore, may be said to have proved entirely abortive, and the matter has not been heard of since, except for faint echoes from some who may be unfamiliar with the course of the entire investigation.[4]

[1] *AQC* v, 228.
[2] *AQC* xiv, 80.
[3] Rev. W. W. Covey-Crump, *The Hiramic Tradition*, p. 14.
[4] It is curious to note, however, that as late as Gould's *Concise History* (1903), he had not yet discovered the apocryphal nature of this account (cf. *op. cit.*, p. 67).

Another 'false alarm' is the story of Dr. Oliver and the 1715 *Targum*[1] told by the Rev. Morris Rosenbaum in his Discussion of F. J. W. Crowe's paper on 'King Solomon and the Queen of Sheba'.[2] 'In the *Freemasons' Treasury* (p. 288),' Rabbi Rosenbaum tells us, 'he (Oliver) says that the legend of the Master Builder's death is to be found in a translation of the Targum to Chronicles, published at London in 1715.'[3]

Now the Targum to Chronicles, according to the *Jewish Encyclopedia*, 'was first published in 1680 (and 1683) by M. F. Beck . . . and it was again edited, by D. Wilkins in 1715, on the basis of a Cambridge manuscript of 1347. . . . ' Whether this is the Targum to which Oliver referred is uncertain, as he himself does not specifically mention Chronicles, but the coincidence of dates is perhaps significant. However, Rabbi Rosenbaum was of the opinion that, so far as he could discover, 'there has never been an English translation of this Targum published'. Moreover, in respect to the particular Targum in question, 'I have, however, read this through most carefully', says the Rabbi, referring no doubt to the original text, 'and find that it contains nothing at all bearing upon the Builder's death.'[4]

Analogous interest in a possible 'operative' allusion to the death of H.A.B. appears to have been engendered by a casual footnote in a paper in *AQC*, wherein reference was made to 'a statement in the Official Bulletin of the Supreme Council for the S.J. [Southern Jurisdiction], U.S., vii, 200, to the effect that the builders of Strasburg Cathedral "clearly represented" (apparently by a picture in stone) the scene of the death of Hiram'.[5] Actual reference to the periodical in question, however, only discloses a statement made in an oration by F. LeBlanc, in the course of an exposition of various Masonic and quasi-Masonic symbols alleged to be seen in connection with many European churches and cathedrals. As part of this exposition, the orator simply said: 'At Strasburg, in the first days of the construction of the Cathedral, the scene of the death of Hiram was clearly represented.' Unfortunately, no documentation of any sort was offered, and, in the absence of any direct or even indirect evidence, the veracity of the allusion is left in very serious doubt.

---

[1] TARGUM: 'The Aramaic translation of the Bible'—*Jew. Enc.*, xii, 57.
[2] *AQC* xix.
[3] *AQC* xix, 124.
[4] *AQC* xix, 124.
[5] Wm. H. Upton, *AQC* vii, 123.

It is moreover significant that J. G. Findel, the learned Editor of the German Masonic publication *Die Bauhütte*, and author of the well-known *History of Freemasonry* (London 1865), in which he plays the protagonist of the German *Steinmetzen* origin of modern Free-masonry—*contra* that of the British Freemasons—and who would have been the logical and natural supporter of a Strasburg origin for the Hiramic Legend, has absolutely nothing to say with regard to such a possibility, even as a theory. And Dr. Herbert Poole, on the other side of the Channel, it might be further noted, had occasion to remark at one time, in more positive terms, while writing on 'The Antiquity of the Craft', that 'the Steinmetzen tradition appears to contain no trace whatever of the Hiram legend'.[1]

A very similar blind alley was a statement alleged to have been made at one time by the Rev. A. F. A. Woodford, who is reported to have said (*in Wm. A. Paine's paraphrase*) 'that the Legend of the 3° was of very ancient usage amongst the Operative Masons, and that years ago he saw an old operative lodge token or seal of the 14th cent. which referred to Hiram Abiff, in an unmistakable way. . . . '[2]

Now, this is an excellent example of the mis-quotations that are sometimes made in the name of highly respected and reputable students, but which, on more careful investigation, are found to be entirely erroneous and to lead to entirely false conclusions. We find, in fact, that W. J. Hughan also quotes the Woodford assertion, as reported above, but apparently verbatim this time, from a statement Woodford had made in the *Freemasons' Magazine* for Dec. 28, 1867, in which the latter had said, in the course of a discussion on the antiquity of the *Royal Arch Degree*, that this 'Degree existed in effect long before Ramsay's time. . . . ' And, after an omitted passage, indicated by the dots, Woodford went on to make the statement which Paine has apparently misquoted and misunderstood, but which in Woodford's own words was to the effect that 'we have numismatic evidence of the antiquity of the second part of the Third Degree, coeval with the operative lodge of York Masons, *certainly in the fifteenth century*'. (Woodford's italics this time, but of no significance in the present discussion.)[3] But what *is* of significance

[1] *AQC* li, 19.
[2] Wm. A. Paine, 'Masonry and King Solomon's Temple'. *The Builder*, 1917, p. 101.
[3] W. J. Hughan, *Origin of the English Rite of Freemasonry* (1884). New and revised edition, Leicester, 1909, p. 80.

in this verbatim quotation of Woodford's remark, is that his reference to the 'second part of the Third Degree', is *not* a reference to our present Hiramic Legend in the Craft, as mistakenly suggested by Paine, but to the Royal Arch Degree, which for a time was thought to have been a portion and a 'completion' of the Third Degree itself—a 'second part', so to speak—and which allegedly came to be divorced from it at a later time, to form a separate Degree, in accordance with a 'mutilation theory' that was popular in some circles at one time, but now largely forgotten.

The 'numismatic evidence' to which the Rev. Woodford refers may have been a medal or coin; but, whether lodge token or seal, medal or coin, and whether the reference was intended to be to the Craft Hiramic Legend or to the Royal Arch Legend, 'the numismatic evidence of the date mentioned has not been traced', Hughan wrote, in 1884, and it has not made its appearance since, to my knowledge, and thus one more blind alley must be racked up for the record.

Still another 'false alarm' centres itself, interestingly enough, in a novel and a resulting grand opera, as well as in several accounts of a purported Hiramic Legend from an alleged mid-Eastern source, as in the Hayter Lewis episode, and all having to do with the same essential theme. This was briefly alluded to in a preceding chapter, and is in connection with a project said to have been initiated by the French writer Gerard de Nerval, who is supposed to have planned, about 1848, the libretto for a grand opera on the subject of King Solomon's Temple, in collaboration with Alexander Dumas, and for which Meyerbeer was to have furnished the music.[1] The project itself never materialized, but the plot of the projected opera is given in Nerval's *Voyage en Orient*, under the title, 'History of the Queen of the Morning, and Soliman, Prince of the Djinns', and is available in an English translation in volume two of *The Women of Cairo*, by the same author (London, 1929). It purports (seriously or not) to be a tale heard told by an Arab storyteller in a Stamboul café, but the profusion of Hiramic details with which it abounds—it could all have hardly originated in Arabic legendary lore—indicates it to be the product of Nerval's creative imagination, based perhaps on some knowledge of then-current French Masonic lore, rather than being a genuine importation from the Orient.

C. W. Heckethorn tells a similar story in his *Secret Societies of all*

[1] See the commentary by W. H. Rylands, *AQC* xiv, 179.

Ages and Countries (London, 1875, vol. i, p. 241 *et seq.*) which has all the earmarks of having been 'lifted', without acknowledgement, from Nerval's account, and with a few interpolated details for good measure, and all of which gives the unwary reader the air of a genuine 'tradition'. A palpably similar tale, again, is told by Max Heindel in his *Freemasonry and Catholicism*, presenting it confidently as 'the Masonic legend', but which he in turn had very obviously and uncritically 'lifted' from Heckethorn—a striking illustration of 'the blind leading the blind'.[1] But even the usually critical scholar, W. H. Rylands, seems to have been taken in for a time by this story, and only discovered, some dozen years later, the true source of the Heckethorn account.[2] G. W. Speth, also, appears to have entertained a similarly erroneous opinion of it, but speaking this time very diffidently, his source of information being admittedly 'at third hand'. He had been told, he had occasion to say in the course of a discussion of the previously mentioned paper by Prof. Johnston, that 'a version of the Hiramic legend is a well-known tale in the bazaars of the Orient, and forms part of the stock-in-trade of the public narrators'—an obvious though unconscious reference to the Nerval yarn. 'But my friend had been told so by a friend, etc. etc.,' continues Speth, 'and I can only give the story for what it is worth. It seems to me, however,' he goes on to say, 'that here we have a more promising field for research than the seventeenth-century literature has proved itself to be',[3] and in this he is perhaps right, though the 'promising field', in all these years, has so far unfortunately failed to yield its harvest. J. S. M. Ward, it is true, has expressed himself as saying that this Nerval story 'contains a core of genuine tradition', but the reasons he gives (if one may call them 'reasons') are not very convincing.[4]

G. S. Draffen has also delivered himself of an opinion very similar to Speth's, in referring to a French work found in the Library of the Grand Lodge of Scotland, by Georges de Norval [*sic*], recounting some tales supposed to have been heard around the coffee-houses in the Middle East, and one of which, Draffen thinks, 'bears such a striking resemblance to the Hiramic Legend that it cannot be

[1] Max Heindel, *Freemasonry and Catholicism*. Oceanside, California, 1919, ch. III.
[2] Cf. *AQC* ii, 65 and xiv, 180.
[3] *AQC* xii, 148.
[4] J. S. M. Ward, *Who was Hiram Abiff?* London, 1925, p. 178.

discounted as a possible source of the legend of our present Third Degree'.[1] But discounted it certainly must be, in my opinion, since the 'striking resemblance' can be so easily explained.

Some theories propounded

It is to the credit of the Rev. W. W. Covey-Crump that he has made at least a realistic effort, in his *The Hiramic Tradition*, to discuss most if not all the major theories that have been propounded at one time or another towards a solution of the question of the Tradition's origin, albeit some of his own conclusions seem to be as faulty as those he criticizes and dismisses as unlikely. This is probably inevitable in any serious discussion of such a cloudy problem as the one we are now facing (the present work included). Nevertheless, this excellent little book deserves to be read in its entirety for such information and inspiration as it may provide.[2]

He begins by disagreeing with Cart de Lafontaine in the latter's opinion that the 'Legend is distinctly a part of the Operative system',[3] and says pointedly that the all-important question to be answered is: 'Did operative masons at any time prior to the eighteenth century say that Hiram or any other ancient Master of their Craft was killed?' If they did, he could agree with Speth that this may have had something to do with the 'foundation' and 'completion' sacrifice which at one time was a builder's tradition, as Speth has shown—later softened (so Covey-Crump thinks) into the story of a plot to extort a secret, rather than a sacrifice to secure the structure's permanence. Attempts have been made, it is true, to connect the Hiramic Drama with some analogous happening among the builders or architects of mediaeval Europe. Many violent deaths of builders or architects, for one cause or another, are of course on record, and the possible connection of one or another of them with the Hiramic Drama has been espoused by some writers at different times, but the direct connection seems to me (and apparently to Covey-Crump as well) somewhat nebulous, though suggestive.

The murder of the artisan

There is the story, for instance, given by Rebold in his *Freemasonry in Europe*, which has suggested to some a possible source for the

[1] *AQC* lxxii, 41.
[2] See also his 'Scriptural Evidence concerning Hiram', *AQC* xliii.
[3] Dorset Masters' Lodge *Transactions*, 1925–6.

Hiramic Drama.[1] In 1080 A.D., Rebold tells us, 'the bishop of Utrecht, desirous of constructing a great cathedral, sought the aid of the leading architect of that city, a man named Plebel, and obtained from him the necessary plans for the proposed construction. Having obtained possession of these papers, the bishop dismissed Plebel, and, desirous of passing himself as the author of the plans, and engage in directing the labors of the workmen without having been initiated into the secrets of the art, sought, by all sorts of menaces and promises, to wring from the son of the architect Plebel, a young master mason, the secrets and manner (*arcanum magisterium*) of laying foundations. . . . The architect, indignant at a perfidy so base on the part of one whom the people regarded as their supreme spiritual adviser, on learning of the perjury of his son, determined to prevent the divulging of the secret of his art, and thereupon, having obtained an opportunity, killed the bishop.'

There is also, of course, the well-known story of the Roslyn Pillar, sometimes referred to as the 'Prentice Pillar', recounted and illustrated in Mackey's *Encyclopedia*, and which deserves to be repeated here, especially because of a curious 'concluding remark'. This story has reference to a certain fluted column in the Chapel of Roslyn Castle, in Scotland, highly ornamented with a floral garland twining itself around the pillar, all carved out of the solid stone. 'The legend,' says the encyclopedia, 'is that when the plans of the chapel were sent from Rome, the master builder . . . had to go to Rome for further instructions. . . . During his absence, a clever apprentice, the only son of a widow, either from memory or from his own invention, carved and completed the beautiful pillar. When the master returned and found the work completed, furious with jealous rage, he killed the apprentice, by striking him a frightful blow on the forehead with a heavy setting-maul. In testimony of the truth of the legend,' we are told, 'the visitor is shown three heads in the west part of the chapel—the master's, the apprentice's, with the gash on his forehead, and the widow's.'[2]

The account concludes with the confident assertion: 'There can be but little doubt that this legend referred to that of the Third Degree, which is thus shown to have existed, at least substantially,

[1] Emmanuel Rebold, *A General History of Free-Masonry in Europe.* Boston, 1875, p. 299.
[2] Mackey's *Encyclopedia of Freemasonry*, ii, 794. *S.v.* PRENTICE PILLAR. The illustration is in vol. iii, p. 1440.

at that early period.' Just what 'early period' is here referred to is not clearly specified, but Roslyn Chapel, it may be noted, was started in 1446.[1] However, the conclusion that the legend of the Prentice Pillar must necessarily go back to the date of construction of the Pillar itself is obviously a *non sequitur*. The three heads, especially, could have been added later, perhaps even much later.[2] But be that as it may, G. G. Coulton has seen fit to tell the same story, with a few embellishments, in his *Art and the Reformation*, but thinks it may be apocryphal (as an historical event, not as a legend). He also gives a slightly different version cited by A. Kerr, who adds: 'An almost similar tradition is preserved at Melrose, in connexion with the building of the east window of the abbey church.'[3]

A somewhat similar story, prevalent on the Continent, is told by Thomas Hope, with respect to Apollodorus, a Greek architect employed by the Romans, and 'who fell a sacrifice to the professional jealousy of that Roman imperial artist Adrian'.[4] And still another such story is told of the two rose windows of the Cathedral at Rouen, and of two stone gates built at Stendal.[5]

Still another story along the same lines is told us by Dr. Oliver; one which, he thinks, 'affords a presumptive evidence that the legend of the third degree was used by the masons who built our cathedral and collegiate churches in the eleventh and twelfth centuries'. Whether or not the 'presumptive evidence' is favourable to the validity of the conclusion offered—which is extremely doubtful—the story itself is at least indicative of the type of tradition that

---

[1] John Harvey, *The Gothic World*. London, 1950, p. 44.

[2] In this connection, G. S. Draffen, Grand Librarian of the Grand Lodge of Scotland, writes me, in response to a query: 'The Chapel of Roslyn, according to Father Hay's *Genealogie of the Saint-Clairs of Rosslyn* . . . was begun in 1446. When Sir William St. Clair . . . died in 1484 the Collegiate Church . . . was still unfinished. . . . There does not seem to be any record of the date of the carving of the three heads to which you refer. One might assume that they were done about 1480–90.'

[3] G. G. Coulton, *Art and the Reformation*. Oxford, 1928. Coulton makes no mention of the 'three heads', but Kerr does.

Part I of *Art and the Reformation* is also available as a paperback with the title of *Medieval Faith and Symbolism* (New York, 1958), and is of special significance to Masonic readers.

The reference to the Prentice Pillar in both editions is on pp. 219–220 and Appendix 14.

[4] Thos. Hope, *Historical Essay on Architecture*. London, 1840, p. 60.

[5] Geo. W. Bullamore, *AQC* xxxviii, 80.

has grown up with our churches and cathedrals. It is a tradition, once again, of mutilation, sacrifice, and death, such as is recounted of the transept window of Lincoln Cathedral (built *c.* 1220–1250[1]). It is said that this window was the pride and joy of the Master Mason in charge of the works, but its excellence and beauty was overshadowed and eclipsed by the work of an apprentice, so that the Master Mason in despair 'cast himself from the scaffold, and was dashed in pieces on the stones below. This destruction of the master by the apprentice,' comments Dr. Oliver—'indirect destruction' might have been a better phrase—'may have a reference to some secret legend existing amongst the masons who constructed these edifices; for it could have no relation to the facts; because the same occurrence could scarcely have happened in every cathedral that was built in this or any other country, which retains a similar tradition', and which may with some probability, in his opinion, be traced to the legend of the third degree, as indicated by the word which signified, "the builder is smitten".'[2]

Here, again, it may be remarked that the prior existence of a quasi-Hiramic legend is only assumed, in order to account for the known builders' tradition of death and mutilation; whether the assumption is justified is another matter. It might be thought, instead, that the existence of building traditions such as those here recounted may have given an idea to our later legendists, which came to be incorporated into our Hiramic Tradition at some time and under some circumstances at present not known.

The Ancient Mysteries

The Rev. Joseph Fort Newton believes he has found a clear connection between our modern mysteries, as expressed in the Hiramic Drama, and the beliefs and ceremonies of the Dionysian Artificers, who, he thought, were the actual builders (or, at least, took part in the building) of King Solomon's Temple. They were, in fact, he tells us, 'an order of builders who erected temples, stadia, and theatres in Asia Minor, and who were at the same time an order of the Mysteries under the tutelage of Bacchus before that worship declined, as it did later in Athens and Rome, into mere revelry'. In this he follows, but too uncritically, Da Costa's *The Dionysian*

---

[1] Harvey, *The Gothic World*, p. 75.
[2] Oliver, Introduction to Hutchinson's *The Spirit of Masonry*. New York Edition, 1903, p. 19.

Artificers,[1] and finds that the latter organization 'united the art of architecture with the old Egyptian drama of faith, representing in their ceremonies the murder of Dionysius by the Titans, and his return to life. So that,' he concludes, 'blending the symbols of Astronomy with those of Architecture, by a slight change made by a natural process, how easy for the master-artist of the temple-builders to become the hero of the ancient drama of immortality.'[2]

A very pretty theory, on the surface, and one in which the few known facts with respect to the Dionysian *Mysteries*, on the one hand, are cleverly blended with some straggling references to the Dionysian *Artificers*, on the other, to create a semblance of a well-supported demonstration. In point of fact, however, the very meagre references to the Dionysian Artificers in da Costa provide us with a very thinly-drawn picture of that organization, if organization it was, and a much too slender basis for the erection upon it of a theory of Hiramic origin.

Other writers on the subject, however, merely content themselves with noting the similarity in symbolism and philosophy—and sometimes even in dramatic content, as in the Osirian Mysteries—between our Hiramic Drama and that of the ancient disciplines; merely assuming, somehow, that some line of direct transmission *must* necessarily lie between them to account for this similarity. But such an assumption, lacking supporting evidence, does not lie well with the more historically-minded.

Thomas à Becket

The Becket theory advanced by W. J. Williams may now come in for brief discussion,[3] although, despite the several curious analogies between the Becket story and the Hiramic Drama, we may perhaps agree with Covey-Crump in that there is no sure connection between the two.

H. L. Haywood, however, has offered the suggestion that 'the fact that three knights, described at the time as "the three ruffians", murdered the fifty-three-year-old prelate by beating him over the head after demanding that he "give them his word", threatened to

[1] Cf. Hippolyto Joseph da Costa, *The Dionysian Artificers* (1820). Los Angeles, 1936 edition.

[2] Joseph Fort Newton, *The Builders*. Cedar Rapids, Iowa, 1916, p. 77. (Not to be confused with the periodical *The Builder*, reference to which has also been made.)

[3] *AQC* xli, 'Archbishop Becket and the Masons' Company of London'.

bury him in the rubbish, and that his body was buried in a spot between a memorial to John the Baptist on one side and John the Evangelist on the other, the two forming parallel lines, must have had a peculiar interest to men in the Masons' Companies', but the suggestion, put in this form, and obviously 'doctored' to give it an air of verisimilitude, may perhaps not have been intended to be taken too literally, and Williams, in his more realistic account, makes no such analogies or allusions. Haywood, however, did seriously think it possible that the root of the Hiramic Drama could have been in this martyrdom of Thomas à Becket; and this possibility, he gravely maintains, 'is reinforced by the fact that the Masons' City Companies had St. Thomas as their Patron, went in procession to his chapel on his day, and supported St. Thomas' Hospitals'. And further, 'the theory that the Lodges inherited the story from a memorial ceremony performed by City Company Masons at St. Thomas chapels', he thinks, 'is not incredible. . . . '[1] But so far it remains only a theory, and the tempting reference to the 'two parallel lines' of the two Saints John appears to be inaccurate, to say the least. The paper by Williams, to which reference has been made, contains the following excerpt:

'It is not long ago that Masonic Lodges were dedicated to those two Saints who were described as "The two grand parallels in Masonry".'[2] Then follows a quotation from W. H. Hutton's *Thomas Becket* (1910), giving a pertinent description of Canterbury Cathedral, where Becket was murdered:

'Beneath was the crypt containing on the South side an altar dedicated to St. Augustine the Apostle of England, and on the North side the altar of St. John the Baptist. Between these two altars in the crypt S. Thomas was buried. . . . The altar stone was prized on which the Saint had said his first Mass and of it an altar was made that was dedicated to S. John the Evangelist.'[3]

It is evident that the imaginary analogy in Haywood's mind may have arisen from a too hasty reading of the Williams paper.

The Templar theory

As to this latter theory, Covey-Crump allows that there is 'a fair possibility that in Scotland some *knights* (Thory), or *clerics* (Ward),

[1] Mackey's *Encyclopedia of Freemasonry*, iii, pp. 1186, 1210–1211.
[2] This is still true of American Lodges in general.
[3] *AQC* xli, 143.

or *serving brethren* (Mackey), may have communicated to Masons a story about Hiram which had originally been a story about Molay. . . . ' (the last Grand Master of the Knights Templar, burnt at the stake in 1314, through connivance of Philip, King of France, and Pope Clement V). And, regarding the suggested identification of our Three Ruffians as the 'renegades who were principal witnesses against the Templars in France, . . . Reghellini's account (quoted by Mackey in his *Encyc.*, 736),[1] of these three men is curiously suggestive, though unauthenticated'.

A somewhat similar story to Reghellini's is reproduced by Oliver from a Dutch work, which adds some details which are even more 'curiously suggestive', and is as follows:

'Some time before the total destruction of the order of the Templars, a certain junior prior of Montfaucon, called Carolus de Monte Carmel, was murdered by three traitors, whereby it is thought that the first death-blow was struck at the Order; from the events which accompanied and followed this murder, some are of the opinion that the mystical and ritual part of a great portion of Freemasonry is derived; for the prior was murdered by three traitors, and by this murder an irreparable loss was inflicted on the Order. The murderers of Charles de Monte Carmel concealed his body under the earth, and in order to mark the spot, planted a young thorn-tree upon it. The knights of the temple, in searching for the body, had their attention drawn to that particular spot by the tree, and in that manner they discovered his remains,' etc.[2]

One never knows how many similar details may have been suggested by the Hiramic Tradition *post facto*, rather than the reverse, and, despite these many 'curiously suggestive' circumstances in both the above accounts, the Templar Theory in general is not now seriously considered in Masonic circles.

The 'political' theory

The greatest amount of space, and perhaps with some amount of sympathy, is expended by Covey-Crump in favour of what might be called the political background of the Hiramic Legend, in English

---

[1] This page reference is to the 1874 Philadelphia edition. It is in the current edition *s.v.* SQUIN DE FLEXIAN.
    Cf. Covey-Crump, *The Hiramic Tradition*, p. 88.
[2] Oliver, Introduction to Hutchinson's *The Spirit of Masonry*. New York Edition, 1903, pp. 29–30. The story is said to have been 'quoted in the "Freemasons' Quarterly Review" for the present year' (probably 1843).

history, though not in Jewish. A correspondingly great amount of space is generally devoted to this theory in our literature, which may perhaps be some indication of its universal appeal.

This theory has its connection with the Cromwellian rebellion and the execution of the Stuart King Charles I, and the subsequent Jacobite revolution of 1688. The suggestion has been put forward, for example, that the execution of the King in 1649 may have been allegorized by his partisans under the guise of the Hiramic Drama for purposes of concealed commemoration. As to that, says Covey-Crump, a strong case can be adduced in favour of the hypothesis of a Stuart partisanship within the Craft in the seventeenth century, as shown by H. B. Hextall. But while Covey-Crump himself does not go quite so far, 'there certainly does seem a fair possibility', he thinks, 'that a sequel of some kind—involving a tragedy—was about that time somehow subjoined to the story of "Aynon" which had come down in the Ancient Charges, and thenceforward was orally transmitted, either in Gilds or Lodges, until it finally became incorporated in our ceremonies'.[1]

The theory has had a certain amount of appeal as something intrinsically plausible, and by no means impossible, especially because of the fairly close concurrence between the political events narrated and the beginning of our Grand Lodge system; and also— and perhaps superlatively—because of the occurrence of these political events during that very Century of Transition when intellectuals such as Elias Ashmole and other known partisans of the King were coming into the Craft as 'Accepted' Masons. Some support for the theory has even been found in the very names of our Three Ruffians, as one commemorative detail, among others. But it should be borne in mind that, while in the United States and the British Isles we know these 'Ruffians' under one set of names in the Craft, they go by totally different names—not even remotely analogous to ours—in other Jurisdictions and in other Rites, and it would be strange indeed if, among this heterogeneous collection, some accidental similarity of sound could not be detected with a little auto-suggestion. Thus, from among some of these ruffianly triads—Hoben, Starke, and Oterfut—Hoben, Gibs, and Gravelot— Akiroh, Kurmavil, and Gravelot—'the most obvious', Covey-Crump thinks, seriously, 'is that Kurmavil (or Romvil) refers to Cromwell', while Ireton (Cromwell's son-in-law and one of the

[1] Covey-Crump, *The Hiramic Tradition*, ch. x.

21

chief regicides) reminds us of Akiroh; and Grey of Groby (one of the first three Commissioners who signed the warrant for the execution of Charles I) reminds us of Gravelot. Thus Covey-Crump is found to fall under the somewhat prevalent delusion, for all his iconoclasm in other and perhaps sounder directions.

Among the triads mentioned, it might be remarked in passing, the names of Hoben, Starke, and Oterfut obviously refer to the now-obsolete Rite of Memphis.[1] In the Rite of Mizraim, now also obsolete, the names are still more impossible—Haemdath, Haghebomoth, and Hakhibouth![2] The names Akirop, Romvel, and Gravelot have also been found in some old rituals of the Ancient and Accepted Scottish Rite.[3]

Still other suggestions, even more fanciful, for the attempted identification of our Three Ruffians with their imagined historical counterparts, have also been put forward elsewhere.

A quite opposite view, but one that also hopes to connect the Hiramic Drama with the Cromwellian rebellion, is the one that sees the Puritan party, instead of that of the Royalists, as the proponents of the Legend. In the opinion of Dr. Rosedale, who put forward this theory, the Puritan party, after the restoration of Charles II, 'adopted Masonry in order to carry on not only their religious practices but their political and social movements with secrecy. That the Parliamentarians . . . lived in the belief that some day they would regain their position, is evident, though it was unsafe to assert it too openly. They found it necessary to use allegories for the purpose, and from no source were the allegories more easily drawn than from the Old Testament, with which they were so conversant. . . . Thus, no doubt, sprang up the Hiramic legend, formulated by men who were learned in Scriptural allusions as well as in Masonic lore.'[4]

Of this theory, Covey-Crump says, justifiably, 'it is ingenious and plausible, but in the absence of confirmatory evidence (concerning either of the two intriguing parties) it is to my mind unconvincing'. As to the later Jacobite revolution, he says, 'if certain

---

[1] See the *Collectanea* of the Grand College of Rites of the U.S.A., vol. 6, part 2, p. 148.
[2] *Collectanea*, vol. 6, part 1, p. 74.
[3] Mackey's *Encyclopedia of Freemasonry*, s.v. ASSASINS OF THE THIRD DEGREE, i, 109.
[4] *AQC* xxxiii, 12.

Royalists did really call themselves "Sons of a Bereft Wife", as alleged by Oliver (in *Freem. Treas.*, 284), one may fairly ask: Why did they thus apply to themselves an expression derived from I Kings vii. 14 unless a story that Hiram had been murdered was already known in England at that time?' And as to who could have played the role of the dead spouse of the 'widow' in this allegation is another historical enigma, since neither Charles II, the so-called James III, nor his son Prince Charles Edward, readily fill the bill. Mackey himself has supported the name of James II, who died in 1701, and whose widow survived him till 1718, but 'the eighteenth century is much too late for the birth of the Hiramic Tradition', Covey-Crump reminds us. 'Nevertheless,' he continues, 'a bare possibility does remain that the Hiramic Tradition had in some way a Jacobite application,[1] and that it was with the object of concealing that connection from Anderson, that the famous holocaust of Masonic documents was effected in 1720. . . . '[2]

As has been briefly noticed, W. B. Hextall has given this political theory some serious thought in his paper on 'The Hiramic Legend and the Ashmolean Theory', wherein he lists fourteen 'possible origins' for the Hiramic Legend that had been suggested by others. He, himself, however, favours only one of them, namely, the 'political reference to the death of King Charles I, generally known as the Ashmolean theory, because of the usual corollary, that it was invented by, or originated with, Elias Ashmole'.[3] The latter

---

[1] For a general discussion of the historical circumstances surrounding this theory, see the article 'Stuart Masonry' in Mackey's *Encyclopedia*, vol. ii; 'Jacobite Freemasonry', in Waite's *New Encyclopedia of Freemasonry*, vol. i; and 'Oliver Cromwell and Freemasonry' in Mackey's *History of Freemasonry*, vol. ii, ch. 32. The reader, however, may well bear the sane advice of Bernard E. Jones in mind, when he says: 'The more interesting and plausible the stories relating to the Jacobite legend are made, the more they must be treated with suspicion.' (*Freemasons' Guide and Compendium*, p. 190).

[2] 'This Year (1720), at some *private* Lodges, several very valuable *Manuscripts* (for they had nothing yet in Print) concerning the Fraternity, their Lodges, Regulations, Charges, Secrets, and Usages . . . were too hastily burnt by some scrupulous Brothers, that those Papers might not fall into strange Hands.'— Dr. Anderson, *Book of Constitutions*, 1738, p. 111. In this connection, Hextall calls attention to the still more illuminating footnote in Preston's *Illustrations of Masonry*, ascribing the burning to 'a fear of making discoveries prejudicial to the interests of Masonry'.

[3] *Transactions*, Leicester Lodge of Research No. 2429, vol. 12, p. 125. The paper has also been reprinted in *British Masonic Miscellany*, vol. x.

circumstance, no doubt, serves to give this theory an added appeal, and Hextall accordingly approves the basic principles of 'Stuart Masonry', as it is sometimes called, and of Ashmole's connection with it, because of the latter's well-known role as a staunch supporter of the king, and as a favourite at court and the recipient of many royal privileges and appointments, and as a student, on the other hand, of esoteric science in many of its branches. But all that Hextall asks the reader to do is to assume as a starting-point 'that the Legend of Hiram Abif was known to members of the Craft for many years before the above date [1717], and had been established as a portion of the Masonic ritual'. But this, of course, is only begging the question. Once we have made these two all-important assumptions, and granted their validity, there is little else of any fundamental importance to search for, except to establish the identity of the person mostly concerned with the development of the Legend and the ritual which is based upon it, and which, of course, is what Hextall was trying to accomplish. But he is forced to admit that 'whether Elias Ashmole had as much to do with the invention of the Hiramic Legend as has been supposed, must remain for the present an unsolved problem', though he still thinks that 'the probabilities appear as yet to point towards Ashmole as the man'.[1]

In this connection it might be remarked that when Ragon is quoted as having stated unequivocally that it was actually Ashmole who had created the Third Degree—at a time when, we now know, the Third Degree as such could not possibly have been in existence—all he may have had in mind was not the Third Degree, as a ceremony, but only the *Legend* now associated with it.

The Compagnonnage Theory

Searching for the origin of our Hiramic Legend somewhat further back than the events just recounted, we come to the Compagnonnage Theory.

R. F. Gould has given the story of the Compagnonnage the greatest amount of attention, both in his larger *History of Freemasonry* (vol. i, ch. 5), and in his more recent single-volume *Concise History* (pp. 45–61), an account which, however, A. E. Waite unjustly claims to be 'utterly uncritical'. W. H. Rylands, also, has written extensively 'On the Legend of the Compagnonnage' in the *Transactions* of Quatuor Coronati (vols. i and ii), and Lionel Vibert

[1] Hextall, Leicester *Transactions*, vol. 12, pp. 125, 149–150.

has followed this up on its historical side, in the same journal (vol. xxxiii), leading to an important commentary by J. E. S. Tuckett.

'The Compagnonnage,' Vibert tells us, 'is the name given to that association of French journeymen—originally restricted to the four building trades of the stonemasons, carpenters, joiners and locksmiths, but expanding until it included almost every craft of importance in the country. . . . ' Our information with respect to this association comes originally from a publication in 1841 of the *Livre du Compagnonnage* by Agricol Perdiguier, a member of the joiner sub-division. Later information is also furnished by other writers (Vibert gives a bibliography), but it is the earlier 1841 disclosures that are the most significant for our purpose, since the question of greater antiquity as between Freemasonry and the Compagnonnage, and the possibility of 'borrowing', in one direction or the other, soon forces itself upon our attention.

The association of the Compagnonnage comprises three main divisions, each of which claims a legendary 'Founder'—King Solomon, Maître Jacques, and Maître Soubise, respectively—each of whom in turn is supposed to have conferred a 'Charge' on his own followers, who thereafter have come to be known as the 'Sons' of their particular Founder. Now all these three legendary Founders are said to have had some connection with King Solomon's Temple —therein arises our primary interest—and all three divisions of the Compagnonnage lay claim to an origin resulting from the building of that Temple.

These are very briefly and inadequately some of the outward points of similarity between the two organizations—the French Compagnonnage and the British Masonic fraternity—but Gould lists no less than forty-one of them, some of which are naturally more significant to us than others.[1] Those so far mentioned happen to be only of an organizational character, but there are others that have to do with terms used, grades, ceremonies of induction, customs and practices—and *legends*. It is with the last that we are here the most concerned, for among these, strangely enough, is the possession, by the Compagnonnage, as amongst us, of a Hiramic Legend. Certainly not *the* Hiramic Legend—that would be almost

---

[1] R. F. Gould, *History of Freemasonry*, i, pp. 249–250.
   It appears that the Compagnonnage 'still exists in France today, though in a slightly modified form'. See Peter Fischel's paper in *AQC* vol. 79, which offers some new information not previously provided in our literature.

too much to expect—but *a* Hiramic Legend. But even with this qualification, the comparison is noteworthy.

'The stonemasons [of the Sons of Solomon],' says Perdiguier, a member of that larger Division and of the joiner sub-division, 'are accounted the most ancient of the Compagnons. An ancient fable has obtained currency amongst them relating, according to some, to Hiram; according to others, to Adonhiram; wherein are represented crimes and punishments; but I leave this fable for what it is worth.' He in fact tells us very little else about his own Sons of Solomon, either because there is very little else to tell, in the realm of legendary lore, or through an understandable reticence, as Gould suggests.[1] But Perdiguier does quote, apparently verbatim, from an account current among the Sons of Maître Jacques— whence the need for the same reticence might not have been felt incumbent upon him—and according to which, 'Maître Jacques, one of the first masters of Solomon, and a colleague of Hiram, . . . hearing that Solomon had summoned to himself all famous men, he passed into Egypt, and thence to Jerusalem. . . . Having received an order from the chief master to construct two columns, he sculptured them with such art and taste that he was accepted a master' in turn. In this legendary 'history', the subsequent murder of Hiram is also mentioned; and the joiners belonging to the Sons of Maître Jacques, Perdiguier tells us, 'wear white gloves, because, as they say, they did not steep their hands in the blood of Hiram', and a dog is said to have discovered the place where the body of Hiram, architect of the Temple, lay under the rubbish.[2]

Perdiguier furthermore tells us that the Sons of Solomon call themselves *Compagnons Etrangers*, or 'strangers', 'foreigners', and explains that the term 'came from the fact that almost all the stonemasons employed at the Temple were not of Judea, but of Tyre and the neighbouring countries'. To which Gould makes the obvious comment that we thus find 'in the legend of the murder of Hiram, the blame resting, according to the followers of Jacques and Soubise, with the *Enfants de Salomon*', Hiram having in fact lost his life (according to their legend, as in ours) at the hands of his own countrymen.[3]

[1] We are reminded of Covey-Crump's similar citing of the Hiramic Legend in Prichard's *Masonry Dissected*, also 'for what it is worth'.
[2] Gould, *Concise History*, p. 59.
[3] Gould, *Concise History*, p. 59.

In a third edition of the work of Perdiguier (1857), there is an illustration, which Rylands reproduces, and in which we see Solomon, Maître Jacques, and Maître Soubise, with their followers, the latter of whom are preparing to disperse to other parts of the world, the Temple having now been completed. Standing alongside of King Solomon is a figure holding a pair of compasses extended. Rylands takes this figure to represent Hiram, from a Song furnished by Perdiguier elsewhere, and which has the words: 'On the horizon brilliant with fire, Hiram with a compass in his hand, seems to trace for you the outline of the shores and banks of Jordan'.[1]

Antiquity of the Compagnonnage Legend

From these and numerous other details in his forty-page exposition, Gould concludes that 'in the Compagnonnage and in English Freemasonry are numerous coincidences, which occur too frequently, and are too strongly marked to be purely accidental'. He infers from all this, in his larger and earlier multi-volume *History*, that the legends and practices of the Compagnonnage are the earlier of the two, but later he appears to have had some change of heart, and speaks more conservatively. But he also adds: 'As it is improbable, not to say impossible, that this corps [the Sons of Solomon] was wholly without a legend at the beginning of the present century,[2] I find a difficulty in believing that it was suddenly discarded—to make room for the Hiramic myth—at the instance of some companions who also happened to be Freemasons,'[3] as had been suggested by others. Gould therefore suggests, as a plausible inference, that this prior Legend, which the Compagnons must have possessed at the beginning of the nineteenth century, must have been a Hiramic one. (Precisely the same argument, it may be observed, has been made, and with equally good reason, for the prior existence of the Hiramic Legend in the English Freemasonry prior to its first notice in Anderson's *Constitutions* of 1723, bearing in mind the inherent conservatism of British Freemasonry.)

The proposition, whether the priority of time with regard to the

---

[1] Rylands, *AQC* i, 156–157.

[2] No doubt he means the 19th, not the 20th century.

[3] Gould, *Concise History*, pp. 58–59.

Throughout his exposition, Gould, unlike the other commentators, anglicizes the word *compagnon* to 'companion', and *compagnonnage* to 'companionage,' but I have substituted the original French form, for the sake of uniformity.

Hiramic Legend belongs to the Compagnonnage or to the Masonic institution, has been a matter of grave dispute, but the resemblances between some portions of the Legend in the two institutions are striking in the extreme—this much has been admitted even by most of the opponents of the Compagnonnage Theory. The question therefore deserves holding in mind, if for no other reason than the theoretical possibility at least that further research may some day disclose the prior existence of the Hiramic Myth in the Compagnonnage, thereby pushing the problem of its appearance in the Masonic system back a step. But only a step, and only as far as Freemasonry is concerned, as Arthur E. Waite has pointed out, since the origin of the myth in the Compagnonnage itself would still continue to be in question.

Despite the fact that the information from Perdiguier comes to us fairly late in the day, there are earlier disclosures with regard to the Compagnonnage, resulting from the condemnation of the institution by the ecclesiastical Doctors of the Sorbonne, that go back to the middle of the seventeenth century. These actually appear to furnish us with the earliest documentary evidence of the Compagnonnage and its customs and practices, its initiations and ceremonies. But by this time their Legend—whatever it may have been—must already have been well established. Legends, it has been observed— that is, genuine legends—do not get themselves 'composed' like a poem or a play. They take time to grow, often from very simple beginnings—as we know from our own *Old Charges*—and the variety of detail they contain in their later period frequently indicates a measure of the period of growth. All this is very much to the point in considering the possible antiquity of the Compagnonnage Hiramic Legend *vis-à-vis* the Masonic.

But W. H. Rylands comes to the conclusion that these legends of the Compagnonnage cannot be considered to be anterior to analogous ones found in Freemasonry. While the French institution itself may be believed to have originated about the twelfth to the fourteenth centuries, it is not certain, he points out, as to when their Legend itself might have originated. Gould had thought at one time that this might have gone back as far as the tenth century, but Rylands on the other hand was of the opinion that it was much more recent, probably not earlier than the seventeenth.

Lionel Vibert's view is much to the same effect as Rylands', but the discussion by Tuckett draws the sting from much of Vibert's (and therefore also of Rylands') argument. Tuckett calls attention to the fact (previously suggested by Gould, in his later *Concise History*) that 'neither Perdiguier nor any other of the Compagnonnage authorities state that, prior to the late introduction of a *Masonic* Hiramic Legend, the Compagnonnage was destitute of *all* knowledge of H.A.B.', and Tuckett himself is of the opinion that a prior Hiramic Legend of their own was in fact in the possession of the Compagnons.[1] In support, he cites approvingly the opinion expressed by Count Goblet d'Alviella (author of *The Migration of Symbols*, 1894—the Hibbert Lectures for 1891): 'I am more inclined than many of our English brethren,' says the Count, 'to believe in the genuineness of the legends retained by the French Compagnonnage. . . . These unquestionably bear, in their rules as well as in their ceremonial and way of thinking, the stamp of the Middle Ages.'[2]

Certainly we can feel at one with W. H. Rylands in his somewhat reluctant view that we here find, as a common denominator at least, one more Solomonic tradition, with its Hiramic counterpart, while we can still further appreciate the suggestion of R. F. Gould, again to say the very least, as to the possible derivation of the Compagnonnage from the same sources of origin as our own Freemasonry. This last bifurcated indication may prove the most promising of all —time will tell—but if so, it may also disclose, at some point anterior to the diverging of the two forks—the French and the British—a common Hiramic origin of genuine antiquity.

But, in view of this well-attested possession by the Compagnonnage of a Hiramic Legend—whatever its source—it is difficult to understand the statement of Dr. Herbert Poole to the effect that the Hiramic Legend 'has *no* parallel outside of English Masonry, and that it is of little further use looking for one'.[3]

The Mediaeval Miracle Play

Turning back now to the British Isles, and bearing in mind the 'Miracle' and 'Morality' plays that used to be performed in the Middle Ages, particularly the ones that were assigned to the various Guilds for presentation as part of their traditional duties, a favourite speculation with regard to the Hiramic Drama has been the very natural thought that some one of these plays—they were always

[1] *AQC* xxxiii, 224.
[2] *AQC* xiii, 80.
[3] *AQC* li, 17. 'The Antiquity of the Craft'.

drawn from some event or account in the Old or New Testament—may very well contain the germ from which our own Drama may have originated and developed. Robert Race, in fact, dissects the Hiramic Drama with this thought in mind, and thinks that our story, far from representing an historical event, as many still believe it does, is in reality nothing more than the libretto of a religious drama—one of those Mystery or Miracle plays that we know to have been in the habit of being enacted in the Middle Ages. But as an historical event, he says, it is impossible to believe that 'at the height of day, 12 o'clock noon, it was possible for a man to come here (and since the Temple was not quite completed, a lot of workmen would certainly be about) to be attacked at one gate, then at another, and finally knocked down at the third gate bleeding, and no one the wiser.'[1] (Of course, it could have been Sunday. Or Christmas).

But even as a play, Race thinks that it may have been presented 'not of necessity in Masonic circles only, but in many and various societies long years ago'. This certainly opens up many possibilities, but unfortunately no evidence of the existence of such a play has been successfully brought forward, among the many morality plays that are well known.

Ernest E. Thiemeyer has accordingly endeavoured at some length to demolish this theory of Robert Race's, in a series of articles on 'The Hiramic Legend and the Medieval Stage',[2] though the negative argument he attempts to put forward is difficult to follow, and to that extent unconvincing. But he comes to the conclusion (however arrived at) that the Hiramic Legend 'has not been invented in the fictional sense', and cannot therefore be considered as the plot of a mere play. We shall later on consider his own contribution to this question of origins at a somewhat more appropriate place in this discussion.

A more positive approach is the one offered by E. Conder, Jr., in a detailed and well-documented paper on 'The Miracle Play', where he lists a great many of such plays—all he could find after a very exhaustive search—and he connects them with the various

[1] Robert Race, 'The Legend of the Third Degree'. *British Masonic Miscellany*, compiled by George M. Martin; Dundee, ix, 84–133.

The greater part of this volume ix (also vol. x) is devoted to a discussion of subjects covered by the present work.

Race's paper originally appeared in the Leicester Lodge of Research *Transactions* for 1920–21.

[2] *The Builder*. Anamosa, Iowa. Vol. xii (1926), pp. 72, 109, 130, 170, 200.

Guilds to whom the presentation of these plays had been assigned around the country as a traditional practice. But, he says pointedly, as a conclusion, 'I am unable to trace any foundation for the Hiramic Legend in any of the MS. Plays or interludes that exist.'[1]

Covey-Crump does entertain the thought, in his discussion of the Thomas à Becket story, that the occurrence 'in 1170, or let us say some Miracle Play subsequently founded thereupon, might have resulted in our Masonic Tradition', and he cites, in a footnote, that 'Wm. Fitzstephen, a contemporary and biographer of Becket, apparently refers to such a Miracle Play, as being performed in London within twenty years of the event.' But the meaningful 'apparently' should be noted,[2] and the Librarian of the Chapter Library at Canterbury Cathedral writes, in answer to a query, that, while Miracle Plays did take place at the Cathedral, 'my research [aided by the advice of two experts] is unable to find any reference to a play dealing with Archbishop Becket's death.'[3]

However—if one wishes to continue speculating on this particular theme, and in a direction this time somewhat opposed to the theory of Robert Race—the suggestion arises that the Masonic play, if there ever was one, need not necessarily have been a *public* performance like these Miracle and Morality plays of the Guilds. Such a Masonic play may well have been of an esoteric character, meant for inner circles only, and transmitted purely by oral tradition and therefore not available in written form.[4] This suggestion of mine is made all the more plausible by the comment made by a Mr. A. W. Pollard, in a letter addressed to W. J. Williams, author of the paper on Becket that has been cited, making reference to Sir Edmund Chambers' *The Medieval Stage*, to the effect that no such Miracle Play is mentioned, beyond what 'seems to have been a pageant in dumb show rather than a proper miracle play'. Furthermore, he adds—and this is the significant passage to which I would like to call the reader's attention—'it is possible that speaking plays about Becket were not encouraged as raising awkward questions as to the relations of Church and State'.[5] There is, still

[1] *AQC* xiv, 60–82.
[2] Covey-Crump, *The Hiramic Tradition*, p. 75.
[3] *AQC* xli, 146.
[4] Covey-Crump appears to have had a similar idea. Cf. *The Hiramic Tradition*, p. 18.
[5] *AQC* xli, 146.

further, the historical fact that, towards the end of the sixteenth century, as Tuckett tells us, 'the Miracle Plays and Moralities which had for a long time been performed in English in various parts of the country were beginning to disappear, being finally suppressed by James I' (1566–1625). Any attempt to inaugurate such a Miracle play—either of the Becket or Hiramic type—after that date, in the face of the royal proscription, would necessarily have had to be *sub rosa* and of an underground character.

'It may also be remarked,' Tuckett says, turning the argument around, 'that in the *publicly* performed Miracle Plays, the Masons do not seem to have taken a share commensurate with their importance as a Gild. This would be natural,' Tuckett thought, 'if their greatest effort in that direction was kept secret.' And by 'greatest effort', it must be pointed out, Tuckett had obviously the esoteric prototype of the Hiramic Drama in mind.[1]

Tuckett's fame, it may be mentioned, rests largely on his demonstration of the esoteric character of the 'substitute' name of the Master Builder, in the *Old Charges* story of King Solomon's Temple, as we have had occasion to review. For the moment, it is only necessary to point out (but perhaps as a coincidence only) that this royal suppression of Miracle plays above-mentioned came shortly after the time of the 1551 suppression of the Taverner Bible, with its *last* mention of the untranslated double name of Hiram Abiff, after which this double name disappeared from public view in that particular form, in the later English translations of the Bible. The double name, and the Miracle Play surrounding it, may have both gone underground at about the same time, generally speaking, and for the same reason, to be preserved henceforth only as an esoteric Masonic tradition.

While on the subject of esoteric plays, as a possible suggestion from which the Hiramic Drama may have become elaborated, we may consider the theory proposed by R. I. Clegg—in his discussion of Herbert Poole's paper on 'Masonic Ritual and Secrets before 1717'—wherein he points to 'the early ceremonies of the Church and particularly those spectacles which have been associated with the period of Easter, . . . showing as a pageant the search for the Master and then the illumination wrought by His Resurrection.' Thus Moss, in the introduction of his edition of 'Everyman', 'recounts that centuries ago, at Easter time, a representation was

[1] *AQC* xxxvi, 180, 189.

given in the Church of a search for the missing Master; that the evergreen was used at the grave; and that some of the linen clothes used at the tomb were brought back as evidence of the discovery.' As another example, Clegg cites Tunnison, whose book on the *Dramatic Traditions of the Dark Ages* was published by the University of Chicago, and who gives many examples of plays presented by craftsmen for hundreds of years in the Near East. The nature of these plays is not elaborated upon, however, and the suggestion may bear further investigation, particularly because of the Near Eastern location.[1]

Parenthetically it might be remarked that it may have been some such set of circumstances as those recounted by R. I. Clegg, Moss, and Tunnison, that may have prompted William Hutchinson to develop the theory that the Legend of the Third Degree was a Christian institution, designed solely to perpetuate Christian beliefs[2] —a theory which Mackey correctly observes was completely refuted at the Union of 1813, when the Christian references in the rituals of the preceding century came to be entirely eradicated in favour of a purely non-sectarian expression of Masonic faith and principles.[3]

A changed direction

Whatever the merit in the Miracle play and associated religious dramas as nuclei out of which may have arisen our Hiramic Drama, the suggestion has been offered—and from more than one important source—that this attempt to track down the origin of the Hiramic Legend to its imagined source in some particular tradition or practice of the operative Masons, whether of England or of France, or in some mediaeval Masonic or Guild play, is altogether futile and unnecessary, since our own Traditions may very well have grown up on an entirely different kind of soil, and have been fertilized by a quite different set of elements. Thus Ernest T. Thiemeyer, in the article on 'The Hiramic Legend and the Medieval Stage' that has already been briefly alluded to, puts out the thought that, 'if any conclusions as to its origin and growth are to be reached, the present line of research must be abandoned and the field of ethnography investigated.' This he has himself done, in a serious attempt

[1] *AQC* xxxvii, 29–30.
[2] William Hutchinson, *The Spirit of Masonry* (1775). Oliver Edition (1843), New York 1903. Lecture ix.
[3] A. G. Mackey, *The History of Freemasonry*, i, 137.

at interpreting the Hiramic Myth as a genuine relic of primitive mythology and folklore, after the manner of Frazer's *The Golden Bough* and similar works of that character. And as a result, he comes to the conclusion that the Myth is a genuine survival of primitive group thinking—'a natural outgrowth of ritual requirements', as he puts it—which finally became incorporated into a Masonic ritual at some time or period so far undetermined.[1] It is this last element in our investigation that we are most desirous of reaching.

It would seem obvious, however, that Thiemeyer's folk-lore theory and Robert Race's Morality Play theory are not mutually exclusive, but that, if some elements of the Hiramic Myth are indeed 'a product of the thought processes of a social group', preserved from more primitive times through the instrumentality of popular folklore and mythology, these elements could very well have incarnated themselves in the body of a folk-drama, on the one hand, as well as in a ritual, on the other, and in these two forms may have passed on to a time when, as now, both the drama and the ritual are found incorporated in a single rite.

Some such approach and methodology is the one proposed by the late R. J. Meekren, in a paper on 'The Age of the Master's Part'.[2] This is another one of those papers that must be read and mulled over in its entirety, together with the important discussion that follows it, in which some very eminent investigators had taken part, and some of whom took issue with some of Meekren's thoughts and arguments, perhaps because they had failed to understand his meaning. The extensive 'Reply' or rebuttal which Meekren then furnishes to these comments is in effect an elaboration of the paper itself, in an effort to further that understanding. All this is almost impossible to adequately summarize, but an attempt must be made to refer to some of its highlights.

Our customary method of search, says Meekren, has generally been for some specific prototype of *our* particular Hiramic legend and myth, and the search appears so far to have led nowhere, he thinks, so much so that it has raised the interesting question as to

---

[1] *The Builder*, xii (1926), p. 203. Thiemeyer's treatment is of additional interest, at one point, because of his discussion of the Hiramic Drama as found in various Jurisdictions, British, French, and American, illustrating some of the variations and embellishments found therein. See *op. cit.*, p. 74 *et seq.*

[2] *AQC* lxxii.

whether or not we may have been looking for the wrong thing in the wrong place and with the wrong methods (as in the well-known analogy of the blind man searching in a dark room for a black cat that isn't there). Meekren, in fact, points out that, in previous investigations of the subject by others, search has been made 'in various places, and especially in the Talmuds, for something like the legend of the degree. But the search was fruitless—nothing of the kind was found. This because the seekers . . . were looking for a legend or myth about King Solomon's building activities when it was a ritual that should have been sought, and this much nearer home than Jerusalem.' He thinks, in fact, that 'there is a quite considerable amount of evidence that the rite embodied in the present forms of the third degree was known prior to the formation of the Grand Lodge, and even that the putative hero of the myth as now told was referred to in some places, though not so certainly'.[1]

But what he sets out to prove is not so much that the Third Degree, as an integrated ceremony, is ancient, 'but that its substance has existed from the very beginning of Masonic ritual— whenever that may have been'. To that end he returns again and again to his central thesis, which is that 'for origin, we must go to anthropology and folk-lore, for the germinal nucleus embedded in our present-day ceremonies are, as I have said elsewhere, nothing but folk-lore, the folk-lore of a segregated group'.[2]

He adds, however, realistically enough, that 'it would take a treatise of considerable length to set it out in coherent form. I have been working,' he says, 'on a preliminary sketch of such a treatise for twenty years and more, but do not think I shall be able to complete it. [He died, in fact, after a long illness, before he was able to do so.] I should like to pass on the work done and the material collected to others, if any there be who would be interested.'[3]

The central core of the Meekren thesis is that no one 'is fully equipped to discuss the origins of Masonic ritual who has not a comprehensive knowledge of the facts collected under the heads of anthropology and folk-lore'. The essential difference, on the other hand, between his own *modus operandi* and the one we have been accustomed to pursue is very well expressed in the following

[1] *AQC* lxxii, 28.
[2] *Ibid.*, 49–50.
[3] *Ibid.*, 53. As a bibliographical comment, I might add that his voluminous notes, passed on to his co-worker A. J. B. Milborne, are now in my possession.

statement: 'The historian,' says Meekren, 'may be likened to the lawyer who presents his case in court. The anthropological student is like the detective who proceeds on clues and odds and ends of information, however come by.'[1] He might have added—and this would undoubtedly be in keeping with his viewpoint—that the latter method of procedure may not even result in producing any evidence that would be admissible in a court of law, and might fail to impress the jury to the point of bringing in a favourable verdict, and yet could actually be nearer the truth of the matter, whatever that truth might be.[2]

We could in this connection bear in mind the somewhat plaintive comment of G. W. Speth on this question of possible theories as to the origin of the Hiramic Myth. 'For generations,' he points out, 'Freemasons greedily swallowed any tale which writers chose to indite: we are to-day more critical, but have we not gone to the other extreme? Do we not foolishly refuse to even entertain any supposition, however natural in itself, unless we can produce absolute proof in black and white of its correctness? Let us, by all means, make a distinction between what is proved up to the hilt and what is only highly probable, but let us cease to assert that nothing is possible which is not capable of Euclidian demonstration.'[3]

The Noah Legend
A prototype of the Hiramic

Our final investigation in the direction of a search for some quasi-Hiramic tradition or legend that may possibly have ante-dated the true-Hiramic takes us to a fairly recent discovery of a long-lost document—the now-famous *Graham MS*. But the discussion requires some preliminary remarks for its better comprehension and appreciation, though many readers may undoubtedly be well-acquainted with the situation. The latest contribution to the subject in our literature is the excellent paper by J. M. Harvey, and most of the material in the present concluding section is taken from my own contribution to the discussion of Harvey's paper.[4]

[1] *AQC* lxxii, 47.
[2] As before, I have taken the liberty of repeating what I had previously said in my Note in *AQC* lxxiii, 118.
[3] *AQC* xii, 148.
[4] The Graham MS., 1726, analysed. *AQC* vol. 80.

If we look back into our past records, there is some evidence that in the early days of our speculative Masonry, and perhaps much earlier, there was a Noah tradition that has since been lost to craft Masonry, though resuscitated to some small extent in a few of the so-called 'Higher Degrees'. But in 1726—less than a decade after the creation of our first Grand Lodge—there appeared an advertisement in a newspaper which made reference, seriously or not, to a 'Society of Ante-diluvian Masons'. The advertisement itself is obviously in the form of a 'skit', or parody, or perhaps even an open mockery—in the style of the procession of the Scald Miserables of approximately the same era—but it is so full of ideas that are of significance to us today, as reflecting the analogous ideas entertained as of 1726, that the entire account is not without interest. Not the least of this interest is contained in the signature—no doubt fictitious—appended to the advertisement, and in some of the details connected with the suggested Noachic or 'antediluvian' tradition. I therefore give the advertisement in full, as originally presented by Henry Sadler in 1910 in his Inaugural Address as W. M. of Quatuor Coronati Lodge of Research No. 2076, London:

'ANTEDILUVIAN MASONRY

This is to give Notice,

To all Masons who have been made after the Antediluvian manner.

That there will be a Lodge held at the Ship Tavern in Bishopsgate Street tomorrow the 24th of this instant June, being the Feast of St. John the Baptist, the Forerunner of—who laid the first parallel Line—there not being Brethren enough assembled the last year to make a true and perfect Lodge.

There will be several Lectures on Ancient Masonry, particularly on the Signification of the Letter G, and how and after what Manner the Antediluvian Masons form'd their Lodges, showing what Innovations have lately been introduced by the Doctor[1] and some other of the Moderns, with their Tape, Jacks, Moveable Letters, Blazing Stars, &c., to the great Indignity of the Mop and Pail.

There will likewise be a Lecture giving a particular Description of the Temple of Solomon, showing which way the Fellow Crafts got into the Middle Chamber to receive their Wages, and proving

---

[1] Obviously Dr. Desaguliers, not Dr. Anderson.

22

without lettering or giving the first or second, that the two Pillars of the Porch were not cast in the Vale of Jehosaphat but elsewhere: and that neither the Honorary, Apollonian, or Free and Accepted Masons know anything of the matter; with the whole History of the Widow's Son killed by the Blow of a Beetle, afterwards found three Foot East, three Foot West, and three Foot perpendicular, and the necessity there is for a Master to well understand the Rule of Three.

Lastly; there will be an Oration in the Henlean stile, on the Antiquity of Signs, Tokens, Points, Gripes, Knuckles, Wrists, Righthands, bare-bended knees, naked left Breast, Bibles, Compasses, Squares, Yellow Jackets, Blue Breeches, Mosaick Pavements, dented Ashlers, broached Turnels, Jewels,movable and immovable, bow-bound Boxes, oblong-Squares, cassia, and mossy Graves, delivered neither sitting nor standing naked nor cloathed, but in due Form, concluding with a genuine Account of Penalties, Throats, Tongues, Hearts, Sands, Cables, Shoars, Tides, Bodies burnt, Ashes, Winds, solemn Obligations, etc.

N.B.—The Wax Chandler near Pall Mall will provide three great Lights and a Gormogon to keep off the Cowin and Evesdroppers.

By Order of the Fraternity
Lewis Giblin, M.B.N.

The Eulogium on Masonry will not be deferred on any account.'[1]

The particular newspaper in which this advertisement is said to have appeared is not specified, and has not up to now been found; and 'whether there ever was a Society of Antediluvian Masons', says Henry Sadler, himself, in comment, 'I cannot positively say, but I have been told by one of our members, who is not likely to be mistaken, that he has seen mention of them somewhere. . . .'— which may or may not mean anything (bearing in mind the Hayter Lewis episode), since no further word respecting these 'Antediluvian Masons' appears to have come up since. But that the Noachic or Antediluvian tradition itself was seriously entertained in some quarters at the period in question is indicated in some way by a letter dated 1735 which the Grand Master, Lord Weymouth, ordered to be sent to the Provincial Grand Master at Calcutta and in which the presumed old-Indian 'Noachidae'—the supposed followers or 'Sons of Noah', (that is, the followers of the Noachic

[1] *AQC* xxiii, 325.

Precepts)—are referred to, and requesting information as to the possible 'Remains of Old Masonry'—presumably antediluvian— that might perhaps still be found in that ancient land.[1]

At about the same period—and in the first chapter of his 1738 *Book of Constitutions*—Dr. Anderson, in reciting 'The History of Masonry . . . from the Creation to Grand Master Nimrod', makes reference to the 'Noachidae' in the above sense, and explains the word, in a footnote, as being 'the first Name of *Masons*, according to some old Traditions'. And in the first of his 'Old Charges', he tells us that 'A MASON is obliged by his Tenure to observe the Moral Law, as a true Noachida.'[2] Knoop and Jones have similarly discussed the various precepts that some Masonic and non-Masonic writers have identified with the designation 'Noachian', and they find that the adjective 'has been traced as early as 1678 (O.E.D.), and the word "Naochidae" ', they think, 'may be equally old'.[3]

All this explanatory material with respect to the Noachidae and the probable existence of a Noachic tradition among the early speculative Masons is for the purpose of developing in the reader a just appreciation of the discovery that was made in 1936 in the form of the *Graham MS.*, and its influence upon our understanding of the Hiramic Legend in its possibly prior form.

The manuscript in question first came to light in modern times when exhibited by the Rev. H. I. Robinson at his initiation, having been found among the papers left by his father, also a Mason, and was described by Dr. Herbert Poole, who brought it to the notice of the members of Quatuor Coronati a few months later, and who described this find as being, in his opinion, 'the most important document which we possess among the material surviving for the student of Masonry from the "ritual" point of view'. Dr. Poole also presented a photographic reproduction of the manuscript, in the *AQC* Transactions for 1937, and analysed it critically, comparing it with two others of a somewhat similar character.

As to the dating on the manuscript, it is found to be somewhat ambiguous, but is now generally accepted as representing the year 1726, following the suggestion of Douglas Knoop. But the MS. appears to be only a copy of a still older original, and, in the opinion of J. Heron Lepper (with which Dr. Poole appeared to agree), was

[1] *AQC* xi, 35. See also *AQC* xlvi, 370.
[2] *QCA* vii, 4, 143.
[3] *AQC* lvi, 44.

'a genuine Masonic production of a period not later than the early seventeenth century' and possibly of Scottish origin.

The dating of this manuscript is fully discussed in the Rev. Dr. Poole's paper in *AQC* vol. 50. The date itself is written in the following manner

2

176

and, says Dr. Poole, 'we might reasonably accept this as 1726 were it not that the authorities at both the British Museum and the Public Record Office . . . were . . . inclined to date the handwriting as of considerably earlier—by perhaps as much as 50 years.'

The manuscript presents numerous ideas, practices, and symbolical allusions as of the period in question; and, associated with the Noachic Legend itself, there is a Legend which comes immediately after, connected with 'Bazalliell', the builder of the Tabernacle of Moses in the Wilderness, and with 'two younger brothers' of 'king alboyne'. It appears that these two princes (according to the Legend) had expressed their desire to be instructed by Bezaleel in the noble science of architecture, and the latter is said to have 'agreed conditionally [that] they were not to discover it [to others] without another to themselves to make a trible [triple] voice'. And they accordingly took an oath to that effect. Now, after Bezaleel's death, the inhabitants thereabout 'did think that the secrets of masonry had been totally Lost . . . for none knew the secrets thereof Save these two princes and they were so sworn at their entering not to discover it without another to make a trible voice. . . .'

So here we have at least three elements of our Hiramic Legend, having to do with

(a) a builder, this time of a Tabernacle which is accepted in Masonic tradition (as among biblical scholars generally) to have been a pattern for the later construction of King Solomon's Temple:

(b) secrets connected with the art of building, or Masonry as it was then called; secrets which were now shared by three personages, and which were not to be divulged except by concerted action of all three:

(c) after the death of one of these three (the builder himself), the secrets of Masonry were now considered to have been effectively 'lost', since they could now no longer be passed on, and would surely become lost in fact to future generations.

As to the Noachic Legend itself, which seems to be so intimately intertwined with elements of the Legend of Bezaleel in our own Hiramic Legend, the portion that is of specific interest to us, rendered into modernized English and somewhat adapted, for greater appreciation, is as follows:

> We have it by tradition and yet some reference to Scripture that Shem, Ham, and Japheth went to their father Noah's *grave* to try if they could *find anything about him* that would *lead them* to a veritable *secret* that this famous preacher had. . . . Now *these three men* had already agreed among themselves that *if they did not find* the very thing itself, that *the first thing* that they did find *was to be* for them *as a secret.* . . . So they came to the grave, and finding nothing save the dead body almost entirely consumed away, they *took* a grip at a *finger* and it came away; so from *joint to joint*; so to the *wrist*; and so to the *elbow*. So they *reared* up the dead body and supported it, setting foot to foot, knee to knee, breast to breast, cheek to cheek, and hand to back, and cried out, 'Help, oh father!' As if they had said, 'O Father of Heaven, help us now, for our earthly father cannot.' So they laid the dead body down again, not knowing what else to do. Then one of them said, 'There is yet marrow in this bone,' and the second said, 'but a dry bone,' and the third said, 'it stinketh'. *So they agreed to give it a name*, as it is known to Freemasonry to this day. . . .

The knowledgeable Craftsman can easily identify for himself which elements in the above account have significance for our present Legend, as a possible and probable point of origin. As to the probable 'name', in this account, as of 1726 or earlier, this 'substitute word' is well known to students of Masonic ritual and its history, but its specific identification is not essential to the present discussion.

It is perhaps additionally significant that, in this *Graham MS.*, the story of the building of King Solomon's Temple, as it comes down to us from all the *Old Charges* since the *Cooke MS.*, comes in immediately after these stories of Bezaleel and of Noah, while elements of all three stories are now found telescoped into one, in our present Legend.

Commenting on the above circumstances, Dr. Poole asks: 'Is it possible that we have here an earlier version of the story, which was later (say, during the seventeenth century) transferred to Hiram? . . . One thing seems to me to be settled beyond any reasonable doubt,' he goes on to say, after his rhetorical and self-answering question, and that is 'that the Hiram story, and perhaps the Noah variant too, was known in the Craft in its amplest form at least 21 years before the formation of the Grand Lodge of England.' This would bring it down to the year 1696. Dr. Poole no doubt had the *Edinburgh Register House MS.*, in mind, endorsed 1696, wherein the 'fyve points of fellowship' are mentioned, among other matters of consequence.

Geo. Bullamore, in the course of the discussion of Dr. Poole's paper, commenting in similar fashion on the possible existence at one time of a Noachic tradition, alongside of a Hiramic, makes a pertinent suggestion that may have some merit. 'The earlier church-builders,' he thinks, 'using much timber, might have based their traditions on the sons of Noah and of Bezaleel,' one of whom built the wooden ark and the other, the Tabernacle of Moses. But 'a later invasion of stone cutters established at Westminster might promulgate a legend connected with the Temple' of Solomon, built of stone. And when the latter organization, at Westminster, 'was well established, the substituted secrets of the sons of Noah could be made to coincide with the substitutions of the Temple craftsmen', and that, he thinks, is how the transformation of the Noachic into the Hiramic may have come about.

Other attempts to explain the substitution of the Hiramic for the Noachic tradition have based themselves on a reference to the Miracle plays of the guilds. Thus, J. R. Rylands, in his study of 'Early Freemasonry in Wakefield', calls attention to a series of Mystery plays that were produced in that town by various crafts and guilds as late as 1576, one of which was a 'Noah' Play, portrayed in a somewhat comic spirit. Another such 'Noah' Play seems to have been produced at Newcastle.[1]

Dr. Poole rejected one or two of the theories that had been proposed, to connect the Noah play with the Hiramic Drama, but admitted that 'it is possible that the suggestions of an association between the Noah *Play* and the Hiram *legend*' might have arisen 'from a confusion between the Play with its emphasis on the ludicrous, and the story with its emphasis on the necromantic'. Similar confusions, in fact, are not unknown in the Masonic legacy. The two antediluvian pillars, so consistently alluded to in all the *Old Charges*, beginning with the *Cooks MS.*—later to be confused with and

[1] *AQC* lvi, 207–208.

replaced by the two pillars of Solomon, but still retaining their characteristic capacity to resist fire and flood—are a case in point.

'All ideas as to how the Hiramic legend came into free-masonry,' says Bernard E. Jones, in his extremely readable *Freemasons' Guide and Compendium* (1950), 'were considerably affected by the discovery of the *Graham MS.* . . .'—and no wonder.

'It is reasonable,' he says, 'to raise the possibility of the Hiramic legend having been at one stage of its evolution a legend of Noah and his sons and that, in that or some other form, it might well go back to early medieval times. . . . An eighteenth-century tradition . . . was to the effect that Ham's eldest son, Nimrod . . . was G.M. of all masons and a builder of many cities in Shinaar. But its existence is one more indication that Noah and his family had Masonic association in the minds of at least some early speculatives.

'With a fair amount of plausible conjecture it is possible now to reconstruct the process by which the Hiramic legend may *possibly* have found its way into freemasonry. The medieval operatives knew of King Solomon's Temple and of Solomon's architect; there is a bare possibility that some of them or their priestly scribes might have known the necromantic legend of Noah and his son Ham. Some of the Rosicrucians, and other delvers into the mystic who came into freemasonry in the 1700's, were probably aware of the Noah story, and it is not impossible that they gave it a dramatic setting. Later editors, aware of all the foregoing, would be able to introduce the name of Hiram, the Biblical character intimately concerned with Solomon's great project. Forthwith Hiram was formed into an architect,[1] and made the centre of a story that fitted well into the setting of King Solomon's Temple. The grisly and necromantic elements were not discarded, but they were softened, and the story was given an apt moral and closely related to the existing five points of fellowship. If this is a reasonable reconstruction, the Hiramic legend might easily have its roots in three distinct places: in the *Old Charges*, in the "black art" story of Noah and his son, and in the association between Hiram, the metal-worker, and King Solomon.'[2]

---

[1] However, this was no 'innovation'. Hiram has been known as an architect—though not so specified in the King James Bible—in an old tradition preserved at least as far back as the time of the Septuagint translation. See *ante*, pp. 135, 136, 271.

[2] Bernard E. Jones, *op. cit.*, pp. 314–318.

But a more incisive demonstration comes from the pen of Count Goblet d'Alviella—previously mentioned in connection with the legends of the Compagnonnage, and author of *The Migration of Symbols*, a work highly esteemed in professional circles, and with the spirit of which the proposed demonstration has much in common—and this is to the effect that the science of Mythology, as amply illustrated in *The Migration*, 'teaches that names are much more easily altered or exchanged than legends; the hero varies, the myth remains'.[1] The personality of Noah in the present instance has now become merged into the personality of Hiram, with only a change of name; the myth, in some important details at least, remains essentially the same.

Four years after the transcribing of the *Graham MS.*—assuming the 1726 dating to be correct—but an unknown number of years after the original from which the *Graham* is supposed to have been copied—Samuel Prichard presented the Hiramic form of the legend in his *Masonry Dissected* (1730), but 'the evidence of the *Graham MS.* and Prichard's publication', says Dr. Poole, 'seems to prove conclusively that the legend must have been widely current in Masonic circles *a good deal earlier* (his italics) than the dates of either of these, though, as to how much earlier, we can only guess'.[2] Prichard's version is given in short form in Covey-Crump's *The Hiramic Tradition*—'for what it may be worth', as the latter is careful to indicate—and is given in somewhat longer form in Dr. Poole's presentation of the *Graham MS.* in *AQC*, as an indication of the possible connection between the Noachic and the Hiramic. But it is presented complete in the Knoop, Jones, and Hamer collection, *The Early Masonic Catechisms*, and has been given, with the same reservation as indicated by Covey-Crump, at the end of Chapter V in the present work.

The commentary of Knoop and Jones on the above, in their *Genesis of Freemasonry*, is very much to the point. 'The marked similarity between the Noah story and the Hiram story in its oldest-known form [the Prichard version] is very striking; both have the same main *motif*—the attempt to obtain a secret from a dead body, and both have the same subsidiary *motif*—the intention to provide a substituted secret, failing the discovery of a genuine one. Where either story originally came from, or how it became associated with

[1] Cited in another connection by J. E. S. Tuckett, *AQC* xxxiii, 224.
[2] *AQC* lxi, 131.

masonry, is unknown. . . . The stories of Noah and Hiram call to mind the fact that in biblical instances of the miraculous restoration of life,[1] the prophet or apostle lay full length upon the body and breathed into its face. In the case of Elisha, who raised the son of the Shunammite woman . . . complete coincidence between living and dead was established twice, first by placing mouth to mouth, eyes to eyes and hands to hands, and secondly by stretching at full length upon the body. It is thus not impossible that the original stories of Noah and Hiram may have been those of attempts to restore these men to life, because their secrets had died with them.'[2]

In the *Edinburgh Register House MS.*, also found in *The Early Masonic Catechisms*, and dated 1696, the five points of fellowship are listed as follows: foot to foot, knee to knee, heart to heart, hand to hand, and ear to ear. 'We would suggest, though only tentatively,' Knoop and Jones say, in comment, 'that the five points of fellowship may have originated in practices connected with witchcraft or some other superstition, of which there was then no lack in Scotland.[3] In the second half of the [seventeenth] century, to judge by the date of most of the surviving Scottish versions of the *MS. Constitutions of Masonry*, the Scottish lodges adopted the Old Charges and caused them to be read to the entered apprentices at their admission. It is not inconceivable that, in order to provide the fellow crafts with some kind of corresponding "history", and perhaps to supply an explanation of the "five points" for the benefit of the increasing number of non-operative masons, a story was elaborated. This was possibly done, in part at least, by the utilisation of existing traditions. The Noah story, with its distinctly necromantic flavour, may have been formulated first and the Hiram story, further removed from witchcraft, but, in its oldest known form, very similar in its *motifs* to the Noah story, perhaps followed later. In each case a very minor character in the legendary history of the *MS. Constitutions of Masonry* was made the principal figure of the story.'[4]

And so, for the present at least, the matter rests.

[1] Cf. *I Kings* xvii, 17–23; *II Kings* iv, 34–35; *Acts* xx, 9–12.
[2] Knoop and Jones, *The Genesis of Freemasonry*. Manchester, 1949, pp. 90–91.
[3] 'For instance in 1623 Patrick Ruthven, believing himself to have been bewitched, was treated by Isobel Haldane: "scho com in to the bed and strauchit hir self above him, hir heid to his heid, hir handis ower him, and so forth, mumbling sum wordis; he knew nocht quhat they war".'—Knoop and Jones, *op. cit.*, p. 277. Cited from Pitcairn, *Criminal Trials in Scotland*, ii, 537.
[4] *Loc. cit.*

INDEX

Abbreviations